Navigating the Waters: An Exploration of International Law and the Laws of the Sea

THIRDY VENTENILLA

Copyright © 2024 by Thirdy.Ventenilla

All rights reserved. No part of this publication may be reproduced, distributed, or transmitted in any form or by any means, including photocopying, recording, or other electronic or mechanical methods, without the prior written permission of the publisher, except in the case of brief quotations embodied in critical reviews and certain other noncommercial uses permitted by copyright law.

For permission requests, write to the publisher at the address below:

Trendah Books Publishing House
262 Lawrence St., Brgy. San Jose
San Miguel, Bulacan, 3011
Philippines
thirdyventenilla@gmail.com

This textbook is intended to provide educational information on the topic of exploration of International Law and the Laws of the Sea. While every effort has been made to ensure the accuracy of the information presented, the publisher and author make no representations or warranties with respect to the completeness, accuracy, or suitability of the contents for any particular purpose. The information is provided on an "as is" basis. The publisher and author shall have no liability to any person or entity with respect to any loss or damage caused or alleged to be caused directly or indirectly by the information contained in this textbook.

Cover design and Interior layout by **Ace Graphics**

ISBN: 9798320693194
Imprint: **Trendah Law Books**

NAVIGATING THE WATERS

DEDICATION

This book is dedicated to my mom, Emelina Roura Ventenilla, whose unwavering love, encouragement, and support have been the guiding light on my journey of writing and exploration. Your boundless kindness and belief in my abilities have fueled my passion for knowledge and creativity. Thank you for being my inspiration and my rock. This achievement is as much yours as it is mine.

Contents

Contents vi
ACKNOWLEDGMENTS ix
Chapter 1. Introduction 10
  Definition of International Law 10
  Significance of International Law in the Modern World 15
  Importance of Understanding the Laws of the Sea 19
  Purpose and Scope of the Book 26
Chapter 2. Foundations of International Law 35
  Historical Development of International Law 35
  Sources of International Law 46
  Principles of International Law 48
Chapter 3. The Concept of the Sea in International Law 56
  Definition and Classification of the Seas and Oceans 56
  Historical Perspective: Evolution of Maritime Law 70
  Key Concepts: Territorial Waters, Exclusive Economic Zones (EEZs), and High Seas 95
Chapter 4. The United Nations Convention on the Law of the Sea (UNCLOS) 103
  Overview of UNCLOS 103
  Structure and Main Provisions of UNCLOS 106
  Structure and Main Provisions 113
  Controversies and Challenges in Implementing UNCLOS 129
Chapter 5. Sovereignty and Jurisdiction 140
  Territorial Waters: Rights and Responsibilities 140

Exclusive Economic Zones (EEZs) and Continental Shelves............. 152

International Straits and Transit Passage 162

Archipelagic States: Special Regimes... 171

Chapter 6. Navigation and Freedom of the Seas 188

Innocent Passage 188

Freedom of Navigation and Overflight 209

Military Activities in the Exclusive Economic Zone 223

Chapter 7. Marine Resources and Environmental Protection 233

Exploitation of Marine Resources: Fisheries and Mining................. 233

Environmental Protection and Conservation 247

Liability and Compensation for Environmental Damage 260

Chapter 8. Dispute Settlement Mechanisms 275

Diplomatic Negotiation and Mediation 275

Arbitration 293

International Court of Justice (ICJ).. 302

Specialized Tribunals and Arbitral Panels 313

Chapter 9. Contemporary Issues and Emerging Challenges 325

Climate Change and its Impact on Maritime Boundaries 325

Piracy and Maritime Terrorism... 337

Illegal, Unreported, and Unregulated (IUU) Fishing 353

Technological Advancements: Opportunities and Risks 372

Chapter 10. Conclusion 388

Recap of Key Points... 388

Future Prospects for the Laws of the Sea 392

Call to Action: Strengthening Compliance and Cooperation............ 395

Glossary of Terms 401

ACKNOWLEDGMENTS

I would like to express my sincere gratitude to all those who contributed to the creation of this book, "Navigating the Waters: An Exploration of International Law and the Laws of the Sea." Your support, encouragement, and expertise have been invaluable throughout this journey. Thank you for your unwavering dedication and belief in this project.

Chapter 1.
Introduction

Definition of International Law

International law refers to the set of rules, agreements, and conventions that govern relations between states and other international actors. It encompasses a wide range of legal principles and norms designed to regulate conduct in the international arena. From treaties to customary practices, international law serves as the foundation for cooperation, diplomacy, and conflict resolution among nations.

The scope of international law extends beyond traditional state-to-state interactions to encompass a variety of subjects, including human rights, environmental protection, trade, and armed conflict. Its reach extends to both governmental and non-governmental entities, shaping behavior and interactions at the global level.

The evolution of international law can be traced back to ancient civilizations, but it has significantly developed over time, particularly in the modern era. Historical milestones such as the Peace of Westphalia in 1648 and the establishment of the United Nations in 1945 have shaped the evolution of international legal norms and institutions.

International law draws its authority from various sources, including treaties, customary practices, judicial decisions, and scholarly writings. Treaties, also known as conventions or agreements, are formal agreements between states that establish legal obligations and rights. Customary international law arises from consistent state practice accepted as law, while judicial decisions and scholarly writings contribute to the development and interpretation of legal norms.

Several key principles underpin international law, including sovereignty, equality of states, peaceful coexistence, and non-intervention. Sovereignty emphasizes the independence and autonomy of states within their territorial boundaries, while the principle of equality ensures that all states have equal standing under the law.

Treaties play a central role in international law, serving as binding agreements between states. They establish legal rights and obligations, define the scope of cooperation, and provide mechanisms for dispute resolution. Treaties can address a wide range of issues, from trade and commerce to human rights and the environment.

Customary international law consists of unwritten rules derived from consistent state practice, which is followed out of a sense of legal obligation. It reflects the general and consistent behavior of states over time and is binding on all states, regardless of whether they have explicitly consented to it.

In addition to treaties and customary law, soft law instruments such as declarations, resolutions, and guidelines also contribute to the development of international norms and standards. While not legally binding, soft law can influence state behavior, shape public opinion, and pave the way for future legal developments.

Jurisdiction refers to a state's authority to exercise legal power over persons, property, or events within its territory or beyond its borders. International law regulates jurisdictional matters to prevent conflicts between states and ensure the orderly resolution of disputes.

Territorial sovereignty is a fundamental principle of international law that asserts a state's exclusive authority and control over its territory and airspace. It encompasses both land and maritime domains and is enshrined in numerous international treaties and conventions.

Extraterritorial jurisdiction refers to a state's authority to apply its laws and regulations to persons or activities outside its territory. This concept raises complex legal issues, particularly in the context of transnational crimes, human rights violations, and environmental protection.

States are held accountable under international law for their actions or omissions that violate international norms or obligations. State responsibility entails the duty to make reparations for harm caused to other states or entities and can arise from various forms of wrongful conduct, including breaches of treaties, violations of customary law, and internationally wrongful acts.

State immunity is a principle of international law that shields states from the jurisdiction of foreign courts and legal proceedings. It reflects the notion of sovereign equality among states and serves to safeguard states from undue interference in their internal affairs.

Diplomatic immunity grants certain privileges and immunities to diplomats and diplomatic missions accredited to foreign states. It ensures the smooth conduct of international relations by protecting diplomats from arrest, prosecution, and civil lawsuits in the host country.

International organizations, such as the United Nations and the International Monetary Fund, enjoy certain immunities under international law to enable them to fulfill their functions effectively. These immunities shield international organizations from legal proceedings in domestic courts and safeguard their assets and operations from interference by host states.

Statehood is a legal status accorded to entities that possess defined territory, a permanent population, a government, and the capacity to enter into relations with other states. Recognition by other states is not a prerequisite for statehood, but it can confer legitimacy and facilitate participation in international affairs.

Recognition of governments involves the acknowledgment by other states of the legitimacy and authority of a particular regime or administration. While recognition is a political act, it can have legal implications for state-to-state relations and the conduct of international affairs.

Self-determination is a principle of international law that recognizes the right of peoples to freely determine their political status and pursue their economic, social, and cultural development. It has been invoked by various peoples and regions seeking independence or autonomy from colonial rule or foreign domination.

Secession refers to the process by which a part of a state's territory seeks to become an independent sovereign entity. The legal implications of secession are complex and often contentious, raising questions of territorial integrity, minority rights, and the principle of self-determination.

The recognition of states and governments is a key aspect of international relations and diplomacy, influencing state-to-state interactions, treaty-making, and participation in international organizations. Recognition can be expressed through formal diplomatic channels or implied through conduct and practice.

Declaratory theory holds that recognition merely acknowledges the existence of a state or government that already possesses the attributes of statehood. In contrast, constitutive theory suggests that recognition is a constitutive act that creates or confirms the legal status of a state or government.

State succession refers to the transfer of rights, obligations, and assets from one state to another as a result of a change in sovereignty, such as independence, annexation, or dissolution. International law provides principles and rules to govern the succession of states and ensure continuity in legal relations.

The acquisition and loss of territory by states are governed by principles of international law, including occupation, prescription, cession, and accretion. These principles determine the legal basis for territorial claims, boundary disputes, and the resolution of conflicts over land and maritime boundaries.

Recognition of boundaries between states is essential for maintaining territorial integrity, peace, and stability. International law provides principles and mechanisms for the delimitation and demarcation of boundaries, including treaties, arbitration, and judicial settlement.

Maritime boundaries delimit the jurisdictional zones of coastal states in the oceans and seas, including territorial waters, exclusive economic zones (EEZs), and continental shelves. These boundaries are established through treaties, customary practices, and international law, often based on principles of equity, proximity, and relevant geographical features.

Territorial waters extend up to 12 nautical miles from a state's coastline and are subject to the full sovereignty of the coastal state. Within this zone, the coastal state exercises exclusive jurisdiction over navigation, fishing, and resource exploitation, subject to certain rights of innocent passage for foreign vessels.

Exclusive economic zones extend up to 200 nautical miles from a state's coastline and grant the coastal state exclusive rights to exploit and manage natural resources, including fish stocks, minerals, and energy resources. Other states enjoy freedom of navigation and overflight in the EEZ, but must respect the coastal state's rights and regulations.

Continental shelves are underwater extensions of a state's land territory, extending beyond its territorial waters and potentially rich in mineral and hydrocarbon resources. Coastal states have sovereign rights to explore and exploit the resources of their continental shelves, subject to certain limitations and obligations under international law.

The high seas refer to areas of the oceans and seas beyond the jurisdiction of any state, where all states enjoy freedom of navigation, overflight, fishing, and scientific research. The high seas are governed by principles of freedom, equality, and the common heritage of mankind, as enshrined in international treaties and conventions.

In conclusion, international law provides a comprehensive framework for regulating relations between states and other international actors, including the establishment and recognition of boundaries. From territorial sovereignty to maritime delimitation, the principles and rules of international law play a crucial role in maintaining peace, stability, and cooperation in the global community. Understanding the legal principles and mechanisms governing boundaries is essential for resolving disputes, promoting cooperation, and upholding the rule of law in the international arena.

Significance of International Law in the Modern World

International law serves as the cornerstone of global governance, providing a framework for interaction between states and promoting peaceful resolution of disputes. In today's interconnected world, where nations are increasingly interdependent, the significance of international law cannot be overstated.

The proliferation of global challenges, such as climate change, terrorism, and pandemics, underscores the need for a comprehensive legal framework that transcends national boundaries. International law offers a mechanism for cooperation and collective action in addressing these pressing issues.

Moreover, in an era characterized by rapid globalization and technological advancements, the reach and impact of state actions extend far beyond their borders. International law plays a crucial role in regulating the conduct of states and ensuring accountability for violations.

Economic globalization has led to the integration of markets and the expansion of international trade and investment. International trade law, as a subset of international law, facilitates commerce by establishing rules and norms governing trade relations between states.

Similarly, the emergence of supranational organizations such as the United Nations (UN), the World Trade Organization (WTO), and the International Criminal Court (ICC) underscores the growing importance of international law as a means of promoting cooperation and maintaining peace and security.

The rise of non-state actors, including multinational corporations, non-governmental organizations (NGOs), and international terrorist groups, further complicates the global landscape. International law provides mechanisms for addressing the actions of these entities and holding them accountable for their conduct.

Human rights violations remain a persistent challenge in many parts of the world. International human rights law sets forth universal standards of human dignity and provides a framework for addressing atrocities and promoting accountability for perpetrators.

In the context of armed conflict, international humanitarian law governs the conduct of parties to conflict and seeks to mitigate the impact of war on civilians and combatants alike. Adherence to these principles is essential for minimizing human suffering and upholding the rule of law during times of conflict.

The proliferation of weapons of mass destruction (WMDs) poses a grave threat to international peace and security. International arms control treaties and agreements seek to prevent the spread of WMDs and promote disarmament efforts to reduce the risk of catastrophic conflict.

Environmental degradation and resource depletion are global challenges that require collective action and cooperation among states. International environmental law provides a framework for addressing these issues and promoting sustainable development practices.

Transnational crime, including human trafficking, drug trafficking, and cybercrime, poses significant challenges to global security and stability. International legal instruments and cooperation mechanisms are essential for combating these illicit activities and holding perpetrators accountable.

The principle of state sovereignty remains a fundamental tenet of international law, but it is increasingly tempered by the recognition of shared responsibilities and obligations among states. Sovereignty is no longer seen as an absolute right but as a concept that must be balanced with other considerations, such as human rights and the common good.

International law also plays a vital role in promoting democracy, good governance, and the rule of law at the national level. By establishing norms and standards for state behavior, international law helps to foster accountable and transparent governance structures.

Globalization has led to increased cultural exchange and interaction among peoples from diverse backgrounds. International cultural heritage law seeks to protect and preserve the world's cultural heritage, fostering mutual respect and understanding among nations.

In the realm of international trade, the proliferation of regional trade agreements and economic blocs underscores the importance of international law as a tool for promoting economic integration and facilitating cross-border commerce.

The growth of the digital economy and the proliferation of information and communication technologies (ICTs) pose new challenges for international law. Issues such as data privacy, cybersecurity, and intellectual property rights require innovative legal solutions that reflect the realities of the digital age.

The COVID-19 pandemic has highlighted the interconnectedness of global health and the need for coordinated responses to public health emergencies. International health regulations and cooperation mechanisms are essential for addressing pandemics and mitigating their impact on global health and economies.

Migration and refugee flows are increasingly prevalent in today's world, driven by factors such as conflict, poverty, and climate change. International refugee law and human rights law provide protections for refugees and asylum seekers, ensuring their rights and dignity are respected.

International law also plays a critical role in addressing the challenges of sustainable development and combating poverty and inequality. Through initiatives such as the Sustainable Development Goals (SDGs), international law seeks to promote inclusive and equitable development that benefits all people.

The pursuit of peace and conflict resolution is a central objective of international law. Diplomatic efforts, peace treaties, and conflict mediation mechanisms are essential tools for preventing and resolving disputes between states and promoting stability and security.

The advent of space exploration and the growing commercialization of outer space raise new legal questions and challenges. International space law governs the use and exploration of outer space, ensuring peaceful cooperation and the responsible use of space resources.

The protection of cultural heritage and the environment in times of armed conflict is a pressing concern for the international community. International humanitarian law and cultural heritage law provide safeguards for cultural sites and environmental resources during times of conflict.

In the realm of international finance and investment, legal frameworks such as international investment agreements and dispute settlement mechanisms provide protections for investors and promote stability and predictability in the global economy.

International law also plays a critical role in addressing transnational challenges such as terrorism and organized crime. Legal instruments and cooperation mechanisms are essential for combating these threats and promoting security and stability at the global level.

The protection of human rights and fundamental freedoms is a core principle of international law. International human rights law provides a framework for promoting and protecting the rights of individuals and groups, ensuring dignity and equality for all.

The rule of law is essential for promoting peace, stability, and development at the national and international levels. International law provides a framework for establishing legal norms and institutions that uphold the rule of law and ensure accountability for violations.

The proliferation of armed conflicts and civil unrest in various parts of the world underscores the importance of international humanitarian law in protecting civilians and minimizing the impact of war on vulnerable populations.

The increasing interconnectedness of the global economy underscores the need for international cooperation and coordination in addressing economic challenges such as financial crises, trade disputes, and currency fluctuations.

International law also plays a crucial role in promoting gender equality and empowering women and girls around the world. Legal frameworks and international conventions seek to eliminate discrimination and promote equal rights and opportunities for all individuals, regardless of gender.

In conclusion, the significance of international law in the modern world cannot be overstated. From promoting peace and security to protecting human rights and addressing global challenges, international law serves as a vital tool for advancing common interests and fostering cooperation among nations.

Importance of Understanding the Laws of the Sea

Understanding the laws of the sea holds profound importance, particularly exemplified by the complex and contentious South China Sea dispute. This maritime territorial conflict involves multiple nations and embodies the intricate interplay of historical claims, geopolitical interests, and international law.

The South China Sea, rich in natural resources and vital for global trade, has become a focal point of tension due to overlapping claims by China, Vietnam, the Philippines, Malaysia, Brunei, and Taiwan. The dispute underscores the significance of maritime law in resolving territorial disputes and ensuring stability in the region.

At the heart of the South China Sea dispute lies the interpretation and application of the United Nations Convention on the Law of the Sea (UNCLOS), a comprehensive legal framework governing maritime rights and boundaries. The competing claims highlight the complexities of UNCLOS and the challenges of reconciling national interests with international law.

UNCLOS establishes the legal framework for defining maritime zones, such as territorial waters, exclusive economic zones (EEZs), and the continental shelf. The South China Sea dispute involves disputes over these maritime boundaries, highlighting the importance of UNCLOS in clarifying rights and obligations of coastal states.

The South China Sea dispute also raises questions about the legal status of disputed features, such as islands, rocks, and low-tide elevations, under UNCLOS. These legal determinations have significant implications for the extent of maritime entitlements and resource exploitation in the region.

Additionally, the South China Sea dispute has led to disputes over freedom of navigation and overflight, as well as concerns about militarization of disputed features. These issues underscore the importance of upholding navigational freedoms and ensuring compliance with international law to maintain peace and stability in the region.

The South China Sea dispute demonstrates the need for effective mechanisms for dispute resolution and peaceful settlement of maritime disputes. UNCLOS provides avenues for arbitration, conciliation, and judicial settlement, highlighting the importance of adherence to international law in resolving complex disputes.

Furthermore, the South China Sea dispute has broader geopolitical implications, affecting regional security dynamics and the balance of power in the Asia-Pacific region. Understanding the laws of the sea is essential for navigating these complex geopolitical realities and promoting stability and cooperation among coastal states.

The South China Sea dispute also underscores the importance of multilateral cooperation and diplomatic dialogue in addressing maritime disputes. Regional initiatives such as the Association of Southeast Asian Nations (ASEAN) and the Code of Conduct in the South China Sea (COC) demonstrate the value of collective efforts to manage tensions and uphold international law. Moreover, the South China Sea dispute highlights the need for enhanced maritime security cooperation and confidence-building measures among littoral states. Maritime law enforcement, joint patrols, and information-sharing mechanisms can help mitigate risks of conflict and promote maritime safety and security.

The South China Sea dispute presents challenges to the rule-based international order and the principles of peaceful coexistence and respect for sovereign rights. Understanding the laws of the sea is essential for upholding these principles and preventing unilateral actions that could escalate tensions and undermine regional stability.

Additionally, the South China Sea dispute underscores the importance of legal clarity and predictability in maritime affairs. Uncertainty over legal rights and obligations can fuel tensions and increase the risk of conflict, highlighting the need for consistent interpretation and application of international law.

The South China Sea dispute also highlights the role of international institutions and mechanisms in addressing maritime disputes. UNCLOS provides the legal framework for resolving disputes, while institutions such as the International Court of Justice (ICJ) and the International Tribunal for the Law of the Sea (ITLOS) offer avenues for adjudication and dispute settlement.

The South China Sea dispute underscores the interconnectedness of maritime security, economic development, and environmental protection. UNCLOS promotes sustainable development and the conservation of marine resources, emphasizing the importance of responsible stewardship of the marine environment in resolving maritime disputes.

Furthermore, the South China Sea dispute raises concerns about the militarization of maritime disputes and the risk of armed conflict. Adherence to international law and confidence-building measures are essential for de-escalating tensions and preventing the use of force in resolving maritime disputes. The South China Sea dispute also underscores the importance of engaging with non-state actors, including civil society organizations and academic institutions, in promoting dialogue and building consensus on maritime issues. Public awareness and participation are essential for fostering transparency and accountability in maritime governance.

Moreover, the South China Sea dispute highlights the need for capacity-building and technical assistance to enhance the capabilities of coastal states in managing their maritime resources and addressing maritime challenges. International cooperation and assistance can help build the capacity of states to effectively implement UNCLOS and other relevant legal instruments.

The South China Sea dispute underscores the importance of balancing competing interests and promoting equitable solutions that respect the rights and interests of all stakeholders. UNCLOS provides the legal framework for negotiating maritime boundaries and resolving disputes through peaceful means, emphasizing the principles of equity and fairness.

Additionally, the South China Sea dispute highlights the importance of regional cooperation in addressing shared challenges and promoting mutual understanding and trust among neighboring states. Regional initiatives such as joint resource development projects and marine scientific research cooperation can help build confidence and foster cooperation in the region.

The South China Sea dispute also underscores the need for comprehensive approaches to maritime security that address not only traditional security threats but also non-traditional challenges such as piracy, illegal fishing, and environmental degradation. Multilateral cooperation and capacity-building efforts are essential for promoting maritime security and stability in the region.

Moreover, the South China Sea dispute underscores the importance of promoting a rules-based international order that upholds the principles of sovereignty, territorial integrity, and peaceful resolution of disputes. Adherence to international law and respect for the rights of all states are essential for preventing conflicts and maintaining regional stability.

The South China Sea dispute also highlights the importance of promoting confidence-building measures and preventive diplomacy to reduce tensions and prevent the escalation of conflicts. Dialogue, transparency, and cooperation are essential for building trust and promoting peaceful resolution of maritime disputes.

Additionally, the South China Sea dispute underscores the importance of promoting maritime safety and security to ensure the free flow of commerce and navigation in the region. International cooperation in areas such as search and rescue, maritime law enforcement, and maritime domain awareness can help address common security challenges and promote stability in the region.

Furthermore, the South China Sea dispute highlights the need for enhanced regional cooperation in addressing maritime environmental challenges such as pollution, overfishing, and habitat destruction. Sustainable resource management and marine conservation efforts are essential for preserving the ecological integrity of the South China Sea and promoting long-term sustainability.

The South China Sea dispute also underscores the importance of upholding the rights of coastal states and ensuring equitable access to maritime resources. UNCLOS provides a legal framework for determining maritime boundaries and resolving disputes through peaceful means, emphasizing the principles of equity and fairness.

Moreover, the South China Sea dispute highlights the importance of promoting transparency and accountability in maritime governance to prevent the abuse of power and the escalation of conflicts. Adherence to international law and respect for the rights of all states are essential for maintaining regional stability and promoting peaceful resolution of disputes.

Additionally, the South China Sea dispute underscores the need for promoting dialogue and cooperation among all stakeholders to address shared challenges and promote mutual understanding and trust. Regional initiatives such as joint resource development projects and marine scientific research cooperation can help build confidence and foster cooperation in the region.

The South China Sea dispute also highlights the importance of promoting a rules-based international order that upholds the principles of sovereignty, territorial integrity, and peaceful resolution of disputes. Adherence to international law and respect for the rights of all states are essential for preventing conflicts and maintaining regional stability.

Moreover, the South China Sea dispute underscores the importance of promoting confidence-building measures and preventive diplomacy to reduce tensions and prevent the escalation of conflicts. Dialogue, transparency, and cooperation are essential for building trust and promoting peaceful resolution of maritime disputes.

Additionally, the South China Sea dispute highlights the importance of promoting maritime safety and security to ensure the free flow of commerce and navigation in the region. International cooperation in areas such as search and rescue, maritime law enforcement, and maritime domain awareness can help address common security challenges and promote stability in the region.

Furthermore, the South China Sea dispute underscores the need for enhanced regional cooperation in addressing maritime environmental challenges such as pollution, overfishing, and habitat destruction. Sustainable resource management and marine conservation efforts are essential for preserving the ecological integrity of the South China Sea and promoting long-term sustainability.

The South China Sea dispute also underscores the importance of upholding the rights of coastal states and ensuring equitable access to maritime resources. UNCLOS provides a legal framework for determining maritime boundaries and resolving disputes through peaceful means, emphasizing the principles of equity and fairness.

Moreover, the South China Sea dispute highlights the importance of promoting transparency and accountability in maritime governance to prevent the abuse of power and the escalation of conflicts. Adherence to international law and respect for the rights of all states are essential for maintaining regional stability and promoting peaceful resolution of disputes.

Additionally, the South China Sea dispute underscores the need for promoting dialogue and cooperation among all stakeholders to address shared challenges and promote mutual understanding and trust. Regional initiatives such as joint resource development projects and marine scientific research cooperation can help build confidence and foster cooperation in the region.

The South China Sea dispute also highlights the importance of promoting a rules based international order that upholds the principles of sovereignty, territorial integrity, and peaceful resolution of disputes. Adherence to international law and respect for the rights of all states are essential for preventing conflicts and maintaining regional stability.

Moreover, the South China Sea dispute underscores the importance of promoting confidence-building measures and preventive diplomacy to reduce tensions and prevent the escalation of conflicts. Dialogue, transparency, and cooperation are essential for building trust and promoting peaceful resolution of maritime disputes.

Furthermore, the South China Sea dispute highlights the importance of promoting maritime safety and security to ensure the free flow of commerce and navigation in the region. International cooperation in areas such as search and rescue, maritime law enforcement, and maritime domain awareness can help address common security challenges and promote stability in the region.

Furthermore, the South China Sea dispute underscores the need for enhanced regional cooperation in addressing maritime environmental challenges such as pollution, overfishing, and habitat destruction. Sustainable resource management and marine conservation efforts are essential for preserving the ecological integrity of the South China Sea and promoting long-term sustainability.

The South China Sea dispute also underscores the importance of upholding the rights of coastal states and ensuring equitable access to maritime resources. UNCLOS provides a legal framework for determining maritime boundaries and resolving disputes through peaceful means, emphasizing the principles of equity and fairness.

Moreover, the South China Sea dispute highlights the importance of promoting transparency and accountability in maritime governance to prevent the abuse of power and the escalation of conflicts. Adherence to international law and respect for the rights of all states are essential for maintaining regional stability and promoting peaceful resolution of disputes.

Purpose and Scope of the Book

The purpose of this book is to provide a comprehensive exploration of international law and the laws of the sea, examining their significance, principles, and applications in the modern world. Through detailed analysis and case studies, this book aims to elucidate the complexities of international legal frameworks and their implications for global governance and cooperation.

By delving into various case studies and examples, this book seeks to illustrate the practical relevance of international law and the laws of the sea in addressing real-world challenges and conflicts. Through empirical evidence and historical context, readers will gain insights into how legal principles are applied in different contexts and their impact on state behavior and international relations.

The scope of this book encompasses a wide range of topics within international law and the laws of the sea, including state sovereignty, territorial disputes, maritime boundaries, navigation rights, environmental protection, and dispute resolution mechanisms. Through a multidisciplinary approach, this book examines legal, political, economic, and social dimensions of these issues to provide a holistic understanding of their significance and implications.

Case studies will include landmark legal disputes and conflicts, such as the South China Sea dispute, the Arctic sovereignty dispute, and the legal framework governing maritime piracy. By analyzing these cases in depth, readers will gain insights into the complexities of contemporary international legal issues and the challenges of resolving disputes in a globalized world.

The South China Sea dispute serves as a compelling case study for understanding the complexities of maritime territorial disputes and the application of international law in resolving such conflicts. With multiple claimants and overlapping maritime claims, this dispute underscores the challenges of reconciling competing interests and upholding the principles of international law.

In the South China Sea dispute, the interpretation and application of the United Nations Convention on the Law of the Sea (UNCLOS) play a central role in defining maritime boundaries and rights. By examining the legal arguments and positions of the parties involved, readers can gain insights into the complexities of UNCLOS and its implications for maritime governance.

Another example that will be explored in this book is the Arctic sovereignty dispute, which involves competing claims over the vast resources of the Arctic region. With the melting of polar ice caps due to climate change, the Arctic has become increasingly accessible for resource exploitation, leading to tensions among Arctic states over territorial claims and jurisdictional rights.

The Arctic sovereignty dispute highlights the importance of international legal frameworks, such as UNCLOS and the Arctic Council, in governing resource development and environmental protection in the region. By analyzing the legal instruments and mechanisms available for addressing disputes in the Arctic, readers can gain insights into the challenges and opportunities of Arctic governance.

Piracy in the Horn of Africa serves as another case study for examining the application of international law in addressing transnational maritime crimes. With the rise of piracy off the coast of Somalia in the early 21st century, the international community mobilized efforts to combat this threat through legal frameworks such as UNCLOS and the United Nations Security Council resolutions.

The piracy case study highlights the role of international cooperation and collective action in addressing maritime security challenges. By examining the legal responses to piracy and the effectiveness of international counter-piracy efforts, readers can gain insights into the complexities of maritime law enforcement and the challenges of combating transnational maritime crimes.

In addition to these specific case studies, this book will also examine broader themes and trends within international law and the laws of the sea, such as the evolution of legal norms and principles, the role of international institutions and mechanisms, and the impact of globalization and technological advancements on maritime governance.

Through comparative analysis and interdisciplinary perspectives, this book aims to provide readers with a comprehensive understanding of the complexities and nuances of international law and the laws of the sea. By examining legal principles in different contexts and their practical applications, readers can gain insights into the dynamic nature of international legal regimes and their implications for global governance and cooperation.

The purpose of this book is not only to provide an academic analysis of international law and the laws of the sea but also to offer practical insights and recommendations for policymakers, practitioners, and stakeholders involved in maritime affairs. By drawing on empirical evidence and best practices, this book aims to inform decision-making processes and contribute to the development of effective legal frameworks and policies for addressing contemporary maritime challenges.

Through detailed case studies and examples, this book will illustrate the complexities and nuances of international law and the laws of the sea, providing readers with a deeper understanding of their significance and implications in the modern world. By examining real-world conflicts and legal disputes, readers can gain insights into the challenges and opportunities of navigating the complex landscape of international maritime governance.

The scope of this book is broad, encompassing a wide range of topics within international law and the laws of the sea. From state sovereignty and territorial disputes to navigation rights and environmental protection, this book will explore the diverse legal issues and challenges facing the international community in the maritime domain.

By analyzing legal principles and precedents, this book aims to provide readers with a comprehensive understanding of the legal frameworks governing maritime affairs and their implications for state behavior and international relations. Through comparative analysis and case studies, readers can gain insights into the complexities of international maritime law and the challenges of navigating the evolving legal landscape.

One of the key objectives of this book is to highlight the role of international institutions and mechanisms in shaping maritime governance and resolving disputes. From the International Maritime Organization (IMO) to regional organizations such as the European Union (EU) and ASEAN, this book will examine the role of multilateral cooperation in addressing maritime challenges and promoting peace and security at sea.

Additionally, this book will explore the impact of globalization and technological advancements on maritime governance and state behavior. From the proliferation of maritime trade and transportation to the rise of cyber threats and unmanned maritime systems, this book will analyze the implications of these trends for international law and the laws of the sea.

Through empirical research and case studies, this book will provide readers with practical insights and recommendations for addressing contemporary maritime challenges. Whether it is piracy off the coast of Somalia, territorial disputes in the South China Sea, or environmental degradation in the Arctic, this book will offer actionable strategies for promoting maritime security, sustainability, and cooperation.

Furthermore, this book will examine the role of non-state actors, such as civil society organizations and private companies, in shaping maritime governance and addressing maritime challenges. From marine conservation initiatives to corporate social responsibility efforts, this book will highlight the contributions of non-state actors to promoting sustainable and responsible maritime practices.

In addition to analyzing legal frameworks and case studies, this book will also explore the broader geopolitical and geostrategic dimensions of maritime affairs. From great power competition to regional security dynamics, this book will examine the political and military implications of maritime disputes and the challenges of maintaining peace and stability at sea.

Through interdisciplinary perspectives and comparative analysis, this book aims to provide readers with a holistic understanding of international law and the laws of the sea. By examining legal, political, economic, and social dimensions of maritime affairs, readers can gain insights into the complexities and challenges of navigating the global maritime domain.

One of the unique features of this book is its focus on practical applications and policy implications. By drawing on empirical research and case studies, this book aims to provide readers with actionable insights and recommendations for addressing contemporary maritime challenges and promoting effective maritime governance.

The scope of this book is not limited to specific regions or issues but encompasses a wide range of topics within international law and the laws of the sea. Whether it is maritime security, environmental protection, or maritime boundary delimitation, this book will provide readers with a comprehensive overview of the legal frameworks governing maritime affairs.

Through detailed case studies and examples, this book will illustrate the practical relevance of international law and the laws of the sea in addressing real-world challenges and conflicts. By examining legal principles and precedents in different contexts, readers can gain insights into the complexities of maritime governance and the challenges of resolving disputes at sea.

One of the key objectives of this book is to promote dialogue and cooperation among policymakers, practitioners, and stakeholders involved in maritime affairs. By providing a platform for knowledge exchange and collaboration, this book aims to contribute to the development of effective legal frameworks and policies for addressing contemporary maritime challenges.

Additionally, this book will explore emerging issues and trends within international law and the laws of the sea, such as the impact of climate change on maritime security and the rise of maritime hybrid threats. By analyzing these trends and their implications, readers can gain insights into the evolving nature of maritime governance and the challenges of adapting legal frameworks to changing realities.

Moreover, this book will examine the role of regional and international organizations in promoting maritime cooperation and addressing maritime challenges. From the IMO to the United Nations Convention on the Law of the Sea (UNCLOS), this book will analyze the contributions of multilateral institutions to shaping maritime governance and resolving disputes at sea.

Through comparative analysis and case studies, this book

will provide readers with practical insights and recommendations for addressing contemporary maritime challenges. Whether it is piracy off the coast of Somalia, territorial disputes in the South China Sea, or environmental degradation in the Arctic, this book will offer actionable strategies for promoting maritime security, sustainability, and cooperation.

Furthermore, this book will explore the role of non-state actors, such as civil society organizations and private companies, in shaping maritime governance and addressing maritime challenges. From marine conservation initiatives to corporate social responsibility efforts, this book will highlight the contributions of non-state actors to promoting sustainable and responsible maritime practices.

In addition to analyzing legal frameworks and case studies, this book will also examine the broader geopolitical and geostrategic dimensions of maritime affairs. From great power competition to regional security dynamics, this book will analyze the political and military implications of maritime disputes and the challenges of maintaining peace and stability at sea.

Through interdisciplinary perspectives and comparative analysis, this book aims to provide readers with a holistic understanding of international law and the laws of the sea. By examining legal, political, economic, and social dimensions of maritime affairs, readers can gain insights into the complexities and challenges of navigating the global maritime domain.

One of the unique features of this book is its focus on practical applications and policy implications. By drawing on empirical research and case studies, this book aims to provide readers with actionable insights and recommendations for addressing contemporary maritime challenges and promoting effective maritime governance.

The scope of this book is not limited to specific regions or issues but encompasses a wide range of topics within international law and the laws of the sea. Whether it is maritime security, environmental protection, or maritime boundary delimitation, this book will provide readers with a comprehensive overview of the legal frameworks governing maritime affairs.

Through detailed case studies and examples, this book will illustrate the practical relevance of international law and the laws of the sea in addressing real-world challenges and conflicts. By examining legal principles and precedents in different contexts, readers can gain insights into the complexities of maritime governance and the challenges of resolving disputes at sea.

One of the key objectives of this book is to promote dialogue and cooperation among policymakers, practitioners, and stakeholders involved in maritime affairs. By providing a platform for knowledge exchange and collaboration, this book aims to contribute to the development of effective legal frameworks and policies for addressing contemporary maritime challenges.

Additionally, this book will explore emerging issues and trends within international law and the laws of the sea, such as the impact of climate change on maritime security and the rise of maritime hybrid threats. By analyzing these trends and their implications, readers can gain insights into the evolving nature of maritime governance and the challenges of adapting legal frameworks to changing realities.

Moreover, this book will examine the role of regional and international organizations in promoting maritime cooperation and addressing maritime challenges. From the IMO to the United Nations Convention on the Law of the Sea (UNCLOS), this book will analyze the contributions of multilateral institutions to shaping maritime governance and resolving disputes at sea.

Through comparative analysis and case studies, this book will provide readers with practical insights and recommendations for addressing contemporary maritime challenges. Whether it is piracy off the coast of Somalia, territorial disputes in the South China Sea, or environmental degradation in the Arctic, this book will offer actionable strategies for promoting maritime security, sustainability, and cooperation.

Furthermore, this book will explore the role of non-state actors, such as civil society organizations and private companies, in shaping maritime governance and addressing maritime challenges. From marine conservation initiatives to corporate social responsibility efforts, this book will highlight the contributions of non-state actors to promoting sustainable and responsible maritime practices.

Chapter 2.
Foundations of International Law

Historical Development of International Law

The historical development of international law can be traced back to ancient civilizations such as Mesopotamia, Egypt, Greece, and Rome. These early societies developed rudimentary legal systems and codes of conduct to regulate relations between city-states, empires, and foreign traders, laying the foundation for principles of reciprocity, fairness, and mutual respect in interstate relations.

Greek City-States: In ancient Greece, city-states like Athens and Sparta established treaties, alliances, and diplomatic protocols to manage conflicts and promote cooperation among independent polities. Greek philosophers such as Plato and Aristotle articulated theories of natural law and justice that influenced later conceptions of international legal norms and principles.

Roman Law: The Roman Empire codified and systematized legal principles governing relations between states and individuals through the development of Roman law. Roman jurists such as Gaius and Ulpian formulated doctrines of *jus gentium* (law of nations) and *jus naturale* (natural law), which recognized common principles of justice and equity applicable to all human beings, regardless of nationality or citizenship.

Medieval Europe: During the Middle Ages, European monarchs and feudal lords relied on customary law, feudal obligations, and religious authority to govern interstate relations and resolve disputes. The Catholic Church played a central role in mediating conflicts and promoting peace through papal bulls, concordats, and ecclesiastical courts, establishing norms of *jus inter gentes* (law among nations) based on Christian ethics and principles of charity and forgiveness.

Feudalism and Sovereignty: The rise of feudalism and the consolidation of state power in medieval Europe gave rise to notions of sovereignty, territoriality, and the principle of *cuius regio, eius religio* (whose realm, his religion). Feudal monarchs asserted exclusive jurisdiction over their territories and subjects, resisting external interference and asserting their independence from papal authority and imperial claims.

Peace of Westphalia: The Peace of Westphalia in 1648 marked a turning point in the development of international law, establishing the principles of state sovereignty, territorial integrity, and non-interference in domestic affairs as foundational norms of the modern international order. The treaties of Westphalia ended the Thirty Years' War in Europe and laid the groundwork for the modern state system based on the principles of legal equality and diplomatic recognition among sovereign states.

Treaty Law: The emergence of treaty law as a primary source of international legal obligations furthered the development of international law during the early modern period. European states concluded bilateral and multilateral treaties to regulate trade, diplomacy, and territorial disputes, codifying rules of conduct and mechanisms for dispute resolution among sovereign entities.

Colonial Expansion: The age of colonial expansion in the 16th to 19th centuries brought new challenges and opportunities for international law, as European powers extended their influence and control over overseas territories and indigenous peoples. The doctrine of discovery, conquest, and terra nullius (empty land) provided legal justifications for colonial expansion and the dispossession of indigenous lands and resources, leading to conflicts and debates over the rights and responsibilities of colonial powers.

Natural Law: Enlightenment thinkers such as Hugo Grotius and Emer de Vattel articulated theories of natural law and the law of nations based on reason, morality, and the social contract, challenging traditional notions of divine right and absolute sovereignty. Their works, including Grotius' "The Law of War and Peace" and Vattel's "The Law of Nations," laid the intellectual foundations for modern international law by emphasizing the importance of consent, reciprocity, and justice in interstate relations.

Peace Congresses: The 19th century saw the emergence of peace congresses, diplomatic conferences, and international organizations dedicated to promoting peace, disarmament, and arbitration as alternative means of resolving conflicts between states. The Congress of Vienna in 1815 and the Hague Conferences of 1899 and 1907 established norms and mechanisms for diplomatic negotiation, arbitration, and the peaceful settlement of disputes, paving the way for the development of international law as a codified and institutionalized system of rules and procedures.

Codification Efforts: The codification of international law gained momentum in the late 19th and early 20th centuries with the establishment of international commissions and codification bodies tasked with drafting treaties, conventions, and model laws to standardize and clarify legal norms in areas such as maritime law, diplomatic immunity, and state responsibility. Notable examples include the Hague Conventions on the Laws and Customs of War and the creation of the Permanent Court of Arbitration in The Hague.

League of Nations: The creation of the League of Nations in 1919 marked a significant milestone in the institutionalization of international law and collective security mechanisms. The League's Covenant established principles of collective security, peaceful dispute resolution, and the promotion of international cooperation, albeit with limited effectiveness due to the absence of major powers such as the United States and the Soviet Union.

Interwar Period: The interwar period witnessed continued efforts to strengthen international law and institutions in response to the devastation of World War I and the rise of totalitarian regimes. The Kellogg-Briand Pact of 1928 renounced war as an instrument of national policy, while the establishment of the Permanent Court of International Justice provided a forum for adjudicating interstate disputes and clarifying legal principles.

Second World War: The outbreak of World War II exposed the weaknesses of the existing international legal order and highlighted the need for stronger mechanisms of conflict prevention and resolution. The atrocities of the Holocaust and the widespread violations of human rights and humanitarian law underscored the importance of establishing universal norms and institutions to protect human dignity and promote peace and justice. The Nuremberg and Tokyo Trials held after the war established the principle of individual criminal responsibility for war crimes, crimes against humanity, and genocide, laying the groundwork for the development of international criminal law and the establishment of the International Criminal Court.

United Nations: The founding of the United Nations in 1945 marked a renewed commitment to the promotion of international peace, security, and cooperation through collective action and multilateral diplomacy. The UN Charter established the legal framework for the organization, emphasizing principles of sovereign equality, non-interference, and the peaceful settlement of disputes, while providing mechanisms for collective security, peacekeeping, and humanitarian intervention.

Universal Declaration of Human Rights: The adoption of the Universal Declaration of Human Rights in 1948 affirmed the inherent dignity and inalienable rights of all human beings, regardless of race, nationality, or creed, laying the foundation for the modern human rights regime. The UDHR enshrined principles of equality, freedom, and justice as universal values to be upheld by all member states of the United Nations, setting standards for individual and collective action to promote and protect human rights.

Decolonization and Self-Determination: The process of decolonization in the mid-20th century led to the emergence of new states and peoples seeking self-determination and independence from colonial rule. The United Nations played a central role in supporting decolonization efforts through resolutions, treaties, and diplomatic initiatives aimed at facilitating peaceful transitions to self-government and promoting the rights of indigenous peoples to land, resources, and cultural heritage.

Cold War Era: The Cold War era (1945-1991) was characterized by ideological rivalry, geopolitical competition, and nuclear brinkmanship between the United States and the Soviet Union, which posed challenges to the principles of international law and collective security. The Cuban Missile Crisis of 1962 and the construction of the Berlin Wall highlighted the dangers of superpower confrontation and the need for effective mechanisms of crisis management and arms control to prevent catastrophic conflict.

Decolonization and New States: The post-colonial period witnessed the emergence of new states in Asia, Africa, and the Middle East, as former colonies gained independence and sought recognition as sovereign entities in the international community. The United Nations played a pivotal role in admitting new members and mediating disputes over borders, resources, and self-determination, while promoting economic development, human rights, and social justice in newly independent nations.

Cold War Conflicts: The Cold War era was also marked by proxy wars, regional conflicts, and interventions in the developing world, as superpowers sought to extend their influence and contain perceived threats to their security and interests. The Korean War, Vietnam War, and conflicts in Afghanistan, Angola, and Nicaragua reflected the dynamics of Cold War competition and the complexities of international law in addressing asymmetric conflicts and non-state actors.

United Nations Treaties: The United Nations played a central role in codifying and expanding international law through the negotiation and adoption of multilateral treaties and conventions on a wide range of subjects, including human rights, disarmament, environmental protection, and the law of the sea. Treaties such as the Genocide Convention, the Convention on the Elimination of All Forms of Discrimination against Women (CEDAW), and the Kyoto Protocol established binding legal obligations for states and provided frameworks for cooperation and compliance monitoring.

International Court of Justice: The establishment of the International Court of Justice (ICJ) in 1945 provided a permanent forum for the peaceful settlement of disputes between states and the interpretation of international law. The ICJ, also known as the World Court, has jurisdiction to hear cases submitted by states voluntarily or through compulsory means such as treaties, providing authoritative interpretations of legal principles and contributing to the development of customary international law.

Humanitarian Law: The development of humanitarian law, also known as the law of armed conflict or international humanitarian law (IHL), aimed to mitigate the effects of armed conflict on civilians, prisoners of war, and other non-combatants, and to regulate the conduct of belligerents in times of war. The Geneva Conventions of 1949 and their Additional Protocols established rules governing the treatment of war victims, the protection of medical personnel and facilities, and the prohibition of certain weapons and tactics in warfare, reflecting the principles of humanity, neutrality, and proportionality in the conduct of hostilities.

Environmental Law: The emergence of environmental law as a distinct field of international law responded to growing concerns about environmental degradation, pollution, and unsustainable resource use in the 20th century. The United Nations Conference on the Human Environment in 1972 and the Rio Earth Summit in 1992 catalyzed international efforts to address global environmental challenges through treaties, agreements, and action plans, leading to the establishment of institutions such as the United Nations Environment Programme (UNEP) and the adoption of landmark treaties such as the Convention on Biological Diversity and the Kyoto Protocol.

Law of the Sea: The development of the law of the sea as a specialized branch of international law was spurred by increasing maritime activities, technological advancements, and disputes over ocean resources in the 20th century. The United Nations Convention on the Law of the Sea (UNCLOS) of 1982 codified rules and principles governing maritime zones, navigation rights, resource exploitation, and environmental protection, providing a comprehensive legal framework for the management and governance of the world's oceans and seas.

Human Rights Law: The expansion of human rights law in the post-war period reflected a growing recognition of the universality and indivisibility of human rights as fundamental freedoms and entitlements inherent to all individuals, regardless of nationality, race, or religion. The Universal Declaration of Human Rights and subsequent human rights treaties established legal standards and mechanisms for promoting and protecting civil, political, economic, social, and cultural rights, while holding states accountable for human rights violations and abuses through international monitoring, reporting, and accountability mechanisms.

International Criminal Law: The emergence of international criminal law as a distinct field of law addressed the need to hold individuals accountable for the most serious crimes under international law, including genocide, crimes against humanity, war crimes, and aggression. The establishment of ad hoc and hybrid tribunals such as the International Criminal Tribunal for the former Yugoslavia (ICTY), the International Criminal Tribunal for Rwanda (ICTR), and the Special Court for Sierra Leone (SCSL) paved the way for the creation of the International Criminal Court (ICC) in 2002, which has jurisdiction over individuals accused of committing international crimes within its mandate.

Humanitarian Intervention: The concept of humanitarian intervention, or the use of military force for humanitarian purposes, raised ethical, legal, and political questions about the legitimacy and legality of intervention in the internal affairs of sovereign states to prevent or halt mass atrocities. Debates over the responsibility to protect (R2P) doctrine and the use of force in situations of grave humanitarian crises underscored the tensions between state sovereignty and the international community's duty to protect populations at risk of genocide, ethnic cleansing, or other mass atrocities.

Globalization and Interdependence: The process of globalization and interdependence in the 21st century has posed new challenges and opportunities for international law, as states, non-state actors, and transnational networks navigate complex issues such as economic integration, migration, cybersecurity, and climate change. The proliferation of international agreements, regional arrangements, and cross-border activities has underscored the need for coordinated action and cooperation to address shared challenges and promote sustainable development, peace, and security in an increasingly interconnected world.

Technological Advances: Rapid advancements in technology, including digital communications, artificial intelligence, biotechnology, and space exploration, have raised novel legal and ethical questions about the governance of emerging technologies and their impact on human rights, privacy, and security. The development of norms, standards, and regulatory frameworks for emerging technologies remains a pressing challenge for international law and policymakers seeking to balance innovation with accountability and societal well-being.

Cybersecurity and Information Law: The rise of cyber threats, including cybercrime, espionage, and warfare, has highlighted the need for international cooperation and legal responses to address vulnerabilities in cyberspace and protect critical infrastructure, data, and privacy rights. Efforts to develop norms of responsible state behavior in cyberspace and enhance cyber resilience through capacity-building, information-sharing, and diplomatic dialogue have become priorities for states and international organizations grappling with the evolving threat landscape.

Space Law: The exploration and commercialization of outer space have raised legal questions about the governance of space activities, resource exploitation, environmental protection, and the peaceful uses of outer space. The Outer Space Treaty of 1967 established principles of space exploration, non-appropriation of celestial bodies, and peaceful coexistence in outer space, laying the groundwork for subsequent treaties, guidelines, and regulatory frameworks to govern space activities and ensure the sustainable and equitable use of space resources.

Migration and Refugee Law: The global migration crisis has underscored the need for international cooperation and legal frameworks to address the rights and protection of migrants, refugees, and asylum seekers fleeing conflict, persecution, and poverty. The adoption of the Global Compact for Safe, Orderly and Regular Migration and the Global Compact on Refugees reflects efforts to enhance international cooperation, burden-sharing, and protection mechanisms for vulnerable populations on the move, while addressing the root causes of displacement and promoting sustainable solutions.

Climate Change Law: The existential threat of climate change has spurred international efforts to mitigate greenhouse gas emissions, adapt to changing environmental conditions, and promote sustainable development strategies that are resilient to climate impacts. The Paris Agreement of 2015, which aims to limit global warming to well below 2 degrees Celsius and pursue efforts to limit it to 1.5 degrees Celsius, represents a landmark multilateral agreement to combat climate change and mobilize global action to transition to low-carbon, climate-resilient economies.

Health Law and Pandemic Response: The COVID-19 pandemic has highlighted the importance of health law, pandemic preparedness, and international cooperation in responding to global health emergencies. The World Health Organization (WHO) and other international health agencies have played a central role in coordinating response efforts, sharing information, and mobilizing resources to contain the spread of the virus, ensure equitable access to vaccines and medical supplies, and address the social and economic impacts of the pandemic on vulnerable populations.

Humanitarian Law and Conflict Resolution: Armed conflicts and humanitarian crises continue to pose challenges to international law and efforts to promote peace, security, and human rights. The protection of civilians, humanitarian access, and compliance with international humanitarian law remain critical priorities for conflict resolution efforts, peacekeeping operations, and humanitarian assistance programs aimed at alleviating suffering and addressing the root causes of violence and instability.

Trade Law and Economic Governance: The globalization of trade and investment has led to the development of international trade law and economic governance frameworks aimed at promoting free trade, economic integration, and sustainable development. Multilateral trade agreements such as the World Trade Organization (WTO) agreements, regional trade blocs, and bilateral trade agreements establish rules and procedures for trade liberalization, tariff reduction, and dispute settlement, while addressing issues such as labor rights, environmental protection, and intellectual property rights.

Human Rights Enforcement and Accountability: The promotion and protection of human rights require effective mechanisms of enforcement and accountability to address violations and ensure redress for victims. International and regional human rights courts and tribunals, national human rights institutions, truth and reconciliation commissions, and transitional justice mechanisms play crucial roles in holding perpetrators accountable, providing reparations to victims, and fostering reconciliation and social cohesion in post-conflict societies.

Civil Society and Public Advocacy: Civil society

organizations, human rights defenders, and grassroots movements play vital roles in promoting awareness, advocacy, and accountability in the field of international law. Their efforts to monitor compliance with international legal standards, document human rights abuses, and mobilize public support for justice and accountability contribute to the strengthening of international norms and institutions, while amplifying the voices of marginalized and vulnerable communities in the global arena.

Educational and Capacity-Building Initiatives: Education and capacity-building initiatives are essential for enhancing awareness, understanding, and compliance with international law among diverse stakeholders, including government officials, legal practitioners, academics, civil society organizations, and the general public. Training programs, workshops, seminars, and online courses provide opportunities for individuals to acquire knowledge, skills, and practical tools for applying international legal principles in their respective fields and contexts. These initiatives also foster networks of collaboration, exchange, and mutual support among practitioners and experts, promoting best practices, innovation, and continuous learning in the field of international law.

By investing in education and capacity-building, states and organizations can strengthen their institutional capacity, promote a culture of respect for the rule of law, and contribute to the advancement of global peace, justice, and sustainable development. Moreover, educational initiatives aimed at raising awareness about international law and human rights can empower individuals to advocate for their rights, hold governments and institutions accountable, and participate actively in democratic processes and decision-making at local, national, and international levels.

In addition to formal education and training programs, public outreach activities, media campaigns, and community engagement initiatives play vital roles in disseminating information about international law and promoting public awareness and engagement. By reaching out to diverse audiences through accessible and culturally relevant channels, such initiatives can bridge gaps in understanding, foster dialogue, and build trust between governments, communities, and international organizations, thereby strengthening social cohesion, resilience, and cooperation in addressing global challenges.

Furthermore, international cooperation and partnerships are essential for leveraging resources, expertise, and best practices to support educational and capacity-building initiatives in the field of international law. Bilateral and multilateral partnerships, academic exchanges, and institutional collaborations facilitate the sharing of knowledge, expertise, and resources among states, universities, research institutions, and civil society organizations, promoting mutual learning, innovation, and collaboration in advancing the rule of law and human rights worldwide.

In conclusion, education and capacity-building are indispensable tools for promoting awareness, understanding, and compliance with international law, as well as fostering a culture of peace, justice, and respect for human rights in diverse societies. By investing in education, training, and public outreach, stakeholders can empower individuals and communities to contribute meaningfully to the promotion and protection of international legal norms and values, thus advancing the collective goal of building a more just, peaceful, and sustainable world for present and future generations.

Sources of International Law

The sources of international law are the origins from which international legal rules derive their authority and legitimacy. These sources provide the basis for the creation, interpretation, and application of international legal norms. There are generally recognized sources of international law, which include:

Treaties: Treaties, also known as conventions, agreements, or protocols, are formal written agreements concluded between states or international organizations. Treaties can be bilateral (between two parties) or multilateral (involving multiple parties) and cover a wide range of subjects, including human rights, trade, environment, and security. Treaties are binding upon the parties that have ratified or acceded to them and are considered primary sources of international law.

Customary International Law: Customary international law consists of established practices and norms that are followed consistently by states out of a sense of legal obligation (*opinio juris*). Customary law arises from the general and consistent practice of states over time and is evidence of a legal obligation binding on all states, regardless of whether they have explicitly consented to it through treaties.

General Principles of Law: General principles of law recognized by civilized nations are another source of international law. These principles include fundamental concepts of justice and equity that are common to legal systems around the world, such as the principle of non-retroactivity, the principle of good faith, and the principle of estoppel. General principles of law serve as supplementary sources of international law and are applied by international tribunals and courts to resolve disputes and fill gaps in treaty and customary law.

Judicial Decisions and Scholarly Writings: Decisions of international tribunals, such as the International Court of Justice (ICJ), and the jurisprudence of other international and regional courts and tribunals contribute to the development of international law by interpreting and applying legal principles to specific cases and disputes. Similarly, scholarly writings and opinions of legal experts, academics, and practitioners provide valuable insights and interpretations of international legal norms and principles, which may influence the development and evolution of international law over time.

Equity: Equity refers to the principles of fairness, justice, and good conscience that guide the resolution of disputes and the interpretation of legal norms in international law. While equity is not a formal source of law, it plays a significant role in the decision-making process of international tribunals and courts, especially when legal rules are unclear or conflicting. Equity allows for flexible and context-specific solutions to complex legal issues, taking into account the interests and needs of all parties involved.

These sources of international law interact and complement each other, shaping the development, interpretation, and application of international legal norms in a dynamic and evolving global legal system. By recognizing and respecting these sources, states, international organizations, and other actors contribute to the stability, predictability, and effectiveness of the international legal order.

Principles of International Law

Sovereignty is a fundamental principle of international law that emphasizes the independence and autonomy of states within their territorial boundaries. It encompasses the exclusive right of states to govern their internal affairs, make and enforce laws, and engage in diplomatic relations with other states. Sovereignty also entails the principle of non-interference, which prohibits states from intervening in the domestic affairs of other states without their consent, except in limited circumstances such as self-defense or with authorization from the United Nations Security Council.

Territorial Integrity: Territorial integrity is a principle of international law that recognizes the inviolability of states' territorial boundaries and prohibits the use of force or coercion to alter the borders of states. It is enshrined in the UN Charter and other international instruments, reflecting the importance of preserving stability, peace, and security by respecting existing borders and territorial arrangements. Violations of territorial integrity, such as annexation, occupation, or territorial aggression, are considered breaches of international law and may trigger diplomatic or legal responses by the international community.

Non-Intervention: The principle of non-intervention

prohibits states from interfering in the internal affairs of other states or engaging in actions that threaten their political independence, territorial integrity, or sovereignty. Non-intervention encompasses a wide range of activities, including military intervention, economic coercion, political subversion, and support for insurgent movements, and is grounded in the principle of sovereign equality and mutual respect among states. While the principle of non-intervention is fundamental to the maintenance of international peace and security, it is not absolute and may be subject to exceptions such as humanitarian intervention or collective self-defense authorized by the United Nations.

Peaceful Settlement of Disputes: The principle of peaceful settlement of disputes underscores the importance of resolving conflicts and disputes between states through peaceful means, such as negotiation, mediation, arbitration, and judicial settlement, rather than resorting to force or coercion. It is enshrined in Article 2(3) and Chapter VI of the UN Charter, which require states to seek peaceful solutions to international disputes and refrain from threatening or using force against the territorial integrity or political independence of any state. Peaceful settlement mechanisms promote the rule of law, stability, and cooperation among states by providing orderly and predictable processes for resolving conflicts and preventing their escalation into armed conflict.

Good Faith: The principle of good faith, or pacta sunt servanda (agreements must be kept), is a fundamental principle of international law that requires states to fulfill their treaty obligations in good faith and refrain from acts that would undermine the purpose or object of a treaty. It is codified in Article 26 of the Vienna Convention on the Law of Treaties, which states that "every treaty in force is binding upon the parties to it and must be performed by them in good faith." Good faith requires states to interpret treaties in accordance with their ordinary meaning, object, and purpose, and to refrain from acts that would defeat the intended purpose or undermine the legitimate expectations of the parties.

Equity: Equity is a principle of international law that emphasizes fairness, justice, and good conscience in the resolution of disputes and the interpretation of legal norms. It serves as a supplementary source of law and allows for flexible and context-specific solutions to complex legal issues, taking into account the interests and needs of all parties involved. Equity enables international tribunals and courts to adapt legal rules and principles to changing circumstances and to achieve just and equitable outcomes in individual cases.

Estoppel: Estoppel is a principle of international law that prevents states from denying or asserting facts or legal positions that are inconsistent with their previous statements, conduct, or representations. It operates to prevent unfairness or injustice where one party has relied on the words or actions of another party to their detriment. Estoppel may arise in various contexts, including diplomatic negotiations, treaty interpretation, and state responsibility, and is based on principles of fairness, reliance, and consistency in international relations.

Acquired Rights: The principle of acquired rights recognizes the legal rights and obligations that arise from the conduct or status of states over time, even in the absence of formal agreement or acknowledgment. It encompasses rights acquired through historical practice, custom, or long-standing usage, as well as rights derived from treaties, agreements, or other legal instruments. Acquired rights may include territorial claims, fishing rights, navigation rights, and other entitlements that have been recognized and respected by the international community over time.

Peaceful Coexistence: Peaceful coexistence is a principle of international law that emphasizes the importance of harmonious relations, mutual respect, and non-interference among states with different political systems, ideologies, or cultural backgrounds. It promotes tolerance, dialogue, and cooperation as means of resolving differences and preventing conflicts between states, while respecting their diversity and sovereignty. Peaceful coexistence is a cornerstone of international diplomacy and conflict resolution, underpinning efforts to build trust, confidence, and cooperation among nations in pursuit of common goals and interests.

Reciprocity: Reciprocity is a principle of international law that governs the mutual exchange of rights, privileges, and obligations between states on the basis of equality and mutual benefit. It entails the expectation that states will treat each other in a manner consistent with the norms and standards of international law, and that they will reciprocate actions and concessions made by other states. Reciprocity serves as a basis for the negotiation and implementation of international agreements, treaties, and arrangements, as well as for the maintenance of stable and mutually beneficial relations between states. It encourages states to comply with their international obligations, uphold their commitments, and respect the rights and interests of other states in order to foster trust, cooperation, and reciprocity in their interactions.

Self-Defense: The principle of self-defense is a customary and treaty-based right enshrined in Article 51 of the UN Charter, which recognizes the inherent right of states to defend themselves against armed attack. Self-defense allows states to use force, including military action, in response to an armed attack or imminent threat of attack, when necessary and proportionate to repel the aggression and restore security. Self-defense may be exercised individually or collectively, and it is subject to the principles of necessity, proportionality, and immediacy, as well as to notification to the UN Security Council, if applicable.

Countermeasures: Countermeasures are measures taken by states in response to wrongful acts of other states in order to induce compliance with international law and protect their own rights and interests. They are governed by the principle of necessity, proportionality, and non-retaliation, and they must be directed against the responsible state rather than innocent third parties. Countermeasures may include diplomatic protests, economic sanctions, retorsions, and other lawful means of coercion aimed at inducing the responsible state to cease its wrongful conduct and provide redress for the harm caused.

State Responsibility: The principle of state responsibility establishes the legal obligations of states for their internationally wrongful acts, whether attributable to the state itself or to its organs, agents, or entities under its authority or control. It is codified in the International Law Commission's Articles on Responsibility of States for Internationally Wrongful Acts, which define the elements of state responsibility, including the wrongful act, attribution, breach of international obligation, and the consequences thereof. State responsibility entails duties such as cessation, reparation, and guarantees of non-repetition, as well as the obligation to cooperate in the settlement of disputes and the enforcement of international law.

Erga Omnes Obligations: *Erga omnes* obligations are obligations owed by states to the international community as a whole, rather than to specific states or individuals, and they arise from peremptory norms of international law (jus cogens). These obligations entail duties such as the prohibition of genocide, slavery, and aggression, as well as the protection of fundamental human rights and the environment. Erga omnes obligations are considered fundamental principles of international law and give rise to rights of enforcement and compliance by other states and the international community as a whole.

Solidarity: Solidarity is a principle of international law that emphasizes collective action, mutual assistance, and shared responsibility among states and peoples in addressing common challenges and promoting common interests. It reflects the recognition that global problems such as poverty, inequality, climate change, and pandemics require collective solutions and cooperation across borders, cultures, and interests. Solidarity encourages states to work together in pursuit of shared goals, to support each other in times of need, and to uphold the principles of fairness, justice, and human dignity in their relations with one another.

Common Heritage of Mankind: The principle of the common heritage of mankind recognizes that certain resources and areas of the earth, such as the deep seabed, outer space, and Antarctica, are the common heritage of all humankind and should be managed and preserved for the benefit of present and future generations. It is based on the idea that certain resources and areas possess unique characteristics or value to humanity as a whole and should therefore be protected from exploitation, appropriation, or degradation by individual states or private actors. The principle of the common heritage of mankind imposes obligations on states to cooperate in the management and conservation of these resources and to ensure their equitable and sustainable use for the benefit of all.

Prohibition of Aggression: The principle of the prohibition of aggression prohibits states from using force or the threat of force against the territorial integrity, political independence, or sovereignty of other states, except in self-defense or when authorized by the UN Security Council. It is enshrined in Article 2(4) of the UN Charter and reflects the fundamental principle of the sovereign equality of states and the peaceful settlement of disputes. The prohibition of aggression aims to prevent the outbreak of armed conflict and to maintain international peace and security by prohibiting acts of aggression and promoting the peaceful resolution of disputes through diplomatic means.

Non-Use of Force: The principle of the non-use of force, also known as the pacific settlement of disputes, emphasizes the importance of resolving disputes between states through peaceful means and refraining from the threat or use of force to settle international disputes. It is enshrined in Article 2(4) of the UN Charter and reflects the commitment of states to respect the sovereignty, territorial integrity, and political independence of other states. The non-use of force principle underscores the central role of diplomacy, negotiation, mediation, arbitration, and judicial settlement in resolving conflicts and promoting international cooperation and stability.

Prohibition of the Threat of Force: The principle of the

prohibition of the threat of force prohibits states from using the threat of force as a means of resolving disputes or achieving political objectives. It is closely related to the prohibition of aggression and the non-use of force and reflects the principle of peaceful coexistence and the peaceful settlement of disputes. The prohibition of the threat of force aims to prevent the escalation of tensions and the outbreak of armed conflict by prohibiting states from engaging in coercive or intimidating behavior that undermines the security and stability of other states.

Principle of Non-Discrimination: The principle of non-discrimination requires states to treat individuals and other states equally and without discrimination based on race, ethnicity, nationality, religion, gender, or other prohibited grounds. It is enshrined in various international human rights instruments, such as the Universal Declaration of Human Rights and the International Convention on the Elimination of All Forms of Racial Discrimination, and it is recognized as a fundamental principle of international law. The principle of non-discrimination promotes equality, dignity, and respect for human rights by prohibiting discriminatory practices and ensuring equal protection under the law for all individuals and groups.

Protection of Human Rights: The protection of human rights is a core principle of international law that recognizes the inherent dignity and worth of every individual and seeks to safeguard their fundamental rights and freedoms from abuse, discrimination, and violation. It is enshrined in various international human rights instruments, including the Universal Declaration of Human Rights, the International Covenant on Civil and Political Rights, and the International Covenant on Economic, Social and Cultural Rights. The protection of human rights obligates states to respect, protect, and fulfill the rights of all individuals within their jurisdiction and to take measures to prevent and remedy human rights violations.

Right to Self-Determination: The principle of the right to self-determination affirms the right of people to freely determine their political status, pursues their economic, social, and cultural development, and freely disposes of their natural wealth and resources. It is enshrined in Article 1 of the UN Charter and is recognized as a fundamental principle of international law. The right to self-determination applies to peoples living under colonial domination, foreign occupation, or alien subjugation, as well as to indigenous peoples and minorities, and it obligates states to respect the territorial integrity and political independence of other states while promoting the exercise of the right to self-determination.

Chapter 3.
The Concept of the Sea in International Law

Definition and Classification of the Seas and Oceans

The seas and oceans cover approximately 71% of the Earth's surface and play a crucial role in global ecosystems, climate regulation, and human activities such as transportation, trade, and resource extraction. The term "sea" generally refers to a large body of saltwater that is partially enclosed by land, while the term "ocean" refers to the vast expanse of saltwater that covers most of the Earth's surface and is divided into major ocean basins such as the Atlantic, Pacific, Indian, and Arctic Oceans.

Classification of Seas and Oceans by Size: Seas and oceans vary in size, depth, and geographical features and they can be classified based on their size and location. The largest and deepest ocean, the Pacific Ocean, covers more than one-third of the Earth's surface and contains the deepest point on Earth, the Mariana Trench. The Atlantic Ocean, the second-largest ocean, is known for its vast expanse and important role in global shipping and trade routes. The Indian Ocean, located between Africa, Asia, Australia, and the Middle East, is characterized by its warm waters and diverse marine ecosystems. The Arctic Ocean, situated in the polar region, is the smallest and shallowest of the world's oceans and is covered by sea ice for much of the year.

Classification of Seas and Oceans by Geographic Location: Seas and oceans can also be classified based on their geographic location and proximity to continents and landmasses. Marginal seas are semi-enclosed bodies of water that are partially surrounded by land and connected to larger oceans, such as the Mediterranean Sea, the Caribbean Sea, and the South China Sea. These seas serve as important transit routes for maritime trade and are home to diverse marine life and ecosystems. In contrast, open oceans are vast expanses of water that are not significantly influenced by landmasses and are characterized by deep-sea currents, marine biodiversity, and geological features such as mid-ocean ridges and abyssal plains.

Classification of Seas and Oceans by Salinity: Seas and oceans can also be classified based on their salinity, or the concentration of dissolved salts and minerals in the water. The saltiness of seawater varies depending on factors such as evaporation, precipitation, and freshwater inputs from rivers and glaciers. The average salinity of seawater is around 3.5%, with higher salinity levels in subtropical and tropical regions and lower salinity levels in Polar Regions and near river mouths. Variations in salinity can affect marine ecosystems, ocean circulation patterns, and the distribution of marine species, making it an important factor in understanding the dynamics of the seas and oceans.

Classification of Seas and Oceans by Depth Zones: Seas and oceans can also be classified based on their depth zones, which include the continental shelf, continental slope, and continental rise, abyssal plain and deep-sea trenches. The continental shelf is the shallow, submerged portion of the continental margin that extends from the shoreline to the shelf break, where it drops off steeply into deeper waters. The continental slope is the steep descent from the shelf break to the abyssal plain, characterized by underwater cliffs and canyons. The continental rise is the gentle slope at the base of the continental slope, where sediment transported from the shelf accumulates. The abyssal plain is the flat, sediment-covered seafloor of the deep ocean, while deep-sea trenches are narrow, elongated depressions in the ocean floor formed by tectonic activity and subduction zones.

Classification of Seas and Oceans by Temperature: Seas and oceans can also be classified based on their temperature regimes, which vary with latitude, depth, and ocean currents. The surface temperature of the oceans ranges from freezing temperatures in polar regions to tropical temperatures near the equator, with seasonal variations influenced by factors such as sunlight, wind, and ocean circulation patterns. Below the surface, ocean temperatures decrease with depth due to the absence of sunlight and the mixing of water masses with different temperatures. The thermocline is the boundary layer between warmer surface waters and colder deep waters, where temperature gradients are most pronounced and significant changes in temperature occur.

Classification of Seas and Oceans by Productivity: Seas and oceans can also be classified based on their productivity, or the ability to support marine life and ecosystems. Productivity is influenced by factors such as nutrient availability, sunlight, and ocean currents, which determine the abundance and diversity of marine species and ecosystems. Coastal seas and upwelling zones are often highly productive due to nutrient-rich waters and favorable environmental conditions for phytoplankton growth, which forms the base of the marine food chain. In contrast, oligotrophic oceans are characterized by low nutrient levels and limited productivity, particularly in regions with low upwelling and limited nutrient inputs from land. Understanding the productivity of seas and oceans is essential for fisheries management, marine conservation, and ecosystem-based approaches to ocean governance.

Classification of Seas and Oceans by Ecological Zones: Seas and oceans can also be classified based on ecological zones, which represent distinct habitats and ecosystems that support a wide variety of marine species and biodiversity. These ecological zones include coastal zones, estuaries, coral reefs, mangrove forests, seagrass beds, pelagic zones, and benthic zones. Coastal zones are dynamic environments where land and sea meet, characterized by diverse habitats such as rocky shores, sandy beaches, and salt marshes, which provide important breeding, feeding, and nursery grounds for marine species. Estuaries are transitional zones where freshwater rivers meet the salty waters of the ocean, creating unique habitats for fish, birds, and other wildlife.

Coral reefs are underwater ecosystems formed by colonies of coral polyps, which support a rich diversity of marine life and provide valuable ecosystem services such as coastal protection, fisheries habitat, and tourism revenue. Mangrove forests are coastal wetlands dominated by salt-tolerant trees and shrubs, which provide essential habitat for fish, birds, and other wildlife, as well as important ecosystem services such as coastal protection, carbon sequestration, and water filtration. Sea grass beds are underwater meadows of grass-like plants that provide habitat for a wide variety of marine species, including fish, crustaceans, and sea turtles, as well as important ecosystem services such as nutrient cycling, sediment stabilization, and habitat for commercially important fisheries species.

Pelagic zones are open ocean environments where marine species such as fish, sharks, whales, and dolphins roam freely in the water column, while benthic zones are the seafloor habitats inhabited by bottom-dwelling organisms such as corals, sponges, and shellfish. Understanding the ecological zones of seas and oceans is essential for marine conservation, ecosystem-based management, and sustainable development of marine resources.

Classification of Seas and Oceans by Legal Status: Seas and oceans can also be classified based on their legal status and jurisdictional regimes, which determine the rights and responsibilities of states and other actors in these areas. The United Nations Convention on the Law of the Sea (UNCLOS) provides the primary framework for the legal regime of the seas and oceans, establishing rules and principles governing the rights and obligations of states with respect to maritime zones, navigation, marine resource exploitation, environmental protection, and dispute resolution. Under UNCLOS, maritime zones are divided into internal waters, territorial seas, contiguous zones, exclusive economic zones (EEZs), continental shelves, and the high seas, each with its own set of rights and responsibilities for coastal states and other states. Internal waters are the waters on the landward side of the baseline from which the territorial sea is measured, subject to the full sovereignty of the coastal state. Territorial seas are the waters adjacent to the coast of a state, extending up to 12 nautical miles from the baseline, within which the coastal state exercises sovereignty and jurisdiction over various activities, including navigation, fishing, and environmental protection.

Contiguous zones are the waters beyond the territorial sea, extending up to 24 nautical miles from the baseline, where the coastal state may exercise limited control for the purpose of preventing and punishing violations of its customs, fiscal, immigration, and sanitary laws and regulations. Exclusive economic zones (EEZs) are the waters adjacent to the territorial sea, extending up to 200 nautical miles from the baseline, within which the coastal state has sovereign rights and jurisdiction over living and non-living marine resources, as well as jurisdictional rights over other activities such as environmental protection, scientific research, and marine pollution control. Continental shelves are the submerged prolongations of the coastal landmass, extending beyond the territorial sea and EEZ, where coastal states have sovereign rights over the exploration and exploitation of natural resources such as oil, gas, and minerals.

The high seas are the waters beyond the EEZ and continental shelf, where all states enjoy freedom of navigation, overflight, fishing, and scientific research, subject to certain international legal obligations such as the duty to protect the marine environment and to cooperate in the conservation and management of shared living resources. The classification of seas and oceans by legal status reflects the complex interplay of international law, state practice, and geopolitical interests in the governance of maritime spaces and resources, and it underscores the importance of UNCLOS as the primary legal framework for regulating activities in the seas and oceans and promoting cooperation and peaceful coexistence among states.

Classification of Seas and Oceans by Environmental Features: Seas and oceans can also be classified based on their environmental features and characteristics, which include factors such as temperature, salinity, biodiversity, and ecological productivity. These environmental features vary widely depending on factors such as latitude, depth, ocean currents, and proximity to land, and they play a critical role in shaping marine ecosystems and habitats, as well as influencing human activities and interactions with the marine environment. For example, tropical seas and oceans are characterized by warm temperatures, high salinity, and high biodiversity, supporting a wide variety of marine species such as coral reefs, fish, and marine mammals, as well as important ecosystems such as mangrove forests and seagrass beds.

In contrast, polar seas and oceans are characterized by cold temperatures, low salinity, and seasonal sea ice cover, creating unique habitats for species adapted to extreme conditions such as polar bears, seals, and penguins, as well as important ecosystems such as sea ice communities and ice shelves. Understanding the environmental features of seas and oceans is essential for marine conservation, ecosystem management, and sustainable development, as well as for assessing the potential impacts of human activities such as fishing, shipping, pollution, and climate change on marine ecosystems and biodiversity.

By classifying seas and oceans based on their environmental features, scientists, policymakers, and stakeholders can better understand the complex interactions between natural processes and human activities in the marine environment and develop effective strategies for mitigating environmental impacts and promoting the long-term health and sustainability of marine ecosystems and resources.

Classification of Seas and Oceans by Geographic Regions: Seas and oceans can also be classified based on geographic regions, which reflect the unique characteristics, ecosystems, and human activities found in different parts of the world's oceans. These geographic regions include the Arctic Ocean, Atlantic Ocean, Indian Ocean, Pacific Ocean, Southern Ocean, and various marginal seas and ocean basins. The Arctic Ocean, located in the polar region, is characterized by its sea ice cover, extreme cold temperatures, and unique marine ecosystems adapted to harsh environmental conditions. The Atlantic Ocean, situated between the Americas to the west and Europe and Africa to the east, is known for its vast expanse, diverse marine life, and important role in global shipping and trade routes.

The Indian Ocean, bordered by Africa to the west, Asia to the north, and Australia to the east, is characterized by its warm waters, rich biodiversity, and strategic importance for maritime trade and transportation. The Pacific Ocean, the largest and deepest ocean, is bounded by Asia and Australia to the west, the Americas to the east, and the Arctic and Southern Oceans to the north and south, respectively, and is known for its vast expanse, diverse marine ecosystems, and dynamic ocean currents. The Southern Ocean, also known as the Antarctic Ocean, surrounds the continent of Antarctica and is characterized by its cold temperatures, strong winds, and unique marine ecosystems, including abundant krill and whales.

Marginal seas and ocean basins, such as the Mediterranean Sea, Caribbean Sea, South China Sea, and Gulf of Mexico, are semi-enclosed bodies of water that are partially surrounded by land and connected to larger oceans, and they are characterized by their unique physical, biological, and geopolitical features. By classifying seas and oceans based on geographic regions, scientists, policymakers, and stakeholders can better understand the regional dynamics and challenges facing different parts of the world's oceans and develop tailored strategies for conservation, management, and sustainable use of marine resources.

Classification of Seas and Oceans by Tectonic Plate Boundaries: Seas and oceans can also be classified based on tectonic plate boundaries, which represent the dynamic interactions between the Earth's lithosphere, or outer shell, and the underlying asthenosphere, or semi-fluid layer. These plate boundaries include divergent boundaries, where tectonic plates move away from each other, convergent boundaries, where tectonic plates collide and subduct beneath one another, and transform boundaries, where tectonic plates slide past each other horizontally. Divergent boundaries occur along mid-ocean ridges, where new oceanic crust is formed through volcanic activity and magma upwelling, creating submarine mountain ranges and rift valleys.

Convergent boundaries occur where oceanic and continental plates collide, leading to the formation of deep-sea trenches, volcanic arcs, and mountain ranges, as well as subduction zones where oceanic crust is forced beneath continental crust. Transform boundaries occur along fracture zones and transform faults, where tectonic plates slide past each other horizontally, causing earthquakes and the lateral movement of crustal material. Understanding the tectonic plate boundaries of seas and oceans is essential for understanding processes such as seafloor spreading, subduction, and plate tectonics, as well as for assessing geohazards such as earthquakes, tsunamis, and volcanic eruptions that can impact marine ecosystems, coastal communities, and human activities.

Classification of Seas and Oceans by Economic Resources: Seas and oceans can also be classified based on their economic resources and potential for commercial exploitation, including fisheries, oil and gas reserves, mineral deposits, and renewable energy sources. Fisheries are a valuable economic resource found in seas and oceans worldwide, providing food, livelihoods, and income for millions of people around the world. Commercial fishing operations target a wide variety of marine species, including finfish, shellfish, and crustaceans, using a range of fishing methods such as trawling, longlining, and purse seining. Oil and gas reserves are another important economic resource found in seas and oceans, particularly in offshore areas such as continental shelves and deep-sea basins, where hydrocarbon deposits are trapped beneath the seafloor and can be extracted through drilling and production operations. Mineral deposits such as manganese nodules, polymetallic sulfides, and cobalt-rich crusts are also found on the seafloor of certain areas, particularly in deep-sea regions with hydrothermal vents, seamounts, and abyssal plains.

Renewable energy sources such as wind, wave, and tidal energy have the potential to provide clean and sustainable power from seas and oceans, harnessing natural forces such as wind, waves, and tides to generate electricity and reduce dependence on fossil fuels. By classifying seas and oceans based on their economic resources, policymakers, investors, and stakeholders can better understand the value and potential of marine resources and develop strategies for sustainable management, conservation, and exploitation of these resources for the benefit of present and future generations.

Classification of Seas and Oceans by Ecological Vulnerability: Seas and oceans can also be classified based on their ecological vulnerability to human activities and environmental stressors, including pollution, habitat destruction, overfishing, climate change, and ocean acidification. Coastal and marine ecosystems such as coral reefs, mangrove forests, and sea grass beds are particularly vulnerable to human impacts due to their proximity to human populations, coastal development, and pollution inputs from land-based sources such as urban runoff, industrial discharge, and agricultural runoff.

Overfishing and destructive fishing practices such as bottom trawling, dynamite fishing, and illegal fishing can also degrade marine ecosystems and deplete fish stocks, leading to loss of biodiversity, ecosystem services, and livelihoods for coastal communities. Climate change and ocean acidification pose additional threats to seas and oceans, impacting marine species and habitats through changes in temperature, ocean chemistry, sea level rise, and extreme weather events.

Classification of Seas and Oceans by Cultural Significance:

Seas and oceans can also be classified based on their cultural significance to human societies, including indigenous peoples, coastal communities, and maritime cultures around the world. Throughout history, seas and oceans have played a central role in shaping human cultures, identities, and traditions, serving as sources of inspiration, livelihoods, and spiritual connections to the natural world. Coastal and maritime cultures have developed unique knowledge, skills, and practices for navigating, fishing, and living in harmony with the marine environment, passing down traditional knowledge and customs from generation to generation.

Indigenous peoples, such as the Inuit, Maori, and Pacific Islanders, have deep cultural connections to the seas and oceans, relying on them for sustenance, transportation, and cultural practices such as fishing, whaling, and storytelling. Coastal communities and fishing villages around the world have developed distinctive cultural traditions, festivals, and rituals centered on the sea, celebrating its bounty and honoring its importance in their lives and livelihoods.

Maritime cultures such as sailors, fishermen, and seafarers have long been celebrated in literature, art, and folklore, embodying the spirit of adventure, exploration, and resilience in the face of the unknown. By classifying seas and oceans based on their cultural significance, scholars, policymakers, and communities can better understand the diverse ways in which human societies have interacted with and been shaped by the marine environment, as well as the importance of preserving and celebrating cultural heritage for future generations.

Classification of Seas and Oceans by Political Boundaries: Seas and oceans can also be classified based on political boundaries and jurisdictional regimes established by coastal states and international agreements, which determine the rights and responsibilities of states and other actors in these areas. Maritime boundaries are defined lines that delimit the jurisdictional zones of coastal states and allocate rights and responsibilities for activities such as navigation, fishing, resource exploitation, and environmental protection. Maritime boundaries can be classified into territorial seas, exclusive economic zones (EEZs), continental shelves, and international waters, each governed by different legal frameworks and principles of international law. Territorial seas extend up to 12 nautical miles from the baseline of a coastal state and are subject to the full sovereignty and jurisdiction of that state, including the regulation of navigation, fishing, and environmental protection. Exclusive economic zones (EEZs) extend up to 200 nautical miles from the baseline of a coastal state and grant that state sovereign rights and jurisdiction over living and non-living marine resources, as well as jurisdictional rights over other activities such as environmental protection, scientific research, and marine pollution control.

Continental shelves are the submerged prolongations of the coastal landmass, extending beyond the territorial sea and EEZ, where coastal states have sovereign rights over the exploration and exploitation of natural resources such as oil, gas, and minerals. International waters, also known as the high seas, are the waters beyond the EEZ and continental shelf, where all states enjoy freedom of navigation, overflight, fishing, and scientific research, subject to certain international legal obligations such as the duty to protect the marine environment and to cooperate in the conservation and management of shared living resources.

By classifying seas and oceans based on political boundaries, states, and international agreements, policymakers, and stakeholders can better understand the legal frameworks and principles governing maritime areas and develop strategies for cooperation, conflict resolution, and sustainable management of marine resources.

Classification of Seas and Oceans by Conservation Status: Seas and oceans can also be classified based on their conservation status and the level of protection afforded to marine ecosystems, habitats and species. Marine protected areas (MPAs) are designated areas of seas and oceans that are managed and regulated to conserve biodiversity, protect habitats, and sustainably manage natural resources. MPAs can include a variety of conservation zones such as marine reserves, national parks, wildlife sanctuaries, and no-take zones, each with its own set of management objectives and regulations.

Marine protected areas can be established by coastal states, regional organizations, or international agreements and they play a crucial role in conserving marine biodiversity, enhancing fisheries productivity, and promoting ecosystem resilience in the face of threats such as overfishing, habitat destruction, pollution, and climate change. By classifying seas and oceans based on their conservation status and the extent of marine protected areas, scientists, policymakers, and conservationists can identify priority areas for conservation, allocate resources more effectively, and develop strategies for expanding and strengthening marine protected area networks to ensure the long-term health and sustainability of marine ecosystems and resources for future generations.

Classification of Seas and Oceans by Access and Governance: Seas and oceans can also be classified based on access and governance arrangements, which determine the rights and responsibilities of states, non-state actors, and international organizations in managing and regulating activities such as navigation, fishing, resource exploitation, and environmental protection. Access to seas and oceans is governed by a complex set of legal frameworks and principles, including international law, coastal state jurisdiction, regional agreements, and customary practices, which establish rules and procedures for the exercise of rights and the resolution of disputes in maritime areas. Governance arrangements for seas and oceans involve a wide range of actors, including coastal states, flag states, port states, international organizations, non-governmental organizations (NGOs), and indigenous peoples, each with its own roles, responsibilities, and interests in promoting sustainable management, conservation, and development of marine resources. International organizations such as the International Maritime Organization (IMO), the Food and Agriculture Organization (FAO), and the United Nations Environment Programme (UNEP) play a crucial role in setting standards, coordinating actions, and providing technical assistance to states and other stakeholders in addressing maritime issues such as shipping safety, fisheries management, marine pollution, and ecosystem conservation.

Regional organizations such as the European Union (EU), the African Union (AU), and the Association of Southeast Asian Nations (ASEAN) also play important roles in regional seas governance, promoting cooperation, coordination, and collective action among member states to address shared challenges and opportunities in maritime areas. Non-state actors such as civil society organizations, research institutions, industry associations, and private sector companies also contribute to ocean governance through advocacy, research, capacity building, and corporate social responsibility initiatives.

Indigenous peoples and local communities often have traditional knowledge, customary practices, and cultural values that inform marine governance and resource management decisions, and their participation and engagement are essential for achieving sustainable and equitable outcomes in seas and oceans. By classifying seas and oceans based on access and governance arrangements, policymakers, and stakeholders can better understand the legal frameworks, institutional mechanisms, and governance processes that shape decision-making and outcomes in maritime areas, as well as identify opportunities for collaboration, innovation, and improvement in ocean governance at local, national, regional, and global levels.

Classification of Seas and Oceans by Risk and Vulnerability: Seas and oceans can also be classified based on the risks and vulnerabilities they face from natural hazards, human activities, and environmental changes, including factors such as climate change, pollution, habitat destruction, overfishing, invasive species, and extreme weather events. Coastal and marine ecosystems are particularly vulnerable to these threats due to their proximity to human populations, urban development, and industrial activities, as well as their role in providing essential ecosystem services such as coastal protection, fisheries habitat, and carbon sequestration. Climate change poses significant risks to seas and oceans through impacts such as sea level rise, ocean warming, ocean acidification, changes in precipitation patterns, and increased frequency and intensity of extreme weather events such as hurricanes, typhoons, and storm surges.

Pollution from sources such as plastic debris, oil spills, chemical contaminants, and nutrient runoff can degrade water quality, harm marine life, and disrupt ecosystem functioning in seas and oceans, affecting human health, livelihoods, and well-being. Habitat destruction from activities such as coastal development, dredging, sand mining, and bottom trawling can degrade critical habitats such as coral reefs, mangrove forests, and seagrass beds, reducing biodiversity, ecosystem resilience, and coastal protection services.

Overfishing and illegal, unreported, and unregulated (IUU) fishing can deplete fish stocks, disrupt food webs, and undermine the sustainability of fisheries and marine ecosystems, threatening food security, livelihoods, and economic development. Invasive species such as marine pests, pathogens, and predators can disrupt native ecosystems, outcompete native species, and alter ecosystem dynamics, leading to ecological imbalances and biodiversity loss. By classifying seas and oceans based on their risks and vulnerabilities, scientists, policymakers, and stakeholders can identify priority areas for action, allocate resources effectively, and develop strategies for risk reduction, adaptation, and resilience-building to address current and future challenges in marine environments.

Classification of Seas and Oceans by Connectivity and Interdependence: Seas and oceans can also be classified based on their connectivity and interdependence with other marine and terrestrial ecosystems, as well as with human societies and economies around the world. Marine ecosystems are interconnected through complex networks of ecological processes, ocean currents, migratory pathways, and nutrient cycles, which link coastal and offshore habitats, species populations, and biological communities in seas and oceans.

Terrestrial ecosystems such as rivers, wetlands, forests, and estuaries are connected to marine ecosystems through freshwater inputs, sediment transport, and nutrient runoff, which influence water quality, habitat quality, and biodiversity in coastal and marine environments. Human societies and economies are also interconnected with seas and oceans through a wide range of activities such as shipping, fishing, tourism, energy production, and trade, which depend on marine resources, services, and infrastructure for their viability and sustainability.

Coastal communities rely on seas and oceans for food, livelihoods, transportation, recreation, and cultural identity, while inland populations benefit from marine resources such as fish, oil, gas, minerals, and renewable energy sources. By classifying seas and oceans based on their connectivity and interdependence, scientists, policymakers, and stakeholders can better understand the ecological, social, and economic linkages between marine and terrestrial systems, as well as the implications of human activities and decisions for the health, resilience, and sustainability of seas and oceans and the well-being of present and future generations.

Historical Perspective: Evolution of Maritime Law

Maritime law has ancient roots, dating back to civilizations such as ancient Egypt, Greece, Rome, and Mesopotamia, where maritime activities such as shipping, trade, and navigation played vital roles in commerce, diplomacy, and cultural exchange. These ancient civilizations developed maritime codes, customs, and practices to regulate maritime activities, resolve disputes, and ensure the safety and security of seafarers and vessels. For example, the Code of Hammurabi, one of the earliest known legal codes dating back to ancient Mesopotamia around 1754 BCE, included provisions governing maritime commerce, shipwrecks, and maritime contracts, reflecting the importance of maritime trade and navigation in ancient societies.

Medieval Maritime Law: During the Middle Ages, maritime law continued to evolve as European nations such as Venice, Genoa, and the Hanseatic League emerged as maritime powers, dominating trade routes and commercial activities in the Mediterranean Sea, Baltic Sea, and North Sea. These maritime cities developed their own legal systems, known as maritime or admiralty law, to govern maritime activities such as shipping, trade, and navigation, establishing courts and tribunals to adjudicate maritime disputes and enforce maritime contracts. The Consulate of the Sea, established in the 13th century in maritime cities such as Barcelona and Valencia, compiled maritime customs and practices into written codes, known as the "Maritime Consulate Ordinances," which served as early examples of maritime law codification in Europe.

Development of the Law of the Sea: The development of the law of the sea accelerated during the Age of Exploration and Discovery in the 15th and 16th centuries, as European powers such as Spain, Portugal, England, and the Netherlands expanded their maritime empires and established colonial outposts and trading posts around the world. These colonial powers asserted control over vast stretches of the seas and oceans, claiming sovereignty and jurisdiction over maritime territories, resources, and trade routes. The principle of *mare liberum* (freedom of the seas), advocated by Dutch jurist Hugo Grotius in his seminal work *"Mare Liberum"* in 1609, challenged the exclusive claims of coastal states and asserted the rights of all nations to navigate, fish, and trade freely in the high seas, laying the groundwork for the modern law of the sea.

Emergence of Admiralty Courts: The emergence of admiralty courts in maritime nations such as England and the Netherlands during the early modern period played a crucial role in the development and enforcement of maritime law. Admiralty courts, also known as maritime courts or vice-admiralty courts, were established to adjudicate maritime disputes, including cases involving shipping, salvage, collisions, piracy, and maritime contracts. These specialized courts applied principles of maritime law, custom, and equity to resolve disputes fairly and efficiently, contributing to the development of a coherent body of maritime law and jurisprudence.

Rise of Commercial Maritime Law: The rise of commercial maritime law in the 17th and 18th centuries reflected the growing importance of maritime trade and commerce in global economic affairs. Merchant communities, shipowners, and traders developed specialized legal rules and practices to facilitate maritime transactions, manage risks, and protect investments in shipping and trade. Maritime insurance, for example, emerged as a vital tool for managing risks associated with maritime commerce, with the development of institutions such as Lloyd's of London and the Lloyd's Register of Shipping providing insurance coverage, risk assessment, and classification services for ships and cargoes.

Colonial Expansion and Maritime Law: The colonial expansion of European powers during the Age of Exploration and Colonialism had profound implications for maritime law and governance. European colonial powers established colonial outposts, trading posts, and settlements in distant lands, asserting control over maritime territories, resources, and trade routes. The doctrine of *terra nullius* (land belonging to no one) and the principle of *res nullius* (resources belonging to no one) were used to justify European claims to newly discovered lands and resources, leading to conflicts with indigenous peoples and rival colonial powers over territorial sovereignty, maritime boundaries, and exclusive economic zones.

Codification of Maritime Law: The codification of maritime law began in the 19th century with the publication of comprehensive legal codes and statutes governing maritime activities and transactions. National governments and international organizations such as the International Maritime Organization (IMO) played key roles in codifying maritime law, harmonizing legal standards, and promoting uniformity in maritime regulations and practices. The adoption of international conventions and treaties, such as the Hague Rules (1924) on carriage of goods by sea, the SOLAS Convention (1914) on maritime safety, and the MARPOL Convention (1973) on marine pollution, established common rules and standards for maritime activities and operations, enhancing safety, security, and environmental protection in the seas and oceans.

Modernization of Admiralty Law: The modernization of admiralty law in the 20th century reflected changes in maritime technology, trade patterns, and legal practices, as well as efforts to adapt to emerging challenges such as piracy, terrorism, and environmental pollution. Admiralty courts and tribunals expanded their jurisdiction to address new types of maritime disputes, including cases involving maritime terrorism, oil spills, marine pollution, and offshore drilling accidents, applying principles of international law, maritime conventions, and domestic statutes to ensure accountability, compensation, and redress for victims and affected parties.

International Maritime Conventions and Treaties: The proliferation of international maritime conventions and treaties in the 20th and 21st centuries reflects the increasing globalization of maritime activities and the need for international cooperation and coordination in regulating maritime affairs. International organizations such as the International Maritime Organization (IMO), the United Nations Convention on the Law of the Sea (UNCLOS), and the International Labour Organization (ILO) have played central roles in negotiating, adopting, and implementing maritime conventions and treaties on a wide range of issues such as maritime safety, security, environmental protection, labor standards, and fisheries management.

UNCLOS and the Modern Law of the Sea: The United Nations Convention on the Law of the Sea (UNCLOS), adopted in 1982 and entered into force in 1994, represents a landmark achievement in the development of the modern law of the sea, providing a comprehensive legal framework for the governance of the world's oceans and seas. UNCLOS establishes rules and principles governing maritime zones, navigation rights, marine resource exploitation, environmental protection, and dispute resolution, balancing the interests and rights of coastal states, flag states, and other stakeholders in maritime affairs. UNCLOS codifies customary international law and establishes new legal concepts such as exclusive economic zones (EEZs), continental shelves, and the common heritage of mankind, reflecting the evolving needs and aspirations of the international community in managing and conserving the oceans and their resources.

Evolution of Maritime Security Law: The evolution of maritime security law in the 21st century reflects growing concerns about maritime threats such as piracy, terrorism, organized crime, and weapons proliferation, as well as efforts to enhance maritime security cooperation and coordination among states and international organizations. Maritime security law encompasses a wide range of legal instruments, initiatives, and mechanisms aimed at preventing, deterring, and responding to security threats in the maritime domain, including measures such as naval patrols, port security, maritime surveillance, intelligence sharing, and counterterrorism operations.

International conventions and agreements such as the International Ship and Port Facility Security (ISPS) Code, the Djibouti Code of Conduct, and the United Nations Security Council resolutions on piracy off the coast of Somalia have established legal frameworks and standards for enhancing maritime security and combating transnational maritime threats. Regional initiatives such as the Gulf of Guinea Commission, the Indian Ocean Rim Association (IORA), and the Regional Cooperation Agreement on Combating Piracy and Armed Robbery against Ships in Asia (ReCAAP) facilitate cooperation and coordination among coastal states, international organizations, and maritime stakeholders to address common security challenges and promote maritime stability and security in key maritime regions.

Maritime Environmental Law and Regulation: The development of maritime environmental law and regulation reflects growing concerns about marine pollution, habitat destruction, overfishing, and climate change, as well as efforts to promote sustainable and responsible stewardship of the oceans and their resources. International conventions and agreements such as the International Convention for the Prevention of Pollution from Ships (MARPOL), the London Convention on the Prevention of Marine Pollution by Dumping of Wastes and Other Matter, and the United Nations Framework Convention on Climate Change (UNFCCC) establish legal frameworks and standards for protecting the marine environment, reducing pollution, conserving biodiversity, and mitigating the impacts of climate change on oceans and coastal areas. National governments and regional organizations also enact domestic laws and regulations to implement international commitments, address specific environmental challenges, and promote sustainable development in maritime areas.

Legal Challenges in the Arctic: The Arctic region presents unique legal challenges and opportunities due to its changing environmental conditions, resource potential, geopolitical significance, and indigenous rights. As the Arctic ice melts and sea ice retreats, new opportunities emerge for shipping, resource exploration, and commercial activities in the region, raising questions about sovereignty, jurisdiction, and environmental protection in the Arctic Ocean. The legal status of the Northwest Passage and the Northern Sea Route, for example, remains a subject of debate among Arctic states, indigenous peoples, and the international community, with implications for navigation rights, environmental protection, and indigenous rights in the region. The Arctic Council, established in 1996, provides a forum for Arctic states and indigenous peoples to discuss common interests, address shared challenges, and promote sustainable development in the Arctic region, while international agreements such as the Agreement on the Conservation of Polar Bears and the Agreement on Cooperation on Marine Oil Pollution Preparedness and Response in the Arctic address specific environmental and safety concerns in the region.

Legal Frameworks for Marine Biodiversity Conservation: The conservation and sustainable use of marine biodiversity are governed by a complex array of international and national legal frameworks, including conventions, treaties, regulations, and guidelines aimed at protecting marine ecosystems, species, and habitats from threats such as overexploitation, habitat degradation, pollution, and climate change. International instruments such as the Convention on Biological Diversity (CBD), the Convention on the Conservation of Migratory Species of Wild Animals (CMS), and the Convention on Wetlands of International Importance (Ramsar Convention) establish legal obligations and principles for conserving and managing marine biodiversity at the global, regional, and national levels, promoting cooperation, collaboration, and capacity building among states and stakeholders.

Regional agreements and initiatives such as the Coral Triangle Initiative, the Mediterranean Action Plan, and the Pacific Islands Regional Ocean Policy provide frameworks for addressing specific biodiversity hotspots, ecosystems, and species of regional significance, fostering partnerships, and sharing best practices for marine conservation and sustainable management.

Legal Frameworks for Fisheries Management: Fisheries management is governed by a complex set of international and national legal frameworks aimed at ensuring the sustainable use and conservation of marine fisheries resources, promoting responsible fishing practices, and preventing overfishing, illegal fishing, and bycatch. International instruments such as the United Nations Fish Stocks Agreement, the FAO Code of Conduct for Responsible Fisheries, and the Port State Measures Agreement establish legal principles and standards for fisheries management, including measures such as quota allocations, gear restrictions, closed seasons, and marine protected areas, to maintain fish stocks at sustainable levels and protect marine ecosystems and biodiversity. Regional fisheries management organizations (RFMOs) such as the International Commission for the Conservation of Atlantic Tunas (ICCAT), the Northwest Atlantic

Fisheries Organization (NAFO), and the Western and Central Pacific Fisheries Commission (WCPFC) coordinate and regulate fishing activities in specific ocean regions, implementing conservation and management measures, conducting scientific research, and monitoring compliance with fisheries regulations.

Legal Frameworks for Marine Spatial Planning: Marine spatial planning (MSP) is an increasingly important tool for managing competing uses and activities in marine areas, including shipping, fishing, offshore energy development, tourism, conservation, and marine protected areas. MSP is governed by a combination of national laws, regulations, policies, and international guidelines aimed at promoting sustainable development, protecting marine ecosystems, and minimizing conflicts among users and stakeholders. International organizations such as the International Maritime Organization (IMO), the United Nations Educational, Scientific and Cultural Organization (UNESCO), and the United Nations Environment Programme (UNEP) provide guidance and best practices for MSP, encouraging states to adopt integrated and ecosystem-based approaches to marine planning, engage stakeholders in decision-making processes, and consider the cumulative impacts of human activities on marine environments.

Legal Frameworks for Marine Spatial Data Infrastructure: Marine spatial data infrastructure (MSDI) is a framework for organizing, sharing, and analyzing spatial data and information about the marine environment, including maps, charts, satellite imagery, and scientific data, to support decision-making, planning, and management of marine resources and activities. MSDI is governed by a combination of national policies, standards, and regulations, as well as international agreements and initiatives aimed at promoting data sharing, interoperability, and accessibility among governments, research institutions, industry, and civil society. International organizations such as the International Hydrographic Organization (IHO), the International Oceanographic Data and Information Exchange (IODE), and the Group on Earth Observations (GEO) provide guidance and technical assistance for developing and implementing MSDI, encouraging states to establish national marine spatial data infrastructures, share data with other countries, and contribute to global databases and records.

The Influence of Customary Law: Throughout history, customary law has played a significant role in shaping maritime practices and regulations. Customary law refers to unwritten legal principles and norms that emerge from consistent and widespread state practice, accepted as binding by states out of a sense of legal obligation. In the maritime context, customary law has evolved through centuries of maritime trade, navigation, and exploration, reflecting the shared practices, customs, and traditions of seafaring nations. Customary maritime law covers a wide range of issues, including navigational rights, salvage, collision, piracy, and marine pollution, providing a flexible and adaptable framework for regulating maritime activities and resolving disputes in the absence of formal legal instruments.

The Role of Treaties and Conventions: Treaties and conventions have been instrumental in shaping the modern framework of maritime law. These international agreements are negotiated and adopted by states to establish binding rules and standards for regulating specific aspects of maritime activities. Over the centuries, maritime treaties and conventions have addressed a wide range of issues, including navigation, safety, pollution prevention, fisheries management, and the law of the sea. Key examples include the International Convention for the Safety of Life at Sea (SOLAS), the International Convention for the Prevention of Pollution from Ships (MARPOL), and the United Nations Convention on the Law of the Sea (UNCLOS). These treaties and conventions provide a foundation for international cooperation and coordination in addressing common maritime challenges and promoting the sustainable use and conservation of marine resources.

The Role of National Legislation: National legislation also plays a crucial role in the development and enforcement of maritime law. Each coastal state has the sovereign authority to enact laws and regulations governing maritime activities within its territorial waters and exclusive economic zone (EEZ). National legislation may address a wide range of issues, including maritime safety, pollution prevention, fisheries management, port operations, and maritime security. Additionally, many coastal states have established admiralty courts or specialized tribunals to adjudicate maritime disputes and enforce maritime laws. National legislation must comply with international treaties and conventions to which the state is a party, ensuring consistency and coherence in the regulation of maritime activities.

The Impact of Technological Advances: Technological advances have significantly influenced the evolution of maritime law. Throughout history, innovations such as the compass, sextant, steam engine, and radio have revolutionized maritime navigation, communication, and transportation, leading to changes in maritime practices, regulations, and legal standards. In the modern era, technologies such as satellite navigation systems, electronic chart displays, automatic identification systems (AIS), and remote sensing technologies have further transformed the maritime industry, enhancing safety, efficiency, and environmental protection in maritime operations. However, technological advancements also present new challenges and risks, such as cyber threats, autonomous vessels, and underwater resource extraction, which require innovative legal responses and regulatory frameworks to address.

The Evolution of Maritime Security: The evolution of maritime security threats has prompted adaptations in maritime law and governance. Historically, piracy, armed robbery at sea, and maritime terrorism has posed significant challenges to maritime safety, security, and commerce. In response, states and international organizations have developed legal frameworks and mechanisms to combat maritime crime, enhance maritime domain awareness, and protect critical maritime infrastructure. The International Maritime Organization (IMO) has adopted a series of international conventions and protocols, such as the International Ship and Port Facility Security (ISPS) Code and the

Djibouti Code of Conduct, to strengthen maritime security measures and promote international cooperation in combating maritime threats. Additionally, regional initiatives, such as the Regional Cooperation Agreement on Combating Piracy and Armed Robbery against Ships in Asia (ReCAAP) and the Yaoundé Code of Conduct in West and Central Africa, facilitate cooperation among coastal states in addressing maritime security challenges in specific regions.

The Rise of Environmental Concerns: Environmental concerns have increasingly shaped maritime law and policy in response to growing threats such as marine pollution, habitat destruction, and climate change. Pollution from shipping, oil spills, chemical discharges, and marine debris poses significant risks to marine ecosystems, biodiversity, and human health. In recent decades, international efforts to address marine pollution have led to the adoption of conventions and protocols such as MARPOL, the London Convention, and the Basel Convention, which establish rules and standards for the prevention, reduction, and control of marine pollution from various sources. Additionally, the United Nations Framework Convention on Climate Change (UNFCCC) and the Paris Agreement aim to mitigate climate change impacts on oceans and coastal areas by reducing greenhouse gas emissions and promoting adaptation measures.

The Protection of Marine Biodiversity: The protection of marine biodiversity has emerged as a priority area in maritime law and governance. Marine biodiversity encompasses a wide range of species, habitats, and ecosystems, including coral reefs, mangroves, sea grasses, and deep-sea vents, which provide essential ecosystem services such as food, oxygen production, carbon sequestration, and coastal protection. Threats such as overfishing, habitat destruction, pollution, and climate change have led to declines in marine biodiversity, prompting international efforts to conserve and sustainably manage marine ecosystems and species. The Convention on Biological Diversity (CBD), the Convention on the Conservation of Migratory Species of Wild Animals (CMS), and the Convention on Wetlands of International Importance (Ramsar Convention) are among the key international instruments aimed at protecting marine biodiversity and promoting sustainable use of marine resources.

Maritime Archaeology and Cultural Heritage: Maritime archaeology plays a crucial role in uncovering and preserving the cultural heritage of the seas and oceans. Underwater archaeological sites, shipwrecks, submerged landscapes, and ancient artifacts provide valuable insights into human history, trade networks, navigation techniques, and maritime cultures. However, these cultural heritage sites are often at risk from natural processes, human activities, and looting. Legal frameworks such as the UNESCO Convention on the Protection of the Underwater Cultural Heritage seek to protect and manage underwater archaeological sites, promote scientific research and exploration, and prevent the illicit trafficking of underwater cultural artifacts. National governments, maritime museums, research institutions, and heritage organizations collaborate to survey, document, and conserve underwater cultural heritage, ensuring that these treasures are preserved for future generations.

Maritime Boundary Delimitation: Maritime boundary delimitation is a complex legal and technical process used to establish the outer limits of coastal states' maritime zones, including territorial waters, exclusive economic zones (EEZs), and continental shelves. Disputes over maritime boundaries arise due to overlapping claims, conflicting interpretations of international law, and competing interests in maritime resources and territories. Legal principles such as equidistance, equitable principles, and relevant circumstances guide the delimitation process, which may involve negotiations, mediation, arbitration, or adjudication by international courts and tribunals. The United Nations Convention on the Law of the Sea (UNCLOS) provides a legal framework for maritime boundary delimitation, establishing rules and procedures for resolving disputes and promoting cooperation among coastal states in delineating their maritime boundaries.

Maritime Security and Counter-Piracy Measures: Maritime security is a paramount concern for coastal states, international organizations, and the global shipping industry, given the persistent threat of piracy, armed robbery at sea, and maritime terrorism in key maritime regions. Piracy, in particular, poses significant risks to maritime safety, security, and commerce, affecting shipping routes, trade flows, and the livelihoods of seafarers. International efforts to combat piracy and maritime crime have led to the deployment of naval patrols, the establishment of high-risk areas, and the adoption of best management practices by shipping companies to deter and prevent pirate attacks. Additionally, international legal frameworks such as the United Nations Convention on the Law of the Sea (UNCLOS), the Convention for the Suppression of Unlawful Acts against the Safety of Maritime Navigation (SUA Convention), and the Djibouti Code of Conduct provide legal mechanisms for prosecuting pirates, enhancing maritime domain awareness, and promoting regional cooperation in combating piracy and maritime terrorism.

Maritime Labour Law and Seafarers' Rights: Maritime labour law governs the rights and responsibilities of seafarers, shipowners, and maritime employers, ensuring fair and decent working conditions, wages, and social protections for seafarers engaged in international shipping. The International Labour Organization (ILO) sets international standards for maritime labour through conventions such as the Maritime Labour Convention (MLC), which establishes minimum requirements for seafarers' employment, working conditions, accommodation, health care, and social security. The MLC aims to protect seafarers from exploitation, ensure their welfare and well-being at sea, and promote compliance with international labour standards by flag states, shipowners, and maritime administrations. Additionally, national laws and regulations supplement international standards, addressing specific issues such as crewing, certification, repatriation, and occupational safety and health in the maritime industry.

Maritime Dispute Resolution Mechanisms: Maritime disputes may arise between states, shipowners, insurers, and other maritime stakeholders over issues such as collisions, salvage, pollution, and contractual disputes. Effective dispute resolution mechanisms are essential for resolving conflicts, minimizing legal uncertainties, and maintaining the stability and integrity of the maritime industry. Various dispute resolution mechanisms exist, including litigation in national courts, arbitration, mediation, and alternative dispute resolution (ADR) procedures. International conventions and agreements such as the International Convention on Salvage (SALVAGE Convention) and the International Convention on Civil Liability for Oil Pollution Damage (CLC Convention) provide legal frameworks for resolving maritime disputes and allocating liability among parties involved in maritime incidents. Additionally, specialized maritime arbitration institutions, such as the London Maritime Arbitrators Association (LMAA) and the Singapore Chamber of Maritime Arbitration (SCMA), offer neutral and efficient forums for resolving complex maritime disputes through arbitration proceedings, ensuring impartiality, expertise, and confidentiality in dispute resolution.

Maritime Insurance and Risk Management: Maritime insurance plays a critical role in managing risks associated with maritime commerce, providing financial protection and compensation for ship owners, cargo owners, and maritime stakeholders against losses, liabilities, and damages arising from maritime incidents such as collisions, groundings, fires, and marine casualties. Marine insurance contracts, known as policies, cover various risks, including hull and machinery damage, cargo loss or damage, third-party liabilities, pollution cleanup costs, and personal injury claims. Insurance underwriters, brokers, and P&I clubs offer specialized marine insurance products and services tailored to the needs of the maritime industry, ensuring that vessels, cargoes, and operations are adequately insured against potential risks and liabilities. Risk management practices such as risk assessment, loss prevention, and claims management help mitigate maritime risks, improve safety performance, and reduce insurance premiums for maritime businesses and operators.

Maritime Cybersecurity: Maritime cybersecurity is a growing concern in the digital age, as the maritime industry increasingly relies on digital technologies, connectivity, and data exchange for vessel operations, cargo management, and supply chain logistics. Cyber threats such as malware, ransomware, phishing attacks, and cyber espionage pose significant risks to maritime safety, security, and operational continuity, potentially compromising vessel systems, navigation equipment, and critical infrastructure. To address these risks, maritime stakeholders implement cybersecurity measures such as network security, access controls, encryption, and incident response protocols to detect, prevent, and mitigate cyber threats and vulnerabilities. International organizations such as the International Maritime Organization (IMO) and the International Telecommunication Union (ITU) develop guidelines, standards, and best practices for maritime cybersecurity, promoting awareness, capacity-building, and cooperation among states and stakeholders to enhance cyber resilience and protect maritime assets and operations from cyber-attacks.

Maritime Emergency Response and Crisis Management: Maritime emergency response and crisis management involve preparedness, coordination, and response activities to address maritime incidents, accidents, and emergencies, such as ship collisions, oil spills, fires, and natural disasters. Effective emergency response and crisis management require robust planning, training, and coordination among maritime stakeholders, including coastal states, port authorities, shipping companies, emergency responders, and environmental agencies, to minimize the impacts of maritime incidents on human lives, the marine environment, and maritime infrastructure. International conventions and agreements, such as the International Convention on Oil Pollution Preparedness, Response and Co-operation (OPRC Convention) and the International Convention on Maritime Search and Rescue (SAR Convention), establish legal frameworks and procedures for maritime emergency response and coordination, promoting cooperation and assistance among states and stakeholders in managing maritime emergencies and protecting lives, property, and the marine environment.

Maritime Spatial Planning: Maritime spatial planning (MSP) is a strategic and participatory process for allocating and managing maritime space and resources to achieve sustainable development, economic growth, and environmental protection in coastal and marine areas. MSP aims to balance competing interests and uses of maritime space, such as shipping, fishing, tourism, energy production, conservation, and recreation, through spatial zoning, designation of marine protected areas, and integrated coastal management approaches. Coastal states and maritime regions develop MSP frameworks, plans, and policies to guide decision-making, promote stakeholder engagement, and ensure coherence and compatibility of maritime activities and uses. International organizations such as the UNESCO Intergovernmental Oceanographic Commission (IOC) and the European Union (EU) provide guidance and support for MSP initiatives worldwide, fostering cooperation, knowledge exchange, and capacity-building among states and stakeholders in implementing MSP and integrated coastal management approaches.

Maritime Governance and Institutional Frameworks: Maritime governance refers to the structures, processes, and mechanisms for decision-making, policy formulation, and implementation in the maritime domain, involving multiple stakeholders, institutions, and levels of government. Effective maritime governance requires clear mandates, roles, and responsibilities among government agencies, regulatory bodies, industry associations, civil society organizations, and other stakeholders to address diverse and interconnected maritime issues, such as safety, security, environmental protection, and sustainable development. Coastal states develop maritime governance frameworks, laws, and policies to establish legal and institutional arrangements for managing maritime activities, enforcing regulations, and promoting cooperation and coordination among stakeholders. International organizations such as the IMO, the United Nations Environment Programme (UNEP), and the Food and Agriculture Organization (FAO) provide guidance, technical assistance, and capacity-building support for strengthening maritime governance, fostering collaboration, and achieving shared objectives in the maritime domain.

Maritime Diplomacy and International Cooperation: Maritime diplomacy plays a crucial role in promoting peace, stability, and cooperation among states and stakeholders in maritime regions, addressing common challenges, and resolving disputes through dialogue, negotiation, and diplomatic means. Coastal states engage in maritime diplomacy to assert their maritime rights and interests, negotiate maritime boundary agreements, and participate in international forums and organizations to shape maritime policies, norms, and regulations. Multilateral and bilateral cooperation mechanisms, such as joint commissions, maritime security dialogues, and regional agreements, facilitate collaboration and confidence-building measures among states in addressing maritime security threats, promoting maritime safety, and enhancing maritime governance. Track-two diplomacy initiatives, academic exchanges, and maritime research networks also contribute to building trust, fostering dialogue, and promoting understanding among maritime nations and stakeholders, strengthening cooperation and partnership in the maritime domain.

Maritime Cultural Heritage Preservation: Maritime cultural heritage preservation encompasses efforts to safeguard and promote the rich cultural heritage associated with maritime history, traditions, and artifacts, including shipwrecks, navigational instruments, maritime museums, and intangible cultural practices. Maritime cultural heritage provides valuable insights into human interactions with the sea, maritime technologies, navigation techniques, trade routes, and cultural exchanges throughout history, contributing to our understanding of maritime cultures and identities. Coastal states, heritage organizations, and maritime museums collaborate to identify, document, and protect maritime cultural heritage sites and artifacts, ensuring their conservation and interpretation for future generations. International conventions such as the UNESCO Convention on the Protection of the Underwater Cultural Heritage and the UNESCO Convention for the Safeguarding of the Intangible Cultural Heritage establish legal frameworks and guidelines for maritime cultural heritage preservation, promoting cooperation, capacity-building, and public awareness of the importance of maritime cultural heritage in sustaining cultural diversity and promoting intercultural dialogue.

Maritime Tourism and Sustainable Development: Maritime tourism plays a significant role in promoting economic growth, job creation, and cultural exchange in coastal and island communities, offering recreational opportunities such as cruising, yachting, diving, and coastal tourism. However, unsustainable tourism practices, such as overdevelopment, pollution, habitat destruction, and cultural commodification, can threaten marine ecosystems, coastal communities, and cultural heritage sites, undermining the long-term sustainability of maritime tourism destinations. Sustainable tourism initiatives such as ecotourism, community-based tourism, and marine protected areas (MPAs) promote responsible tourism practices, environmental conservation, and community engagement, ensuring that tourism development benefits local folks.

Maritime Connectivity and Digitalization: Maritime connectivity and digitalization are transforming the maritime industry by enabling seamless communication, data exchange, and collaboration among ships, ports, logistics providers, and maritime stakeholders. Digital technologies such as Internet of Things (IoT), artificial intelligence (AI), blockchain, and big data analytics enhance operational efficiency, safety, and sustainability in maritime transportation, enabling real-time monitoring, predictive maintenance, and optimization of vessel operations and logistics processes. Maritime digitalization initiatives such as e-navigation, electronic documentation, and port community systems streamline maritime operations, reduce administrative burdens, and improve supply chain visibility and resilience. Collaborative platforms and digital marketplaces facilitate transactions, bookings, and information-sharing among maritime actors, promoting transparency, efficiency, and competitiveness in the maritime industry.

Maritime Innovation Hubs and Clusters: Maritime innovation hubs and clusters are emerging as focal points for research, entrepreneurship, and collaboration in the maritime industry, bringing together startups, academia, industry players, and investors to drive technological innovation and digital transformation in maritime sectors such as shipping, port operations, logistics, and marine engineering. Innovation hubs provide infrastructure, resources, and support services for startups and innovators to develop and commercialize maritime technologies, products, and solutions, fostering a culture of innovation and entrepreneurship in the maritime ecosystem. Clusters promote knowledge exchange, networking, and collaboration among maritime stakeholders, facilitating joint research projects, pilot tests, and technology adoption initiatives to address common challenges and seize opportunities for growth and competitiveness in the global maritime market.

Maritime Sustainability and Corporate Social Responsibility: Maritime sustainability and corporate social responsibility (CSR) are increasingly important considerations for maritime businesses, shipping companies, and port operators, as stakeholders demand greater accountability, transparency, and environmental stewardship in maritime operations and supply chains. Sustainable practices such as emissions reduction, energy efficiency, waste management, and green shipping technologies help mitigate the environmental impact of maritime activities, reduce carbon emissions, and promote ecological resilience in marine ecosystems. Corporate social responsibility initiatives such as community engagement, stakeholder consultation, and social investment contribute to the well-being and development of coastal communities, fostering inclusive and sustainable growth in maritime regions. Certification schemes such as ISO 14001 (Environmental Management Systems) and ISO 26000 (Social Responsibility) provide frameworks for integrating sustainability and CSR principles into maritime business operations, ensuring compliance with international standards and best practices while creating long-term value for society and the environment. These aspects collectively contribute to the evolution and transformation of maritime industries, shaping their future direction and sustainability in the global economy.

Maritime Energy Efficiency and Renewable Energy: Maritime energy efficiency and the adoption of renewable energy sources are key priorities for reducing greenhouse gas emissions, mitigating climate change impacts, and promoting sustainable maritime transportation. Energy-efficient ship design, propulsion systems, and operational practices help minimize fuel consumption, reduce carbon emissions, and enhance the environmental performance of vessels. Technologies such as shore power, cold ironing, and hybrid propulsion systems enable ships to connect to onshore power sources and switch to cleaner energy sources while at berth, reducing air pollution and noise in port areas. Renewable energy solutions such as wind propulsion, solar panels, and hydrogen fuel cells offer alternatives to conventional fossil fuels, providing clean and sustainable power sources for vessels and maritime infrastructure. Industry initiatives such as the International Maritime Organization's (IMO) Energy Efficiency Design Index (EEDI) and the Global Maritime Energy Efficiency Partnerships (GloMEEP) promote energy-efficient practices and technologies in the maritime sector, fostering innovation, collaboration, and sustainability in maritime transportation.

Maritime Risk Management and Resilience: Maritime risk management involves identifying, assessing, and mitigating risks and uncertainties associated with maritime activities, operations, and investments to enhance resilience, safety, and business continuity in the maritime sector. Risk management frameworks and methodologies such as risk assessment, scenario analysis, and contingency planning help maritime stakeholders anticipate and respond to potential hazards, threats, and disruptions, including natural disasters, geopolitical tensions, cyber-attacks, and market volatility. Resilience-building measures such as redundancy, diversification, and adaptive capacity enable maritime organizations to withstand shocks, recover quickly from disruptions, and adapt to changing conditions in the maritime environment. Collaboration among governments, industry associations, insurers, and risk experts facilitates information-sharing, best practices exchange, and capacity-building in maritime risk management, promoting a culture of safety, preparedness, and resilience across the maritime industry.

Maritime Insurance and Liability: Maritime insurance and liability regimes play a crucial role in managing risks, protecting assets, and ensuring financial security for maritime stakeholders, including ship owners, cargo owners, port operators, and insurers. Marine insurance covers a wide range of risks associated with maritime activities, including hull and machinery insurance, protection and indemnity (P&I) insurance, cargo insurance, and liability insurance, providing compensation for losses, damages, and liabilities arising from maritime incidents, accidents, and perils. Liability regimes such as the Athens Convention Relating to the Carriage of Passengers and Their Luggage by Sea and the International Convention on Civil Liability for Bunker Oil Pollution Damage establish legal frameworks and liability limits for compensating victims and addressing environmental damage caused by maritime accidents and pollution incidents. Maritime insurers, classification societies, and legal experts collaborate to develop insurance products, risk assessment tools, and legal frameworks to address emerging risks, promote safety, and ensure compliance with international regulations and industry standards in the maritime sector.

Maritime Heritage Tourism and Cultural Diplomacy: Maritime heritage tourism and cultural diplomacy promote the preservation, interpretation, and promotion of maritime cultural heritage assets, including historic ships, maritime museums, lighthouses, and coastal landmarks, as valuable resources for education, recreation, and cultural exchange. Maritime heritage sites and attractions attract visitors, researchers, and enthusiasts from around the world, generating economic benefits, fostering community pride, and raising awareness of maritime history, traditions, and identities. Cultural diplomacy initiatives such as maritime festivals, exhibitions, and heritage trails promote cross-cultural understanding, dialogue, and cooperation among maritime nations and communities, strengthening people-to-people ties and fostering goodwill and friendship in the maritime domain. Public-private partnerships, heritage organizations, and tourism agencies collaborate to develop sustainable tourism strategies, heritage preservation plans, and visitor experiences that celebrate and showcase maritime cultural heritage, ensuring its conservation and appreciation for future generations.

Maritime Health and Well-being: Maritime health and well-being initiatives aim to promote the physical, mental, and social well-being of seafarers, maritime workers, and their families, addressing health challenges such as fatigue, stress, loneliness, and occupational hazards associated with maritime employment and seafaring lifestyles. Seafarers' health and well-being are critical for ensuring safe and efficient maritime operations, maintaining crew morale and productivity, and safeguarding human rights and social justice in the maritime industry. Maritime health programs and services provide medical care, counseling, and support services to seafarers and maritime workers, addressing their health needs and concerns both onboard and ashore. International organizations such as the International Labour Organization (ILO) and the World Health Organization (WHO) develop guidelines, standards, and recommendations for promoting seafarers' health and well-being, advocating for improved working and living conditions, access to healthcare, and social protection for maritime workers worldwide.

Maritime Education and Capacity Building: Maritime

education and capacity building initiatives aim to enhance the knowledge, skills, and competencies of maritime professionals, policymakers, and stakeholders to address emerging challenges, seize opportunities, and promote sustainable development in the maritime sector. Maritime education institutions, academies, and training centers offer a wide range of programs and courses in areas such as maritime law, policy, management, technology, and environmental stewardship, preparing students and professionals for careers in shipping, port management, marine science, and maritime law enforcement. Capacity-building programs and initiatives provide technical assistance, training, and mentorship to coastal states, port authorities, and maritime organizations, strengthening their institutional capacity, regulatory frameworks, and human resources to effectively manage maritime activities, enforce regulations, and promote sustainable development. International partnerships, donor agencies, and development projects support maritime education and capacity-building efforts, fostering collaboration, knowledge sharing, and innovation in the maritime domain to achieve shared goals and objectives for maritime sustainability and prosperity.

Maritime Governance and Policy Development: Maritime governance and policy development involve the formulation, implementation, and evaluation of laws, regulations, and policies to govern maritime activities, protect maritime resources, and promote sustainable development in the maritime domain. Effective maritime governance frameworks ensure coherence, coordination, and accountability in maritime decision-making processes, involving multiple stakeholders, government agencies, and civil society organizations in policy development and implementation. Coastal states develop national maritime policies, laws, and strategies to address maritime challenges such as safety, security, environmental protection, and resource management, aligning with international conventions, agreements, and best practices in the maritime domain. Regional and international organizations provide technical assistance, capacity-building, and policy advice to support maritime governance and policy development efforts, fostering cooperation, harmonization, and convergence of maritime regulations and standards at the global, regional, and national levels.

Maritime Technology Transfer and Innovation: Maritime technology transfer and innovation initiatives promote the exchange, adoption, and adaptation of innovative technologies, solutions, and best practices to address maritime challenges, improve operational efficiency, and enhance sustainability in the maritime sector. Technology transfer programs facilitate the sharing of knowledge, expertise, and technologies among maritime stakeholders, fostering collaboration, capacity-building, and technology diffusion in areas such as shipbuilding, maritime engineering, navigation systems, and environmental monitoring. Innovation ecosystems, such as technology parks, incubators, and accelerators, provide support and resources for startups, entrepreneurs, and researchers to develop and commercialize maritime technologies, products, and services, driving technological advancements and digital transformation in the maritime industry. Public-private partnerships, industry consortia, and research networks promote collaboration and investment in maritime R&D, innovation clusters, and technology demonstration projects.

Maritime Security Cooperation and Capacity Building: Maritime security cooperation and capacity building initiatives aim to address common security threats and challenges in the maritime domain, such as piracy, armed robbery at sea, maritime terrorism, and illicit trafficking, through collaborative efforts among coastal states, international organizations, and maritime stakeholders. Maritime security cooperation mechanisms such as joint patrols, information sharing, and capacity-building programs enhance maritime domain awareness, surveillance, and response capabilities, enabling states to detect, deter, and respond to maritime security threats effectively. Capacity-building initiatives provide training, technical assistance, and equipment support to maritime law enforcement agencies, coast guards, and navies, strengthening their capabilities to enforce maritime laws, combat transnational crime, and protect maritime assets and interests. Regional and international frameworks such as the Djibouti Code of Conduct, the Yaoundé Code of Conduct, and the United Nations Convention on the Law of the Sea (UNCLOS) promote cooperation, collaboration, and coordination among states in addressing maritime security challenges and promoting peace, stability, and security in the maritime domain.

Maritime Disaster Preparedness and Response: Maritime disaster preparedness and response involve planning, coordination, and cooperation among coastal states, port authorities, emergency responders, and international organizations to prevent, prepare for, and respond to maritime disasters, including ship collisions, oil spills, natural disasters, and environmental emergencies. Disaster preparedness measures such as risk assessment, contingency planning, and emergency drills help maritime stakeholders identify vulnerabilities, develop response plans, and build resilience to potential disasters, reducing their impact on human lives, the marine environment, and maritime infrastructure. Effective response mechanisms such as incident command systems, mutual aid agreements, and international assistance frameworks enable rapid mobilization and coordination of resources, expertise, and support in response to maritime disasters, facilitating search and rescue operations, pollution response, and humanitarian assistance efforts.

International conventions and agreements such as the International Convention on Oil Pollution Preparedness, Response and Co-operation (OPRC Convention) and the International Convention on Maritime Search and Rescue (SAR Convention) establish legal frameworks and protocols for international cooperation and assistance in maritime disaster preparedness and response, promoting solidarity, cooperation, and mutual assistance among states and stakeholders in times of crisis. These aspects collectively contribute to the resilience, sustainability, and prosperity of maritime industries and communities, shaping their future trajectory and impact in the global economy

Key Concepts: Territorial Waters, Exclusive Economic Zones (EEZs), and High Seas

Territorial waters refer to the coastal state's sovereignty and jurisdictional zone extending up to 12 nautical miles (22.2 kilometers) from its baseline, including the airspace above and the seabed and subsoil below. Within this zone, the coastal state exercises full sovereignty and exclusive jurisdiction over its territorial sea, subject to international law, including the United Nations Convention on the Law of the Sea (UNCLOS).

Historical Development: The concept of territorial waters has evolved over centuries, reflecting changes in maritime practices, legal norms, and state sovereignty. Historically, states claimed varying extents of territorial waters, from cannon shot limits to three nautical miles, before the establishment of the modern 12-nautical-mile limit codified in UNCLOS.

Sovereignty and Rights: In territorial waters, the coastal state enjoys sovereignty over its natural resources, including fish stocks, mineral resources, and energy reserves, as well as jurisdictional authority to enforce its laws, regulations, and customs controls. Foreign vessels enjoy the right of innocent passage through territorial waters, subject to certain restrictions and conditions.

Regulation of Navigation: While foreign vessels have the right of innocent passage through territorial waters, coastal states have the authority to regulate and control navigation, including imposing safety, security, and environmental regulations, conducting maritime surveillance, and enforcing customs and immigration laws within their territorial sea.

Protection of Coastal State Interests: Territorial waters serve as a critical zone for the protection of the coastal state's security, sovereignty, and economic interests, enabling the state to assert control over its maritime domain, safeguard its territorial integrity, and manage activities within its coastal waters effectively.

Legal Framework: The legal framework governing territorial waters is primarily based on customary international law and treaty provisions, including UNCLOS, which codifies the rights and obligations of coastal states and foreign vessels in territorial seas, providing a comprehensive regime for the governance of maritime zones.

Disputes and Challenges: Territorial waters often become subject to disputes and challenges between neighboring states over boundary delimitation, resource exploitation, and navigation rights, leading to diplomatic negotiations, legal proceedings, and conflict resolution mechanisms to resolve conflicting claims and interests in accordance with international law.

Case Studies: Several historical and contemporary case studies illustrate the significance and implications of territorial waters, including disputes such as the Falklands/Malvinas Islands dispute between Argentina and the United Kingdom and the South China Sea disputes involving multiple claimants and overlapping maritime claims.

Coastal State Responsibilities: Coastal states have certain responsibilities in their territorial waters, including ensuring the safety of navigation, preventing pollution, protecting the marine environment, and preserving biodiversity, as well as cooperating with neighboring states and international organizations to address common challenges and promote sustainable maritime development.

Future Trends and Developments: With ongoing developments in maritime technology, geopolitics, and environmental conservation, the governance and management of territorial waters are likely to face new challenges and opportunities, requiring innovative approaches, cooperative frameworks, and adaptive strategies to address emerging issues and promote maritime security, stability, and sustainability in the 21st century.

Definition and Establishment: Exclusive Economic Zones (EEZs) are maritime zones extending up to 200 nautical miles

(370.4 kilometers) from the baseline of the coastal state, as defined by UNCLOS. Within the EEZ, the coastal state has sovereign rights and jurisdiction over the exploration, exploitation, conservation, and management of natural resources, including fish stocks, mineral resources, and energy reserves.

Historical Context: The concept of EEZs emerged as part of the negotiations leading to the adoption of UNCLOS in 1982, reflecting the need to balance coastal state rights with the interests of other states in the development and utilization of marine resources beyond national jurisdiction.

Sovereign Rights and Jurisdiction: In the EEZ, the coastal state enjoys sovereign rights for the purpose of exploring, exploiting, conserving, and managing living and non-living resources, as well as jurisdiction over marine scientific research, environmental protection, and law enforcement activities.

Rights of Other States: While the coastal state has exclusive rights and jurisdiction in its EEZ, other states enjoy certain freedoms and rights, including the freedom of navigation and overflight, the laying of submarine cables and pipelines, and the conduct of marine scientific research, subject to the coastal state's consent and regulations.

Regulation of Activities: Coastal states have the authority to regulate and control activities within their EEZs, including fishing, seabed mining, offshore energy exploration, and marine scientific research, through licensing, permitting, and environmental impact assessment processes, as well as monitoring, surveillance, and enforcement measures.

Environmental Protection: EEZs are critical areas for marine biodiversity and ecosystem conservation, requiring coastal states to implement measures to protect and preserve the marine environment, including the establishment of marine protected areas (MPAs), the regulation of fishing activities, and the prevention of pollution from land-based and maritime sources.

Resource Management: Coastal states are responsible for the sustainable management and utilization of resources within their EEZs, including fisheries management, mineral exploitation, and energy production, to ensure long-term ecological integrity, economic viability, and social equity.

International Cooperation: While coastal states have primary responsibility for the management of their EEZs, international cooperation and collaboration are essential for addressing shared challenges and promoting sustainable development in adjacent and overlapping maritime zones, including joint fisheries management, scientific research cooperation, and marine environmental protection initiatives.

Legal Framework: The legal framework governing EEZs is primarily established by UNCLOS, which sets out the rights and obligations of coastal states and other states in EEZs, providing a comprehensive regime for the governance and management of maritime resources and activities in these zones.

Disputes and Challenges: EEZs often become subject to disputes and challenges between coastal states over boundary delimitation, resource allocation, and jurisdictional rights, leading to diplomatic negotiations, legal proceedings, and conflict resolution mechanisms to resolve conflicting claims and interests in accordance with international law.

Case Studies: Numerous case studies highlight the significance and complexities of EEZs, including disputes such as the South China Sea disputes involving multiple claimants and overlapping maritime claims, as well as cooperation mechanisms such as the joint management of fisheries resources in the North Atlantic Ocean.

Marine Scientific Research: EEZs are important areas for marine scientific research, providing opportunities for studying marine ecosystems, biodiversity, and geology, as well as understanding ocean dynamics, climate change impacts, and marine resource potential, through collaborative research initiatives and data-sharing arrangements among coastal states and the international scientific community.

Maritime Security: EEZs are also critical areas for maritime security and law enforcement, requiring coastal states to maintain maritime domain awareness, conduct surveillance and monitoring activities, and enforce laws and regulations to combat illegal activities such as piracy, smuggling, and illegal fishing within their EEZs.

Economic Development: EEZs play a vital role in supporting economic development and livelihoods in coastal communities, providing opportunities for sustainable fisheries, aquaculture, tourism, and offshore industries, as well as promoting trade, investment, and job creation in maritime sectors.

Future Prospects: With increasing pressures and demands on marine resources and ecosystems, the governance and management of EEZs are likely to face new challenges and opportunities in the coming years, requiring innovative approaches, adaptive strategies, and international cooperation to address emerging issues and promote sustainable development in

Definition and Characteristics: The high seas, also known as the open ocean or international waters, refer to the vast expanses of the ocean beyond the exclusive economic zones (EEZs) of coastal states, where no single state exercises sovereignty or jurisdiction. The high seas are considered part of the global commons, belonging to all humanity and subject to the freedoms and rights enshrined in international law, including the United Nations Convention on the Law of the Sea (UNCLOS).

Legal Status: The legal status of the high seas is governed by the principle of freedom of the high seas, which grants all states the freedoms of navigation, overflight, fishing, laying of submarine cables and pipelines, and conducting scientific research in the high seas, subject to certain limitations and regulations prescribed by international law.

Common Heritage of Mankind: The high seas are regarded as the common heritage of mankind, belonging to all states and future generations, and are therefore subject to the principle of equitable and sustainable utilization, conservation, and management for the benefit of present and future generations.

Regulation and Management: While the high seas are considered a global commons, certain activities and resources in the high seas are subject to regulation and management by international organizations and agreements, including fisheries management, marine pollution prevention, and deep-sea mining, to ensure sustainable use and conservation of marine resources and ecosystems.

Freedom of Navigation: One of the fundamental freedoms of the high seas is the freedom of navigation, which allows ships and aircraft of all states to traverse the high seas without interference, subject to the rules and regulations of international maritime law, including safety of navigation, collision avoidance, and environmental protection.

Freedom of Overflight: The freedom of overflight extends to aircraft of all states, allowing them to fly over the high seas without interference, subject to the rules and regulations of international aviation law, including air traffic management, safety standards, and airspace sovereignty of coastal states.

Freedom of Fishing: The freedom of fishing allows vessels of all states to engage in fishing activities in the high seas, subject to the conservation and management measures adopted by regional fisheries management organizations (RFMOs) and international agreements to prevent overexploitation and ensure sustainable fisheries.

Freedom of Scientific Research: The high seas provide opportunities for scientific research and exploration of the marine environment, biodiversity, and resources, including oceanography, marine biology, and geology, through international collaboration, data-sharing, and research expeditions conducted in accordance with international scientific norms and protocols.

Protection of the Marine Environment: While the high seas are generally beyond the jurisdiction of coastal states, they are subject to international obligations and commitments to protect and preserve the marine environment, including measures to prevent marine pollution, mitigate climate change impacts, and conserve marine biodiversity in accordance with international conventions and agreements.

Challenges and Threats: Despite the legal framework and

principles governing the high seas, they face various challenges and threats, including illegal, unreported, and unregulated (IUU) fishing, marine pollution, piracy, illicit trafficking, and overexploitation of marine resources, highlighting the need for enhanced international cooperation, governance, and enforcement mechanisms to address these issues effectively.

Marine Scientific Research: The high seas are important areas for marine scientific research, providing opportunities for studying oceanographic processes, marine ecosystems, biodiversity, and resource potential, as well as understanding climate change impacts, ocean circulation patterns, and deep-sea environments through collaborative research initiatives and data-sharing arrangements among states and the international scientific community.

Maritime Security and Law Enforcement: The high seas are also critical areas for maritime security and law enforcement, requiring international cooperation and coordination to combat illegal activities such as piracy, armed robbery at sea, drug trafficking, and human smuggling, as well as to enforce international regulations and standards for safety of navigation, marine pollution prevention, and conservation of marine resources.

Deep-sea Mining: The high seas are increasingly becoming the focus of interest for deep-sea mining activities, as technological advancements and rising demand for strategic minerals and metals drive exploration and exploitation of seabed mineral resources, including polymetallic nodules, crusts, and sulfides, raising concerns about environmental impacts, biodiversity loss, and regulatory gaps in the governance of deep-sea mining activities.

Future Governance and Management: With growing pressures and demands on the high seas, the governance and management of these global commons are likely to face new challenges and opportunities in the coming years, requiring enhanced international cooperation, coordination, and innovation to address emerging issues and promote sustainable use and conservation of marine resources and ecosystems for the benefit of all humanity.

These key concepts of territorial waters, exclusive economic zones (EEZs), and the high seas form the foundation of maritime governance and management, shaping the legal, policy, and institutional frameworks for the sustainable use and conservation of marine resources and ecosystems on a global scale.

Chapter 4.
The United Nations Convention on the Law of the Sea (UNCLOS)

Overview of UNCLOS

The United Nations Convention on the Law of the Sea (UNCLOS) is an international treaty that was adopted in 1982 after nearly a decade of negotiations involving the United Nations and the international community. UNCLOS replaced several earlier conventions and customary international law principles governing the use and management of the world's oceans and seas.

Scope and Objectives: UNCLOS aims to establish a comprehensive legal framework for the governance of all aspects of the world's oceans and seas, including maritime boundaries, navigation rights, marine resource management, environmental protection, scientific research, and dispute resolution. It seeks to balance the interests of coastal states, landlocked states, and the international community in the sustainable use and conservation of marine resources and ecosystems.

Key Provisions: UNCLOS consists of 320 articles and 9 annexes, covering a wide range of maritime issues, including the delimitation of maritime zones, the rights and duties of states in various maritime zones, the protection and preservation of the marine environment, the exploitation of marine resources, the regulation of navigation and overflight, and the settlement of disputes through peaceful means.

Universal Participation: UNCLOS has achieved near-universal acceptance and participation, with 168 parties to the convention, including most coastal states, landlocked states, and major maritime powers. The convention serves as the primary legal framework for the governance of the world's oceans and seas, providing rights and obligations for all states and stakeholders.

Codification of International Law: UNCLOS represents a landmark achievement in the codification and development of international law relating to the oceans and seas, consolidating and elaborating existing customary international law principles and establishing new legal norms and standards to address emerging challenges and developments in maritime affairs.

Principles and Concepts: UNCLOS is based on several fundamental principles and concepts, including the principle of the freedom of the seas, the principle of the common heritage of mankind, the principle of the peaceful settlement of disputes, and the principle of cooperation among states in the management and conservation of marine resources.

Legal Regime for Maritime Zones: UNCLOS establishes a legal regime for the delimitation and governance of maritime zones, including internal waters, territorial seas, contiguous zones, exclusive economic zones (EEZs), continental shelves, and the high seas, defining the rights and obligations of coastal states and other states in each zone.

Protection of the Marine Environment: UNCLOS contains provisions for the protection and preservation of the marine environment, including measures to prevent marine pollution from land-based and maritime sources, regulate marine scientific research, and conserve marine biodiversity and ecosystems in accordance with the precautionary principle and the ecosystem approach.

Settlement of Disputes: UNCLOS provides for the settlement of disputes related to the interpretation and application of the convention through peaceful means, including negotiation, mediation, conciliation, arbitration, and adjudication before international courts and tribunals, such as the International Court of Justice (ICJ) and the International Tribunal for the Law of the Sea (ITLOS).

Implementation and Enforcement: UNCLOS requires states parties to implement and enforce the provisions of the convention in their national laws and regulations, as well as to cooperate with other states and international organizations in promoting compliance, monitoring, and enforcement of UNCLOS rules and standards.

Adaptation to Change: UNCLOS includes mechanisms for periodic review and adaptation to changing circumstances and developments in maritime affairs, allowing states parties to amend the convention through formal procedures and to adopt additional protocols or agreements to address emerging issues and challenges.

Global Governance Framework: UNCLOS serves as the cornerstone of the global governance framework for the oceans and seas, providing a legal basis for cooperation, coordination, and collaboration among states and stakeholders in addressing shared challenges and promoting sustainable development, peace, and security in maritime regions around the world.

Achievements and Impact: Since its adoption, UNCLOS has had a significant impact on the development and regulation of maritime activities, contributing to the peaceful settlement of maritime disputes, the protection of marine biodiversity, the promotion of sustainable fisheries, and the conservation of marine resources and ecosystems on a global scale.

Challenges and Limitations: Despite its achievements, UNCLOS faces challenges and limitations in its implementation and enforcement, including unresolved maritime disputes, gaps in governance and regulation, compliance issues, and the need for enhanced capacity-building, technical assistance, and international cooperation to address emerging maritime threats and vulnerabilities effectively.

Future Prospects: UNCLOS continues to play a central role in shaping the governance and management of the world's oceans and seas, with ongoing efforts to strengthen its implementation, enforcement, and adaptation to evolving challenges and opportunities in maritime affairs, including climate change impacts, technological advancements, and geopolitical shifts.

Structure and Main Provisions of UNCLOS

The Preamble of UNCLOS sets out the objectives, principles, and purposes of the convention, emphasizing the peaceful use and conservation of the oceans and seas for the benefit of present and future generations, as well as the promotion of international cooperation and solidarity in maritime affairs.

Part I - Introduction: Part I of UNCLOS provides general provisions and definitions, including the definition of key terms and concepts used throughout the convention, such as the baseline, territorial sea, exclusive economic zone, continental shelf, and high seas.

Part II - Territorial Sea and Contiguous Zone: Part II of UNCLOS establishes the legal regime for the territorial sea and contiguous zone, defining the breadth of the territorial sea, the rights and duties of coastal states and foreign vessels, and the jurisdictional authority of coastal states to enforce their laws and regulations in these zones.

Part III - Straits Used for International Navigation: Part III of UNCLOS addresses the legal regime for straits used for international navigation, including the rights and obligations of coastal states and transit states in international straits, as well as the principle of transit passage for foreign vessels through straits used for international navigation.

Part IV - Archipelagic States: Part IV of UNCLOS sets out special regimes for archipelagic states, including the definition and delimitation of archipelagic baselines, the establishment of archipelagic waters and routes, and the rights and duties of archipelagic states and foreign vessels in archipelagic waters.

Part V - Exclusive Economic Zone and Continental Shelf: Part V of UNCLOS establishes the legal regime for the exclusive economic zone (EEZ) and continental shelf, defining the breadth of the EEZ and continental shelf, the rights and duties of coastal states and other states in these zones, and the jurisdictional authority of coastal states to regulate and manage marine resources and activities within their EEZs and continental shelves.

Part VI - High Seas: Part VI of UNCLOS addresses the legal regime for the high seas, including the freedoms of navigation, overflight, fishing, laying of submarine cables and pipelines, and conducting scientific research in the high seas, as well as the responsibilities of states to cooperate in the conservation and management of high seas resources.

Part VII - Islands: Part VII of UNCLOS contains provisions relating to islands, including the definition and classification of islands, the determination of maritime zones around islands, and the rights and duties of states concerning islands and their maritime zones.

Part VIII - Regime of the Territorial Sea, Contiguous Zone, and EEZ for the Purpose of Navigation and Overflight: Part VIII of UNCLOS sets out the legal regime for navigation and overflight in the territorial sea, contiguous zone, and EEZ, including the rights and duties of coastal states and foreign vessels, the regulation of navigation and overflight, and the settlement of disputes related to navigation and overflight.

Part IX - Enclosed or Semi-Enclosed Seas: Part IX of UNCLOS addresses the legal regime for enclosed or semi-enclosed seas, including the rights and duties of coastal states and other states in enclosed or semi-enclosed seas, the delimitation of maritime boundaries, and the protection and preservation of the marine environment in these seas.

Part X - Right of Access of Landlocked States to and from the Sea and Freedom of Transit: Part X of UNCLOS establishes the rights of landlocked states to access and from the sea and the freedoms of transit through the territory of transit states, including the negotiation of agreements between landlocked states and transit states to facilitate access to and from the sea.

Part XI - The Area: Part XI of UNCLOS addresses the legal regime for the Area, defined as the seabed and ocean floor and subsoil thereof beyond the limits of national jurisdiction, and its resources, including the regime for the exploration and exploitation of mineral resources in the Area, the establishment of the International Seabed Authority (ISA) as the competent authority for the Area, and the equitable sharing of benefits derived from activities in the Area.

Part XII - Protection and Preservation of the Marine Environment: Part XII of UNCLOS contains provisions for the protection and preservation of the marine environment, including measures to prevent, reduce, and control marine pollution from land-based and maritime sources, regulate activities with potential environmental impacts, and promote the conservation and sustainable use of marine biodiversity and ecosystems.

Part XIII - Marine Scientific Research: Part XIII of UNCLOS addresses the legal regime for marine scientific research, including the rights and duties of states to conduct marine scientific research in the marine environment, the regulation of marine scientific research activities, and the exchange of scientific data and information among states and international organizations.

Part XIV - Development and Transfer of Marine Technology: Part XIV of UNCLOS contains provisions for the promotion and facilitation of the development and transfer of marine technology, including measures to enhance scientific research and technological innovation, promote cooperation in marine technology development, and facilitate access to marine technology for developing states.

Part XV - Settlement of Disputes: Part XV of UNCLOS establishes procedures for the settlement of disputes related to the interpretation and application of the convention, including negotiation, mediation, conciliation, arbitration, and adjudication before international courts and tribunals, such as the International Court of Justice (ICJ) and the International Tribunal for the Law of the Sea (ITLOS).

Part XVI - General Provisions: Part XVI of UNCLOS contains general provisions relating to the interpretation and implementation of the convention, including the obligation of states parties to act in good faith, the principle of non-discrimination, and the obligation to cooperate in the promotion and implementation of the convention.

Part XVII - Final Provisions: Part XVII of UNCLOS contains final provisions relating to the signature, ratification, accession, and entry into force of the convention, as well as the depositary and registration of instruments of ratification, accession, and declaration.

Annexes: UNCLOS includes nine annexes containing supplementary provisions and technical details on various aspects of the convention, including the delimitation of maritime boundaries, the establishment of baselines, the regulation of maritime activities, and the protection of the marine environment.

Review Conference: UNCLOS provides for a review conference to be convened at regular intervals to review the implementation and effectiveness of the convention, as well as to consider amendments and updates to reflect new developments and emerging challenges in maritime affairs.

Interpretation and Application: The interpretation and application of UNCLOS are guided by the principles of customary international law, treaty interpretation, and the object and purpose of the convention, as well as relevant decisions and judgments of international courts and tribunals, including the International Court of Justice (ICJ) and the International Tribunal for the Law of the Sea (ITLOS).

Implementation Measures: States parties to UNCLOS are required to take appropriate measures to implement the provisions of the convention in their national laws and regulations, as well as to cooperate with other states and international organizations in promoting compliance, monitoring, and enforcement of UNCLOS rules and standards.

Monitoring and Reporting: UNCLOS establishes mechanisms for monitoring and reporting on the implementation and enforcement of the convention, including the submission of periodic reports by states parties to the convention to the United Nations Secretary-General and relevant international bodies, as well as the review and assessment of compliance with UNCLOS obligations and commitments.

Capacity Building and Technical Assistance: UNCLOS recognizes the importance of capacity building and technical assistance for states, particularly developing states and small island developing states, to effectively implement and enforce the provisions of the convention, including support for legal and institutional reforms, training programs, and technical cooperation initiatives.

International Cooperation and Partnerships: UNCLOS encourages states parties to engage in international cooperation and partnerships to address shared challenges and promote sustainable development in maritime regions, including joint research and monitoring programs, collaborative resource management initiatives, and regional cooperation frameworks.

Non-State Actors: UNCLOS recognizes the role of non-state actors, including civil society organizations, the private sector, and academic institutions, in supporting the implementation and enforcement of the convention, promoting public awareness and participation, and contributing to research, innovation, and capacity-building efforts in maritime affairs.

Civil Society Engagement: UNCLOS encourages states parties to engage with civil society organizations and stakeholders in the development, implementation, and review of national policies and programs related to the convention, including public consultations, stakeholder dialogues, and participatory decision-making processes.

Regional and Subregional Cooperation: UNCLOS recognizes the importance of regional and subregional cooperation mechanisms in addressing specific maritime challenges and opportunities, including trans boundary pollution, marine resource management, maritime security, and disaster risk reduction, through regional seas programs, regional fisheries management organizations, and other regional initiatives.

Global Partnerships: UNCLOS encourages states parties to participate in global partnerships and initiatives to address cross-cutting issues and promote sustainable development in maritime regions, including the United Nations Decade of Ocean Science for

Sustainable Development, the Sustainable Development Goals (SDGs), the Paris Agreement on climate change, and the Sendai Framework for Disaster Risk Reduction.

Adaptation to Change: UNCLOS recognizes the need for adaptive governance and management approaches to address emerging challenges and opportunities in maritime affairs, including climate change impacts, technological advancements, geopolitical shifts, and socioeconomic changes, requiring flexibility, innovation, and collaboration among states and stakeholders.

Comprehensive Review: UNCLOS provides for a comprehensive review of the implementation and effectiveness of the convention to be conducted at regular intervals, taking into account new developments, emerging issues, and best practices in maritime governance and management, as well as the evolving needs and priorities of states and stakeholders.

Enhanced Coordination: UNCLOS encourages enhanced coordination and coherence among relevant international and regional organizations, bodies, and initiatives involved in maritime governance and management, including the United Nations system, regional economic communities, specialized agencies, and non governmental organizations, to maximize synergies, minimize duplication, and promote collective action in addressing maritime challenges.

Capacity Development: UNCLOS emphasizes the importance of capacity development for states, particularly developing states and small island developing states, to effectively implement and enforce the provisions of the convention, including support for legal and institutional reforms, human resource development, technology transfer, and knowledge sharing initiatives.

Sustainable Financing: UNCLOS recognizes the need for sustainable financing mechanisms to support the implementation and enforcement of the convention, including contributions from states parties, international organizations, private sector partners, philanthropic foundations, and other sources, as well as innovative financing instruments and mechanisms to mobilize resources and investments for maritime governance and management.

Public Awareness and Education: UNCLOS promotes public awareness and education on the importance of the oceans and seas, the rights and responsibilities of states under the convention, and the role of individuals, communities, and societies in promoting sustainable development and conservation of marine resources and ecosystems, through educational programs, outreach campaigns, and media initiatives.

Youth Engagement: UNCLOS encourages the active engagement and participation of youth in marine conservation and sustainable development initiatives, including youth-led campaigns, projects, and networks focused on ocean literacy, marine pollution prevention, marine biodiversity conservation, and climate change adaptation and mitigation in maritime regions.

Indigenous Peoples and Local Communities: UNCLOS recognizes the rights and interests of indigenous peoples and local communities in the sustainable use and conservation of marine resources and ecosystems, including their traditional knowledge, customary practices, and cultural values related to the oceans and seas, and encourages their meaningful participation and involvement in decision-making processes affecting their livelihoods and well-being.

Gender Equality and Women's Empowerment: UNCLOS promotes gender equality and women's empowerment in maritime governance and management, including the full and equal participation of women in decision-making processes, leadership roles, and employment opportunities in maritime sectors, as well as the integration of gender perspectives in policies, programs, and projects.

Structure and Main Provisions

Preamble: The preamble of UNCLOS sets out the foundational principles and objectives of the convention, emphasizing the importance of the rule of law, peaceful cooperation, and sustainable development in maritime affairs.

Part I - Introduction and General Provisions: Part I of UNCLOS contains introductory provisions and general principles, including definitions of key terms, the scope of application, and basic principles guiding the interpretation and implementation of the convention.

Part II - Territorial Sea and Contiguous Zone: Part II establishes the legal regime for the territorial sea and contiguous zone, defining the breadth of the territorial sea, the rights and duties of coastal states and foreign vessels, and the jurisdictional authority of coastal states to enforce their laws and regulations in these zones.

Part III - Straits Used for International Navigation: Part III addresses the legal regime for straits used for international navigation, including the rights and obligations of coastal states and transit states in international straits, as well as the principle of transit passage for foreign vessels through straits used for international navigation.

Part IV - Archipelagic States: Part IV sets out special regimes for archipelagic states, including the definition and delimitation of archipelagic baselines, the establishment of archipelagic waters and routes, and the rights and duties of archipelagic states and foreign vessels in archipelagic waters.

Part V - Exclusive Economic Zone (EEZ) and Continental Shelf: Part V establishes the legal regime for the EEZ and continental shelf, defining the breadth of the EEZ and continental shelf, the rights and duties of coastal states and other states in these zones, and the jurisdictional authority of coastal states to regulate and manage marine resources and activities within their EEZs and continental shelves.

Part VI - High Seas: Part VI addresses the legal regime for

the high seas, including the freedoms of navigation, overflight, fishing, laying of submarine cables and pipelines, and conducting scientific research in the high seas, as well as the responsibilities of states to cooperate in the conservation and management of high seas resources.

Part VII - Islands: Part VII contains provisions relating to islands, including the definition and classification of islands, the determination of maritime zones around islands, and the rights and duties of states concerning islands and their maritime zones.

Part VIII - Regime of Navigation and Overflight: Part VIII sets out the legal regime for navigation and overflight in the territorial sea, contiguous zone, and EEZ, including the rights and duties of coastal states and foreign vessels, the regulation of navigation and overflight, and the settlement of disputes related to navigation and overflight.

Part IX - Enclosed or Semi-Enclosed Seas: Part IX addresses the legal regime for enclosed or semi-enclosed seas, including the rights and duties of coastal states and other states in enclosed or semi-enclosed seas, the delimitation of maritime boundaries, and the protection and preservation of the marine environment in these seas.

Part X - Right of Access for Landlocked States: Part X establishes the rights of landlocked states to access and from the sea and the freedoms of transit through the territory of transit states, including the negotiation of agreements between landlocked states and transit states to facilitate access to and from the sea.

Part XI - The Area: Part XI addresses the legal regime for the Area, defined as the seabed and ocean floor and subsoil thereof beyond the limits of national jurisdiction, and its resources, including the regime for the exploration and exploitation of mineral resources in the Area, the establishment of the International Seabed Authority (ISA) as the competent authority for the Area, and the equitable sharing of benefits derived from activities in the Area.

Part XII - Protection and Preservation of the Marine

Environment: Part XII contains provisions for the protection and preservation of the marine environment, including measures to prevent, reduce, and control marine pollution from land-based and maritime sources, regulate activities with potential environmental impacts, and promote the conservation and sustainable use of marine biodiversity and ecosystems.

Part XIII - Marine Scientific Research: Part XIII addresses the legal regime for marine scientific research, including the rights and duties of states to conduct marine scientific research in the marine environment, the regulation of marine scientific research activities, and the exchange of scientific data and information among states and international organizations.

Part XIV - Development and Transfer of Marine Technology: Part XIV contains provisions for the promotion and facilitation of the development and transfer of marine technology, including measures to enhance scientific research and technological innovation, promote cooperation in marine technology development, and facilitate access to marine technology for developing states.

Part XV - Settlement of Disputes: Part XV establishes procedures for the settlement of disputes related to the interpretation and application of the convention, including negotiation, mediation, conciliation, arbitration, and adjudication before international courts and tribunals, such as the International Court of Justice (ICJ) and the International Tribunal for the Law of the Sea (ITLOS).

Part XVI - General Provisions: Part XVI contains general provisions relating to the interpretation and implementation of the convention, including the obligation of states parties to act in good faith, the principle of non-discrimination, and the obligation to cooperate in the promotion and implementation of the convention.

Part XVII - Final Provisions: Part XVII contains final provisions relating to the signature, ratification, accession, and entry into force of the convention, as well as the depositary and registration of instruments of ratification, accession, and declaration.

Annexes: UNCLOS includes nine annexes containing supplementary provisions and technical details on various aspects of the convention, including the delimitation of maritime boundaries, the establishment of baselines, the regulation of maritime activities, and the protection of the marine environment.

Review Conference: UNCLOS provides for a review conference to be convened at regular intervals to review the implementation and effectiveness of the convention, as well as to consider amendments and updates to reflect new developments and emerging challenges in maritime affairs.

As we further explore the structure and main provisions of UNCLOS, we gain a deeper understanding of the legal framework governing the oceans and seas.

Interpretation and Application: The interpretation and application of UNCLOS are guided by the principles of customary international law, treaty interpretation, and the object and purpose of the convention, as well as relevant decisions and judgments of international courts and tribunals, including the International Court of Justice (ICJ) and the International Tribunal for the Law of the Sea (ITLOS).

Implementation Measures: States parties to UNCLOS are required to take appropriate measures to implement the provisions of the convention in their national laws and regulations, as well as to cooperate with other states and international organizations in promoting compliance, monitoring, and enforcement of UNCLOS rules and standards.

Monitoring and Reporting: UNCLOS establishes mechanisms for monitoring and reporting on the implementation and enforcement of the convention, including the submission of periodic reports by states parties to the convention to the United Nations Secretary-General and relevant international bodies, as well as the review and assessment of compliance with UNCLOS obligations and commitments.

Capacity Building and Technical Assistance: UNCLOS

recognizes the importance of capacity building and technical assistance for states, particularly developing states and small island developing states, to effectively implement and enforce the provisions of the convention, including support for legal and institutional reforms, training programs, and technical cooperation initiatives.

International Cooperation and Partnerships: UNCLOS encourages states parties to engage in international cooperation and partnerships to address shared challenges and promote sustainable development in maritime regions, including joint research and monitoring programs, collaborative resource management initiatives, and regional cooperation frameworks.

Non-State Actors: UNCLOS recognizes the role of non-state actors, including civil society organizations, the private sector, and academic institutions, in supporting the implementation and enforcement of the convention, promoting public awareness and participation, and contributing to research, innovation, and capacity-building efforts in maritime affairs.

Civil Society Engagement: UNCLOS encourages states parties to engage with civil society organizations and stakeholders in the development, implementation, and review of national policies and programs related to the convention, including public consultations, stakeholder dialogues, and participatory decision-making processes.

Regional and Subregional Cooperation: UNCLOS recognizes the importance of regional and subregional cooperation mechanisms in addressing specific maritime challenges and opportunities, including transboundary pollution, marine resource management, maritime security, and disaster risk reduction, through regional seas programs, regional fisheries management organizations, and other regional initiatives.

Global Partnerships: UNCLOS encourages states parties to participate in global partnerships and initiatives to address cross-cutting issues and promote sustainable development in maritime regions, including the United Nations Decade of Ocean Science for Sustainable Development, the Sustainable Development Goals

(SDGs), the Paris Agreement on climate change, and the Sendai Framework for Disaster Risk Reduction.

Adaptation to Change: UNCLOS recognizes the need for adaptive governance and management approaches to address emerging challenges and opportunities in maritime affairs, including climate change impacts, technological advancements, geopolitical shifts, and socioeconomic changes, requiring flexibility, innovation, and collaboration among states and stakeholders.

Comprehensive Review: UNCLOS provides for a comprehensive review of the implementation and effectiveness of the convention to be conducted at regular intervals, taking into account new developments, emerging issues, and best practices in maritime governance and management, as well as the evolving needs and priorities of states and stakeholders.

Enhanced Coordination: UNCLOS encourages enhanced coordination and coherence among relevant international and regional organizations, bodies, and initiatives involved in maritime governance and management, including the United Nations system, regional economic communities, specialized agencies, and non-governmental organizations, to maximize synergies, minimize duplication, and promote collective action in addressing maritime challenges.

Capacity Development: UNCLOS emphasizes the importance of capacity development for states, particularly developing states and small island developing states, to effectively implement and enforce the provisions of the convention, including support for legal and institutional reforms, human resource development, technology transfer, and knowledge sharing initiatives.

Sustainable Financing: UNCLOS recognizes the need for sustainable financing mechanisms to support the implementation and enforcement of the convention, including contributions from states parties, international organizations, private sector partners, philanthropic foundations, and other sources, as well as innovative financing instruments and mechanisms to mobilize resources and investments for maritime governance and management.

Public Awareness and Education: UNCLOS promotes public awareness and education on the importance of the oceans and seas, the rights and responsibilities of states under the convention, and the role of individuals, communities, and societies in promoting sustainable development and conservation of marine resources and ecosystems, through educational programs, outreach campaigns, and media initiatives.

Youth Engagement: UNCLOS encourages the active engagement and participation of youth in marine conservation and sustainable development initiatives, including youth-led campaigns, projects, and networks focused on ocean literacy, marine pollution prevention, marine biodiversity conservation, and climate change adaptation and mitigation in maritime regions.

Indigenous Peoples and Local Communities: UNCLOS recognizes the rights and interests of indigenous peoples and local communities in the sustainable use and conservation of marine resources and ecosystems, including their traditional knowledge, customary practices, and cultural values related to the oceans and seas, and encourages their meaningful participation and involvement in decision-making processes affecting their livelihoods and well-being.

Gender Equality and Women's Empowerment: UNCLOS promotes gender equality and women's empowerment in maritime governance and management, including the full and equal participation of women in decision-making processes, leadership roles, and employment opportunities in maritime sectors, as well as the integration of gender perspectives in policies, programs, and projects related to the oceans and seas.

Transfer of Marine Technology: UNCLOS emphasizes the importance of promoting and facilitating the transfer of marine technology to developing states and small island developing states, including through capacity-building initiatives, technology transfer agreements, and knowledge-sharing platforms, to enhance their capabilities in marine scientific research, marine resource management, and marine environmental protection.

South-South Cooperation: UNCLOS encourages South-South cooperation among developing states and small island developing states to share experiences, lessons learned, and best practices in maritime governance and management, including through joint projects, technical assistance programs, and regional cooperation frameworks, to address common challenges and achieve shared objectives in sustainable development and conservation of marine resources and ecosystems.

These provisions highlight the comprehensive and holistic approach of UNCLOS towards promoting cooperation, sustainable development, and the rule of law in maritime affairs.

Significance and Impact of UNCLOS on International Relations

Foundation of International Cooperation: UNCLOS serves as the cornerstone of international cooperation and collaboration in maritime affairs, providing a comprehensive legal framework for the governance and management of the world's oceans and seas.

Promotion of Peaceful Relations: UNCLOS contributes to the promotion of peaceful relations among states by establishing clear rules and procedures for the settlement of disputes related to maritime boundaries, navigation rights, and resource management.

Prevention of Conflicts: UNCLOS helps prevent conflicts and tensions between states by providing mechanisms for the peaceful resolution of disputes through negotiation, mediation, arbitration, and adjudication, thereby reducing the risk of armed conflict and instability in maritime regions.

Protection of Sovereignty and Jurisdiction: UNCLOS safeguards the sovereignty and jurisdiction of coastal states over their territorial waters, exclusive economic zones (EEZs), and continental shelves, while also ensuring the rights and freedoms of navigation and overflight for all states in accordance with international law.

Promotion of Maritime Security: UNCLOS contributes to the promotion of maritime security by establishing rules and standards for the prevention and suppression of illegal activities at sea, including piracy, maritime terrorism, drug trafficking, and illicit trafficking in arms and weapons of mass destruction.

Facilitation of Maritime Trade and Commerce: UNCLOS facilitates maritime trade and commerce by providing a stable legal framework for the conduct of international shipping, navigation, and trade, including the establishment of rights and obligations of states and shipping companies in accordance with international law.

Protection of Marine Environment: UNCLOS promotes the protection and preservation of the marine environment by establishing rules and standards for the prevention and control of marine pollution, the conservation and management of marine resources, and the protection of marine biodiversity and ecosystems.

Promotion of Sustainable Development: UNCLOS promotes sustainable development in maritime regions by balancing the economic, social, and environmental dimensions of maritime activities, including the equitable sharing of benefits derived from the exploration and exploitation of marine resources and the promotion of ecosystem-based approaches to marine resource management.

Enhancement of Scientific Research: UNCLOS enhances scientific research and cooperation in marine science and technology by providing a legal framework for the conduct of marine scientific research, the exchange of scientific data and information, and the sharing of research findings and expertise among states and international organizations.

Protection of Cultural Heritage: UNCLOS protects and preserves the cultural heritage of coastal communities and indigenous peoples by recognizing their rights and interests in the sustainable use and conservation of marine resources and ecosystems, including their traditional knowledge, customary practices, and cultural values related to the oceans and seas.

Promotion of Good Governance: UNCLOS promotes good governance and transparency in maritime affairs by establishing rules and procedures for the exercise of rights and duties of states, the regulation of maritime activities, and the resolution of disputes in accordance with international law and principles of equity and fairness.

Fostering of Diplomatic Relations: UNCLOS fosters diplomatic relations and cooperation among states by providing a platform for dialogue, negotiation, and collaboration on maritime issues of common interest, including the management of shared maritime resources, the protection of the marine environment, and the promotion of maritime safety and security.

Strengthening of Regional Cooperation: UNCLOS strengthens regional cooperation and integration by encouraging states to establish regional and subregional cooperation mechanisms, frameworks, and initiatives to address specific maritime challenges and opportunities, including transboundary pollution, marine resource management, maritime security, and disaster risk reduction.

Enhancement of International Law: UNCLOS enhances the development and codification of international law by contributing to the progressive development of international legal norms and principles governing maritime affairs, including the recognition and protection of customary international law and the adaptation of international law to new challenges and emerging issues in maritime governance and management.

Promotion of Equity and Justice: UNCLOS promotes equity and justice in maritime affairs by recognizing the rights and interests of all states, including coastal states, landlocked states, archipelagic states, and island states, and ensuring the equitable sharing of benefits and responsibilities arising from the use and conservation of marine resources and ecosystems.

Protection of Vulnerable Groups: UNCLOS protects the rights and interests of vulnerable groups, including indigenous peoples, local communities, small-scale fishers, and artisanal miners, by recognizing their traditional knowledge, customary practices, and cultural heritage related to the oceans and seas, and ensuring their meaningful participation and involvement in decision-making processes affecting their livelihoods and well-being.

Promotion of Human Rights: UNCLOS promotes respect for human rights and fundamental freedoms in maritime affairs by upholding the principles of equality, non-discrimination, and non-interference in the exercise of rights and freedoms of navigation, overflight, fishing, and scientific research for all states and peoples in accordance with international law.

Prevention of Environmental Degradation: UNCLOS prevents environmental degradation and depletion of marine resources by establishing rules and standards for the sustainable management and conservation of marine biodiversity and ecosystems, the prevention and control of marine pollution, and the promotion of ecosystem-based approaches to marine resource management.

Facilitation of Disaster Response: UNCLOS facilitates disaster response and humanitarian assistance in maritime regions by providing a legal framework for the coordination and cooperation among states, international organizations, and non-governmental organizations in providing emergency assistance, search and rescue operations, and disaster relief efforts in accordance with international law and humanitarian principles.

Promotion of Maritime Safety: UNCLOS promotes maritime safety and security by establishing rules and standards for the prevention of collisions, groundings, and other accidents at sea, the provision of navigational aids and services, and the regulation of maritime traffic in accordance with international regulations and best practices.

Protection of Endangered Species: UNCLOS protects endangered species and habitats in maritime regions by establishing rules and standards for the conservation and management of marine biodiversity and ecosystems, the establishment of marine protected areas, and the regulation of activities with potential environmental impacts on vulnerable species and habitats.

Promotion of Cultural Exchange: UNCLOS promotes cultural exchange and understanding among states and peoples by facilitating the exchange of ideas, knowledge, and experiences related to maritime traditions, customs, and heritage, including through cultural events, festivals, and exhibitions celebrating the cultural diversity of coastal communities and indigenous peoples.

Facilitation of Economic Development: UNCLOS facilitates economic development and prosperity in maritime regions by providing a stable legal framework for the conduct of maritime trade, investment, and resource exploitation, the establishment of maritime infrastructure and services, and the promotion of entrepreneurship and innovation in maritime sectors.

Protection of Indigenous Rights: UNCLOS protects the rights and interests of indigenous peoples in maritime affairs by recognizing their traditional knowledge, customary practices, and cultural heritage related to the oceans and seas, and ensuring their meaningful participation and involvement in decision-making processes affecting their livelihoods and well-being.

Facilitation of Cultural Preservation: UNCLOS facilitates the preservation and promotion of maritime cultures and traditions by recognizing the cultural rights and heritage of coastal communities and indigenous peoples, including their traditional fishing practices.

Promotion of Scientific Cooperation: UNCLOS promotes scientific cooperation and collaboration among states and international organizations by facilitating the exchange of scientific data, information, and expertise related to marine research, exploration, and monitoring, as well as the establishment of joint research programs and projects to address common scientific challenges and priorities.

Protection of Traditional Knowledge: UNCLOS protects the traditional knowledge and practices of coastal communities and indigenous peoples by recognizing their rights and interests in the sustainable use and conservation of marine resources and ecosystems, and ensuring their participation and involvement in decision-making processes affecting their traditional knowledge and practices.

Promotion of Gender Equality: UNCLOS promotes gender equality and women's empowerment in maritime affairs by recognizing the rights and contributions of women in maritime sectors, including fishing, shipping, and marine resource management, and ensuring their equal participation and representation in decision-making processes and leadership positions.

Facilitation of Technology Transfer: UNCLOS facilitates the transfer of marine technology and expertise to developing states and small island developing states by providing mechanisms for technology transfer, capacity-building, and knowledge-sharing, as well as the establishment of partnerships and networks to promote collaboration and cooperation in marine science and technology. The vulnerable ecosystems and habitats in maritime regions by establishing rules and standards for the conservation and management of marine biodiversity, including the establishment of marine protected areas, the regulation of activities with potential environmental impacts, and the promotion of sustainable use practices.

Promotion of Access to Justice: UNCLOS promotes access to justice and effective remedies for states and individuals affected by violations of maritime rights and obligations by providing mechanisms for the settlement of disputes through negotiation, mediation, arbitration, and adjudication, as well as the enforcement of decisions and judgments of international courts and tribunals.

Enhancement of Maritime Governance: UNCLOS enhances maritime governance and management by providing a legal framework for the regulation and coordination of maritime activities, the establishment of maritime policies and strategies, and the promotion of good governance practices, transparency, and accountability in maritime sectors.

Facilitation of Capacity Development: UNCLOS facilitates capacity development and institutional strengthening for states and regional organizations by providing support for legal and institutional reforms, human resource development, and technical assistance programs, as well as the establishment of training centers and knowledge-sharing platforms to enhance capabilities in maritime governance and management.

Protection of Cultural Heritage Sites: UNCLOS protects cultural heritage sites and artifacts in maritime regions by recognizing the cultural rights and heritage of coastal communities and indigenous peoples, including their traditional fishing grounds, sacred sites, and historical landmarks, and ensuring their preservation and conservation for future generations.

Promotion of Marine Tourism: UNCLOS promotes marine tourism and recreation by establishing rules and standards for the sustainable development and management of coastal and marine tourism activities, including the protection of marine ecosystems, cultural heritage sites, and indigenous territories, and the promotion of responsible tourism practices.

Facilitation of Disaster Risk Reduction: UNCLOS facilitates disaster risk reduction and resilience-building in maritime regions by providing a legal framework for the prevention, mitigation, and preparedness for natural disasters, including tsunamis, hurricanes, and cyclones, as well as the coordination of emergency response and recovery efforts in collaboration with states and international organizations.

Protection of Underwater Cultural Heritage: UNCLOS protects underwater cultural heritage sites and artifacts by establishing rules and standards for the conservation and management of submerged archaeological sites, shipwrecks, and other cultural remains, and ensuring their preservation and protection from looting, vandalism, and illicit trade.

Promotion of Marine Conservation: UNCLOS promotes marine conservation and biodiversity conservation by establishing rules and standards for the establishment of marine protected areas, the regulation of activities with potential environmental impacts, and the promotion of sustainable use practices, including ecosystem-based approaches to marine resource management.

Facilitation of Sustainable Fisheries: UNCLOS facilitates sustainable fisheries management and conservation by establishing rules and standards for the regulation of fishing activities, the conservation of fish stocks and marine ecosystems, and the promotion of responsible fishing practices, including the prevention of overfishing, illegal fishing, and bycatch.

Protection of Marine Mammals: UNCLOS protects marine mammals and other marine species by establishing rules and standards for the conservation and management of marine biodiversity, including the protection of critical habitats, migration routes, and breeding grounds, and the regulation of activities with potential environmental impacts on vulnerable species and populations.

Promotion of International Cooperation: UNCLOS promotes international cooperation and collaboration among states, international organizations, and non-governmental actors in addressing common challenges and opportunities in maritime affairs, including the conservation and sustainable use of marine resources, the protection of marine environment, and the promotion of maritime safety and security.

Enhancement of Maritime Connectivity: UNCLOS enhances maritime connectivity and trade by providing a legal framework for the establishment of shipping lanes, navigation routes, and maritime infrastructure, as well as the facilitation of transit passage and freedom of navigation for commercial vessels and shipping companies.

Promotion of Blue Economy: UNCLOS promotes the development of the blue economy by establishing rules and standards for the sustainable use and exploitation of marine resources, including fisheries, aquaculture, renewable energy, seabed mining, and marine biotechnology, as well as the promotion of investment, innovation, and entrepreneurship in maritime sectors.

Protection of Marine Ecosystem Services: UNCLOS protects the ecosystem services provided by marine ecosystems, including food security, climate regulation, coastal protection, and cultural heritage, by establishing rules and standards for the conservation and sustainable management of marine biodiversity, as well as the restoration and rehabilitation of degraded ecosystems.

Promotion of Maritime Heritage Tourism: UNCLOS promotes maritime heritage tourism and recreation by recognizing the cultural significance of coastal and marine heritage sites, including shipwrecks, lighthouses, and maritime museums, and encouraging their preservation, interpretation, and promotion for public enjoyment and education.

Enhancement of Maritime Security: UNCLOS enhances maritime security and stability by establishing rules and standards for the prevention and suppression of illicit activities at sea, including piracy, maritime terrorism, drug trafficking, and illegal fishing, as well as the promotion of maritime domain awareness, law enforcement cooperation, and border control measures.

Promotion of Disaster Resilience: UNCLOS promotes disaster resilience and adaptation in maritime regions by establishing rules and standards for the prevention, mitigation, and preparedness for natural disasters, including tsunamis, hurricanes, and cyclones, as well as the coordination of emergency response and recovery efforts in collaboration with states and international organizations.

Protection of Marine Cultural Heritage: UNCLOS protects marine cultural heritage sites and artifacts by establishing rules and standards for the conservation and management of underwater archaeological sites, shipwrecks, and other cultural remains, as well as the prevention of looting, vandalism, and illicit trade in marine artifacts.

Promotion of Sustainable Tourism: UNCLOS promotes sustainable tourism and recreation in maritime regions by establishing rules and standards for the sustainable development and management of coastal and marine tourism activities, including the protection of marine ecosystems, cultural heritage sites, and indigenous territories, and the promotion of responsible tourism practices.

Enhancement of Maritime Connectivity: UNCLOS enhances maritime connectivity and trade by providing a legal framework for the establishment of shipping lanes, navigation routes, and maritime infrastructure, as well as the facilitation of transit passage and freedom of navigation for commercial vessels and shipping companies.

Controversies and Challenges in Implementing UNCLOS

Territorial Disputes: One of the primary challenges in implementing UNCLOS laws is the existence of territorial disputes among states over maritime boundaries, islands, and resources. These disputes often lead to tensions, conflicts, and diplomatic standoffs, making it difficult to enforce international law and resolve disputes peacefully.

Overlapping Claims: Many coastal states assert overlapping claims to maritime zones such as territorial waters, exclusive economic zones (EEZs), and continental shelves, leading to competing interests and legal uncertainties. Resolving these overlapping claims requires careful negotiation, compromise, and adherence to international legal principles, which can be challenging to achieve.

Unilateral Actions: Some states unilaterally undertake activities in disputed maritime areas without consulting or obtaining consent from neighboring states, violating the principles of good faith, cooperation, and mutual respect enshrined in international law. These unilateral actions can escalate tensions and undermine efforts to maintain peace and stability in maritime regions.

Resource Exploitation: The exploitation of marine resources, such as fisheries, minerals, and hydrocarbons, often leads to disputes and conflicts among states over the allocation, management, and conservation of these resources. Competing claims to fishing grounds, oil and gas fields, and mineral deposits exacerbate tensions and hinder cooperation in implementing ONT laws.

Illegal, Unreported, and Unregulated (IUU) Fishing: IUU fishing poses a significant challenge to the implementation of ONT laws, as it undermines efforts to conserve and manage marine resources sustainably. IUU fishing depletes fish stocks, damages marine ecosystems, and threatens the livelihoods of coastal communities, requiring coordinated international action to combat this illegal activity effectively.

Maritime Pollution: Pollution of the marine environment, including oil spills, chemical pollution, plastic waste, and marine debris, poses a serious challenge to the implementation of UNCLOS laws aimed at protecting marine ecosystems and biodiversity. Addressing maritime pollution requires enhanced regulation, enforcement, and cooperation among states, industries, and civil society organizations.

Climate Change: Climate change exacerbates existing challenges in implementing UNCLOS laws by altering marine ecosystems, shifting maritime boundaries, and increasing the frequency and intensity of extreme weather events such as storms, hurricanes, and sea-level rise. Adapting to the impacts of climate change requires innovative approaches, resilient infrastructure, and international cooperation.

Armed Conflict: Armed conflict and instability in maritime regions, including piracy, maritime terrorism, and interstate disputes, pose significant challenges to the implementation of UNCLOS laws and the maintenance of peace and security at sea. Addressing the root causes of conflict, promoting dialogue, and building trust among states are essential for resolving maritime disputes peacefully.

Lack of Capacity: Many developing states lack the capacity, resources, and technical expertise to effectively implement UNCLOS laws and fulfill their obligations under international law.

Building institutional capacity, providing technical assistance, and enhancing legal education and training are essential for strengthening the implementation of UNCLOS laws in these states.

Non-State Actors: Non-state actors, including private companies, criminal syndicates, and non-governmental organizations, play a significant role in shaping maritime activities and influencing the implementation of ONT laws. Regulating the activities of non-state actors, promoting corporate responsibility, and engaging civil society are crucial for achieving sustainable and inclusive maritime governance.

Technological Advances: Rapid technological advances, including advancements in navigation, communication, surveillance, and resource exploitation, present both opportunities and challenges for the implementation of UNCLOS laws. Harnessing technology to enhance maritime safety, security, and sustainability while addressing potential risks and vulnerabilities is essential for effective maritime governance.

Cybersecurity Threats: Cybersecurity threats, including cyber-attacks, data breaches, and information warfare, pose a growing challenge to the implementation of UNCLOS laws and the security of maritime infrastructure and operations. Strengthening cybersecurity measures, enhancing information sharing, and promoting international cooperation are critical for addressing these emerging threats.

Human Trafficking and Smuggling: Human trafficking and smuggling of migrants by sea pose serious humanitarian and security challenges, undermining efforts to protect human rights, combat transnational crime, and ensure maritime safety and security. Strengthening legal frameworks, enhancing law enforcement cooperation, and addressing root causes are essential for combating these illicit activities.

Environmental Degradation: Environmental degradation, including habitat destruction, species loss, and ecosystem collapse, threatens the health and resilience of marine ecosystems and compromises the effectiveness of UNCLOS laws aimed at protecting marine biodiversity and ecosystems. Adopting ecosystem-based approaches, promoting sustainable practices, and enforcing environmental regulations are crucial for addressing these challenges.

Illegal Resource Extraction: Illegal resource extraction, including illegal fishing, poaching, and unauthorized seabed mining, undermines efforts to conserve and sustainably manage marine resources, threatening food security, livelihoods, and ecosystem health. Strengthening monitoring, control, and surveillance measures, as well as enhancing international cooperation and coordination, are essential for combating illegal resource extraction.

Corruption and Illicit Activities: Corruption and illicit activities in maritime sectors, including bribery, fraud, and money laundering, undermine the rule of law, erode public trust, and facilitate criminal enterprises at sea. Strengthening transparency, accountability, and governance mechanisms, as well as promoting ethical behavior and integrity, are essential for combating corruption and illicit activities in maritime governance.

Geopolitical Competition: Geopolitical competition and strategic rivalries among states in maritime regions, driven by competing interests in resources, strategic assets, and geopolitical influence, pose challenges to the implementation of UNCLOS laws and the maintenance of peace and stability at sea. Promoting dialogue, confidence-building measures, and cooperative mechanisms are essential for managing maritime tensions and reducing the risk of conflict.

Territorial Encroachments: Territorial encroachments by states in maritime zones claimed by neighboring states, including unauthorized construction, militarization, and resource exploitation, violate international law and undermine efforts to maintain peace, stability, and cooperation at sea. Upholding the principles of sovereignty, territorial integrity, and good neighborliness is essential for preventing territorial encroachments and resolving maritime disputes peacefully.

Sovereignty Claims: Sovereignty claims over disputed

islands, reefs, and shoals in maritime regions, often based on historical, legal, and strategic considerations, contribute to maritime tensions, conflicts, and insecurity. Resolving sovereignty disputes through dialogue, negotiation, and peaceful means in accordance with international law is crucial for maintaining peace and stability in maritime regions.

Boundaries between neighboring states, particularly in areas with overlapping claims and conflicting interests, poses challenges to the implementation of UNCLOS laws and the resolution of maritime disputes. Negotiating equitable and mutually acceptable maritime boundaries based on principles of international law, equity, and fairness is essential for preventing conflicts and promoting cooperation at sea.

Military Activities: Military activities and exercises conducted by states in maritime zones claimed by neighboring states, including freedom of navigation operations, naval patrols, and military maneuvers, can escalate tensions and provoke conflicts. Promoting transparency, confidence-building measures, and dialogue among states.

Maritime Terrorism: The threat of maritime terrorism, including attacks on ships, ports, and maritime infrastructure, poses significant challenges to the implementation of UNCLOS laws and the maintenance of maritime security. Strengthening maritime security measures, enhancing intelligence-sharing and promoting international cooperation are essential for countering the threat of maritime terrorism effectively.

Piracy and Armed Robbery: Piracy and armed robbery at sea remain persistent challenges in certain maritime regions, threatening the safety and security of maritime navigation, trade, and commerce. Enhancing maritime law enforcement, deploying naval patrols, and prosecuting pirates and armed robbers under international law are crucial for combating piracy and ensuring maritime safety.

Humanitarian Crises: Humanitarian crises, including mass migration, refugee flows, and maritime disasters, pose significant challenges to maritime governance and the implementation of

ONT laws. Providing humanitarian assistance, protecting the rights of migrants and refugees, and promoting regional cooperation are essential for addressing humanitarian crises at sea.

Illegal Immigration: Illegal immigration and irregular migration by sea present complex challenges to maritime governance, border control, and human rights protection. Enhancing maritime surveillance, strengthening border security measures, and addressing the root causes of migration are essential for managing illegal immigration and ensuring maritime safety and security.

Maritime Accidents and Pollution: Maritime accidents, including ship collisions, groundings, and oil spills, pose significant risks to marine ecosystems, coastal communities, and maritime infrastructure. Strengthening maritime safety regulations, enhancing emergency response capabilities, and holding responsible parties accountable for pollution incidents are essential for preventing and mitigating maritime accidents and pollution.

Cyber Threats: Cyber threats to maritime infrastructure, including shipping systems, port operations, and navigation networks, pose emerging challenges to maritime security and safety. Strengthening cybersecurity measures, enhancing resilience against cyber-attacks, and promoting international cooperation are essential for addressing cyber threats in maritime domains.

Climate Change Impacts: The impacts of climate change, including sea-level rise, ocean acidification, and extreme weather events, pose significant challenges to maritime governance, coastal management, and marine biodiversity conservation. Implementing adaptation measures, promoting sustainable practices, and reducing greenhouse gas emissions are essential for addressing climate change impacts in maritime regions.

Resource Competition: Competition for marine resources, including fish stocks, minerals, and energy resources, among states and stakeholders, exacerbates tensions and conflicts in maritime regions. Promoting sustainable resource management, fostering cooperation in resource sharing, and resolving disputes through dialogue and negotiation are essential for preventing resource-related conflicts at sea.

Maritime Trafficking: Maritime trafficking in illicit goods, including drugs, weapons, and contraband, poses serious security and law enforcement challenges in maritime regions. Enhancing maritime surveillance, strengthening law enforcement cooperation, and disrupting illicit trafficking networks are essential for combating maritime trafficking effectively.

Illegal Resource Exploitation: Illegal exploitation of marine resources, including overfishing, illegal fishing, and unauthorized seabed mining, threatens marine ecosystems, food security, and sustainable development. Strengthening regulatory frameworks, improving monitoring and enforcement mechanisms, and promoting sustainable resource management are essential for combating illegal resource exploitation in maritime regions.

Transboundary Pollution: Transboundary pollution from land-based sources, including industrial discharges, agricultural runoff, and plastic pollution, poses significant threats to marine ecosystems and biodiversity. Strengthening pollution control measures, promoting waste management initiatives, and implementing international agreements are essential for addressing transboundary pollution in maritime regions.

Armed Conflict: Armed conflict and instability in maritime regions, including civil wars, territorial disputes, and state-sponsored aggression, pose serious threats to maritime security and stability. Promoting dialogue, mediation, and conflict resolution mechanisms, as well as strengthening peacekeeping and peace building efforts, are essential for preventing armed conflict and promoting peace in maritime regions.

Maritime Boundary Disputes: Maritime boundary disputes between neighboring states, including disagreements over the delimitation of territorial waters, EEZs, and continental shelves, pose complex challenges to maritime governance and security. Facilitating dialogue, mediation, and dispute resolution processes, as well as adhering to international legal principles, are essential for resolving maritime boundary disputes peacefully.

Environmental Degradation: Environmental degradation in maritime regions, including habitat loss, pollution, and climate change impacts, threatens marine ecosystems, biodiversity, and ecosystem services. Implementing conservation measures, promoting sustainable practices, and raising awareness about the importance of marine conservation are essential for addressing environmental degradation in maritime regions.

Maritime Security Threats: Maritime security threats, including piracy, maritime terrorism, and transnational organized crime, pose significant risks to maritime navigation, trade, and commerce. Strengthening maritime law enforcement, enhancing intelligence-sharing, and promoting international cooperation are essential for countering maritime security threats effectively.

D.1.37 Illegal Fishing: Illegal, unreported, and unregulated (IUU) fishing poses serious threats to marine ecosystems, fish stocks, and food security in maritime regions. Implementing effective monitoring, control, and surveillance measures, as well as promoting sustainable fishing practices and international cooperation, are essential for combating illegal fishing and ensuring the long-term sustainability of marine resources.

Marine Pollution: Marine pollution from shipping, oil and gas exploration, and coastal development poses significant threats to marine ecosystems, biodiversity, and human health. Strengthening pollution prevention measures, promoting sustainable practices, and enforcing environmental regulations are essential for combating marine pollution and protecting marine environments.

Maritime Safety Risks: Maritime safety risks, including ship collisions, groundings, and accidents, pose serious threats to maritime navigation, trade, and human life at sea. Enhancing maritime safety regulations, promoting risk management practices, and providing training and education for maritime personnel are essential for reducing maritime safety risks and ensuring safe and secure navigation.

Illegal Migration: Illegal migration by sea poses complex challenges to maritime governance, border control, and human rights protection. Strengthening border security measures, enhancing search and rescue capabilities, and addressing the root causes of migration are essential for managing illegal migration and ensuring maritime safety and security.

Maritime Sovereignty Disputes: Disputes over maritime sovereignty, including claims to islands, reefs, and shoals, often lead to tensions and conflicts between neighboring states. Resolving maritime sovereignty disputes requires adherence to international law, including the United Nations Convention on the Law of the Sea (UNCLOS), and diplomatic negotiations aimed at achieving mutually acceptable solutions.

Arctic Governance Challenges: The Arctic region presents unique governance challenges due to its rapidly changing environment, potential for resource extraction, and strategic importance. Managing competing interests in the Arctic, including territorial claims, shipping routes, and environmental conservation, requires international cooperation, multilateral agreements, and sustainable development initiatives.

South China Sea Disputes: The South China Sea is a hotspot for maritime disputes, with overlapping territorial claims among multiple states and strategic rivalries between major powers. Addressing the South China Sea disputes requires a peaceful resolution based on international law, respect for freedom of navigation, and dialogue among claimant states to reduce tensions and promote stability in the region.

Illegal Fishing Practices: Illegal, unreported, and unregulated (IUU) fishing practices pose serious threats to marine ecosystems, food security, and livelihoods in maritime regions worldwide. Combating IUU fishing requires enhanced surveillance, enforcement measures, and international cooperation to deter illegal fishing activities and promote sustainable fisheries management.

Maritime Trafficking Networks: Maritime trafficking networks engage in illicit activities such as human trafficking, drug smuggling, and arms trafficking, posing security threats and undermining the rule of law at sea. Disrupting maritime trafficking networks requires coordinated efforts among law enforcement agencies, intelligence sharing, and targeted operations to dismantle criminal enterprises operating in maritime domains.

Marine Pollution from Shipping: Shipping-related pollution, including oil spills, hazardous waste discharge, and ship emissions, contributes to marine pollution and ecosystem degradation in maritime regions. Implementing regulations such as the International Maritime Organization (IMO) conventions and promoting sustainable shipping practices are essential for reducing the environmental impact of shipping activities and protecting marine ecosystems.

Climate Change Adaptation: Climate change poses significant challenges to maritime governance, including sea-level rise, ocean acidification, and extreme weather events that threaten coastal communities and infrastructure. Adaptation measures, such as coastal protection, sustainable coastal development, and climate-resilient infrastructure, are essential for building resilience to climate change impacts in maritime regions.

Maritime Cybersecurity Risks: Maritime cybersecurity risks, including cyberattacks on port facilities, shipping companies, and maritime infrastructure, pose threats to maritime safety, security, and trade. Strengthening cybersecurity measures, promoting information sharing, and enhancing cyber resilience are critical for mitigating maritime cybersecurity risks and safeguarding maritime operations.

Marine Biodiversity Conservation: Marine biodiversity conservation is essential for maintaining healthy ecosystems, sustainable fisheries, and ecosystem services in maritime regions. Implementing marine protected areas, habitat restoration initiatives, and sustainable fishing practices are crucial for conserving marine biodiversity and ensuring the long-term health of marine ecosystems.

Illegal Seabed Mining: Illegal seabed mining activities,

including unauthorized exploration and extraction of minerals from the seabed, pose threats to marine ecosystems and biodiversity in deep-sea habitats. Strengthening regulatory frameworks, monitoring mechanisms, and enforcement measures are essential for preventing illegal seabed mining and protecting vulnerable marine ecosystems.

Chapter 5.
Sovereignty and Jurisdiction

Territorial Waters: Rights and Responsibilities

Territorial waters are the areas of the sea adjacent to a state's coast, extending up to 12 nautical miles (22.2 kilometers) from its baseline. Within these waters, coastal states exercise sovereignty and have exclusive jurisdiction over certain activities. Here, we will explore the rights and responsibilities associated with territorial waters:

Sovereignty: Coastal states enjoy full sovereignty over their territorial waters, including the seabed, subsoil, and airspace above. This sovereignty allows states to regulate and enforce laws within their territorial waters, subject to international law and treaty obligations.

Innocent Passage: One of the fundamental principles governing territorial waters is the right of innocent passage. According to international law, foreign vessels have the right to traverse through another state's territorial waters, as long as their passage is innocent and does not threaten the peace, security, or sovereignty of the coastal state.

Navigation: Coastal states have the right to regulate navigation and control access to their territorial waters, including the establishment of navigation routes, traffic separation schemes, and pilotage requirements to ensure safe passage and prevent collisions.

Resource Exploitation: Coastal states have the exclusive right to exploit and manage the natural resources found within their territorial waters, including fish stocks, minerals, and energy resources. However, they are also responsible for ensuring sustainable resource management and conservation to prevent overexploitation and depletion.

Environmental Protection: Coastal states have a duty to protect and preserve the marine environment within their territorial waters, including preventing pollution, conserving biodiversity, and mitigating the impacts of human activities on marine ecosystems.

Law Enforcement: Coastal states have the authority to enforce their laws and regulations within their territorial waters, including customs, immigration, and environmental laws. This includes the right to board, inspect, and detain foreign vessels suspected of violating domestic laws or regulations.

Security: Coastal states have a responsibility to maintain the security and defense of their territorial waters, including protecting against threats such as piracy, terrorism, and illicit activities. This may involve deploying coast guard vessels, conducting patrols, and cooperating with neighboring states and international partners.

Customs and Immigration: Coastal states have the authority to enforce customs and immigration laws within their territorial waters, including the inspection of vessels and cargo entering or departing from their ports. This helps prevent smuggling, trafficking, and other illicit activities at sea.

Protection of Indigenous Rights: Coastal states have an obligation to respect the rights of indigenous communities and traditional fishing practices within their territorial waters, in accordance with international human rights standards and indigenous rights agreements.

Treaty Obligations: Coastal states are bound by international treaties and agreements governing the use and management of territorial waters, including the United Nations Convention on the Law of the Sea (UNCLOS) and regional conventions. Compliance with these treaty obligations is essential for maintaining stability, cooperation, and peaceful relations among maritime states.

These rights and responsibilities underscore the importance of territorial waters as a key component of maritime governance, where coastal states exercise sovereignty and jurisdiction in accordance with international law and treaty obligations. Understanding and upholding these principles are essential for promoting maritime security, safety, and cooperation in territorial waters.

Sovereignty: The concept of sovereignty over territorial waters is enshrined in international law, particularly in the United Nations Convention on the Law of the Sea (UNCLOS). Coastal states have the exclusive right to regulate activities within their territorial waters, including fishing, navigation, and resource exploitation. An example of sovereignty in action is the enforcement of fishing regulations by coastal states to prevent overfishing and protect marine ecosystems. For instance, countries like Norway and Iceland closely monitor fishing activities in their territorial waters to ensure compliance with quotas and conservation measures.

Innocent Passage: The right of innocent passage allows foreign vessels to transit through another state's territorial waters, provided their passage is peaceful and non-threatening. One notable case is the USS Wilkes-Barre incident in 1957 when a United States Navy destroyer conducted an innocent passage through Soviet territorial waters in the Black Sea. The incident sparked tensions between the United States and the Soviet Union, highlighting the delicate balance between freedom of navigation and territorial sovereignty.

Navigation: Coastal states have the authority to regulate navigation and establish rules to ensure safe passage through their territorial waters. An example is the creation of traffic separation schemes (TSS) in busy maritime areas to prevent collisions and enhance maritime safety. The Malacca Strait, one of the world's busiest shipping lanes, has designated TSS to facilitate the safe passage of vessels navigating through the narrow strait, reducing the risk of accidents and maritime congestion.

Resource Exploitation: Coastal states have exclusive rights to exploit and manage the natural resources within their territorial waters, including fish stocks, minerals, and energy resources. One significant case is the dispute between Indonesia and neighboring countries over fishing rights in the Natuna Sea. Indonesia, as the coastal state, asserts its sovereignty over the waters surrounding the Natuna Islands and enforces regulations to control fishing activities and protect its marine resources.

`Environmental Protection: Coastal states have a duty to protect the marine environment within their territorial waters, including preventing pollution and conserving biodiversity. An example is the case of the MV Wakashio oil spill in Mauritius in 2020, where a Japanese-owned bulk carrier ran aground and leaked oil into the pristine waters of the island nation's territorial sea. The incident highlighted the importance of prompt response and effective measures to mitigate environmental damage and protect marine ecosystems.

Law Enforcement: Coastal states have the authority to enforce domestic laws and regulations within their territorial waters, including customs, immigration, and environmental laws. In the case of maritime piracy off the coast of Somalia, coastal states and international naval forces conducted joint patrols and law enforcement operations to combat piracy activities within Somali territorial waters, demonstrating the importance of cooperative efforts in maintaining maritime security.

Security: Coastal states are responsible for ensuring the security and defense of their territorial waters against threats such as piracy, terrorism, and illicit activities. An example is the Gulf of Aden, where maritime piracy was rampant in the early 2000s, prompting coastal states and international coalitions to deploy naval assets and implement security measures to protect shipping lanes and deter pirate attacks.

Customs and Immigration: Coastal states have the authority to enforce customs and immigration laws within their territorial waters to prevent smuggling, trafficking, and other illicit activities. In the case of maritime migration across the Mediterranean Sea, coastal states such as Italy and Greece have intercepted migrant vessels in their territorial waters, leading to debates over humanitarian obligations and border control measures.

Protection of Indigenous Rights: Coastal states must respect the rights of indigenous communities and traditional fishing practices within their territorial waters, in accordance with international human rights standards. In New Zealand, the Treaty of Waitangi Tribunal has recognized the rights of Māori indigenous communities to customary fishing rights within their territorial waters, highlighting the importance of indigenous rights in maritime governance.

Treaty Obligations: Coastal states are bound by international treaties and agreements governing the use and management of territorial waters, such as UNCLOS. Compliance with these treaty obligations is crucial for promoting stability, cooperation, and peaceful relations among maritime states. For example, the establishment of maritime boundaries between neighboring states in accordance with UNCLOS has helped prevent conflicts and promote maritime security in various regions worldwide.

These examples and cases illustrate the complex dynamics surrounding the rights and responsibilities associated with territorial waters, highlighting the importance of international law, cooperation, and adherence to legal frameworks in governing maritime domains.

Scientific Research: Coastal states have the authority to regulate and permit scientific research activities within their territorial waters. This includes conducting marine research, biodiversity studies, and oceanographic surveys to better understand marine ecosystems and resources. For example, coastal states often collaborate with research institutions and international organizations to conduct scientific studies in their territorial waters, contributing to global efforts to advance marine science and conservation.

Submarine Cables and Pipelines: Coastal states have the right to regulate the installation and maintenance of submarine cables and pipelines within their territorial waters. These cables and pipelines are essential for telecommunications, energy transmission, and resource exploitation activities. Coastal states may grant permits and impose regulations to ensure the safe and environmentally sound installation and operation of submarine infrastructure.

Protection of Underwater Cultural Heritage: Coastal states have a responsibility to protect and preserve underwater cultural heritage sites within their territorial waters. These sites may include shipwrecks, archaeological remains, and historical artifacts of cultural significance. Coastal states may enact laws and regulations to prevent looting, destruction, or unauthorized salvage of underwater cultural heritage, in accordance with international conventions and guidelines.

Maritime Boundaries: Territorial waters are delimited by maritime boundaries, which are established through agreements between neighboring states or determined based on international law, such as UNCLOS. Disputes over maritime boundaries can arise due to overlapping claims, historical grievances, or conflicting interpretations of international law. Resolving maritime boundary disputes requires diplomatic negotiations, legal interpretations, and adherence to international legal principles.

Transit Passage: In addition to innocent passage, transit passage is another navigational right granted to foreign vessels in straits used for international navigation. Transit passage allows vessels to pass through designated international straits, such as the Strait of Hormuz or the Turkish Straits, without interference, subject to certain regulations aimed at ensuring the safety of navigation and protecting the marine environment.

Protection of Marine Mammals: Coastal states have a duty to protect marine mammals and other marine species within their territorial waters. This includes implementing conservation measures, establishing protected areas, and regulating human activities that may impact marine mammal populations. For example, coastal states may enact laws to prevent disturbance, harassment, or hunting of marine mammals in their territorial waters.

Emergency Response and Search and Rescue: Coastal states are responsible for providing emergency response and search and rescue services within their territorial waters. This includes responding to maritime emergencies, such as shipwrecks, accidents, or natural disasters, and coordinating search and rescue operations to save lives and protect property at sea. Coastal states may establish maritime rescue coordination centers and cooperate with neighboring states and international organizations to enhance maritime safety and security.

Port State Control: Coastal states have the authority to conduct port state control inspections on foreign vessels entering their ports or territorial waters. These inspections aim to ensure compliance with international maritime regulations, safety standards, and environmental requirements. Port state control measures help prevent substandard shipping practices, reduce the risk of marine pollution, and promote maritime safety and security.

Military Activities and Exercises: Coastal states retain the right to regulate and control military activities and exercises conducted within their territorial waters. While foreign military vessels enjoy the right of innocent passage, coastal states may impose restrictions on military activities that threaten their security or sovereignty. Coastal states may require prior notification or authorization for military exercises and may monitor and escort foreign military vessels operating in their territorial waters.

Dispute Resolution Mechanisms: In the event of disputes arising in territorial waters, coastal states may resort to various dispute resolution mechanisms to seek peaceful settlement. This may include diplomatic negotiations, mediation, arbitration, or adjudication through international tribunals or courts. Resolving disputes through peaceful means is essential for maintaining stability, cooperation, and good relations among maritime states.

Protection of Fisheries: Coastal states have a vested interest in the sustainable management and conservation of fisheries resources within their territorial waters. This includes regulating fishing activities, enforcing catch limits and quotas, and combating illegal, unreported, and unregulated (IUU) fishing practices. Coastal states may establish exclusive fishing zones or marine protected areas to safeguard fish stocks and promote ecosystem health.

Maritime Infrastructure Development: Coastal states have the authority to develop maritime infrastructure within their territorial waters to support economic activities, trade, and transportation. This may include the construction of ports, harbors, jetties, and navigational aids to facilitate maritime commerce and enhance connectivity with the global economy. Coastal states may also invest in coastal defense infrastructure to protect their territorial waters from security threats.

Marine Spatial Planning: Coastal states engage in marine spatial planning to optimize the use of marine resources and space within their territorial waters. Marine spatial planning involves assessing competing interests, balancing environmental conservation with economic development, and allocating areas for various activities such as shipping, fishing, tourism, and conservation. Coastal states may develop marine spatial plans in consultation with stakeholders and neighboring states to ensure sustainable and equitable use of marine resources.

Protection of Indigenous Rights: Coastal states recognize and respect the rights of indigenous peoples and local communities residing in coastal areas and exercising traditional fishing rights within their territorial waters. This includes consulting with indigenous representatives, accommodating their cultural practices and customary uses of marine resources, and ensuring their participation in decision-making processes affecting their livelihoods and well-being.

Maritime Boundary Delimitation: Delimiting maritime boundaries between neighboring states requires adherence to international law, including principles such as equity, proportionality, and equitable access to resources. Coastal states engage in negotiations, bilateral or multilateral agreements, and legal proceedings to establish maritime boundaries and clarify their rights and responsibilities in territorial waters. Delimitation agreements contribute to certainty, stability, and peaceful relations between maritime states.

Protection of Critical Infrastructure: Coastal states safeguard critical infrastructure within their territorial waters, such as ports, shipping lanes, and offshore installations, from security threats and acts of sabotage or terrorism. This may involve implementing security measures, surveillance systems, and emergency response protocols to detect, deter, and respond to potential threats to maritime infrastructure. Coastal states collaborate with international partners and share intelligence to enhance maritime security and protect vital maritime assets.

Promotion of Maritime Tourism: Coastal states promote maritime tourism and recreational activities within their territorial waters to stimulate economic growth, create employment opportunities, and showcase cultural and natural heritage. This may involve developing tourist facilities, promoting marine conservation and eco-tourism initiatives, and ensuring the safety and sustainability of maritime tourism activities. Coastal states may collaborate with tourism operators, local communities, and environmental organizations to promote responsible tourism practices and minimize negative impacts on marine ecosystems.

Maritime Heritage Conservation: Coastal states preserve and protect maritime heritage sites within their territorial waters, including underwater archaeological sites, shipwrecks, and historical landmarks of cultural significance. This involves conducting research, surveying, and documenting maritime heritage assets, implementing conservation measures to prevent degradation and looting, and promoting public awareness and appreciation of maritime history and heritage. Coastal states may collaborate with archaeologists, heritage experts, and international organizations to safeguard maritime heritage for future generations.

Enforcement of Fisheries Regulations: Coastal states enforce fisheries regulations within their territorial waters to combat illegal fishing, prevent overexploitation of fish stocks, and promote sustainable fisheries management. This may involve conducting surveillance patrols, inspecting fishing vessels, and prosecuting offenders for violations of fishing laws and regulations. Coastal states may also collaborate with regional fisheries management organizations and neighboring states to coordinate enforcement efforts and share information on illegal fishing activities.

Cultural Heritage Protection: Coastal states recognize the cultural significance of their territorial waters and take measures to protect underwater cultural heritage sites from unauthorized disturbance or destruction. For example, in Greece, the underwater archaeological site of the Antikythera Shipwreck, dating back to the 1st century BC, is protected as a national monument. Coastal states collaborate with archaeologists, heritage organizations, and international bodies to preserve and promote awareness of underwater cultural heritage.

Sustainable Coastal Development: Coastal states implement policies and regulations to promote sustainable coastal development within their territorial waters, balancing economic growth with environmental conservation and social equity. This includes zoning regulations, land-use planning, and coastal management initiatives to prevent coastal erosion, protect habitats, and enhance resilience to natural hazards. Coastal states may also adopt integrated coastal zone management approaches to coordinate development activities and protect coastal ecosystems and communities.

Cultural and Religious Rights: Coastal states respect the cultural and religious rights of indigenous peoples and local communities practicing traditional customs and rituals in their territorial waters. This includes recognizing sacred sites, cultural landscapes, and traditional fishing grounds as integral parts of indigenous heritage and identity. Coastal states consult with indigenous representatives and incorporate traditional knowledge and practices into coastal management and conservation efforts.

Maritime Surveillance and Monitoring: Coastal states

conduct maritime surveillance and monitoring activities within their territorial waters to detect and deter illicit activities, including smuggling, piracy, and illegal fishing. This may involve deploying maritime patrol vessels, aircraft, and surveillance technologies to monitor maritime traffic, detect suspicious behavior, and respond to security threats in real-time. Coastal states may also collaborate with international partners and share intelligence to enhance maritime domain awareness and strengthen maritime security.

Economic Exclusivity: Coastal states enjoy economic exclusivity within their territorial waters, including the exclusive right to exploit and manage natural resources, collect revenue from fisheries, and regulate maritime trade and commerce. This economic exclusivity provides coastal states with opportunities for economic development, job creation, and revenue generation through activities such as fisheries, aquaculture, tourism, and port services.

Maritime Pollution Prevention: Coastal states implement measures to prevent and mitigate maritime pollution within their territorial waters, including oil spills, chemical discharges, and marine litter. This may involve enforcing regulations on ship emissions, ballast water management, and waste disposal, as well as conducting pollution response exercises and cleanup operations to minimize environmental damage and protect marine ecosystems. Coastal states may also collaborate with neighboring states and international organizations to address transboundary pollution issues and promote regional cooperation on marine pollution prevention.

Historical Claims and Sovereignty: Coastal states may assert historical claims and sovereignty over certain areas within their territorial waters based on historical occupation, usage, or cultural ties. Historical claims may be subject to dispute and contested by neighboring states, leading to tensions and conflicts over territorial sovereignty. Resolving historical claims requires careful examination of historical evidence, legal principles, and diplomatic negotiations to reach mutually acceptable solutions and promote stability in maritime regions.

Maritime Education and Training: Coastal states invest in maritime education and training programs to develop skilled professionals and enhance maritime capabilities within their territorial waters. This includes training for maritime law enforcement personnel, search and rescue teams, port officials, and marine scientists, as well as educational initiatives to raise awareness of maritime issues and promote ocean literacy among coastal communities. Maritime education and training contribute to enhancing maritime safety, security, and environmental stewardship in territorial waters.

Maritime Border Control: Coastal states enforce border control measures within their territorial waters to regulate immigration, prevent smuggling, and combat transnational crime. This may involve deploying patrol vessels, conducting maritime patrols, and inspecting vessels and cargo for contraband, illicit substances, and prohibited goods. Coastal states may also collaborate with international partners and share information to enhance border security and prevent cross-border threats in maritime regions.

Maritime Search and Rescue Coordination: Coastal states coordinate maritime search and rescue operations within their territorial waters to respond to distress incidents, emergencies, and disasters at sea. This includes establishing maritime rescue coordination centers, deploying search and rescue assets, and coordinating efforts with neighboring states and international organizations to provide timely assistance to vessels and individuals in distress. Maritime search and rescue coordination save lives, protect property, and ensure the safety of maritime activities in territorial waters.

Promotion of Maritime Safety Culture: Coastal states promote a culture of maritime safety within their territorial waters through education, training, and public awareness campaigns. This includes disseminating information on maritime regulations, safety guidelines, and emergency procedures to mariners, coastal communities, and recreational boaters. Coastal states may also conduct safety inspections, provide navigational aids, and enforce compliance with maritime safety standards to reduce the risk of accidents and incidents in territorial waters.

Exclusive Economic Zones (EEZs) and Continental Shelves

Definition of EEZ: An Exclusive Economic Zone (EEZ) is an area beyond and adjacent to the territorial sea of a coastal state, extending up to 200 nautical miles (370.4 kilometers) from its baseline. Within the EEZ, coastal states have sovereign rights for the purpose of exploring and exploiting, conserving, and managing natural resources, both living and nonliving, of the waters superjacent to the seabed and of the seabed and its subsoil.

Legal Basis of EEZ: The legal basis for establishing EEZs is provided by the United Nations Convention on the Law of the Sea (UNCLOS), which defines the rights and responsibilities of coastal states in their EEZs. UNCLOS grants coastal states exclusive rights to exploit and manage marine resources within their EEZs, while also preserving the freedom of navigation and overflight for all states.

Purpose of EEZs: EEZs are established to extend coastal state jurisdiction over marine resources beyond their territorial seas and promote sustainable development and management of ocean resources. By delineating EEZ boundaries, coastal states can assert control over fisheries, mineral exploration, and other economic activities within their maritime zones.

Resource Management in EEZs: Coastal states have the exclusive right to exploit and manage living and non-living resources within their EEZs, including fish stocks, oil and gas reserves, minerals, and renewable energy sources. Resource management in EEZs involves establishing regulations, quotas, and licensing systems to ensure sustainable exploitation and conservation of marine resources.

Fisheries Management: One of the primary activities

within EEZs is fisheries management, as coastal states regulate fishing activities to prevent overfishing, protect fish stocks, and promote sustainable fisheries. Coastal states may establish fishing quotas, licensing requirements, and conservation measures to manage fish populations and prevent the depletion of marine resources.

Marine Resource Exploration: Coastal states conduct exploration and exploitation activities within their EEZs to harness the potential of marine resources, including oil and gas exploration, mineral mining, and seabed mapping. These activities require careful environmental assessment, risk management, and compliance with regulatory frameworks to minimize environmental impacts and ensure sustainable resource development.

Mineral Resources: EEZs are rich in mineral resources, including polymetallic nodules, manganese crusts, and hydrothermal vent deposits, which hold potential for economic development. Coastal states may grant exploration and exploitation rights to mining companies through licensing agreements, subject to environmental regulations and conservation measures to protect marine ecosystems.

Oil and Gas Exploration: EEZs often contain significant oil and gas reserves, which coastal states exploit through offshore drilling and production activities. Oil and gas exploration within EEZs requires comprehensive environmental impact assessments, safety measures, and emergency response plans to mitigate the risk of spills and accidents and ensure the protection of marine ecosystems.

Renewable Energy: Coastal states explore renewable energy sources within their EEZs, such as wind, wave, and tidal energy, to diversify their energy portfolios and reduce dependence on fossil fuels. Renewable energy projects in EEZs require careful planning, stakeholder engagement, and environmental assessments to minimize ecological impacts and ensure sustainable energy development.

Environmental Protection: Coastal states have a

responsibility to protect the marine environment within their EEZs, including preventing pollution, conserving biodiversity, and mitigating the impacts of human activities. Environmental protection measures may include marine protected areas, pollution control regulations, and habitat restoration initiatives to safeguard sensitive ecosystems and species.

Maritime Boundary Disputes: EEZs can be subject to maritime boundary disputes between neighboring states, particularly in regions with overlapping claims or unresolved historical grievances. Disputes over EEZ boundaries may arise due to conflicting interpretations of UNCLOS provisions, historical claims, or competing resource interests, requiring diplomatic negotiations or legal arbitration to reach resolution.

Joint Development Agreements: In cases where maritime boundary disputes cannot be resolved through bilateral negotiations, coastal states may enter into joint development agreements to cooperatively exploit shared resources within overlapping EEZs. These agreements allow states to share the benefits of resource extraction while avoiding conflicts and promoting regional cooperation.

Arbitration and Legal Proceedings: Coastal states may resort to international arbitration or legal proceedings to resolve disputes over EEZ boundaries or resource rights. UNCLOS provides mechanisms for dispute settlement, including arbitration by international tribunals or adjudication by the International Court of Justice (ICJ), to adjudicate disputes in accordance with international law.

Hydrographic Surveys: Coastal states conduct hydrographic surveys within their EEZs to map the seabed, identify geological features, and assess potential resource deposits. Hydrographic surveys provide valuable data for mineral exploration, offshore infrastructure development, and marine spatial planning, helping coastal states make informed decisions about resource management and development.

Environmental Impact Assessments: Before undertaking any exploration or exploitation activities within their EEZs, coastal states are required to conduct environmental impact assessments (EIAs) to evaluate the potential environmental consequences of proposed projects. EIAs assess the potential impacts on marine ecosystems, biodiversity, and local communities, informing decision-making and regulatory processes to ensure sustainable development.

International Cooperation: Coastal states often collaborate with neighboring states, international organizations, and industry stakeholders to promote sustainable development and management of resources within their EEZs. International cooperation initiatives may include joint research projects, information sharing, capacity building, and the establishment of regional agreements or organizations to address common challenges and promote shared goals.

Integrated Coastal Zone Management: Integrated Coastal Zone Management (ICZM) approaches are employed to coordinate land and sea-based activities within coastal areas, including EEZs, to achieve sustainable development objectives. ICZM frameworks integrate environmental, social, and economic considerations into coastal planning and management processes, balancing competing interests and ensuring the holistic management of coastal resources.

Submarine Cable Protection: Coastal states protect and manage submarine cables and pipelines within their EEZs to ensure the uninterrupted flow of telecommunications, energy, and data transmission. Submarine cables are vital for global connectivity, and coastal states enact regulations and safety measures to prevent damage or disruption to cable infrastructure from human activities or natural hazards.

Maritime Security: Coastal states maintain maritime security within their EEZs to protect against threats such as piracy, terrorism, and illicit activities. Maritime security measures may include surveillance patrols, naval presence, intelligence sharing, and international cooperation to deter and respond to security threats and maintain peace and stability in maritime regions.

Search and Rescue Operations: Coastal states are responsible for conducting search and rescue operations within their EEZs to respond to maritime emergencies, distress incidents, and natural disasters. Search and rescue coordination centers coordinate rescue efforts, deploy assets, and coordinate with neighboring states and international agencies to provide timely assistance and save lives.

Climate Change Resilience: Coastal states within EEZs are increasingly focusing on building resilience to the impacts of climate change, including sea-level rise, ocean acidification, and extreme weather events. Climate change adaptation measures may include coastal defense infrastructure, ecosystem restoration, and community-based resilience strategies to mitigate risks and enhance adaptive capacity in vulnerable coastal areas.

Sustainable Tourism Development: Coastal states leverage the natural beauty and cultural heritage within their EEZs to promote sustainable tourism development, generating economic opportunities while preserving marine ecosystems and cultural sites. Sustainable tourism initiatives prioritize environmental conservation, community engagement, and responsible visitor behavior to minimize negative impacts on marine environments and local communities.

Maritime Transport: EEZs serve as important transit routes for maritime transport, facilitating the movement of goods, passengers, and commodities between ports and regions. Coastal states regulate maritime transport within their EEZs to ensure safety, security, and environmental protection, implementing measures such as vessel traffic management, pollution prevention, and port infrastructure development.

Marine Spatial Planning: Marine spatial planning is used to manage competing uses and activities within EEZs, including shipping lanes, fishing grounds, renewable energy sites, and marine protected areas. Coastal states develop marine spatial plans to optimize resource allocation, minimize conflicts, and promote sustainable development while conserving marine biodiversity and ecosystem services.

Cross-Border Cooperation: Coastal states collaborate with neighboring states and international partners to address transboundary challenges and opportunities within their EEZs, including fisheries management, pollution control, and maritime security. Cross-border cooperation initiatives may involve joint research projects, information sharing, and capacity-building efforts to promote regional stability and prosperity.

Blue Economy Development: EEZs are integral to the development of the blue economy, which encompasses sustainable economic activities related to ocean resources, such as fisheries, aquaculture, renewable energy, tourism, and biotechnology. Coastal states harness the potential of their EEZs to promote blue economy sectors, create jobs, and drive economic growth while ensuring environmental sustainability and social equity.

Marine Biodiversity Conservation: EEZs support diverse marine ecosystems and species, making conservation efforts critical to maintaining ecological integrity and resilience. Coastal states establish marine protected areas, biodiversity hotspots, and conservation zones within their EEZs to safeguard vulnerable habitats, protect endangered species, and preserve marine biodiversity for future generations.

Illegal, Unreported, and Unregulated (IUU) Fishing: Coastal states combat IUU fishing within their EEZs through regulatory enforcement, surveillance, and international cooperation. IUU fishing threatens marine ecosystems, undermines fisheries management efforts, and deprives coastal communities of vital resources. Coastal states collaborate with regional fisheries management organizations, law enforcement agencies, and industry stakeholders to combat IUU fishing and promote sustainable fisheries.

Marine Pollution Prevention: EEZs are vulnerable to various sources of marine pollution, including oil spills, plastic debris, chemical contaminants, and wastewater discharges. Coastal states implement pollution prevention measures, such as oil spill response plans, waste management systems, and pollution monitoring programs, to minimize environmental damage and protect marine ecosystems within their EEZs.

Legal Frameworks and Compliance: Coastal states establish legal frameworks and regulatory regimes to govern activities within their EEZs, ensuring compliance with international law, UNCLOS provisions, and national regulations. Legal frameworks address issues such as resource exploitation, environmental protection, maritime security, and navigation rights, providing clarity and stability for stakeholders operating within EEZs.

Sustainable Aquaculture: Coastal states promote sustainable aquaculture practices within their EEZs to meet growing demand for seafood while reducing pressure on wild fish stocks. Aquaculture operations in EEZs must adhere to environmental standards, stocking densities, and disease management protocols to minimize ecological impacts and ensure food safety and quality.

Scientific Research and Monitoring: EEZs serve as living laboratories for scientific research and monitoring, providing valuable data on marine ecosystems, oceanography, and climate change. Coastal states support scientific research expeditions, monitoring programs, and data-sharing initiatives within their EEZs to advance understanding of marine environments and inform evidence-based decision-making.

Ecosystem-Based Management: Coastal states adopt ecosystem-based management approaches within their EEZs to promote holistic and integrated management of marine resources. Ecosystem-based management considers ecological interactions, cumulative impacts, and social dynamics to sustainably balance multiple uses and values within marine ecosystems, enhancing resilience and ecosystem services.

Capacity Building and Technical Assistance: Coastal states may require capacity building and technical assistance to effectively manage and develop resources within their EEZs, particularly in developing and small island states. International organizations, donor agencies, and bilateral partners provide support for capacity building, training programs, and technical assistance to enhance institutional capabilities and governance frameworks.

Environmental Monitoring and Assessment: Coastal states conduct environmental monitoring and assessment programs within their EEZs to track changes in marine ecosystems, assess the effectiveness of management measures, and detect emerging threats. Environmental monitoring data inform adaptive management strategies, policy revisions, and conservation interventions to address environmental challenges and safeguard marine biodiversity.

Cultural Heritage Preservation: Coastal states protect and preserve cultural heritage sites and indigenous territories within their EEZs, recognizing their cultural, historical, and spiritual significance. Cultural heritage preservation efforts include documenting cultural sites, engaging indigenous communities, and integrating traditional knowledge into marine management plans to safeguard cultural identity and heritage values.

Maritime Domain Awareness: Coastal states enhance maritime domain awareness within their EEZs through surveillance, intelligence gathering, and information sharing to detect and deter illegal activities, safeguard maritime interests, and maintain security. Maritime domain awareness systems integrate radar, satellite imagery, AIS data, and other technologies to monitor vessel movements, detect anomalies, and respond to potential threats.

Intersectoral Coordination: Effective management of EEZs requires intersectoral coordination and collaboration among government agencies, stakeholders, and civil society organizations responsible for fisheries, environment, energy, transportation, and security. Intersectoral coordination mechanisms facilitate integrated decision-making, policy coherence, and stakeholder engagement, promoting sustainable development and governance of EEZs.

Socioeconomic Benefits: EEZs generate socioeconomic benefits for coastal communities and national economies through fisheries, tourism, shipping, and resource extraction activities. Coastal states invest in infrastructure, education, and social programs to maximize the benefits of EEZ resources, alleviate poverty, and enhance livelihoods for coastal populations, fostering economic growth and human development.

Community Participation and Stakeholder Engagement: Coastal states engage local communities, indigenous peoples, and stakeholders in decision-making processes related to EEZ management and development, ensuring their participation, ownership, and empowerment. Community-based management approaches empower local stakeholders to contribute traditional knowledge, cultural values, and social capital to marine governance initiatives, fostering social cohesion and resilience.

Maritime Boundary Delimitation: Coastal states engage in maritime boundary delimitation negotiations with neighboring states to establish clear and mutually agreed-upon boundaries between their respective EEZs and continental shelves. Delimitation processes consider factors such as geographical features, equitable principles, and relevant UNCLOS provisions to resolve overlapping claims and prevent conflicts over resource rights.

Resource Sharing Arrangements: Coastal states may enter into resource sharing arrangements with neighboring states to jointly manage and exploit shared resources within their overlapping EEZs and continental shelves. Resource sharing agreements allocate quotas, revenue-sharing mechanisms, and cooperative arrangements for fisheries, oil and gas reserves, and other natural resources, fostering cooperation and mutual benefit.

Marine Spatial Data Infrastructure: Coastal states develop marine spatial data infrastructure (MSDI) to manage, analyze, and share geospatial data related to their EEZs and continental shelves. MSDI platforms integrate data from various sources, including satellite imagery, bathymetric surveys, and environmental monitoring, to support informed decision-making, policy development, and resource management in maritime domains.

Marine Bioprospecting and Biotechnology: EEZs and continental shelves harbor diverse marine biodiversity, providing opportunities for bioprospecting and biotechnology research to discover novel pharmaceuticals, biomaterials, and biotechnological applications. Coastal states regulate bioprospecting activities through access and benefit-sharing agreements, genetic resource governance frameworks, and bioprospecting permits to ensure equitable and sustainable utilization of marine genetic resources.

Offshore Energy Development: Coastal states explore offshore energy resources within their EEZs and continental shelves, including oil and gas reserves, wind energy, and marine renewables, to diversify energy sources and reduce reliance on fossil fuels. Offshore energy projects undergo environmental impact assessments, regulatory approvals, and stakeholder consultations to address potential environmental risks and social concerns.

Deep-sea Mining Regulation: Coastal states regulate deep-sea mining activities within their EEZs and continental shelves to ensure responsible and sustainable exploitation of mineral resources, such as polymetallic nodules, cobalt-rich crusts, and manganese nodules. Deep-sea mining regulations address environmental impacts, biodiversity conservation, and financial obligations, including royalty payments and liability mechanisms, to protect marine ecosystems and minimize adverse effects.

Ocean Governance Institutions: Coastal states establish ocean governance institutions, such as marine spatial planning agencies, maritime authorities, and fisheries management organizations, to coordinate and implement policies and programs within their EEZs and continental shelves. These institutions facilitate stakeholder engagement, policy coordination, and regulatory enforcement to promote integrated and adaptive management of marine resources.

Marine Spatial Planning Tools: Coastal states utilize marine spatial planning tools, such as Geographic Information Systems

(GIS), remote sensing technologies, and decision support systems, to support evidence-based decision-making and spatial management of activities within their EEZs and continental shelves. Marine spatial planning tools enable visualization, analysis, and modeling of marine data to inform policy development, zoning decisions, and ecosystem-based management approaches.

Climate Change Adaptation Strategies: Coastal states develop climate change adaptation strategies and resilience plans for their EEZs and continental shelves to address the impacts of climate change, such as ocean warming, sea-level rise, and ocean acidification. Adaptation strategies may include habitat restoration, coastal defense infrastructure, and community-based adaptation measures to enhance ecosystem resilience and protect vulnerable coastal communities.

International Cooperation and Partnerships: Coastal states engage in international cooperation and partnerships to address shared challenges and opportunities within their EEZs and continental shelves, including marine pollution, IUU fishing, and maritime security. International cooperation initiatives may involve regional organizations, multilateral agreements, and joint research projects to promote sustainable development, conservation, and governance of marine resources on a global scale.

International Straits and Transit Passage

Definition of International Straits: International straits are narrow passages of water that connect two larger bodies of water, such as seas or oceans, and are used for international navigation. These straits serve as crucial maritime routes for the passage of ships, facilitating trade, transportation, and communication between regions.

Importance of International Straits: International straits play a vital role in global maritime trade, providing shortcuts for vessels to navigate between major water bodies and access key ports and markets. The efficient and unrestricted passage through international straits is essential for maintaining maritime connectivity, economic prosperity, and geopolitical stability.

Legal Framework: The legal regime governing international straits is primarily established by the United Nations Convention on the Law of the Sea (UNCLOS), which sets forth rules and principles regarding the rights and obligations of states in international waters. UNCLOS defines the legal status of international straits and outlines the rights of all states to transit passage through these strategic waterways.

Transit Passage: Transit passage refers to the freedom of navigation and overflight enjoyed by all states, including both coastal and non-coastal states, through international straits used for international navigation. According to UNCLOS, transit passage entails the continuous and expeditious passage of vessels and aircraft through international straits without interference, subject to certain navigational rules and regulations.

Scope of Transit Passage: Transit passage extends to the entire width of the international strait and includes the right of innocent passage through territorial seas within the strait, provided that vessels comply with relevant coastal state regulations and do not engage in activities prejudicial to the peace, good order, or security of the coastal state.

Exercise of Transit Passage Rights: States exercising transit passage rights must respect the sovereignty, jurisdiction, and security of the coastal states bordering the international strait. Vessels transiting through international straits are required to comply with applicable international laws and regulations, including navigational safety measures, environmental protection standards, and customs procedures.

Historical Examples: One of the most well-known international straits is the Strait of Hormuz, located between the Persian Gulf and the Gulf of Oman. The strategic significance of the Strait of Hormuz as a vital maritime chokepoint has led to tensions and disputes over navigation rights, particularly regarding military activities and freedom of passage.

Case Study: Strait of Malacca: The Strait of Malacca, situated between the Malay Peninsula and the Indonesian island of Sumatra, is another critical international strait that facilitates maritime trade between the Indian Ocean and the Pacific Ocean. The Strait of Malacca is one of the busiest waterways in the world, with a significant volume of oil, natural gas, and cargo shipments passing through its narrow channels daily.

Transboundary Cooperation: Coastal states bordering international straits often engage in transboundary cooperation and joint management efforts to ensure the safety, security, and sustainability of maritime navigation. Cooperative initiatives may include the establishment of maritime traffic separation schemes, search and rescue coordination centers, and pollution response mechanisms to address common challenges and enhance maritime governance.

International Agreements: States bordering international straits may enter into bilateral or multilateral agreements to regulate navigation and transit passage through these strategic waterways. These agreements may address issues such as navigational safety, environmental protection, and security cooperation to promote peace, stability, and prosperity in the region.

Freedom of Navigation: Transit passage through international straits is essential for upholding the principle of freedom of navigation, a fundamental tenet of international law that ensures the unimpeded movement of vessels in international waters. Freedom of navigation promotes maritime trade, economic development, and peaceful cooperation among states, contributing to global prosperity and stability.

Navigation Rights of Landlocked States: UNCLOS recognizes the rights of landlocked states to enjoy freedom of transit passage through international straits, ensuring their access to the sea and facilitating their participation in international trade and maritime activities. Landlocked states rely on transit passage rights to connect to global shipping routes and access essential maritime resources.

Security Challenges: International straits are vulnerable to various security challenges, including piracy, terrorism, and maritime disputes, which pose threats to the safety and security of vessels transiting through these critical waterways. Coastal states and international organizations collaborate to address security risks through maritime patrols, information sharing, and capacity-building initiatives to protect shipping lanes and ensure safe passage.

Environmental Protection: International straits are subject to environmental pressures, including pollution, habitat degradation, and marine biodiversity loss, resulting from maritime traffic, industrial activities, and coastal development. Coastal states implement measures to mitigate environmental impacts, such as pollution control regulations, ecosystem restoration projects, and sustainable shipping practices, to preserve the ecological integrity of international straits.

Legal Disputes: Disputes over navigation rights and transit passage through international straits may arise between coastal states and user states, leading to diplomatic tensions and legal disputes. UNCLOS provides mechanisms for the peaceful settlement of disputes, including negotiation, mediation, arbitration, and adjudication, to resolve conflicts and uphold the rule of law in international waters.

Case Study: Bosporus and Dardanelles: The Bosporus and Dardanelles, collectively known as the Turkish Straits, are crucial international waterways connecting the Black Sea to the Mediterranean Sea. The Montreux Convention of 1936 regulates navigation and transit passage through the Turkish Straits, balancing the interests of coastal states and user states while ensuring maritime security and stability in the region.

Sustainable Maritime Development: Coastal states and user states collaborate to promote sustainable maritime development and environmental stewardship in international straits, incorporating principles of ecosystem-based management, integrated coastal zone management, and blue economy approaches. Sustainable maritime development strategies aim to balance economic growth with environmental conservation and social equity, fostering resilience and prosperity in maritime regions.

Maritime Safety and Navigation: Coastal states implement measures to enhance maritime safety and navigation in international straits, including the establishment of maritime traffic management systems, navigational aids, and port facilities to support safe and efficient passage of vessels. International organizations provide technical assistance and capacity-building support to improve maritime infrastructure and promote best practices in navigation and seamanship.

Crisis Management and Contingency Planning: Coastal states develop crisis management and contingency plans to address maritime emergencies, such as oil spills, ship collisions, and natural disasters that may occur in international straits. Emergency response mechanisms involve coordination among government agencies, emergency services, and international partners to mitigate risks, minimize impacts, and ensure timely and effective response to maritime incidents.

Humanitarian Assistance and Disaster Relief: International straits serve as critical transit routes for humanitarian assistance and disaster relief operations during emergencies, such as natural disasters, conflicts, and humanitarian crises. Coastal states facilitate the passage of relief vessels and humanitarian aid convoys through international straits to deliver essential supplies, medical assistance, and support to affected populations, demonstrating solidarity and cooperation in times of crisis.

Arctic Navigation: The Arctic region presents unique challenges and opportunities for navigation and transit passage due to its harsh climate, ice-covered waters, and changing environmental conditions. As Arctic sea ice diminishes and maritime activity increases, coastal states bordering the Arctic Ocean navigate issues of sovereignty, environmental protection, and security in international straits.

Suez Canal: The Suez Canal is one of the world's most

significant international straits, linking the Mediterranean Sea to the Red Sea and providing a vital shortcut for maritime trade between Europe, Asia, and Africa. The canal's strategic location and importance as a major shipping route have made it a focal point for international navigation and transit passage, with millions of tons of cargo passing through annually.

Panama Canal: The Panama Canal is another critical international strait, connecting the Atlantic Ocean to the Pacific Ocean and serving as a key transit route for vessels traveling between the Americas. The canal's construction and operation have had profound impacts on global maritime trade, facilitating the movement of goods and commodities between major markets and contributing to economic development and prosperity in the region.

Legal Principles of Transit Passage: UNCLOS establishes legal principles governing transit passage through international straits, including the requirement for continuous and expeditious passage without delay, the obligation to refrain from activities prejudicial to the peace, good order, or security of the coastal state, and the prohibition of exercises or maneuvers that threaten the safety of navigation.

Submarines and Transit Passage: UNCLOS clarifies the legal status of submarines transiting through international straits, affirming their right to transit passage like other vessels, provided they navigate on the surface and display their flag. Submarines are required to adhere to navigational rules and safety protocols to ensure the safety and security of navigation in international waters.

User States' Obligations: User states exercising transit passage through international straits must respect the rights and interests of the coastal state, including its sovereignty, security, and environmental concerns. User states are prohibited from conducting activities that would undermine the coastal state's authority or pose risks to the safety and security of navigation within the strait.

Coastal State Jurisdiction: Coastal states retain jurisdiction over activities within their territorial seas, including law enforcement, environmental protection, and customs control, even during transit passage by foreign vessels. However, coastal states may not impede or interfere with the lawful exercise of transit passage rights by user states in accordance with UNCLOS provisions.

Military Activities: UNCLOS permits the conduct of military activities during transit passage through international straits, provided they are conducted in a manner consistent with the rights and duties of user states and do not threaten the peace, good order, or security of the coastal state. Military vessels transiting through international straits may exercise self-defense and take necessary measures to ensure their safety and security.

Maritime Security Cooperation: Coastal states and user states collaborate on maritime security initiatives to enhance the safety and security of navigation in international straits, including information sharing, joint patrols, and capacity-building efforts to combat piracy, terrorism, and illicit activities. Maritime security cooperation fosters trust, confidence, and cooperation among states, contributing to regional stability and maritime governance.

International Cooperation Mechanisms: Regional organizations and multilateral agreements provide platforms for international cooperation and dialogue on issues related to international straits, including navigation rights, safety of navigation, and environmental protection. Cooperation mechanisms such as the International Maritime Organization (IMO) and the Association of Southeast Asian Nations (ASEAN) promote cooperation and coordination among coastal states and user states to address common challenges and promote sustainable maritime development.

Transit Passage in Archipelagic Waters: Archipelagic states, which consist of groups of islands and their surrounding waters, also have international straits within their archipelagic waters that connect different parts of the state's territory. UNCLOS recognizes the right of transit passage through archipelagic waters and international straits within archipelagic baselines, subject to certain conditions and regulations established by the archipelagic state.

Freedom of Navigation Operations (FONOPS): Some user states conduct freedom of navigation operations (FONOPS) to assert their rights and challenge excessive maritime claims, including restrictions on transit passage through international straits. FONOPS demonstrate a commitment to upholding freedom of navigation principles and challenging unlawful maritime restrictions, contributing to the maintenance of a rules-based international order and the protection of navigation rights.

Environmental Protection Measures: Coastal states implement environmental protection measures in international straits to mitigate the impacts of maritime traffic on marine ecosystems and habitats. These measures may include the establishment of marine protected areas, pollution control regulations, and ecosystem-based management strategies to conserve biodiversity and promote sustainable use of marine resources.

Maritime Traffic Management Systems: Coastal states deploy maritime traffic management systems in international straits to monitor vessel movements, regulate traffic flow, and prevent collisions or incidents. These systems utilize technologies such as radar, Automatic Identification System (AIS), and Vessel Traffic Services (VTS) to enhance situational awareness and ensure safe and efficient navigation in busy waterways.

Arbitration and Dispute Resolution: In cases of disputes or disagreements between coastal states and user states regarding transit passage rights or other issues related to international straits, UNCLOS provides mechanisms for peaceful dispute resolution, including arbitration, mediation, and negotiation. These mechanisms help states resolve conflicts and reach mutually acceptable solutions to maintain maritime peace and stability.

Case Study: Strait of Gibraltar: The Strait of Gibraltar, located between Spain and Morocco, is a critical international strait connecting the Atlantic Ocean to the Mediterranean Sea.

The strait's strategic location has made it a key transit route for maritime trade and naval operations throughout history, with significant implications for regional security and geopolitics.

Maritime Boundaries in International Straits: Coastal states may establish maritime boundaries within international straits to delimit their respective territorial seas and exclusive economic zones (EEZs) in accordance with UNCLOS principles. Delimitation of maritime boundaries in international straits requires cooperation and negotiation between neighboring states to ensure equitable and peaceful resolution of overlapping claims.

Hydrographic Surveys and Nautical Charts: Coastal states conduct hydrographic surveys and produce nautical charts for international straits to accurately depict navigational hazards, underwater obstacles, and other features that may affect safe navigation. These surveys provide essential information for mariners and maritime authorities to plan and execute transit passages through international straits safely and efficiently.

International Cooperation Agreements: Coastal states bordering international straits may enter into bilateral or multilateral cooperation agreements with neighboring states and user states to address shared challenges and opportunities related to maritime security, safety of navigation, and environmental protection. These agreements promote mutual understanding, confidence-building, and collaborative action to enhance the governance and management of international straits.

Maritime Law Enforcement: Coastal states deploy maritime law enforcement agencies, such as coast guards and naval forces, to enforce laws and regulations in international straits, including safety of navigation rules, customs regulations, and environmental protection measures. Maritime law enforcement ensures compliance with international law and enhances security and safety in international waters, deterring illegal activities and maintaining order.

Archipelagic States: Special Regimes

Definition of Archipelagic States: Archipelagic states are nations composed of multiple islands and their surrounding waters, forming archipelagos or island chains. These states have unique geographical characteristics and face specific challenges in maritime governance and resource management due to the dispersion of their territories across vast oceanic areas.

Legal Status of Archipelagic States: Archipelagic states are recognized under international law as sovereign entities with exclusive rights and jurisdiction over archipelagic waters, including the waters within the baselines connecting the outermost points of the archipelago. The United Nations Convention on the Law of the Sea (UNCLOS) provides a legal framework for the rights and obligations of archipelagic states in managing their maritime zones.

Archipelagic Baselines: Archipelagic states establish baselines to delimit the outer limits of their archipelagic waters, connecting the outermost points of the archipelago's islands and reefs. These baselines serve as the basis for defining the archipelagic state's territorial sea, contiguous zone, exclusive economic zone (EEZ), and other maritime zones in accordance with UNCLOS provisions.

Territorial Sea of Archipelagic States: Archipelagic states have a territorial sea extending up to 12 nautical miles from their baselines, where they exercise full sovereignty, including the right to regulate navigation, fishing, and other activities. UNCLOS recognizes the archipelagic state's sovereignty over its territorial sea and the airspace above it, subject to international law and the rights of other states.

Contiguous Zone: Beyond the territorial sea, archipelagic states may establish a contiguous zone extending up to 24 nautical miles from the baselines, where they exercise limited jurisdiction to enforce customs, immigration, and environmental laws. The contiguous zone allows archipelagic states to extend their control over certain activities and protect their national interests beyond their territorial sea.

Exclusive Economic Zone (EEZ): Archipelagic states are entitled to an exclusive economic zone (EEZ) extending up to 200 nautical miles from their baselines, where they have sovereign rights to explore, exploit, conserve, and manage natural resources, including fisheries, minerals, and energy resources. The EEZ provides archipelagic states with exclusive rights to maritime resources within this zone, subject to certain rights of other states under UNCLOS.

Archipelagic Waters: UNCLOS defines archipelagic waters as the waters enclosed by the archipelagic baselines of an archipelagic state, including its territorial sea, contiguous zone, and internal waters. Archipelagic waters form a single integrated maritime zone under the jurisdiction of the archipelagic state, allowing for the regulation and management of maritime activities within this area.

Freedom of Navigation through Archipelagic Waters: UNCLOS guarantees the right of all states to enjoy freedom of navigation and overflight through archipelagic waters, including the right of innocent passage through the archipelagic sea lanes and air routes designated by the archipelagic state. The principle of freedom of navigation ensures the unimpeded movement of vessels and aircraft through archipelagic waters in accordance with international law.

Archipelagic Sea Lanes: Archipelagic states designate and maintain sea lanes and air routes for international navigation and overflight through their archipelagic waters, ensuring the safety and efficiency of maritime transportation and communication. UNCLOS allows for the establishment of archipelagic sea lanes and air routes to facilitate the passage of vessels and aircraft engaged in international transit through archipelagic waters.

Maritime Zones Management: Archipelagic states implement comprehensive maritime zones management plans to regulate and manage maritime activities within their archipelagic waters, including fisheries management, marine conservation, and maritime security measures. These management plans aim to balance economic development, environmental protection, and national security priorities while respecting international law and the rights of other states.

Environmental Protection Measures: Archipelagic states implement environmental protection measures to conserve marine biodiversity, mitigate pollution, and address environmental challenges within their archipelagic waters. These measures may include the establishment of marine protected areas, pollution control regulations, and ecosystem-based management strategies to promote sustainable use of marine resources and protect fragile ecosystems.

Marine Resource Management: Archipelagic states develop marine resource management strategies to sustainably exploit and manage fisheries, minerals, and other natural resources within their archipelagic waters. These strategies may include fisheries regulations, resource conservation measures, and licensing systems to ensure the responsible utilization of marine resources and equitable distribution of benefits.

Integrated Coastal Zone Management: Archipelagic states adopt integrated coastal zone management (ICZM) approaches to address land-sea interactions, coastal development, and natural resource conservation within their archipelagic territories. ICZM strategies integrate land-use planning, marine spatial planning, and ecosystem management to promote sustainable development and resilience in coastal communities.

Traditional Fishing Rights: Archipelagic states recognize the traditional fishing rights of coastal communities and indigenous peoples within their archipelagic waters, ensuring their access to marine resources for subsistence and cultural purposes. These traditional fishing rights may be regulated through customary laws, community-based management systems, and co-management arrangements to safeguard local livelihoods and cultural heritage.

Archipelagic Defense and Security: Archipelagic states maintain defense and security capabilities to protect their sovereignty, territorial integrity, and national interests within their archipelagic waters. Maritime security measures may include maritime patrols, surveillance operations, and border control measures to deter illegal activities, safeguard maritime borders, and respond to security threats effectively.

Naval Presence and Patrols: Archipelagic states deploy naval forces and maritime law enforcement agencies to patrol and monitor their archipelagic waters, ensuring compliance with national laws and international regulations. Naval presence and patrols contribute to maritime security, safety of navigation, and law enforcement efforts to combat piracy, smuggling, and other maritime crimes.

Search and Rescue Operations: Archipelagic states coordinate search and rescue (SAR) operations within their archipelagic waters to respond to maritime emergencies, including shipwrecks, accidents, and natural disasters. SAR efforts involve collaboration among government agencies, maritime authorities, and international partners to provide timely assistance and save lives at sea.

Regional Cooperation Mechanisms: Archipelagic states engage in regional cooperation mechanisms to address shared challenges and opportunities in maritime governance, security, and sustainable development. Regional organizations, such as the Association of Southeast Asian Nations (ASEAN) and the Pacific Islands Forum (PIF), facilitate dialogue, cooperation, and capacity-building initiatives among archipelagic states and neighboring countries to promote regional stability and prosperity.

Maritime Connectivity and Infrastructure: Archipelagic states invest in maritime connectivity and infrastructure development to enhance transportation, trade, and communication links between islands and mainland regions. Infrastructure projects, such as ports, harbors, and shipping lanes, improve accessibility and connectivity within archipelagic waters, facilitating economic growth, social development, and cultural exchange.

Cultural Heritage Preservation: Archipelagic states preserve and promote their cultural heritage and maritime traditions through cultural heritage conservation programs, educational initiatives, and heritage tourism activities. Cultural heritage preservation efforts celebrate the rich maritime heritage of archipelagic communities and promote awareness of their cultural identity, history, and traditions.

Case Study: Indonesia: Indonesia is the world's largest archipelagic state, comprising thousands of islands scattered across the equatorial archipelago of Southeast Asia. The Indonesian government has implemented special regimes to govern its vast maritime domain, including archipelagic baselines, territorial seas, and exclusive economic zones, in accordance with UNCLOS provisions.

Maritime Boundaries Delimitation: Indonesia has concluded maritime boundary agreements with neighboring states, such as Malaysia, Singapore, and Australia, to delimit maritime boundaries and clarify jurisdictional rights in overlapping maritime areas. These agreements promote peaceful coexistence, cooperation, and mutual respect for sovereignty and territorial integrity among neighboring archipelagic states.

Fisheries Management: Indonesia implements fisheries management measures to regulate and conserve marine resources within its archipelagic waters, including fisheries licensing, seasonal closures, and protected areas. Fisheries management efforts aim to ensure sustainable fish stocks, promote responsible fishing practices, and support the livelihoods of coastal communities dependent on marine resources.

Marine Conservation: Indonesia has established marine protected areas (MPAs) and marine parks to conserve marine biodiversity, protect endangered species, and preserve fragile ecosystems within its archipelagic waters. Marine conservation initiatives contribute to the sustainability of marine ecosystems, enhance resilience to climate change, and promote ecotourism opportunities in coastal areas.

Environmental Protection: Indonesia implements environmental protection measures to address pollution, habitat degradation, and marine pollution within its archipelagic waters, including pollution control regulations, waste management initiatives, and ecosystem restoration projects. Environmental protection efforts aim to mitigate the impacts of human activities on marine ecosystems and promote sustainable development in coastal areas.

Maritime Safety and Security: Indonesia maintains maritime safety and security capabilities to safeguard its archipelagic waters against maritime threats, including piracy, illegal fishing, and transnational crime. Maritime security initiatives involve naval patrols, maritime surveillance, and law enforcement operations to maintain order, combat maritime crimes, and protect national interests.

Search and Rescue Coordination: Indonesia coordinates search and rescue (SAR) operations within its archipelagic waters through the Indonesian Search and Rescue Agency (BASARNAS) and other government agencies. SAR coordination efforts involve rapid response to maritime emergencies, deployment of rescue assets, and coordination with international partners to save lives and ensure maritime safety.

Maritime Connectivity: Indonesia invests in maritime connectivity projects to improve transportation links, facilitate trade, and promote economic development between islands and regions within its archipelagic territory. Maritime connectivity initiatives include port development, ferry services, and shipping lanes to enhance accessibility and mobility for people and goods.

Cultural Heritage Preservation: Indonesia preserves and promotes its rich maritime heritage and cultural traditions through cultural heritage conservation programs, maritime museums, and heritage tourism initiatives. Cultural heritage preservation efforts showcase Indonesia's maritime history, seafaring traditions, and diverse cultural heritage to local and international audiences.

Regional Cooperation: Indonesia participates in regional cooperation mechanisms, such as ASEAN and the Indian Ocean Rim Association (IORA), to address common challenges and opportunities in maritime governance, security, and sustainable development. Regional cooperation initiatives promote dialogue, collaboration, and capacity-building among archipelagic states and neighboring countries to foster regional stability and prosperity.

Case Study: Philippines: The Philippines is an archipelagic state located in Southeast Asia, comprising over 7,000 islands and islets spread across the Philippine archipelago. As an archipelagic state, the Philippines has established special regimes to govern its maritime zones and protect its maritime interests in accordance with international law, including UNCLOS.

Maritime Boundaries Disputes: The Philippines has been involved in maritime boundary disputes with neighboring states, particularly China, over overlapping claims in the South China Sea. These disputes involve competing claims to maritime features, such as islands, reefs, and shoals, and have led to tensions and diplomatic negotiations to resolve conflicting claims and assert maritime rights.

Legal Challenges and Arbitration: The Philippines initiated arbitration proceedings against China under UNCLOS to challenge the legality of China's maritime claims and assert its rights under international law. The arbitration tribunal ruled in favor of the Philippines, invalidating China's nine-dash line claim and affirming the Philippines' sovereign rights and jurisdiction over its maritime zones.

Territorial Sea Baselines: The Philippines has established baselines to delimit its territorial sea and archipelagic waters, connecting the outermost points of its archipelago's islands and reefs. These baselines serve as the basis for defining the Philippines' territorial sea, contiguous zone, and exclusive economic zone (EEZ) in accordance with UNCLOS provisions.

Territorial Sea and Contiguous Zone: The Philippines exercises sovereignty and jurisdiction over its territorial sea extending up to 12 nautical miles from its baselines, where it regulates navigation, fishing, and other activities in accordance with international law. The contiguous zone extends up to 24 nautical miles from the baselines, where the Philippines enforces customs, immigration, and environmental laws.

Exclusive Economic Zone (EEZ): The Philippines is entitled to an exclusive economic zone (EEZ) extending up to 200 nautical miles from its baselines, where it has sovereign rights to explore, exploit, conserve, and manage natural resources, including fisheries, minerals, and energy resources. The EEZ provides the Philippines with exclusive rights to maritime resources within this zone, subject to certain rights of other states under UNCLOS.

Archipelagic Waters Management: The Philippines implements comprehensive maritime zones management plans to regulate and manage maritime activities within its archipelagic waters, including fisheries management, marine conservation, and maritime security measures. These management plans aim to balance economic development, environmental protection, and national security priorities while respecting international law and the rights of other states.

Environmental Conservation: The Philippines has established marine protected areas (MPAs) and marine parks to conserve marine biodiversity, protect endangered species, and preserve fragile ecosystems within its archipelagic waters. These conservation efforts aim to sustain marine ecosystems, enhance resilience to climate change, and promote sustainable use of marine resources.

Maritime Security Operations: The Philippines conducts maritime security operations to safeguard its archipelagic waters against maritime threats, including piracy, illegal fishing, and transnational crime. Maritime security measures involve naval patrols, maritime surveillance, and law enforcement operations to maintain maritime order, combat maritime crimes, and protect national interests.

International Cooperation: The Philippines engages in international cooperation mechanisms to address shared maritime challenges and opportunities, including piracy, maritime terrorism, and environmental protection. Bilateral and multilateral cooperation initiatives promote dialogue, collaboration, and capacity-building among archipelagic states and neighboring countries to enhance maritime security and governance.

Case Study: Indonesia-Malaysia Archipelagic Waters: Indonesia and Malaysia share maritime boundaries in the archipelagic waters of the Malacca Strait and the Sulu Sea. Both countries have established special regimes to govern their respective archipelagic waters and manage maritime cooperation and security in the region.

Maritime Boundary Delimitation: Indonesia and Malaysia have concluded maritime boundary agreements to delimit their respective territorial seas, exclusive economic zones (EEZs), and continental shelves in the overlapping maritime areas. These agreements provide clarity on jurisdictional boundaries and promote peaceful cooperation and mutual respect for sovereignty and territorial integrity.

Joint Patrols and Cooperation: Indonesia and Malaysia conduct joint maritime patrols and cooperation initiatives to address common challenges, including piracy, illegal fishing, and maritime security threats, in the archipelagic waters of the Malacca Strait and the Sulu Sea. Joint patrols enhance maritime security, promote law enforcement, and strengthen bilateral relations between the two countries.

Marine Resource Management: Indonesia and Malaysia collaborate on marine resource management and fisheries conservation measures in their shared archipelagic waters, including joint surveillance, monitoring, and enforcement operations to combat illegal, unreported, and unregulated (IUU) fishing activities. Cooperation in marine resource management promotes sustainable fisheries and protects marine ecosystems in the region.

Search and Rescue Coordination: Indonesia and Malaysia coordinate search and rescue (SAR) operations in the archipelagic waters of the Malacca Strait and the Sulu Sea to respond to maritime emergencies and save lives at sea. SAR coordination involves joint exercises, information sharing, and mutual assistance agreements to enhance maritime safety and security in the region.

Environmental Protection Measures: Indonesia and Malaysia implement environmental protection measures to address pollution, habitat degradation, and marine conservation in their shared archipelagic waters. These measures include pollution control regulations, marine protected areas, and ecosystem restoration projects to preserve marine biodiversity and promote sustainable development.

Cross-Border Cooperation: Indonesia and Malaysia engage in cross-border cooperation initiatives to promote economic development, tourism, and cultural exchange in the border regions adjacent to their archipelagic waters. Cross-border projects and initiatives enhance connectivity, people-to-people ties, and socio-economic opportunities for communities living in the border areas.

Legal Frameworks and Agreements: Indonesia and Malaysia have established legal frameworks and bilateral agreements to govern maritime cooperation, security, and environmental protection in their shared archipelagic waters. These agreements provide mechanisms for dispute resolution, joint management, and cooperation to address common challenges and promote regional stability.

Regional Engagement: Indonesia and Malaysia actively participate in regional forums and organizations, such as ASEAN and the Indian Ocean Rim Association (IORA), to promote regional cooperation, dialogue, and capacity-building in maritime governance, security, and sustainable development. Regional engagement enhances maritime security, fosters trust, and strengthens regional resilience to maritime threats and challenges.

Future Prospects: The future prospects for cooperation between Indonesia and Malaysia in managing their shared archipelagic waters remain promising, with opportunities for further collaboration, joint initiatives, and mutual benefits in maritime governance, security, and sustainable development. Continued dialogue, cooperation, and partnership are essential to address emerging maritime challenges and promote peace, stability, and prosperity in the region.

Case Study: Philippines-Indonesia Archipelagic Borders: The Philippines and Indonesia share maritime boundaries in the Celebes Sea and the Mindanao Sea, where their archipelagic waters overlap. Both countries have established special regimes to govern their respective maritime zones and address maritime security and cooperation in the region.

Maritime Boundary Negotiations: The Philippines and Indonesia engage in maritime boundary negotiations to delimit their respective territorial seas, exclusive economic zones (EEZs), and continental shelves in the overlapping maritime areas. These negotiations aim to establish clear jurisdictional boundaries and promote peaceful cooperation and mutual respect for sovereignty.

Joint Patrols and Cooperation: The Philippines and Indonesia conduct joint maritime patrols and cooperation initiatives to address common maritime challenges, including piracy, illegal fishing, and maritime security threats, in the archipelagic waters of the Celebes Sea and the Mindanao Sea. Joint patrols enhance maritime security, promote law enforcement, and strengthen bilateral relations between the two countries.

Fisheries Management: The Philippines and Indonesia collaborate on fisheries management and conservation measures in their shared archipelagic waters, including joint surveillance, monitoring, and enforcement operations to combat illegal fishing activities. Cooperation in fisheries management promotes sustainable fisheries and protects marine resources in the region.

Search and Rescue Coordination: The Philippines and Indonesia coordinate search and rescue (SAR) operations in the archipelagic waters of the Celebes Sea and the Mindanao Sea to respond to maritime emergencies and save lives at sea. SAR coordination involves joint exercises, information sharing, and mutual assistance agreements to enhance maritime safety and security in the region.

Environmental Protection Measures: The Philippines and Indonesia implement environmental protection measures to address pollution, habitat degradation, and marine conservation in their shared archipelagic waters. These measures include pollution control regulations, marine protected areas, and ecosystem restoration projects to preserve marine biodiversity and promote sustainable development.

Cross-Border Cooperation: The Philippines and Indonesia engage in cross-border cooperation initiatives to promote economic development, tourism, and cultural exchange in the border regions adjacent to their archipelagic waters. Cross-border projects and initiatives enhance connectivity, people-to-people ties, and socio-economic opportunities for communities living in the border areas.

Legal Frameworks and Agreements: The Philippines and Indonesia have established legal frameworks and bilateral agreements to govern maritime cooperation, security, and environmental protection in their shared archipelagic waters. These agreements provide mechanisms for dispute resolution, joint management, and cooperation to address common challenges and promote regional stability.

Regional Engagement: The Philippines and Indonesia actively participate in regional forums and organizations, such as ASEAN and the Coral Triangle Initiative (CTI), to promote regional cooperation, dialogue, and capacity-building in maritime governance, security, and sustainable development. Regional engagement enhances maritime security, fosters trust, and strengthens regional resilience to maritime threats and challenges.

Future Prospects: The future prospects for cooperation between the Philippines and Indonesia in managing their shared archipelagic waters remain promising, with opportunities for further collaboration, joint initiatives, and mutual benefits in maritime governance, security, and sustainable development. Continued dialogue, cooperation, and partnership are essential to address emerging maritime challenges and promote peace, stability, and prosperity in the region.

Case Study: Malaysia-Philippines Archipelagic Borders: Malaysia and the Philippines share maritime boundaries in the Sulu Sea and the Celebes Sea, where their archipelagic waters intersect. Both countries have established special regimes to govern their respective maritime zones and address maritime security and cooperation in the region.

Maritime Boundary Negotiations: Malaysia and the Philippines engage in maritime boundary negotiations to delimit their respective territorial seas, exclusive economic zones (EEZs), and continental shelves in the overlapping maritime areas. These negotiations aim to establish clear jurisdictional boundaries and promote peaceful cooperation and mutual respect for sovereignty.

Joint Patrols and Cooperation: Malaysia and the Philippines conduct joint maritime patrols and cooperation initiatives to address common maritime challenges, including piracy, illegal fishing, and maritime security threats, in the archipelagic waters of the Sulu Sea and the Celebes Sea. Joint patrols enhance maritime security, promote law enforcement, and strengthen bilateral relations between the two countries.

Fisheries Management: Malaysia and the Philippines collaborate on fisheries management and conservation measures in their shared archipelagic waters, including joint surveillance, monitoring, and enforcement operations to combat illegal fishing activities. Cooperation in fisheries management promotes sustainable fisheries and protects marine resources in the region.

Search and Rescue Coordination: Malaysia and the Philippines coordinate search and rescue (SAR) operations in the archipelagic waters of the Sulu Sea and the Celebes Sea to respond to maritime emergencies and save lives at sea. SAR coordination involves joint exercises, information sharing, and mutual assistance agreements to enhance maritime safety and security in the region.

Environmental Protection Measures: Malaysia and the Philippines implement environmental protection measures to address pollution, habitat degradation, and marine conservation in their shared archipelagic waters. These measures include pollution control regulations, marine protected areas, and ecosystem restoration projects to preserve marine biodiversity and promote sustainable development.

Cross-Border Cooperation: Malaysia and the Philippines engage in cross-border cooperation initiatives to promote economic development, tourism, and cultural exchange in the border regions adjacent to their archipelagic waters. Cross-border projects and initiatives enhance connectivity, people-to-people ties, and socio-economic opportunities for communities living in the border areas.

Legal Frameworks and Agreements: Malaysia and the Philippines have established legal frameworks and bilateral agreements to govern maritime cooperation, security, and environmental protection in their shared archipelagic waters. These agreements provide mechanisms for dispute resolution, joint management, and cooperation to address common challenges and promote regional stability.

Regional Engagement: Malaysia and the Philippines actively participate in regional forums and organizations, such as ASEAN and the Coral Triangle Initiative (CTI), to promote regional cooperation, dialogue, and capacity-building in maritime governance, security, and sustainable development. Regional engagement enhances maritime security, fosters trust, and strengthens regional resilience to maritime threats and challenges.

Future Prospects: The future prospects for cooperation between Malaysia and the Philippines in managing their shared archipelagic waters remain promising, with opportunities for further collaboration, joint initiatives, and mutual benefits in maritime governance, security, and sustainable development. Continued dialogue, cooperation, and partnership are essential to address emerging maritime challenges and promote peace, stability, and prosperity in the region.

Case Study: Indonesia-Philippines Archipelagic Borders:

Indonesia and the Philippines share maritime boundaries in the Celebes Sea and the Mindanao Sea, where their archipelagic waters intersect. Both countries have established special regimes to govern their respective maritime zones and address maritime security and cooperation in the region.

Maritime Boundary Negotiations: Indonesia and the Philippines engage in maritime boundary negotiations to delimit their respective territorial seas, exclusive economic zones (EEZs), and continental shelves in the overlapping maritime areas. These negotiations aim to establish clear jurisdictional boundaries and promote peaceful cooperation and mutual respect for sovereignty.

Joint Patrols and Cooperation: Indonesia and the Philippines conduct joint maritime patrols and cooperation initiatives to address common maritime challenges, including piracy, illegal fishing, and maritime security threats, in the archipelagic waters of the Celebes Sea and the Mindanao Sea. Joint patrols enhance maritime security, promote law enforcement, and strengthen bilateral relations between the two countries.

Fisheries Management: Indonesia and the Philippines collaborate on fisheries management and conservation measures in their shared archipelagic waters, including joint surveillance, monitoring, and enforcement operations to combat illegal fishing activities. Cooperation in fisheries management promotes sustainable fisheries and protects marine resources in the region.

Search and Rescue Coordination: Indonesia and the Philippines coordinate search and rescue (SAR) operations in the archipelagic waters of the Celebes Sea and the Mindanao Sea to respond to maritime emergencies and save lives at sea. SAR coordination involves joint exercises, information sharing, and mutual assistance agreements to enhance maritime safety and security in the region.

Environmental Protection Measures: Indonesia and the Philippines implement environmental protection measures to address pollution, habitat degradation, and marine conservation in their shared archipelagic waters. These measures include pollution control regulations, marine protected areas, and ecosystem restoration projects to preserve marine biodiversity and promote sustainable development.

Cross-Border Cooperation: Indonesia and the Philippines engage in cross-border cooperation initiatives to promote economic development, tourism, and cultural exchange in the border regions adjacent to their archipelagic waters. Cross-border projects and initiatives enhance connectivity, people-to-people ties, and socio-economic opportunities for communities living in the border areas.

Legal Frameworks and Agreements: Indonesia and the Philippines have established legal frameworks and bilateral agreements to govern maritime cooperation, security, and environmental protection in their shared archipelagic waters. These agreements provide mechanisms for dispute resolution, joint management, and cooperation to address common challenges and promote regional stability.

Regional Engagement: Indonesia and the Philippines actively participate in regional forums and organizations, such as ASEAN and the Coral Triangle Initiative (CTI), to promote regional cooperation, dialogue, and capacity-building in maritime governance, security, and sustainable development. Regional engagement enhances maritime security, fosters trust, and strengthens regional resilience to maritime threats and challenges.

Future Prospects: The future prospects for cooperation between Indonesia and the Philippines in managing their shared archipelagic waters remain promising, with opportunities for further collaboration, joint initiatives, and mutual benefits in maritime governance, security, and sustainable development. Continued dialogue, cooperation, and partnership are essential to address emerging maritime challenges and promote peace, stability, and prosperity in the region.

These paragraphs provide insights into the cooperation and collaboration between Indonesia and the Philippines in managing their shared archipelagic waters, highlighting the importance of bilateral and regional engagement in addressing common maritime challenges and promoting peace, stability, and prosperity in the region. If you have any further questions or specific areas you'd like to explore, feel free to let me know!

Chapter 6.
Navigation and Freedom of the Seas

Innocent Passage

Innocent passage refers to the lawful and uninterrupted transit of ships through the territorial sea of a coastal state in accordance with the rules and principles of international law, particularly as outlined in the United Nations Convention on the Law of the Sea (UNCLOS). According to UNCLOS, innocent passage entails navigation through the territorial sea for the purpose of continuous and expeditious transit, without engaging in activities prejudicial to the peace, good order, or security of the coastal state.

Principles of Innocent Passage: Innocent passage is subject to certain principles and restrictions aimed at safeguarding the sovereignty and security of the coastal state while ensuring the freedom of navigation for foreign ships. These principles include the requirement for continuous and expeditious transit, the prohibition of any threat or use of force against the coastal state, and the obligation to comply with the laws and regulations of the coastal state.

Historical Evolution: The concept of innocent passage has its roots in customary international law and has been recognized and codified in various international treaties and conventions over the centuries. In the past, coastal states asserted broader rights to regulate and control foreign ships' passage through their territorial waters, leading to tensions and conflicts between maritime powers. However, the modern legal framework, particularly under UNCLOS, seeks to balance the rights of coastal states with the freedom of navigation for foreign vessels.

UNCLOS Provisions: UNCLOS provides detailed provisions regarding innocent passage through the territorial sea of coastal states. Article 17 of UNCLOS stipulates that ships of all states enjoy the right of innocent passage through the territorial sea in accordance with the provisions of the convention and international law. Coastal states are required to respect and recognize this right and may not suspend innocent passage arbitrarily or discriminate against foreign ships.

Scope of Innocent Passage: Innocent passage encompasses various activities and actions permissible for foreign ships navigating through the territorial sea of a coastal state. These include but are not limited to navigation, anchoring, fishing, and scientific research, provided that such activities do not pose a threat to the security or interests of the coastal state. However, certain activities, such as military exercises, intelligence gathering, and weapons testing, are not considered innocent and may be prohibited by the coastal state.

Navigation Requirements: Ships conducting innocent passage must adhere to specific navigation requirements to ensure compliance with international law and the safety of navigation. These requirements include maintaining a continuous and expeditious course through the territorial sea, refraining from any activities that could interfere with the coastal state's security or maritime operations, and complying with navigational rules and regulations established by the coastal state.

Notification and Clearance: While UNCLOS does not explicitly require ships to notify or seek clearance from coastal states before conducting innocent passage, some coastal states may impose notification requirements or establish traffic separation schemes to manage maritime traffic and ensure safety. Ships are generally encouraged to communicate with coastal authorities and comply with any instructions or guidance provided to facilitate their passage through the territorial sea.

Case Study: USS Decatur Incident: In 2018, the USS Decatur, a United States Navy destroyer, conducted a freedom of navigation operation (FONOP) near disputed islands in the South China Sea. The USS Decatur was challenged by Chinese naval vessels while navigating within 12 nautical miles of the islands, prompting concerns over the interpretation and application of innocent passage under UNCLOS.

Legal Interpretations: The USS Decatur incident highlighted differing interpretations of innocent passage and freedom of navigation among coastal states and maritime powers. While the United States asserted its rights to conduct FONOPs in accordance with international law, China criticized the USS Decatur's actions as provocative and inconsistent with UNCLOS provisions regarding innocent passage.

Diplomatic Responses: The USS Decatur incident led to diplomatic tensions between the United States and China, with both countries exchanging diplomatic protests and statements regarding the legality and implications of the naval encounter. The incident underscored the complexities and challenges associated with maritime disputes and the interpretation of UNCLOS principles in contested waters.

Arbitration and Dispute Resolution: In cases where disputes arise over the interpretation or application of innocent passage and freedom of navigation, coastal states and maritime powers may resort to diplomatic negotiations, arbitration, or other dispute resolution mechanisms to resolve their differences peacefully. UNCLOS provides avenues for dispute settlement, including arbitration under Annex VII and recourse to the International Court of Justice (ICJ).

Regional Agreements and Practices: In addition to UNCLOS provisions, regional agreements and practices may influence the application of innocent passage and freedom of navigation in specific maritime regions. For example, regional organizations such as the Association of Southeast Asian Nations (ASEAN) have adopted codes of conduct and confidence-building measures to promote stability and cooperation in the South China Sea and other disputed areas.

Navigational Challenges: Navigating through congested or narrow waterways poses challenges for ships conducting innocent passage, particularly in areas with high maritime traffic, adverse weather conditions, or navigational hazards. Ships must exercise caution, maintain situational awareness, and adhere to established navigational rules and procedures to mitigate the risk of accidents or collisions. Coastal states may also implement measures such as traffic separation schemes, designated shipping lanes, and mandatory pilotage to enhance maritime safety and facilitate the smooth flow of vessel traffic.

Environmental Considerations: In addition to safety concerns, ships conducting innocent passage must also consider environmental factors and take measures to minimize their environmental impact while transiting through the territorial sea. This includes complying with regulations on pollution prevention, waste disposal, and ballast water management to protect marine ecosystems and mitigate pollution risks.

Commercial Shipping Operations: Innocent passage is commonly utilized by commercial shipping vessels engaged in international trade and transportation. Cargo ships, container vessels, bulk carriers, and other types of merchant ships rely on innocent passage rights to navigate through territorial seas en route to their destination ports, ensuring the uninterrupted flow of goods and commodities across maritime routes.

Port Access and Maritime Infrastructure: Access to ports and maritime infrastructure is essential for ships conducting innocent passage to refuel, resupply, and undergo repairs or maintenance. Coastal states have a responsibility to provide facilities and services to accommodate visiting foreign vessels and promote port efficiency and logistics connectivity in support of international trade and maritime commerce.

Humanitarian Assistance and Disaster Relief (HADR): Innocent passage may also be utilized for humanitarian assistance and disaster relief (HADR) operations in response to natural disasters, humanitarian crises, or maritime emergencies. Ships carrying relief supplies, medical assistance, and personnel may transit through territorial seas to reach affected areas and provide assistance to those in need, subject to the consent and cooperation of the coastal state.

Freedom of Navigation Operations (FONOPs): Freedom of navigation operations (FONOPs) are conducted by naval forces to assert and demonstrate the rights and freedoms of navigation under international law, including innocent passage through territorial seas. FONOPs are often employed by maritime powers to challenge excessive maritime claims, assert navigational rights, and promote adherence to international norms and standards.

Naval Exercises and Training: Naval exercises and training activities may involve the navigation of ships through territorial seas as part of routine operations or cooperative engagements with foreign navies. These exercises enhance interoperability, promote maritime security cooperation, and contribute to regional stability by fostering mutual understanding and trust among maritime stakeholders.

Legal Interpretations and Disputes: Despite the clarity of UNCLOS provisions on innocent passage, disputes and legal interpretations may arise regarding the scope and application of this principle in specific maritime contexts. Coastal states and maritime powers may differ in their interpretation of navigational rights, security concerns, and sovereignty claims, leading to diplomatic tensions and legal challenges.

Sovereignty and Security Concerns: Coastal states have legitimate interests in safeguarding their sovereignty, security, and territorial integrity within their territorial seas. While UNCLOS recognizes the right of innocent passage, coastal states retain the authority to regulate and control activities that may threaten their security or violate their laws and regulations, subject to the principles of international law and customary practice.

Military Activities and Exercises: The conduct of military activities and exercises during innocent passage remains a contentious issue, particularly in regions with ongoing maritime disputes or geopolitical tensions. Coastal states may view certain military activities, such as surveillance operations or weapons testing, as incompatible with innocent passage and may take measures to monitor, regulate, or restrict such activities within their territorial waters.

Transit Passage through International Straits: Transit passage, as distinct from innocent passage, applies to ships navigating through international straits used for international navigation between one part of the high seas or an exclusive economic zone (EEZ) and another part of the high seas or an EEZ. While transit passage affords ships a broader range of navigational freedoms, it is subject to specific rights and obligations outlined in UNCLOS, including the obligation to refrain from any threat or use of force against the coastal state.

Case Study: Transit Passage in the Strait of Hormuz: The Strait of Hormuz, located between the Persian Gulf and the Gulf of Oman, is a vital international strait through which a significant portion of the world's oil shipments pass. The concept of transit passage is particularly relevant in the context of the Strait of Hormuz, where ships from various countries transit through narrow and congested waters subject to the jurisdiction of coastal states.

Legal and Operational Challenges: Transit passage through international straits presents legal and operational challenges for ships navigating in confined and heavily trafficked waterways. Ships must navigate through designated shipping lanes, avoid collisions with other vessels, and comply with the rules and regulations established by coastal states to ensure safe and efficient passage through the strait.

Military Presence and Security Concerns: The presence of military forces and security concerns in international straits, such as piracy, terrorism, and maritime disputes, may impact the exercise of transit passage rights. Coastal states may impose security measures, conduct military exercises, or establish maritime security zones to protect their territorial integrity and maintain order within the strait, potentially affecting the freedom of navigation for foreign ships.

Diplomatic Engagement and Cooperation: Diplomatic engagement and cooperation among coastal states, maritime powers, and international organizations are essential for addressing legal disputes, resolving conflicts, and promoting the peaceful and orderly transit of ships through international straits. Multilateral agreements, confidence-building measures, and regional initiatives can enhance maritime security and stability in critical waterways.

Environmental Protection and Conservation: International straits are often characterized by sensitive marine ecosystems, biodiversity hotspots, and vulnerable coastal habitats that require special protection and conservation measures. Coastal states and international organizations may implement environmental regulations, establish marine protected areas, and promote sustainable practices to mitigate the environmental impacts of shipping activities in international straits.

Navigational Safety and Risk Management: Navigating through international straits poses challenges for ships due to the presence of navigational hazards, adverse weather conditions, and congested traffic patterns. Ships must employ advanced navigation technologies, adhere to navigational best practices, and maintain vigilance to ensure the safety of navigation and mitigate the risk of accidents or maritime incidents in the strait.

Future Trends and Developments: The future of navigation and freedom of the seas in international straits will be influenced by various factors, including technological advancements, geopolitical dynamics, environmental concerns, and legal developments. Emerging trends such as the digitalization of maritime navigation, the rise of autonomous shipping, and the increasing focus on sustainable shipping practices will shape the future maritime landscape in international straits.

Security Measures and Countermeasures: In some instances, coastal states may impose security measures, such as maritime patrols, surveillance, or vessel inspections, to protect their territorial waters and enforce their sovereignty. While such measures are within the rights of coastal states, they should be exercised in accordance with international law and should not unduly interfere with innocent passage rights.

Challenges to Navigation: Despite the recognition of innocent passage under international law, ships may encounter challenges and obstacles when navigating through certain territorial waters. Coastal states may impose restrictions or requirements on foreign vessels, such as compulsory pilotage, reporting obligations, or prohibitions on specific activities, which could affect the smooth and unhindered passage of ships.

Humanitarian Considerations: Innocent passage rights extend to humanitarian missions and activities conducted by foreign ships, including search and rescue operations, medical assistance, and disaster relief efforts. Coastal states are expected to facilitate and support such humanitarian initiatives, ensuring that ships engaged in these activities are not unduly hindered or delayed during their passage through territorial waters.

Environmental Protection Obligations: Ships conducting innocent passage must adhere to environmental protection obligations and regulations to prevent pollution, minimize environmental impact, and preserve marine ecosystems. Coastal states have a vested interest in ensuring that foreign vessels comply with environmental standards and regulations while transiting through their territorial seas to prevent ecological harm and promote sustainable maritime practices.

Sustainable Shipping Practices: The promotion of sustainable shipping practices, such as reducing emissions, conserving energy, and adopting eco-friendly technologies, aligns with the objectives of innocent passage and contributes to the overall protection of the marine environment. Coastal states may encourage or incentivize ships to adopt sustainable practices during their passage through territorial waters, fostering responsible maritime behavior.

Maritime Boundary Disputes: Maritime boundary disputes between coastal states can impact innocent passage rights, particularly in areas where territorial claims overlap or maritime boundaries remain undefined. Disputes over the delimitation of territorial seas and exclusive economic zones may lead to conflicting interpretations of innocent passage rights and require diplomatic or legal resolution to ensure the unhindered passage of ships.

Legal Interpretations by Coastal States: Coastal states retain the authority to interpret and enforce their laws and regulations within their territorial waters, including those pertaining to innocent passage. While international law provides general principles and guidelines for innocent passage, coastal states may adopt varying interpretations or impose additional requirements on foreign vessels based on their national security concerns and domestic legislation.

Customary International Law: The concept of innocent passage is rooted in customary international law and reflects long-standing maritime practices and traditions. While UNCLOS codifies and elaborates on the rights and obligations associated with innocent passage, customary international law continues to play a significant role in shaping state practice and legal interpretations regarding navigation and freedom of the seas.

Non-Recognition of Innocent Passage: In exceptional cases, certain coastal states may refuse to recognize innocent passage rights or assert restrictive interpretations of UNCLOS provisions, particularly in areas of heightened tension or maritime disputes. Non-recognition of innocent passage may lead to diplomatic protests, legal challenges, or incidents at sea, highlighting the complexities and challenges inherent in maritime law enforcement and compliance.

Engagement with International Organizations: Coastal states, maritime powers, and international organizations play crucial roles in promoting dialogue, cooperation, and adherence to international law regarding innocent passage and freedom of navigation. Engagement with organizations such as the International Maritime Organization (IMO), the International Court of Justice (ICJ), and regional maritime forums facilitates the exchange of best practices, capacity-building initiatives, and dispute resolution mechanisms to address maritime challenges effectively.

Transit Passage through International Straits: Transit passage, as defined in UNCLOS, applies to ships navigating through international straits used for international navigation between one part of the high seas or an exclusive economic zone (EEZ) and another part of the high seas or an EEZ. Unlike innocent passage, which is limited to the territorial sea, transit passage affords ships a broader range of navigational freedoms in international straits, subject to certain rights and obligations outlined in UNCLOS.

Legal Framework: UNCLOS establishes the legal framework for transit passage through international straits, specifying that ships enjoy the right of transit passage through such straits without discrimination and regardless of the flag they fly. Coastal states bordering international straits are required to respect and recognize the right of transit passage and may not suspend or obstruct transit passage arbitrarily.

Scope of Transit Passage: Transit passage entitles ships to traverse international straits expeditiously and without interruption, maintaining a continuous and uninterrupted passage through the strait. Ships may navigate through the strait for the purpose of transit only and may not linger or engage in activities inconsistent with transit passage, such as fishing, surveying, or military exercises.

Non-Suspendable Nature: One of the key features of transit passage is its non-suspendable nature, meaning that coastal states may not suspend or impede the exercise of transit passage rights by foreign ships passing through international straits, even in times of conflict or tension. However, coastal states retain the right to adopt regulations and measures to ensure the safety of navigation and protect their legitimate interests within the strait.

Navigation and Safety Measures: Ships conducting transit passage through international straits must adhere to navigational rules, regulations, and safety measures established by coastal states to ensure the safe and orderly passage of vessels. This includes complying with traffic separation schemes, navigation aids, and other navigational guidelines to mitigate the risk of collisions, accidents, or maritime incidents.

Military Activities and Exercises: While transit passage permits the passage of military ships through international straits, it does not authorize military activities or exercises that are inconsistent with the right of innocent passage. Military activities during transit passage must be conducted in a manner that avoids any threat or use of force against the coastal state and complies with international law and the principles of freedom of navigation.

Case Study: Strait of Hormuz: The Strait of Hormuz, located between the Persian Gulf and the Gulf of Oman, is one of the world's most strategically significant international straits, through which a significant portion of global oil shipments transit. The concept of transit passage is particularly relevant in the context of the Strait of Hormuz, where ships from various countries navigate through narrow and congested waters subject to the jurisdiction of coastal states.

Legal and Operational Challenges: Navigating through international straits poses legal and operational challenges for ships due to the presence of navigational hazards, adverse weather conditions, and congested traffic patterns. Ships conducting transit passage must exercise caution, maintain situational awareness, and comply with navigational rules and safety measures to ensure the safe and efficient passage of vessels through the strait.

Freedom of Navigation Operations (FONOPs): Transit passage rights are often asserted and demonstrated through freedom of navigation operations (FONOPs) conducted by naval forces to challenge excessive maritime claims and assert navigational freedoms under international law. FONOPs in international straits promote adherence to UNCLOS provisions, uphold navigational rights, and discourage unilateral attempts to restrict freedom of navigation.

Diplomatic Engagement and Cooperation: Diplomatic engagement and cooperation among coastal states, maritime powers, and international organizations are essential for addressing legal disputes, resolving conflicts, and promoting the peaceful and orderly transit of ships through international straits. Multilateral agreements, confidence-building measures, and regional initiatives can enhance maritime security and stability in critical waterways, contributing to global peace and security.

Sovereignty and Security Concerns: Coastal states have legitimate interests in safeguarding their sovereignty, security, and territorial integrity within international straits. While transit passage grants ships the right to traverse international straits, coastal states retain certain rights and obligations to regulate maritime traffic, maintain public order, and protect their national interests within the strait. Coastal states may adopt measures such as maritime patrols, surveillance, and security zones to safeguard their sovereignty and ensure the safety and security of navigation.

Navigational Safety and Risk Management: Ensuring navigational safety is paramount in international straits due to the presence of navigational hazards, congested traffic, and adverse weather conditions. Ships transiting through international straits must adhere to established navigational rules, maintain a safe speed and course, and exercise vigilance to avoid collisions, groundings, or other maritime accidents. Coastal states may implement navigational aids, traffic management schemes, and search and rescue capabilities to enhance maritime safety and mitigate the risk of maritime incidents.

Environmental Protection and Conservation: International straits are often located in ecologically sensitive areas with diverse marine ecosystems and vulnerable habitats. Coastal states and international organizations have a responsibility to protect and conserve the marine environment in international straits, including measures to prevent pollution, regulate shipping activities, and promote sustainable maritime practices. Initiatives such as marine protected areas, pollution control programs, and ecosystem monitoring efforts help mitigate the environmental impact of shipping activities and preserve the biodiversity of international straits.

Search and Rescue Operations: International straits are critical transit routes for ships navigating between different maritime regions, making them susceptible to maritime accidents, emergencies, and distress situations. Coastal states bordering international straits have an obligation to provide prompt and effective search and rescue services to ships in distress, regardless of their nationality or flag. Coordination mechanisms, communication protocols, and mutual assistance agreements facilitate timely response and coordination among coastal states and international maritime agencies during search and rescue operations in international straits.

Maritime Security Cooperation: Given the strategic importance of international straits for global trade and maritime security, coastal states and maritime powers engage in cooperative efforts to enhance maritime security, combat maritime threats, and promote regional stability in international straits. Joint patrols, information-sharing arrangements, and capacity-building initiatives strengthen maritime domain awareness, maritime law enforcement capabilities, and counter-terrorism measures in international straits, contributing to the safety, security, and stability of maritime navigation.

Legal Disputes and Arbitration: Disputes over the interpretation and application of transit passage rights in international straits may arise between coastal states and maritime powers, leading to diplomatic tensions or legal proceedings. UNCLOS provides mechanisms for the peaceful settlement of disputes related to transit passage, including arbitration, conciliation, and adjudication before international tribunals or the International Court of Justice (ICJ). Adherence to international law, good-faith negotiations, and respect for established legal principles facilitate the resolution of legal disputes and promote cooperation among states in international straits.

Freedom of Navigation Exercises: Maritime powers conduct freedom of navigation exercises (FONEXs) or freedom of navigation operations (FONOPs) to assert and demonstrate their rights to navigate through international straits and challenge excessive maritime claims that may restrict freedom of navigation. These exercises uphold the principles of international law, promote navigational freedoms, and discourage unilateral attempts to restrict transit passage rights in international straits. Transparency, adherence to international standards, and respect for the rights of coastal states are essential in conducting freedom of navigation exercises in international straits.

Regional Cooperation Mechanisms: Regional organizations and multilateral forums play a crucial role in promoting cooperation, dialogue, and confidence-building measures among coastal states and maritime stakeholders in international straits. Platforms such as the Strait of Hormuz Initiative, the Malacca Strait Patrols, and the Djibouti Code of Conduct facilitate maritime security cooperation, information-sharing, and capacity-building efforts to address common challenges and enhance maritime governance in international straits.

Maritime Connectivity and Trade Routes: International straits serve as vital maritime chokepoints and trade routes, connecting major maritime regions and facilitating the flow of goods, energy resources, and commodities between different continents and economic zones. Enhancing the resilience, efficiency, and sustainability of maritime connectivity in international straits supports global trade, economic development, and prosperity, benefiting coastal states, maritime powers, and the international community as a whole.

Future Challenges and Opportunities: The future of transit passage in international straits will be influenced by emerging trends, challenges, and opportunities in the maritime domain, including technological advancements, geopolitical dynamics, environmental changes, and legal developments. Addressing issues such as maritime security threats, environmental degradation, and jurisdictional disputes requires concerted efforts, cooperation, and innovative solutions from coastal states, maritime powers, and international organizations to ensure the continued safe, secure, and sustainable navigation of ships through international straits.

Historical Context: The concept of transit passage through international straits has its roots in customary international law and historical maritime practices. Throughout history, ships have traversed narrow waterways and strategic passages for trade, navigation, and exploration, often facing challenges and disputes over access and rights of passage. Over time, customary norms and traditions governing the transit of ships through international straits evolved, culminating in the codification of transit passage rights in modern international law, particularly in UNCLOS.

Legal Framework and UNCLOS Provisions: UNCLOS provides a comprehensive legal framework for transit passage through international straits, codifying the rights and obligations of states and ships navigating through these critical maritime chokepoints. Article 38 of UNCLOS defines international straits as straits used for international navigation between one part of the high seas or an exclusive economic zone (EEZ) and another part of the high seas or an EEZ, and establishes the principle of transit passage through such straits.

Scope of Transit Passage: Transit passage grants ships the right to transit through international straits expeditiously and without obstruction, navigating in a continuous and uninterrupted manner through the strait. Unlike innocent passage, which is limited to the territorial sea, transit passage extends throughout the entire width of the strait and encompasses the full range of navigational freedoms necessary for safe and efficient passage.

Non-Suspendable Nature: One of the fundamental principles of transit passage is its non-suspendable nature, meaning that coastal states may not suspend or obstruct transit passage rights by foreign ships passing through international straits, even during times of conflict or tension. Coastal states are obliged to respect and recognize the right of transit passage and may not interfere with the lawful exercise of this right by ships transiting through the strait.

Rights and Obligations of Ships: Ships exercising transit passage through international straits enjoy certain rights and obligations under international law. They have the right to navigate through the strait without interference, maintain a continuous and expeditious passage, and refrain from activities that are inconsistent with transit passage, such as military exercises or resource exploration. Ships must comply with navigational rules, regulations, and safety measures established by coastal states to ensure the safety of navigation and prevent maritime incidents.

Exceptions and Restrictions: While transit passage grants ships broad navigational freedoms in international straits, certain limitations and restrictions may apply under specific circumstances. Coastal states may adopt regulations and measures to ensure the safety of navigation, protect the marine environment, and maintain public order within the strait, provided that such measures are consistent with international law and do not unduly interfere with transit passage rights.

Security Measures and Maritime Security: Coastal states have a legitimate interest in safeguarding their sovereignty, security, and territorial integrity within international straits, particularly in areas of strategic importance or maritime security threats. Coastal states may implement security measures, conduct maritime patrols, and establish security zones to protect their maritime interests and prevent threats such as piracy, terrorism, or illegal activities in the strait.

Military Activities and Exercises: While transit passage permits the passage of military ships through international straits, it does not authorize military activities or exercises that are inconsistent with the right of transit passage. Military activities during transit passage must be conducted in a manner that respects the sovereignty of coastal states, avoids any threat or use of force against the coastal state, and complies with international law and the principles of freedom of navigation.

Case Study: Strait of Gibraltar: The Strait of Gibraltar, located between southern Spain and northern Morocco, is a critical international strait connecting the Mediterranean Sea with the Atlantic Ocean. Transit passage through the Strait of Gibraltar is governed by the legal framework established in UNCLOS, ensuring the unhindered passage of ships between the Mediterranean and the Atlantic, subject to the rights and obligations of coastal states.

Legal Disputes and Dispute Resolution: Disputes over transit passage rights in international straits may arise between coastal states and maritime powers, particularly in areas where territorial claims or maritime boundaries are contested. UNCLOS provides mechanisms for the peaceful settlement of disputes related to transit passage, including negotiation, arbitration, and adjudication before international tribunals or the International Court of Justice (ICJ), promoting the rule of law and the peaceful resolution of maritime disputes.

Diplomatic Engagement and Cooperation: Diplomatic engagement and cooperation among coastal states, maritime powers, and international organizations are essential for addressing legal disputes, resolving conflicts, and promoting the peaceful and orderly transit of ships through international straits. Multilateral agreements, confidence-building measures, and regional initiatives facilitate dialogue, cooperation, and mutual understanding among states with shared interests in international straits.

Environmental Protection and Conservation: International straits are often characterized by sensitive marine ecosystems, biodiversity hotspots, and vulnerable coastal habitats that require special protection and conservation measures. Coastal states and international organizations have a responsibility to protect and conserve the marine environment in international straits, including measures to prevent pollution, regulate shipping activities, and promote sustainable maritime practices.

Maritime Safety and Navigation: Ensuring the safety of navigation is essential for ships transiting through international straits, given the presence of navigational hazards, adverse weather conditions, and congested traffic patterns. Ships must adhere to navigational rules, maintain situational awareness, and exercise caution to avoid collisions, groundings, or other maritime accidents, contributing to the safety and efficiency of maritime navigation in international straits.

Humanitarian Considerations: International straits may serve as critical transit routes for humanitarian assistance and disaster relief (HADR) operations, allowing ships to deliver relief supplies, medical assistance, and personnel to affected areas in times of crisis or emergencies. Coastal states bordering international straits have an obligation to facilitate and support such humanitarian initiatives, ensuring the timely and unhindered passage of ships engaged in HADR operations.

Future Challenges and Opportunities: The future of transit passage in international straits will be shaped by various factors, including technological advancements, geopolitical dynamics, environmental changes, and legal developments.

Technological Advancements: Technological advancements in navigation, communication, and maritime surveillance have the potential to enhance the safety, efficiency, and security of transit passage through international straits. Innovations such as satellite navigation systems, automated vessel traffic management, and unmanned aerial vehicles (UAVs) enable ships to navigate more accurately, monitor traffic patterns, and detect potential threats or hazards in real-time, contributing to safer and more efficient maritime navigation in international straits.

Geopolitical Dynamics: Geopolitical dynamics and regional tensions may impact transit passage rights in international straits, particularly in areas where maritime disputes, territorial claims, or geopolitical rivalries exist. Competition for control over strategic waterways, access to vital resources, and influence over maritime trade routes can lead to friction between coastal states and maritime powers, affecting the exercise of transit passage rights and necessitating diplomatic engagement and conflict resolution mechanisms.

Environmental Changes and Climate Resilience: Climate change and environmental degradation pose significant challenges to the sustainable management and conservation of international straits. Rising sea levels, extreme weather events, and ocean acidification threaten coastal habitats, navigation infrastructure, and marine biodiversity in international straits, necessitating adaptation measures, resilience-building initiatives, and international cooperation to mitigate the impacts of climate change and preserve the ecological integrity of these vital maritime corridors.

Legal Developments and Interpretations: Legal developments and interpretations regarding transit passage rights in international straits may evolve over time in response to changing geopolitical dynamics, environmental concerns, and maritime security threats. Coastal states, maritime powers, and international organizations may seek clarification or reinterpretation of UNCLOS provisions related to transit passage through international straits, leading to legal debates, diplomatic negotiations, or judicial proceedings to clarify rights and obligations under international law.

Multilateral Cooperation and Governance: Multilateral cooperation and governance mechanisms play a crucial role in addressing common challenges and promoting cooperation among coastal states, maritime powers, and international organizations in international straits. Regional agreements, joint initiatives, and collaborative frameworks facilitate dialogue, information-sharing, and capacity-building efforts to enhance maritime security, environmental protection, and navigational safety in international straits, fostering greater cooperation and mutual trust among stakeholders.

Economic Development and Maritime Infrastructure: Economic development and investment in maritime infrastructure can enhance the efficiency, capacity, and resilience of international straits, supporting the sustainable growth of maritime trade and commerce. Investments in port facilities, navigational aids, and maritime services improve the connectivity, accessibility, and safety of international straits, facilitating the seamless flow of goods, energy resources, and commodities through these critical maritime corridors.

Maritime Connectivity and Digitalization: Digitalization and connectivity initiatives in the maritime sector have the potential to transform the management and operation of international straits, optimizing navigation, enhancing situational awareness, and improving the efficiency of maritime traffic management. Digital platforms, smart technologies, and data-driven solutions enable real-time monitoring, decision-making, and coordination among maritime stakeholders, contributing to safer, more sustainable, and resilient maritime navigation in international straits.

Capacity Building and Institutional Strengthening: Capacity building and institutional strengthening efforts are essential for enhancing the capabilities and capacities of coastal states, particularly those with limited resources or technical expertise, to effectively manage and govern international straits. Technical assistance, training programs, and knowledge-sharing initiatives support the development of maritime governance frameworks, regulatory frameworks, and operational capabilities, empowering coastal states to fulfill their obligations and responsibilities in international straits.

Public-Private Partnerships and Stakeholder Engagement: Public-private partnerships (PPPs) and stakeholder engagement initiatives play a vital role in promoting sustainable development, innovation, and best practices in international straits. Collaboration between governments, industry stakeholders, civil society organizations, and academia fosters inclusive decision-making, knowledge exchange, and resource mobilization, driving forward initiatives to address common challenges, leverage opportunities, and promote the shared interests of all stakeholders in international straits.

Maritime Security Cooperation and Counterterrorism: Maritime security cooperation and counterterrorism efforts are crucial for addressing transnational threats, piracy, maritime terrorism, and illicit activities in international straits. Joint patrols, information-sharing mechanisms, and capacity-building initiatives enhance maritime domain awareness, strengthen law enforcement capabilities, and disrupt criminal networks operating in international straits, bolstering the security and stability of these critical maritime corridors.

Promotion of Sustainable Maritime Practices: The promotion of sustainable maritime practices, including environmental protection, conservation, and resource management, is essential for ensuring the long-term viability and resilience of international straits. Coastal states, maritime powers, and international organizations can collaborate to develop and implement sustainable shipping initiatives, pollution prevention measures, and ecosystem-based management approaches, safeguarding the ecological integrity and socio-economic vitality of international straits for future generations.

Community Engagement and Empowerment: Community engagement and empowerment initiatives empower local communities living in coastal areas adjacent to international straits to participate in decision-making processes, contribute to marine conservation efforts, and benefit from sustainable development opportunities. By involving local stakeholders in planning, management, and governance activities, coastal states and international organizations can foster greater ownership, inclusivity, and resilience in the management of international straits, promoting the well-being and livelihoods of coastal communities.

Cultural Heritage Preservation: International straits are often rich in cultural heritage, historical significance, and archaeological treasures, reflecting centuries of human interaction and maritime trade. Efforts to preserve and protect cultural heritage sites, maritime artifacts, and traditional knowledge associated with international straits contribute to the promotion of cultural diversity, heritage tourism, and intercultural dialogue, fostering greater appreciation and understanding of the shared maritime heritage of coastal states and maritime communities.

Adaptive Governance and Resilience: Adaptive governance and resilience-building strategies enable coastal states and maritime stakeholders to anticipate, adapt to, and mitigate the impacts of environmental, economic, and social changes in international straits. Flexible governance frameworks, adaptive management approaches, and participatory decision-making processes enhance the resilience of international straits to emerging challenges and uncertainties, ensuring their continued vitality and sustainability in a rapidly changing world.

Promotion of Peaceful Cooperation and Diplomacy: The promotion of peaceful cooperation, dialogue, and diplomacy is essential for building trust, resolving conflicts, and fostering mutual understanding among coastal states and maritime powers in international straits. Diplomatic engagement, confidence-building measures, and conflict resolution mechanisms promote stability, security, and cooperation in international straits, reducing the risk of tensions, disputes, or escalations that could undermine regional peace and security.

Freedom of Navigation and Overflight

Freedom of navigation and overflight are fundamental principles of international law that uphold the rights of states and vessels to navigate and fly over the high seas, international straits, and airspace beyond national jurisdiction. These rights are enshrined in various international conventions and customary norms, including the United Nations Convention on the Law of the Sea (UNCLOS), which codifies the legal framework governing freedom of navigation and overflight in maritime and aerial domains.

UNCLOS Provisions: UNCLOS establishes the legal framework for freedom of navigation and overflight, defining the rights, obligations, and responsibilities of states and vessels operating in international waters and airspace. Articles 87 to 90 of

UNCLOS specifically address freedom of navigation and overflight, affirming the freedom of all states to navigate ships and aircraft on the high seas, through international straits, and over the exclusive economic zones (EEZs) of coastal states, subject to certain limitations and obligations under international law.

High Seas Freedom: The concept of freedom of navigation on the high seas encompasses the freedom of ships of all states to navigate, transit, and conduct lawful activities in the waters beyond the territorial seas of coastal states. Ships enjoy broad navigational freedoms on the high seas, including the freedom of innocent passage, the freedom of navigation and overflight, the freedom to lay submarine cables and pipelines, the freedom to conduct marine scientific research, and the freedom of fishing on the high seas.

International Straits: Freedom of navigation through international straits is governed by specific legal regimes established in UNCLOS and customary international law. UNCLOS defines international straits as straits used for international navigation between one part of the high seas or an EEZ and another part of the high seas or an EEZ, subject to the right of transit passage for ships and aircraft. Coastal states bordering international straits are required to ensure the right of transit passage for ships and aircraft through the strait without obstruction, subject to certain limitations and regulations to ensure safety and order.

Transit Passage Rights: Transit passage grants ships and aircraft the right to transit through international straits in a continuous and expeditious manner, navigating through the strait without interference or interruption. Coastal states bordering international straits must refrain from suspending or obstructing transit passage rights and may only adopt regulations and measures necessary for the safety of navigation, the prevention of pollution, and the maintenance of public order within the strait.

Case Study: Strait of Hormuz: The Strait of Hormuz, located between the Persian Gulf and the Gulf of Oman, is a vital international strait through which a significant portion of the world's oil exports pass. Freedom of navigation through the Strait of Hormuz is essential for global energy security and maritime trade, as ships transit through the strait to access major oil-producing regions in the Middle East and transport oil and gas to international markets.

Strategic Importance: The strategic importance of the Strait of Hormuz has led to geopolitical tensions and security concerns, particularly in relation to freedom of navigation and overflight in the region. Coastal states bordering the strait, including Iran and Oman, have sovereignty over their respective territorial waters but must ensure the right of transit passage for ships and aircraft transiting through the strait in accordance with international law.

Military Presence: The presence of military forces and naval assets in the vicinity of international straits, such as the Strait of Hormuz, underscores the importance of freedom of navigation and overflight for maintaining regional stability and security. Maritime powers conduct freedom of navigation operations (FONOPs) and joint exercises to assert their rights and demonstrate their commitment to upholding international law in critical maritime chokepoints like the Strait of Hormuz.

Maritime Security Challenges: Maritime security challenges, including piracy, maritime terrorism, and illicit activities, pose threats to freedom of navigation and overflight in international straits and adjacent waters. Coastal states and maritime powers collaborate to address these security challenges through cooperative initiatives, joint patrols, and information-sharing mechanisms to ensure the safety and security of maritime navigation and prevent disruptions to global maritime trade.

Legal Disputes and Arbitration: Disputes over freedom of navigation and overflight rights in international straits may arise between coastal states and maritime powers, leading to diplomatic tensions or legal proceedings. UNCLOS provides mechanisms for the peaceful settlement of disputes related to freedom of navigation and overflight, including arbitration, conciliation, and adjudication before international tribunals or the

International Court of Justice (ICJ), promoting the rule of law and the peaceful resolution of maritime disputes.

Freedom of Navigation Operations: Maritime powers conduct freedom of navigation operations (FONOPs) to assert their rights and challenge excessive maritime claims that may restrict freedom of navigation in international waters, including international straits. FONOPs demonstrate a commitment to upholding international law, challenging unlawful maritime restrictions, and promoting navigational freedoms for all states in accordance with UNCLOS and customary international law.

Freedom of Overflight: In addition to freedom of navigation, freedom of overflight is a fundamental principle of international law that ensures the right of aircraft to fly over international waters, including international straits and the high seas. Coastal states must respect the freedom of overflight for civil and military aircraft, refraining from interference or obstruction unless justified by exceptional circumstances such as national security or safety of air navigation.

Airspace Sovereignty and International Law: While coastal states have sovereignty over their territorial airspace, they are required to ensure the freedom of overflight for civil aircraft in accordance with international law, including the Chicago Convention on International Civil Aviation and customary principles of freedom of overflight. Military aircraft enjoy certain rights and privileges under international law, including the right of innocent passage through foreign airspace, subject to compliance with air traffic control procedures and safety regulations.

Case Study: South China Sea: The South China Sea is a contested maritime region where multiple states claim sovereignty over islands, reefs, and features, leading to disputes over maritime boundaries, territorial sovereignty, and freedom of navigation and overflight. The United States and other maritime powers conduct freedom of navigation operations (FONOPs) in the South China Sea to challenge excessive maritime claims, assert navigational freedoms, and uphold the principles of international law, including UNCLOS.

Regional Cooperation and Confidence-Building: Regional cooperation and confidence-building measures play a crucial role in promoting mutual understanding, dialogue, and cooperation among coastal states, maritime powers, and international organizations in international straits. Platforms such as the ASEAN Regional Forum (ARF), the Indian Ocean Naval Symposium (IONS), and the Western Pacific Naval Symposium (WPNS) facilitate dialogue, information-sharing, and cooperative initiatives to address maritime security challenges and promote stability in international straits.

Maritime Domain Awareness: Maritime domain awareness (MDA) encompasses the ability to monitor, track, and understand activities and developments in the maritime domain, including freedom of navigation and overflight in international straits. Coastal states and maritime powers invest in MDA capabilities, including surveillance systems, reconnaissance assets, and information-sharing networks, to enhance situational awareness, detect potential threats, and respond effectively to maritime security challenges in international straits.

Civilian and Military Cooperation: Civilian and military cooperation is essential for ensuring the effective management and governance of international straits, particularly in areas where security threats and maritime disputes exist. Coastal states and maritime powers collaborate on joint patrols, training exercises, and capacity-building initiatives to enhance maritime security, counter piracy, and combat illegal activities in international straits, fostering trust, cooperation, and interoperability among maritime stakeholders.

Search and Rescue Operations: Search and rescue (SAR) operations are critical for ensuring the safety and security of vessels and aircraft navigating through international straits, especially in cases of maritime accidents, emergencies, or distress situations. Coastal states and maritime powers collaborate on SAR coordination, response planning, and capacity-building efforts to improve preparedness and effectiveness in conducting SAR operations in international waters and airspace.

Humanitarian Assistance and Disaster Response: International straits serve as vital transit routes for humanitarian assistance and disaster response (HADR) operations, enabling the timely delivery of relief supplies, medical assistance, and humanitarian aid to affected communities in times of crisis or natural disasters. Coastal states and maritime powers cooperate on HADR coordination, logistics support, and capacity-building initiatives to enhance the effectiveness and efficiency of humanitarian operations in international straits.

Environmental Protection and Conservation: Environmental protection and conservation efforts are essential for preserving the ecological integrity and sustainability of international straits, which are often characterized by sensitive marine ecosystems, biodiversity hotspots, and vulnerable coastal habitats. Coastal states, maritime powers, and international organizations collaborate on marine conservation initiatives, pollution prevention measures, and ecosystem-based management approaches to mitigate the impacts of human activities and climate change on international straits.

Maritime Safety and Navigation: Ensuring maritime safety and navigation is paramount for preventing maritime accidents, protecting lives and property, and safeguarding the marine environment in international straits. Coastal states and maritime powers invest in navigational aids, maritime infrastructure, and safety regulations to enhance the safety and efficiency of maritime navigation, mitigate navigational hazards, and reduce the risk of maritime incidents in international straits.

Legal Compliance and Enforcement: Legal compliance and enforcement mechanisms are essential for upholding international law, ensuring compliance with UNCLOS provisions, and addressing violations of freedom of navigation and overflight rights in international straits. Coastal states and maritime powers implement legal frameworks, maritime regulations, and enforcement measures to deter unlawful activities, prosecute offenders, and uphold the rule of law in international waters and airspace.

Capacity Building and Training: Capacity building and training programs are instrumental in enhancing the capabilities and capacities of coastal states, particularly those with limited resources or technical expertise, to effectively manage and govern international straits. International organizations, maritime academies, and bilateral partnerships offer training courses, workshops, and technical assistance to support the development of maritime governance frameworks, regulatory capacities, and operational skills required for the sustainable management of international straits.

Data Sharing and Information Exchange: Data sharing and information exchange play a crucial role in enhancing maritime domain awareness, situational awareness, and collaborative decision-making among coastal states, maritime powers, and international organizations operating in international straits. Platforms such as the Automatic Identification System (AIS), Long Range Identification and Tracking (LRIT), and satellite surveillance systems facilitate real-time data sharing, information exchange, and communication among maritime stakeholders, improving the effectiveness and efficiency of maritime operations in international waters and airspace.

Interagency Coordination and Cooperation: Interagency coordination and cooperation are essential for ensuring seamless integration and cooperation among different government agencies, law enforcement authorities, and maritime stakeholders involved in managing and governing international straits. Coastal states establish interagency task forces, joint operations centers, and coordination mechanisms to facilitate cooperation, information-sharing, and joint decision-making on maritime security, safety, and environmental protection initiatives in international straits.

Public Awareness and Education: Public awareness and education campaigns are crucial for raising awareness, promoting understanding, and fostering stewardship of international straits among local communities, maritime stakeholders, and the general public. Coastal states, non-governmental organizations (NGOs), and educational institutions collaborate on outreach programs, educational initiatives, and community engagement activities to educate the public about the significance, challenges, and opportunities associated with international straits, encouraging responsible behavior and sustainable practices.

Scientific Research and Monitoring: Scientific research and monitoring programs contribute to the understanding, management, and conservation of international straits by providing valuable insights into marine ecosystems, biodiversity, and environmental dynamics. Coastal states, research institutions, and international organizations conduct scientific expeditions, monitoring surveys, and research projects to assess the health of international straits, identify emerging threats, and develop evidence-based management strategies for sustainable maritime governance.

Crisis Management and Contingency Planning: Crisis management and contingency planning are essential for preparing coastal states and maritime stakeholders to respond effectively to emergencies, security threats, and natural disasters in international straits. Coastal states develop contingency plans, emergency response protocols, and crisis management frameworks to coordinate multi-agency responses, mobilize resources, and mitigate the impacts of crises on maritime safety, security, and environmental protection in international straits.

Regional Cooperation Mechanisms: Regional cooperation mechanisms play a crucial role in promoting cooperation, dialogue, and coordination among coastal states, maritime powers, and international organizations operating in international straits. Regional forums, joint initiatives, and cooperative frameworks facilitate information-sharing, capacity-building, and collaborative action on shared maritime challenges, promoting stability, security, and prosperity in international straits and the wider region.

Legal Assistance and Capacity Building: Legal assistance and capacity-building initiatives support coastal states and maritime stakeholders in developing and implementing robust legal frameworks, regulatory regimes, and enforcement mechanisms to ensure compliance with international law and UNCLOS provisions governing freedom of navigation and overflight in international straits. International organizations, legal experts, and donor agencies provide technical assistance, legal advice, and capacity-building support to enhance the legal capacities and capabilities of coastal states in managing and governing international straits effectively.

Overflight in international waters and airspace, highlighting the importance of cooperation, legal compliance, capacity-building, and crisis management in ensuring the safety, security, and sustainability of maritime navigation and aviation in international straits. By promoting adherence to international law, fostering regional cooperation, and investing in institutional capacity, coastal states and maritime stakeholders can effectively address emerging challenges, mitigate security threats, and promote the peaceful and orderly use of international straits for the benefit of all.

Interoperability and Standardization: Interoperability and standardization of maritime and aviation practices, procedures, and technologies are essential for ensuring seamless coordination, communication, and cooperation among coastal states and maritime stakeholders operating in international straits. Harmonized regulations, interoperable systems, and common operating procedures facilitate efficient maritime and aviation operations, enhance situational awareness, and improve response capabilities in international waters and airspace.

International Collaboration and Partnerships: International collaboration and partnerships among coastal states, maritime powers, and international organizations are critical for addressing common challenges, advancing shared interests, and promoting sustainable development in international straits. Multilateral initiatives, joint projects, and collaborative platforms foster dialogue, cooperation, and mutual understanding among stakeholders, facilitating coordinated action and collective responses to maritime security threats, environmental challenges, and humanitarian crises in international straits.

Capacity Building and Technical Assistance: Capacity building and technical assistance programs support coastal states and maritime stakeholders in developing and enhancing their capabilities to effectively manage, govern, and safeguard international straits. Training workshops, knowledge-sharing sessions, and technical exchanges provide valuable opportunities for skill development, institutional strengthening, and best practice dissemination, empowering coastal states to fulfill their obligations and responsibilities under international law and UNCLOS provisions.

Maritime Domain Awareness and Surveillance: Maritime domain awareness (MDA) and surveillance capabilities are essential for monitoring, detecting, and responding to maritime security threats, illicit activities, and environmental hazards in international straits. Coastal states and maritime powers invest in surveillance technologies, reconnaissance assets, and information-sharing networks to enhance MDA coverage, improve situational awareness, and facilitate timely and effective responses to maritime incidents and emergencies in international waters.

Public-Private Partnerships (PPPs): Public-private partnerships (PPPs) play a crucial role in enhancing maritime security, promoting environmental stewardship, and supporting sustainable development initiatives in international straits. Collaboration between governments, industry stakeholders, and civil society organizations facilitates resource mobilization, technology transfer, and knowledge exchange, driving innovation, and fostering greater resilience in managing and governing international straits.

Maritime Law Enforcement and Interdiction: Maritime law enforcement and interdiction operations are essential for combating piracy, maritime terrorism, illicit trafficking, and other transnational crimes in international straits. Coastal states and maritime powers conduct joint patrols, maritime interdictions, and law enforcement operations to deter criminal activities, disrupt illicit networks, and uphold the rule of law in international waters, contributing to maritime security and stability in critical maritime chokepoints.

Environmental Monitoring and Protection: Environmental monitoring and protection efforts are integral to preserving the ecological integrity and sustainability of international straits, which are often characterized by rich biodiversity, sensitive marine ecosystems, and vulnerable coastal habitats. Coastal states, scientific institutions, and environmental organizations collaborate on monitoring programs, research projects, and conservation initiatives to assess environmental health, mitigate pollution, and promote ecosystem resilience in international waters.

Sustainable Shipping Practices: Promoting sustainable shipping practices and maritime operations is essential for reducing environmental impacts, enhancing safety, and ensuring the long-term viability of maritime transportation in international straits. Coastal states, port authorities, and shipping companies adopt measures such as emission controls, ballast water management, and fuel efficiency standards to minimize pollution, conserve resources, and mitigate the ecological footprint of shipping activities in international waters.

Maritime Spatial Planning and Management: Maritime spatial planning and management frameworks provide a holistic approach to regulating maritime activities, balancing competing interests, and promoting sustainable development in international straits. Coastal states and maritime stakeholders engage in collaborative planning processes, stakeholder consultations, and ecosystem-based management approaches to allocate maritime resources, manage conflicts, and protect sensitive marine areas in international waters.

International Norms and Best Practices: Upholding international norms and best practices is essential for promoting responsible behavior, enhancing cooperation, and ensuring the peaceful and orderly use of international straits for maritime navigation and aviation. Coastal states, maritime powers, and international organizations adhere to established norms, guidelines, and codes of conduct governing freedom of navigation, overflight, and other maritime activities, fostering trust, confidence, and stability in international waters and airspace.

Maritime Connectivity and Trade Facilitation: Enhancing maritime connectivity and facilitating trade flows are key objectives for promoting economic growth, prosperity, and regional integration in international straits. Coastal states invest in port infrastructure, logistics networks, and trade facilitation measures to improve connectivity, reduce trade barriers, and promote economic development along maritime trade routes, contributing to increased trade volumes and economic opportunities for coastal communities.

Humanitarian Assistance and Disaster Relief (HADR): Strengthening humanitarian assistance and disaster relief (HADR) capabilities is essential for responding effectively to natural disasters and humanitarian crises in international straits. Coastal states, maritime powers, and international organizations collaborate on HADR coordination, preparedness, and response efforts to provide timely and coordinated assistance to affected communities, mitigate the impacts of disasters, and save lives in times of crisis. Joint exercises, training programs, and capacity-building initiatives enhance the readiness and effectiveness of HADR operations in international waters and airspace, ensuring a coordinated and comprehensive response to humanitarian emergencies.

Maritime Security Architecture: Developing a robust maritime security architecture is essential for addressing evolving security challenges, enhancing cooperation, and promoting stability in international straits. Coastal states, maritime powers, and international organizations work together to establish maritime security frameworks, cooperation mechanisms, and information-sharing platforms to coordinate responses to maritime threats, strengthen maritime domain awareness, and build trust among maritime stakeholders operating in international waters.

Maritime Governance and Regulation: Effective maritime governance and regulation are essential for ensuring the sustainable management and governance of international straits, protecting the rights and interests of coastal states, and promoting the safety and security of maritime navigation and aviation. Coastal states establish regulatory frameworks, navigation rules, and safety standards to regulate maritime activities, prevent accidents, and mitigate environmental risks in international waters, contributing to the orderly and sustainable use of international straits.

Maritime Surveillance and Intelligence Sharing: Maritime surveillance and intelligence-sharing capabilities are critical for detecting, monitoring, and responding to security threats, illegal activities, and maritime incidents in international straits. Coastal states, maritime powers, and international organizations invest in surveillance technologies, intelligence analysis, and information-sharing networks to enhance maritime domain awareness, identify potential threats, and coordinate responses to emerging security challenges in international waters and airspace.

Regional Cooperation Initiatives: Regional cooperation initiatives play a vital role in promoting dialogue, trust-building, and cooperation among coastal states, maritime powers, and international organizations in international straits. Regional forums, joint patrols, and collaborative projects facilitate information-sharing, capacity-building, and joint action on maritime security, environmental protection, and humanitarian assistance initiatives, fostering greater stability, resilience, and prosperity in international waters.

Maritime Training and Education: Investing in maritime training and education programs is essential for building the human capacity and technical expertise required to effectively manage and govern international straits. Coastal states, academic institutions, and international organizations offer training courses, workshops, and educational programs to enhance the skills, knowledge, and professionalism of maritime personnel, ensuring the safe, secure, and sustainable use of international straits for maritime navigation and aviation.

Maritime Diplomacy and Conflict Resolution: Maritime diplomacy and conflict resolution efforts are essential for addressing maritime disputes, resolving conflicts, and promoting peaceful cooperation among coastal states, maritime powers, and international organizations operating in international straits. Diplomatic engagement, dialogue, and mediation facilitate the resolution of maritime disputes through peaceful means, promoting mutual understanding, confidence-building, and cooperation among maritime stakeholders in international waters.

Maritime Environmental Protection: Protecting the marine environment and biodiversity of international straits is essential for preserving the ecological integrity and sustainability of these vital maritime corridors. Coastal states, environmental organizations, and international bodies collaborate on marine conservation initiatives, pollution prevention measures, and ecosystem restoration projects to mitigate the impacts of human activities, climate change, and pollution on international straits, promoting the long-term health and resilience of marine ecosystems.

Multilateral Cooperation and Partnerships: Multilateral cooperation and partnerships are essential for addressing common challenges, advancing shared interests, and promoting sustainable development in international straits. Coastal states, maritime powers, and international organizations collaborate on multilateral initiatives, joint projects, and cooperative frameworks to address maritime security threats, environmental challenges, and humanitarian crises, fostering greater resilience, stability, and prosperity in international waters and airspace.

These narratives provide a comprehensive overview of the principles, challenges, and opportunities associated with freedom of navigation and overflight in international waters and airspace, highlighting the importance of cooperation, capacity-building, and diplomatic engagement in ensuring the safety, security, and sustainability of maritime navigation and aviation in international straits. By upholding international law, promoting regional cooperation, and investing in institutional capacity, coastal states and maritime stakeholders can effectively address emerging challenges, mitigate security threats, and promote the peaceful and orderly use of international straits for the benefit of all.

Military Activities in the Exclusive Economic Zone

Overview of Military Activities in the Exclusive Economic Zone (EEZ): The Exclusive Economic Zone (EEZ) is a maritime zone extending up to 200 nautical miles from a coastal state's baselines, where the coastal state holds sovereign rights over natural resources and jurisdiction over certain activities. Military activities within the EEZ raise complex legal and strategic considerations, as they intersect with the rights and interests of coastal states, maritime powers, and international law.

Legal Framework: Under the United Nations Convention on the Law of the Sea (UNCLOS), coastal states have sovereign rights for the purpose of exploring, exploiting, conserving, and managing natural resources within their EEZ. However, UNCLOS also upholds the freedom of navigation and overflight for all states, including military vessels and aircraft, within the EEZ. This creates a delicate balance between coastal state sovereignty and the rights of other states to conduct military activities in international waters.

Freedom of Navigation Operations (FONOPS): Freedom of navigation operations are conducted by maritime powers to challenge excessive maritime claims and assert their rights to navigate and operate in accordance with international law. These operations often involve military vessels conducting innocent passage or other lawful activities within the EEZs of coastal states that assert excessive maritime claims inconsistent with UNCLOS.

Case of the South China Sea: The South China Sea has been a focal point of maritime disputes and military tensions, particularly concerning competing territorial claims and the freedom of navigation. Various countries, including the United States, have conducted freedom of navigation operations in the South China Sea to challenge excessive maritime claims by China and assert the principles of UNCLOS.

Surveillance and Intelligence Gathering: Military activities in EEZs often include surveillance and intelligence gathering operations conducted by maritime powers to monitor maritime traffic, assess regional security threats, and gather information on potential adversaries. These activities are conducted in accordance with international law and are considered essential for maintaining situational awareness and strategic readiness in contested maritime regions.

Anti-Submarine Warfare (ASW) Operations: Anti-submarine warfare operations are conducted by naval forces to detect, track, and neutralize enemy submarines operating in the maritime domain. These operations may involve the deployment of submarines, surface vessels, maritime patrol aircraft, and other assets to detect and counter underwater threats within EEZs and other maritime zones.

Case of the North Atlantic: The North Atlantic region has historically been a strategic area for anti-submarine warfare operations, particularly during the Cold War era when NATO and Warsaw Pact forces conducted extensive submarine patrols and countermeasures to protect vital sea lines of communication and deter potential adversaries.

Maritime Interdiction Operations: Maritime interdiction operations are conducted to enforce maritime security, combat illicit activities, and prevent the proliferation of weapons of mass destruction (WMD) and other contraband at sea. These operations may involve the boarding, inspection, and seizure of vessels suspected of engaging in illegal activities within EEZs and other maritime zones.

Counter-Piracy Operations: Counter-piracy operations are

conducted by naval forces to suppress and deter acts of piracy and armed robbery at sea, particularly in piracy-prone regions such as the Gulf of Aden, the Gulf of Guinea, and the Malacca Strait. These operations may involve the deployment of naval task forces, maritime patrol aircraft, and international cooperation mechanisms to patrol and secure high-risk maritime areas.

Case of the Gulf of Aden: The Gulf of Aden has been a hotspot for piracy and maritime insecurity, prompting multinational naval coalitions such as Combined Task Force 151 to conduct counter-piracy operations and escort merchant vessels through high-risk areas to ensure safe passage and protect maritime trade routes.

Search and Rescue (SAR) Operations: Military forces often play a crucial role in conducting search and rescue operations to assist vessels and aircraft in distress, particularly in remote or hazardous maritime environments. These operations may involve the deployment of naval vessels, maritime patrol aircraft, and specialized search and rescue teams to locate and assist mariners in need of assistance within EEZs and other maritime zones.

Case of the Mediterranean Sea: The Mediterranean Sea is a busy maritime transit route prone to maritime accidents and migrant rescues. Military forces, including coast guards and naval vessels, conduct search and rescue operations to respond to distress calls, save lives at sea, and provide humanitarian assistance to migrants and refugees in the region.

Maritime Security Cooperation: Military activities in EEZs often involve bilateral and multilateral cooperation among coastal states, maritime powers, and regional organizations to enhance maritime security, build capacity, and address common threats and challenges. Joint exercises, training programs, and information-sharing initiatives strengthen interoperability and foster cooperation among naval forces operating in shared maritime domains.

Case of the Western Pacific: The Western Pacific region has witnessed increased maritime security cooperation among countries such as Japan, Australia, the United States, and regional partners to address common security threats, including maritime territorial disputes, illegal fishing, and transnational crime. Joint exercises such as the Rim of the Pacific Exercise (RIMPAC) enhance interoperability and build trust among naval forces operating in the region.

Maritime Humanitarian Assistance and Disaster Response (HA/DR): Military forces often play a crucial role in providing humanitarian assistance and disaster response (HA/DR) in the aftermath of natural disasters, such as hurricanes, tsunamis, and earthquakes, that affect coastal communities within EEZs and other maritime zones. Naval vessels, aircraft, and amphibious units are deployed to deliver emergency relief supplies, medical assistance, and logistical support to affected areas, saving lives and alleviating human suffering.

Case of Typhoon Haiyan: In 2013, Typhoon Haiyan struck the Philippines, causing widespread devastation and loss of life. International military forces, including the United States Navy and other regional partners, conducted Operation Damayan to provide humanitarian assistance and disaster response, delivering relief supplies, medical aid, and engineering support to affected communities in the Philippines.

Maritime Environmental Protection: Military activities in EEZs also include efforts to protect the marine environment, conserve natural resources, and respond to environmental emergencies, such as oil spills and marine pollution incidents. Naval forces may conduct environmental monitoring, pollution surveillance, and cleanup operations to mitigate the impacts of human activities and safeguard fragile marine ecosystems within EEZs and other maritime zones.

Case of the Deepwater Horizon Oil Spill: In 2010, the Deepwater Horizon oil spill in the Gulf of Mexico resulted in one of the largest environmental disasters in history. Military forces, including the United States Coast Guard and Navy, assisted in oil spill response efforts, conducting pollution surveillance, containment operations, and cleanup activities to minimize the ecological damage and protect coastal habitats in the affected area.

Maritime Border Security: Military forces play a critical role in safeguarding maritime borders, protecting territorial integrity, and preventing unauthorized border crossings and incursions within EEZs and other maritime zones. Coast guards, naval patrols, and maritime surveillance assets monitor maritime boundaries, enforce border controls, and intercept illicit activities, such as smuggling, human trafficking, and illegal migration, to maintain maritime security and sovereignty.

Case of Border Incursions: Incidents of maritime border incursions and territorial violations pose challenges to coastal states' sovereignty and territorial integrity, requiring military forces to respond promptly and effectively to assert control, enforce maritime laws, and protect national interests within EEZs and other maritime zones. Diplomatic channels and de-escalation mechanisms are often utilized to address border disputes and prevent potential conflicts from escalating into broader security crises.

Maritime Law Enforcement Operations: Military forces conduct maritime law enforcement operations to uphold national and international laws, regulations, and agreements within EEZs and other maritime zones. These operations may involve the inspection, detention, and prosecution of vessels suspected of engaging in illegal activities, such as smuggling, illegal fishing, and maritime pollution, to maintain maritime order and security.

Case of Illegal, Unreported, and Unregulated (IUU) Fishing: Illegal, unreported, and unregulated (IUU) fishing poses significant challenges to maritime security, environmental sustainability, and economic development in EEZs and coastal waters. Military forces collaborate with coast guards, fisheries authorities, and international organizations to combat IUU fishing through surveillance, interdiction, and enforcement actions, protecting marine resources and livelihoods dependent on sustainable fisheries.

Maritime Counterterrorism Operations: Military forces play a critical role in countering maritime terrorism and preventing terrorist attacks at sea, particularly in strategic maritime chokepoints and high-risk areas vulnerable to terrorist infiltration and maritime sabotage. Naval patrols, maritime security forces, and special operations units conduct counterterrorism operations, intelligence gathering, and interdiction activities to disrupt terrorist networks, deter attacks, and safeguard maritime infrastructure and transportation networks.

Case of Maritime Terrorism Threats: Maritime terrorism threats, including piracy, hijacking, and maritime terrorism, pose serious security risks to international shipping, maritime trade, and port facilities in EEZs and other maritime zones. Military forces collaborate with law enforcement agencies, intelligence services, and international partners to counter maritime terrorism threats through intelligence sharing, joint patrols, and targeted operations, enhancing maritime security and stability in critical maritime regions.

Maritime Domain Awareness (MDA): Military forces contribute to maritime domain awareness (MDA) efforts to monitor, track, and analyze maritime activities, threats, and trends within EEZs and other maritime zones. Integrated surveillance systems, reconnaissance assets, and intelligence fusion centers enable naval forces to enhance situational awareness, detect potential security threats, and respond effectively to maritime incidents and emergencies in real-time.

Case of Maritime Surveillance Systems: Advanced maritime surveillance systems, including radar networks, satellite imagery, and unmanned aerial vehicles (UAVs), provide military forces with the capability to monitor maritime traffic, detect suspicious activities, and enforce maritime laws and regulations within EEZs and other maritime zones. These systems enhance MDA coverage, improve maritime security, and support maritime law enforcement efforts in contested maritime regions.

Maritime Interoperability and Joint Operations: Military forces promote interoperability and conduct joint operations with regional partners and allies to enhance maritime security, crisis response, and collective defense capabilities in EEZs and shared maritime domains. Combined naval exercises, joint patrols, and interoperable command and control systems strengthen military cooperation, build trust, and promote stability in critical maritime regions.

Case of Multinational Naval Task Forces: Multinational naval task forces, such as Combined Task Force 151 in the Gulf of Aden and Combined Maritime Forces in the Western Indian Ocean, demonstrate the effectiveness of coordinated maritime operations and information-sharing mechanisms in countering piracy, maritime terrorism, and other transnational threats in EEZs and international waters.

Maritime Security Assistance and Capacity Building: Military forces provide maritime security assistance and capacity-building support to coastal states and regional partners to strengthen their capabilities to maintain maritime security, combat illicit activities, and respond to maritime emergencies within their EEZs and maritime territories. Training programs, technical assistance, and equipment transfers enhance the operational effectiveness and professionalism of maritime forces, promoting stability and security in shared maritime domains.

Case of Maritime Security Cooperation Programs: Maritime security cooperation programs, such as the US-led Maritime Security Initiative (MSI) in Southeast Asia and the European Union Naval Force Mediterranean (Operation Sophia), demonstrate the importance of international cooperation and capacity-building initiatives in addressing maritime security challenges, enhancing regional stability, and protecting maritime interests in EEZs and international waters. These programs provide training, equipment, and operational support to coastal states and regional partners, strengthening their maritime capabilities and promoting maritime security in strategic maritime regions.

Maritime Border Patrols and Sovereignty Enforcement: Military forces conduct maritime border patrols and sovereignty enforcement operations to protect coastal states' territorial integrity, enforce maritime laws, and assert sovereignty over their EEZs and territorial waters. Naval vessels, coast guard patrols, and maritime surveillance aircraft monitor maritime borders, conduct sovereignty patrols, and intercept unauthorized vessels to prevent illegal activities and safeguard national interests within EEZs and territorial seas.

Case of Border Incursions and Sovereignty Disputes: Border incursions and sovereignty disputes between neighboring states often lead to military tensions and confrontations in maritime zones, requiring military forces to assert control, enforce maritime laws, and protect national sovereignty. Diplomatic negotiations, dispute resolution mechanisms, and confidence-building measures are utilized to address border disputes and prevent escalations in EEZs and territorial waters.

Maritime Law Enforcement and Interdiction Operations: Military forces conduct maritime law enforcement and interdiction operations to combat transnational crime, enforce maritime regulations, and interdict illicit activities, such as drug trafficking, smuggling, and illegal migration, within EEZs and international waters. Naval patrols, interdiction teams, and maritime surveillance assets collaborate with law enforcement agencies to disrupt criminal networks, seize contraband, and maintain maritime security and order.

Case of Drug Interdiction Operations: Drug interdiction operations conducted by military forces aim to disrupt narcotics trafficking networks, intercept drug shipments, and prevent the flow of illegal drugs through maritime routes within EEZs and international waters. Naval vessels, maritime patrol aircraft, and interdiction teams collaborate with law enforcement agencies and international partners to detect, track, and apprehend drug smugglers, reducing the supply of illicit drugs and combating transnational crime at sea.

Maritime Search and Rescue (SAR) Coordination: Military forces play a key role in coordinating maritime search and rescue (SAR) operations to respond to distress calls, emergencies, and maritime incidents within EEZs and international waters. Naval vessels, aircraft, and specialized SAR teams collaborate with coast guard authorities, maritime agencies, and international organizations to conduct search and rescue missions, provide assistance to vessels in distress, and save lives at sea.

Case of Joint SAR Exercises: Joint search and rescue exercises conducted by military forces and civilian agencies demonstrate the importance of interoperability, coordination, and cooperation in responding to maritime emergencies and ensuring effective SAR operations in EEZs and shared maritime domains. These exercises enhance readiness, improve response times, and strengthen maritime safety and security in critical maritime regions.

Maritime Counterterrorism and Security Operations: Military forces conduct maritime counterterrorism and security operations to prevent terrorist attacks, protect critical infrastructure, and deter terrorist threats within EEZs and international waters. Naval patrols, maritime security forces, and special operations units conduct surveillance, intelligence gathering, and interdiction activities to detect and disrupt terrorist activities, safeguard maritime assets, and maintain maritime security and stability.

Case of Maritime Terrorism Threats and Response: Maritime terrorism threats, including attacks on commercial shipping, port facilities, and offshore installations, pose significant security risks in EEZs and international waters, requiring military forces to remain vigilant and proactive in detecting and countering terrorist threats at sea. Intelligence sharing, joint patrols, and maritime security cooperation mechanisms enhance the ability of naval forces to respond effectively to maritime terrorism threats and protect maritime interests.

Maritime Humanitarian Assistance and Disaster Relief (HA/DR) Operations: Military forces conduct maritime humanitarian assistance and disaster relief (HA/DR) operations to provide emergency relief, medical aid, and logistical support to coastal communities affected by natural disasters, humanitarian crises, and maritime emergencies within EEZs and international waters. Naval vessels, amphibious units, and humanitarian teams collaborate with civilian agencies, non-governmental organizations, and international partners to deliver timely assistance and alleviate human suffering in affected areas.

Case of Humanitarian Assistance Operations: Humanitarian assistance operations conducted by military forces in response to natural disasters, such as earthquakes, tsunamis, and hurricanes, demonstrate the critical role of naval forces in providing rapid and effective disaster relief in EEZs and maritime territories. Naval vessels, aircraft, and medical teams deploy emergency supplies, medical personnel, and logistical support to affected communities, demonstrating solidarity, compassion, and international cooperation in times of crisis.

Chapter 7.
Marine Resources and Environmental Protection

Exploitation of Marine Resources: Fisheries and Mining

The exploitation of marine resources, including fisheries and mining activities, plays a vital role in supporting global economies, providing food security, and meeting the growing demand for natural resources. However, the unsustainable exploitation of marine resources poses significant environmental challenges, including overfishing, habitat destruction, and pollution, necessitating effective management and conservation measures to ensure the long-term sustainability of marine ecosystems.

Importance of Fisheries: Fisheries are a critical source of food, income, and livelihoods for millions of people worldwide, particularly in coastal communities and developing countries heavily reliant on marine resources for sustenance and economic development. Sustainable fisheries management practices are essential to maintain fish stocks, preserve biodiversity, and support the livelihoods of artisanal fishers, commercial fleets, and coastal communities dependent on marine resources.

Case of Overfishing: Overfishing, driven by excessive fishing pressure, unsustainable harvesting practices, and illegal, unreported, and unregulated (IUU) fishing activities, has depleted fish stocks, degraded marine habitats, and threatened the ecological balance of marine ecosystems worldwide. The collapse of fisheries, such as the Atlantic cod fishery in Canada and the North Sea, underscores the urgent need for effective fisheries management and conservation measures to prevent further depletion of fish populations and ensure their recovery.

Fisheries Management Strategies: Fisheries management strategies, including catch quotas, fishing gear regulations, marine protected areas, and ecosystem-based approaches, are implemented to regulate fishing activities, conserve fish stocks, and promote sustainable fisheries practices. Collaborative efforts between governments, fisheries stakeholders, and international organizations are essential to develop and implement effective fisheries management plans that balance conservation objectives with socioeconomic considerations.

Case of Sustainable Fisheries Management: Successful examples of sustainable fisheries management, such as the recovery of the Alaskan pollock fishery in the Bering Sea and the implementation of ecosystem-based fisheries management in New Zealand's hoki fishery, demonstrate the effectiveness of science-based approaches, stakeholder engagement, and adaptive management practices in restoring fish stocks and ensuring the long-term sustainability of marine resources.

Challenges of IUU Fishing: Illegal, unreported, and unregulated (IUU) fishing poses significant challenges to fisheries management, conservation efforts, and marine governance, undermining sustainable fisheries practices, eroding fish stocks, and threatening the livelihoods of legitimate fishers. IUU fishing activities, including illegal fishing vessels, transshipment operations, and fish laundering networks, evade detection and enforcement measures, exacerbating overfishing and resource depletion in marine ecosystems.

Case of IUU Fishing Hotspots: IUU fishing hotspots, such as the waters off West Africa, Southeast Asia, and the Southern Ocean, are characterized by rampant illegal fishing activities, weak enforcement capacity, and governance challenges, contributing to the depletion of fish stocks, loss of biodiversity, and socio-economic impacts on coastal communities. International cooperation, surveillance technologies, and enforcement measures are essential to combat IUU fishing and promote sustainable fisheries management in these vulnerable regions.

Impact of Climate Change on Fisheries: Climate change poses additional challenges to fisheries sustainability, altering ocean conditions, shifting fish distribution patterns, and exacerbating existing pressures on marine ecosystems. Rising sea temperatures, ocean acidification, and changes in ocean currents affect fish physiology, productivity, and distribution, posing risks to fish stocks, fisheries-dependent communities, and marine biodiversity.

Case of Coral Reef Degradation: Coral reef degradation, attributed to climate change, overfishing, pollution, and habitat destruction, threatens the ecological integrity and resilience of marine ecosystems, particularly in tropical regions rich in biodiversity and fisheries resources. The loss of coral reefs, such as the Great Barrier Reef in Australia and the Coral Triangle in Southeast Asia, undermines fish habitat, reduces fishery productivity, and jeopardizes the livelihoods of coastal communities dependent on reef fisheries.

Sustainable Aquaculture Practices: Aquaculture, or mariculture, has emerged as a sustainable alternative to wild fisheries, providing a reliable source of seafood, reducing pressure on wild fish stocks, and generating economic opportunities for coastal communities. Sustainable aquaculture practices, including integrated multi-trophic aquaculture (IMTA), land-based recirculating aquaculture systems (RAS), and responsible feed sourcing, minimize environmental impacts, optimize resource use, and enhance the resilience of aquaculture operations to climate change and other stressors.

Case of Sustainable Aquaculture: Sustainable aquaculture initiatives, such as organic shrimp farming in Ecuador, integrated seaweed and shellfish farming in Norway, and land-based salmon aquaculture in Canada, demonstrate the potential of environmentally-friendly aquaculture practices to support food security, promote economic development, and conserve marine resources while minimizing environmental impacts and social risks.

Challenges of Marine Mining: Marine mining, including deep-sea mining and seabed exploration for minerals and precious metals, presents new opportunities and challenges for resource exploitation in the marine environment. The extraction of minerals, such as polymetallic nodules, manganese crusts, and hydrothermal vent deposits, from the ocean floor raises concerns about ecosystem disruption, habitat destruction, and potential impacts on deep-sea biodiversity.

Case of Deep-sea Mining: Deep-sea mining projects, such as those proposed in the Clarion-Clipperton Zone (CCZ) in the Pacific Ocean and the mid-Atlantic Ridge, have sparked debates over the environmental risks, regulatory gaps, and social implications of seabed mining activities in ecologically sensitive and legally complex areas beyond national jurisdiction. The potential impacts of deep-sea mining on marine ecosystems, including benthic communities, hydrothermal vent ecosystems, and deep-sea biodiversity, require comprehensive environmental assessments and precautionary measures to mitigate risks and safeguard ocean health.

Regulatory Framework for Marine Mining: The regulatory framework for marine mining is governed by international law, including UNCLOS, the International Seabed Authority (ISA) regulations, and regional agreements, which establish legal principles, environmental standards, and licensing procedures for deep-sea mining activities. The ISA's regulatory regime aims to ensure the equitable and sustainable management of mineral resources in the international seabed area, balancing the interests of resource exploitation with environmental protection and the common heritage of mankind.

Case of Regulatory Challenges: Regulatory challenges, including jurisdictional disputes, governance gaps, and technological uncertainties, complicate the development and implementation of effective regulatory frameworks for marine mining activities in the high seas and areas beyond national jurisdiction. The absence of a comprehensive legal regime for deep-sea mining poses challenges to the equitable distribution of benefits, environmental conservation, and sustainable development of marine mineral resources.

Environmental Impacts of Marine Mining: Marine mining operations have the potential to cause significant environmental impacts, including habitat destruction, sediment plumes, and chemical pollution, which can disrupt marine ecosystems, alter ocean chemistry, and harm deep-sea biodiversity. The extraction of minerals from the seabed may also release toxic substances, heavy metals, and pollutants into the water column, posing risks to marine life and ecosystem health.

Case of Sediment Plumes: Sediment plumes generated by marine mining activities, such as dredging, drilling, and seabed excavation, can smother benthic habitats, reduce water clarity, and disperse fine particles over large distances, affecting marine organisms, filter feeders, and pelagic species. The dispersal of sediments may also impact marine biogeochemical cycles, alter nutrient dynamics, and disrupt ecosystem functioning, with potential consequences for primary productivity, food webs, and fisheries resources in affected areas.

Biodiversity Conservation and Marine Protected Areas (MPAs): Biodiversity conservation efforts, including the establishment of marine protected areas (MPAs) and ecologically or biologically significant areas (EBSAs), aim to safeguard marine habitats, protect vulnerable species, and preserve marine biodiversity in EEZs and international waters. MPAs serve as vital refuges for marine life, nurseries for fish stocks, and sanctuaries for endangered species, contributing to the resilience and sustainability of marine ecosystems.

Case of Marine Protected Areas: Marine protected areas, such as the *Papahānaumokuākea* Marine National Monument in Hawaii and the *Chagos* Marine Protected Area in the Indian Ocean, demonstrate the effectiveness of spatial conservation measures in conserving marine biodiversity, restoring fish populations, and maintaining ecosystem services in ecologically valuable and vulnerable marine environments. These protected areas support scientific research, promote sustainable tourism, and provide opportunities for education and outreach on marine conservation.

Integrated Coastal Zone Management (ICZM): Integrated coastal zone management (ICZM) approaches aim to reconcile competing interests, address multiple uses, and balance conservation objectives with socio-economic priorities in coastal areas, including fisheries management, aquaculture development, tourism, and infrastructure development. ICZM strategies integrate ecosystem-based management principles, stakeholder participation, and adaptive governance mechanisms to enhance the resilience, sustainability, and equitable use of coastal and marine resources.

Case of ICZM Practices: Successful examples of integrated coastal zone management practices, such as the Wadden Sea National Parks in Germany, Denmark, and the Netherlands, and the Great Barrier Reef Marine Park in Australia, demonstrate the benefits of collaborative governance, adaptive management, and ecosystem-based approaches in preserving coastal habitats, supporting sustainable fisheries, and promoting resilient coastal communities.

Sustainable Seafood Certification and Eco-labeling: Sustainable seafood certification programs and eco-labeling initiatives provide consumers with information on the environmental sustainability, traceability, and responsible sourcing of seafood products, encouraging market demand for sustainably harvested fish and promoting fisheries stewardship practices. Certification schemes, such as the Marine Stewardship Council (MSC) and the Aquaculture Stewardship Council (ASC), certify fisheries and aquaculture operations that meet rigorous sustainability standards, promoting transparency, accountability, and market access for certified products.

Case of Sustainable Seafood Initiatives: Sustainable seafood initiatives, such as the Monterey Bay Aquarium's Seafood

Watch program and the World Wildlife Fund's Smart Fishing Initiative, empower consumers, retailers, and seafood suppliers to make informed choices about sustainable seafood options, supporting fisheries management, reducing environmental impacts, and incentivizing responsible fishing practices. These initiatives raise awareness about sustainable seafood issues, promote market transformation, and drive positive change across the seafood supply chain.

Ecosystem-based Fisheries Management: Ecosystem-based fisheries management (EBFM) approaches recognize the interconnectedness of marine ecosystems, species interactions, and human activities in fisheries management decision-making, integrating ecological, social, and economic considerations to promote sustainable fisheries practices and conserve marine biodiversity. EBFM strategies prioritize the maintenance of ecosystem integrity, the protection of critical habitats, and the resilience of marine ecosystems to climate change and other stressors.

Case of EBFM Implementation: Successful examples of ecosystem-based fisheries management implementation, such as the Icelandic Fisheries Management System and the California Groundfish Collective, demonstrate the effectiveness of ecosystem-based approaches in rebuilding fish stocks, reducing bycatch, and enhancing the ecological and economic sustainability of fisheries. These initiatives integrate scientific research, stakeholder engagement, and adaptive management to address complex fisheries challenges and achieve conservation objectives.

Community-based Fisheries Management: Community-based fisheries management (CBFM) approaches empower local communities, indigenous peoples, and small-scale fishers to participate in fisheries decision-making, resource management, and conservation efforts, recognizing their traditional knowledge, cultural values, and rights-based perspectives on marine resource governance. CBFM initiatives promote community stewardship, social equity, and co-management arrangements that enhance the resilience and sustainability of fisheries while supporting local livelihoods and food security.

Case of Community-based Fisheries Governance: Community-based fisheries governance models, such as the Locally Managed Marine Areas (LMMAs) in the Pacific Islands and the Territorial Use Rights for Fisheries (TURFs) in Chile, demonstrate the effectiveness of participatory approaches, customary practices, and decentralized management systems in empowering local communities to manage marine resources, regulate fishing activities, and conserve coastal ecosystems. These initiatives strengthen social cohesion, build adaptive capacity, and promote self-determination among coastal communities engaged in fisheries management.

Marine Spatial Planning (MSP): Marine spatial planning (MSP) processes facilitate the systematic organization, allocation, and regulation of human activities in marine and coastal areas, including fisheries, aquaculture, shipping, energy development, and conservation, to achieve sustainable development objectives, minimize conflicts, and optimize resource use. MSP initiatives integrate stakeholder engagement, ecosystem-based management principles, and spatial analysis tools to support informed decision-making, promote multi-sectoral collaboration, and ensure the effective governance of marine resources.

Case of Marine Spatial Planning: Marine spatial planning initiatives, such as the European Union's Marine Strategy Framework Directive and Australia's Great Barrier Reef Marine Park Zoning Plan, demonstrate the benefits of spatial planning approaches in balancing competing uses, protecting sensitive habitats, and managing marine resources in a holistic and integrated manner. These initiatives enhance regulatory clarity, reduce user conflicts, and promote the sustainable management of marine ecosystems and coastal waters.

Technological Innovations in Fisheries Management: Technological innovations, including remote sensing, satellite monitoring, electronic monitoring systems, and artificial intelligence, are transforming fisheries management practices by improving data collection, monitoring compliance, and enhancing decision support tools for fisheries management authorities and stakeholders. These technologies enable real-time tracking of fishing vessels, detection of illegal fishing activities, and assessment of fish stocks, supporting evidence-based decision-making, adaptive management, and transparency in fisheries governance.

Ecosystem-based Fisheries Management (EBFM): Ecosystem-based fisheries management (EBFM) is an approach that considers the interactions between species, habitats, and human activities in fisheries management decision-making. By taking into account the broader ecosystem context, EBFM aims to promote sustainable fisheries practices, conserve marine biodiversity, and maintain the resilience of marine ecosystems to environmental change. This approach recognizes that healthy ecosystems are essential for the long-term viability of fisheries and the well-being of coastal communities.

Principles of EBFM: Ecosystem-based fisheries management is guided by several key principles, including precautionary management, adaptive governance, holistic management, and stakeholder engagement. These principles emphasize the importance of using the best available science, incorporating uncertainty into decision making, addressing cumulative impacts, and involving stakeholders in the management process. By embracing these principles, EBFM seeks to balance ecological, social, and economic objectives in fisheries management and ensure the sustainable use of marine resources.

Implementation Challenges: Despite its potential benefits, ecosystem-based fisheries management faces implementation challenges, including data limitations, governance complexities, and institutional barriers. The integration of ecosystem considerations into fisheries management requires comprehensive data on ecosystem dynamics, species interactions, and human activities, which may be lacking in many fisheries. Additionally, the coordination of multiple stakeholders, agencies, and sectors involved in ecosystem-based management can be challenging, requiring collaborative governance mechanisms and institutional reforms.

Case of EBFM Success: Successful examples of ecosystem-based fisheries management, such as the implementation of ecosystem-based management plans in the Gulf of Maine and the Baltic Sea, demonstrate the potential of this approach to rebuild fish stocks, reduce bycatch, and promote ecosystem resilience. These initiatives incorporate ecosystem indicators, reference points, and management strategies tailored to the specific characteristics of each ecosystem, leading to improved ecological outcomes and enhanced fisheries sustainability.

Integrated Multi-Trophic Aquaculture (IMTA): Integrated multi-trophic aquaculture (IMTA) is a sustainable aquaculture practice that involves the simultaneous cultivation of multiple species, including finfish, shellfish, and seaweeds, within the same aquatic environment. IMTA systems utilize the nutrient cycling capabilities of different species to enhance overall productivity, reduce environmental impacts, and optimize resource use. By mimicking natural ecosystems and minimizing waste, IMTA offers a promising approach to sustainable seafood production and coastal zone management.

Benefits of IMTA: Integrated multi-trophic aquaculture offers several environmental, economic, and social benefits compared to conventional monoculture aquaculture systems. IMTA systems improve water quality by recycling excess nutrients and reducing the risk of pollution, enhance biodiversity by providing habitat and food for a variety of species, and increase overall productivity by utilizing multiple trophic levels. Additionally, IMTA can diversify income streams for aquaculture farmers, create employment opportunities, and support resilient coastal communities.

Case of IMTA Implementation: Successful examples of integrated multi-trophic aquaculture implementation, such as salmon-seaweed IMTA systems in Norway and mussel-oyster-seaweed IMTA systems in China, demonstrate the feasibility and effectiveness of this approach in enhancing aquaculture sustainability and resilience. These IMTA systems reduce environmental impacts, increase resource efficiency, and provide economic benefits to farmers, contributing to the transition towards more sustainable and diversified aquaculture practices.

Responsible Feed Sourcing: Responsible feed sourcing is a critical aspect of sustainable aquaculture that addresses the environmental and social impacts associated with feed production, particularly for carnivorous species such as salmon and shrimp. Sustainable feed sourcing practices aim to minimize the reliance on wild-caught fishmeal and fish oil, reduce the use of land-based ingredients, and promote the adoption of alternative protein sources, such as algae, insects, and plant-based proteins.

Certification Programs: Certification programs, such as the Aquaculture Stewardship Council (ASC) and the Best Aquaculture Practices (BAP) certification, set standards for responsible feed sourcing in aquaculture operations, ensuring that feed ingredients are sourced from sustainable and traceable sources. These certification programs promote transparency, accountability, and continuous improvement in feed production practices, encouraging aquaculture producers to adopt more sustainable feed formulations and reduce their environmental footprint.

Case of Sustainable Feed Innovation: Innovations in sustainable feed ingredients, such as the development of insect-based feeds, algae-derived proteins, and microbial additives, offer promising alternatives to conventional fishmeal and soy-based feeds in aquaculture. These novel feed ingredients have lower environmental impacts, higher nutritional value, and reduced reliance on wild-caught fish stocks, contributing to the sustainability and resilience of aquaculture operations worldwide.

Aquaculture Certification and Eco-labeling: Aquaculture certification programs and eco-labeling initiatives, such as the ASC and BAP certification schemes, provide consumers with assurance that farmed seafood products meet rigorous environmental and social standards. By promoting certified aquaculture products, retailers, and consumers can support responsible aquaculture practices, incentivize industry improvements, and contribute to the sustainability of global seafood supply chains.

Role of Government Policies: Government policies and regulations play a crucial role in promoting sustainable aquaculture practices, incentivizing responsible feed sourcing, and addressing environmental and social concerns associated with aquaculture operations. Policy instruments, such as subsidies, incentives, and regulations, can encourage aquaculture producers to adopt sustainable feed sourcing practices, invest in research and innovation, and comply with environmental standards and certification requirements.

International Cooperation: International cooperation and collaboration are essential for addressing the global challenges of sustainable aquaculture, including responsible feed sourcing, certification harmonization, and market access for certified products. Multilateral agreements, regional initiatives, and industry partnerships facilitate knowledge exchange, capacity building, and technical assistance to support the adoption of sustainable feed sourcing practices and improve the environmental performance of aquaculture worldwide.

Illegal, Unreported, and Unregulated (IUU) Fishing: Illegal, unreported, and unregulated (IUU) fishing poses a significant threat to marine resources, food security, and the livelihoods of coastal communities worldwide. IUU fishing involves activities conducted outside of national or international regulations, such as fishing without proper authorization, underreporting catches, or using destructive fishing practices. IUU fishing undermines efforts to conserve fish stocks, combat overfishing, and promote sustainable fisheries management, leading to economic losses, environmental degradation, and social injustice.

IUU Fishing Methods: IUU fishing encompasses a wide range of illegal and unsustainable fishing methods, including overfishing, poaching, bycatch, shark finning, and the use of prohibited gear, such as driftnets and explosives. These destructive practices not only deplete fish populations but also damage marine habitats, disrupt marine ecosystems, and threaten the survival of vulnerable species, including endangered marine mammals, sea turtles, and seabirds.

Global Impacts of IUU Fishing: IUU fishing has significant global impacts on marine biodiversity, food security, and socio-economic development, particularly in developing countries and small island states heavily reliant on fisheries resources. The depletion of fish stocks due to IUU fishing reduces fish availability, increases market prices, and exacerbates food insecurity, disproportionately affecting vulnerable coastal communities and indigenous peoples dependent on fisheries for their livelihoods and cultural identity.

Case of IUU Fishing: The case of illegal, unreported, and unregulated (IUU) fishing in the Southern Ocean, particularly in the waters surrounding Antarctica, highlights the challenges of combating illegal fishing activities in remote and poorly monitored areas. IUU fishing vessels targeting valuable fish species, such as Patagonian toothfish and Antarctic krill, operate under flags of convenience, evade detection by authorities, and exploit regulatory gaps in the management of high seas fisheries, posing a significant threat to marine ecosystems and biodiversity in the region.

International Cooperation to Combat IUU Fishing: International cooperation and collaboration are essential for addressing the global problem of IUU fishing, enhancing maritime surveillance, strengthening port controls, and improving enforcement mechanisms to deter illegal fishing activities and promote responsible fisheries management. Regional fisheries management organizations (RFMOs), intergovernmental agreements, and international initiatives, such as the Port State Measures Agreement (PSMA) and the FAO's International Plan of Action to Prevent, Deter and Eliminate Illegal, Unreported and Unregulated Fishing, provide frameworks for cooperation, information sharing, and capacity building among countries to combat IUU fishing effectively.

Technological Solutions to Combat IUU Fishing: Technological innovations, such as satellite monitoring, vessel tracking systems, and electronic surveillance tools, are increasingly being utilized to combat IUU fishing by enhancing maritime domain awareness, detecting suspicious fishing activities, and monitoring vessel movements in real time. These technologies enable authorities to identify and apprehend IUU fishing vessels, collect evidence for prosecution, and enforce fisheries regulations more effectively, contributing to the prevention and deterrence of illegal fishing practices.

Market-based Approaches to Combat IUU Fishing: Market-based approaches, such as traceability systems, seafood certification programs, and supply chain transparency initiatives, play a crucial role in combating IUU fishing by promoting legal and sustainable seafood sourcing, empowering consumers to make informed choices, and creating market incentives for responsible fisheries practices. Certification schemes, such as the Marine Stewardship Council (MSC) and the Aquaculture Stewardship Council (ASC), certify fisheries and aquaculture operations that meet rigorous sustainability standards, providing assurance to consumers and retailers that seafood products are sourced responsibly and legally.

Case of Market-based Initiatives: The case of the European Union's Illegal, Unreported, and Unregulated (IUU) Regulation and the United States' Seafood Import Monitoring Program (SIMP) demonstrates the effectiveness of market-based initiatives in combating IUU fishing by requiring seafood importers to provide documentation and traceability information for imported seafood products, verifying their legality and origin. These regulations help prevent IUU-caught fish from entering the market, disincentivize illegal fishing practices, and promote sustainable fisheries management globally.

Capacity Building and Fisheries Enforcement: Capacity building initiatives, technical assistance programs, and fisheries enforcement training play a vital role in strengthening the capacity of developing countries and small island states to combat IUU fishing, enhance fisheries surveillance, and enforce fisheries regulations effectively. International organizations, donor agencies, and non-governmental organizations (NGOs) provide support for fisheries monitoring, control, and surveillance (MCS) activities, legal reforms, and institutional strengthening efforts to build the capacity of coastal states to combat IUU fishing and promote sustainable fisheries management.

Civil Society Engagement and Stakeholder Collaboration: Civil society organizations, fishers' associations, and community-based groups play an essential role in combating IUU fishing by raising awareness, advocating for policy reforms, and engaging with governments, industry stakeholders, and international organizations to promote transparency, accountability, and responsible fisheries management practices. Stakeholder collaboration, multi-stakeholder partnerships, and participatory approaches are key to addressing the complex challenges of IUU fishing and fostering collective action for the sustainable management of marine resources.

These examples provide a comprehensive examination of illegal, unreported, and unregulated (IUU) fishing, highlighting its global impacts, challenges, and solutions. By addressing IUU fishing through international cooperation, technological innovations, market-based approaches, capacity building, and stakeholder collaboration, stakeholders can combat illegal fishing activities, promote responsible fisheries management, and safeguard marine biodiversity and food security for present and future generations.

Environmental Protection and Conservation

Environmental protection and conservation are essential for maintaining the health, integrity, and resilience of marine ecosystems, sustaining biodiversity, and safeguarding ecosystem services that support human well-being and livelihoods. By preserving marine habitats, reducing pollution, and mitigating human impacts on marine environments, environmental protection efforts contribute to the sustainability of marine resources and the long-term viability of coastal communities.

Ecosystem-based Management: Ecosystem-based management

(EBM) approaches prioritize the conservation and restoration of marine ecosystems, focusing on the maintenance of ecological processes, biodiversity conservation, and the sustainable use of natural resources. EBM integrates ecological knowledge, stakeholder engagement, and adaptive management strategies to address multiple stressors, such as habitat degradation, pollution, and climate change, and promote ecosystem resilience and sustainability.

Case of Ecosystem-based Management: The Great Barrier Reef Marine Park in Australia exemplifies the implementation of ecosystem-based management principles to conserve and manage a globally significant marine ecosystem. The Great Barrier Reef Marine Park Authority (GBRMPA) employs zoning plans, marine spatial planning, and adaptive management strategies to protect coral reefs, sea grass meadows, and mangrove forests, mitigate threats from climate change and coastal development, and sustainably manage fisheries and tourism activities within the marine park.

Marine Protected Areas (MPAs): Marine protected areas (MPAs) are designated areas of the ocean that are managed to conserve biodiversity, protect critical habitats, and sustainably use marine resources. MPAs serve as refuges for marine species, spawning grounds for fish stocks, and sites for scientific research, education, and recreation. By restricting certain human activities and regulating resource use, MPAs contribute to the resilience and sustainability of marine ecosystems.

Case of Marine Protected Areas: The establishment of the Chagos Marine Protected Area (MPA) in the British Indian Ocean Territory represents one of the world's largest and most remote marine protected areas, encompassing over 640,000 square kilometers of ocean. The Chagos MPA protects coral reefs, sea grass beds, and deep-sea habitats, conserves endangered species, such as the Chagos giant clam and the hawksbill turtle, and supports scientific research on marine biodiversity and ecosystem dynamics.

Marine Spatial Planning (MSP): Marine spatial planning

(MSP) is a systematic process for organizing and regulating human activities in marine and coastal areas to achieve ecological, economic, and social objectives. MSP integrates multiple uses, such as fisheries, shipping, energy development, conservation, and tourism, into spatial plans that balance competing interests, minimize conflicts, and promote sustainable development. By providing a framework for decision-making, stakeholder engagement, and adaptive management, MSP enhances the effectiveness of marine resource management and conservation.

Case of Marine Spatial Planning: The European Union's Marine Strategy Framework Directive (MSFD) and the Marine Spatial Planning Directive (MSPD) demonstrate the application of marine spatial planning principles to promote ecosystem-based management and sustainable development in European marine waters. These directives require member states to develop marine strategies and spatial plans that protect marine biodiversity, reduce pollution, and support blue economy sectors, such as fisheries, aquaculture, and renewable energy.

Pollution Prevention and Control: Pollution prevention and control measures are essential for reducing the impacts of pollution on marine ecosystems, mitigating habitat degradation, and protecting marine biodiversity. Efforts to prevent pollution include the regulation of land-based sources of pollution, such as industrial discharges, agricultural runoff, and urban wastewater, as well as the control of marine litter, oil spills, and chemical contaminants that threaten marine environments.

Case of Pollution Prevention: The Baltic Marine Environment Protection Commission (HELCOM) coordinates efforts among Baltic Sea countries to prevent and control pollution in the Baltic Sea region, which is highly vulnerable to pollution from land-based sources, shipping activities, and industrial discharges. HELCOM implements pollution reduction targets, regulates hazardous substances, and monitors water quality to address eutrophication, oil spills, and marine litter in the Baltic Sea, promoting the sustainable management of this semi-enclosed sea.

Marine Debris Management: Marine debris, including plastics, metals, glass, and other materials, poses a significant threat to marine ecosystems, wildlife, and human health. Efforts to manage marine debris involve prevention, cleanup, education, and policy measures to reduce plastic pollution, remove litter from beaches and coastal waters, and raise awareness about the impacts of marine debris on marine life and ecosystems.

Case of Marine Debris Management: The Ocean Cleanup project, founded by Boyan Slat, aims to develop innovative technologies to remove plastic pollution from the world's oceans, focusing on ocean cleanup systems that passively capture and concentrate plastic debris for collection and recycling. By deploying floating barriers and collection vessels in ocean gyres and coastal areas, the Ocean Cleanup project seeks to remove millions of tons of plastic waste from marine environments and prevent further accumulation of debris.

Marine Habitat Restoration: Marine habitat restoration efforts aim to rehabilitate degraded habitats, such as coral reefs, sea grass beds, and mangrove forests, through active restoration interventions, habitat enhancement, and ecosystem-based approaches. Restoration projects involve coral transplantation, sea grass planting, mangrove reforestation, and coastal habitat rehabilitation to promote biodiversity recovery, enhance ecosystem services, and increase the resilience of marine ecosystems to environmental stressors.

Case of Marine Habitat Restoration: The Coral Restoration Foundation in Florida Keys National Marine Sanctuary conducts coral reef restoration projects to restore degraded coral habitats, enhance reef resilience, and promote coral reef recovery in the Florida Keys. Using coral nurseries, outplanting techniques, and community engagement, the foundation restores coral populations, mitigates the impacts of coral bleaching and disease, and supports the recovery of diverse coral reef ecosystems in the sanctuary.

Marine Species Conservation: Marine species conservation efforts focus on protecting and recovering endangered species, conserving critical habitats, and reducing threats to marine wildlife, such as overfishing, habitat destruction, pollution, and climate change. Conservation measures include the establishment of protected areas, species recovery plans, conservation breeding programs, and international agreements to regulate trade and protect migratory species.

Case of Marine Species Conservation: The conservation of marine turtles, such as the endangered loggerhead, green, and leatherback turtles, involves habitat protection, nesting site management, and fisheries bycatch reduction measures to safeguard nesting beaches, reduce egg poaching, and mitigate threats from fishing gear and marine pollution.

Sustainable Fisheries Management: Sustainable fisheries management practices aim to ensure the long-term viability of fish stocks, maintain ecosystem health, and support the livelihoods of fishing communities. Strategies for sustainable fisheries management include science-based fisheries assessments, ecosystem-based management approaches, catch limits, gear restrictions, and monitoring and enforcement measures to prevent overfishing, minimize bycatch, and promote responsible fishing practices.

Case of Sustainable Fisheries Management: The Marine Stewardship Council (MSC) certification program recognizes fisheries that meet rigorous sustainability standards, including the use of science-based management, stock assessments, and ecosystem considerations to maintain healthy fish populations and minimize environmental impacts. MSC-certified fisheries adhere to principles of sustainable fishing, traceability, and effective management, providing consumers with assurance that seafood products are sourced responsibly and sustainably.

Climate Change Adaptation and Mitigation: Climate change adaptation and mitigation measures are essential for addressing the impacts of climate change on marine ecosystems, including ocean warming, sea level rise, ocean acidification, and extreme weather events. Adaptation strategies involve enhancing the resilience of marine ecosystems, species, and coastal communities to climate-related impacts, while mitigation efforts aim to reduce greenhouse gas emissions and limit global warming to minimize future climate risks.

Case of Climate Change Adaptation: The establishment of climate-resilient marine protected areas (MPAs) and marine spatial planning (MSP) initiatives, such as the Coral Triangle Initiative in Southeast Asia, incorporates climate change adaptation considerations into marine conservation and management efforts. These initiatives identify climate refugia, protect critical habitats, and enhance connectivity between marine protected areas to facilitate species migration and promote ecosystem resilience in the face of climate change.

Ocean Acidification Monitoring and Research: Ocean acidification monitoring and research programs assess the impacts of increasing carbon dioxide (CO_2) levels on marine ecosystems, coral reefs, shellfish populations, and marine biodiversity. Monitoring efforts involve measuring seawater pH, carbonate chemistry, and calcification rates to understand the drivers and consequences of ocean acidification and inform adaptation strategies to mitigate its impacts on marine organisms and ecosystems.

Case of Ocean Acidification Research: The Ocean Acidification Program of the National Oceanic and Atmospheric Administration (NOAA) conducts research and monitoring activities to assess the vulnerability of marine ecosystems to ocean acidification, particularly in high-latitude regions and coastal areas where cold-water corals, shellfish, and calcifying organisms are most affected by decreasing pH levels and carbonate saturation states.

Marine Spatial Planning for Climate Adaptation: Marine spatial planning (MSP) initiatives integrate climate change adaptation considerations into marine resource management and conservation planning processes, identifying climate refugia, designing resilient networks of protected areas, and promoting ecosystem-based approaches to address climate-related impacts on marine biodiversity, habitats, and fisheries.

Case of Marine Spatial Planning for Climate Adaptation: The Coastal Zone Management Program in the United States integrates climate change adaptation considerations into coastal planning and management efforts, utilizing marine spatial planning tools and stakeholder engagement processes to identify climate vulnerabilities, assess adaptation options, and prioritize actions to enhance the resilience of coastal communities and ecosystems to climate change impacts, such as sea level rise, coastal erosion, and storm surge.

Marine Renewable Energy Development: Marine renewable energy technologies, such as offshore wind, wave energy, and tidal energy, offer promising alternatives to fossil fuels for generating clean and renewable energy from the ocean. Marine renewable energy development has the potential to reduce greenhouse gas emissions, enhance energy security, and support the transition to a low-carbon economy while minimizing environmental impacts on marine ecosystems and wildlife.

Case of Marine Renewable Energy Development: The Block Island Wind Farm off the coast of Rhode Island, USA, represents the first offshore wind farm in the United States and demonstrates the feasibility of offshore wind energy development in North American waters. The project consists of five wind turbines with a combined capacity of 30 megawatts, providing clean electricity to the Block Island community and reducing dependence on fossil fuels, thereby contributing to climate change mitigation and renewable energy transition efforts.

Integrated Coastal Zone Management (ICZM): Integrated coastal zone management (ICZM) approaches aim to balance competing uses and interests in coastal areas, such as tourism, recreation, fisheries, conservation, and urban development, while safeguarding coastal ecosystems, habitats, and natural resources. ICZM integrates environmental, social, and economic considerations into planning and decision-making processes to promote sustainable development and resilience in coastal zones.

Case of Integrated Coastal Zone Management: The Wadden Sea Plan in the Netherlands illustrates the implementation of integrated coastal zone management principles to sustainably manage the Wadden Sea, a UNESCO World Heritage Site and Ramsar Wetland of International Importance. The Wadden Sea Plan integrates nature conservation, spatial planning, and sustainable tourism development to protect the ecological integrity of the Wadden Sea ecosystem, mitigate coastal erosion, and enhance public participation in coastal management decisions.

Marine Spatial Data Infrastructure (MSDI): Marine spatial data infrastructure (MSDI) systems facilitate the collection, management, analysis, and sharing of spatial data and information for informed decision-making, marine resource management, and policy development. MSDI systems provide access to geospatial datasets, maps, and tools for stakeholders, researchers, and policymakers to support marine spatial planning, ecosystem-based management, and sustainable development in marine and coastal areas.

Case of Marine Spatial Data Infrastructure: The European Marine Observation and Data Network (EMODnet) initiative establishes marine spatial data infrastructure (MSDI) platforms for sharing marine data and information across European countries and regions. EMODnet provides access to a wide range of marine datasets, including bathymetry, seabed habitats, marine species distributions, and human activities, to support marine spatial planning, environmental assessment, and sustainable management of European marine waters.

Blue Carbon Conservation: Blue carbon ecosystems, such as mangroves, sea grasses, and salt marshes, sequester large amounts of carbon dioxide (CO2) from the atmosphere and store it in coastal sediments and biomass, playing a crucial role in mitigating climate change and reducing greenhouse gas emissions. Blue carbon conservation efforts aim to protect and restore these coastal habitats to enhance carbon sequestration, promote biodiversity conservation, and support climate adaptation and resilience in coastal zones.

Marine Spatial Planning for Biodiversity Conservation:

Marine spatial planning (MSP) initiatives integrate biodiversity conservation objectives into marine resource management and spatial planning processes, identifying priority areas for habitat protection, species conservation, and ecosystem restoration. MSP for biodiversity conservation aims to enhance the representation, connectivity, and resilience of marine ecosystems, safeguarding critical habitats and vulnerable species from anthropogenic threats and environmental stressors.

Case of Marine Spatial Planning for Biodiversity Conservation: The Coral Triangle Initiative (CTI) on Coral Reefs, Fisheries, and Food Security, a multilateral partnership in Southeast Asia, promotes marine spatial planning for biodiversity conservation and sustainable fisheries management in the Coral Triangle region. CTI member countries collaborate to develop marine spatial plans, establish marine protected areas, and implement ecosystem-based management strategies to conserve coral reefs, sea grass beds, and mangrove forests, supporting the region's rich marine biodiversity and coastal communities.

Coastal Erosion and Shoreline Management: Coastal erosion and shoreline management strategies aim to mitigate the impacts of coastal erosion, sea level rise, and storm surge on coastal communities, infrastructure, and natural habitats. Shoreline stabilization measures, such as beach nourishment, dune restoration, and coastal vegetation planting, help protect coastal areas from erosion, maintain natural buffers against storm damage, and preserve the ecological functions of coastal ecosystems.

Case of Coastal Erosion Management: The Netherlands' Delta Works project exemplifies innovative coastal engineering and shoreline management strategies to protect low-lying coastal areas from flooding, storm surge, and sea level rise. The Delta Works includes a system of dams, dikes, and storm surge barriers that protect the Dutch coastline and river deltas from inundation, while enhancing habitat diversity, recreational opportunities, and coastal resilience to climate change impacts.

Marine Spatial Planning for Aquaculture: Marine spatial

planning (MSP) integrates aquaculture planning and management considerations into marine resource management frameworks, identifying suitable sites for aquaculture development, assessing environmental impacts, and regulating aquaculture activities to minimize conflicts with other marine uses and protect sensitive habitats and species.

Case of Marine Spatial Planning for Aquaculture: The Scottish Aquaculture Marine Spatial Planning Pilot Project in Scotland, UK, explores the integration of aquaculture into marine spatial planning processes, balancing the expansion of aquaculture activities with environmental conservation and other marine uses. The pilot project engages stakeholders, assesses environmental sensitivities, and develops spatial plans to guide the sustainable growth of aquaculture while minimizing environmental impacts and promoting ecosystem health.

Ocean Governance and International Cooperation: Ocean governance frameworks and international cooperation mechanisms are essential for addressing transboundary marine issues, promoting sustainable development, and conserving marine biodiversity on a global scale. International agreements, conventions, and organizations, such as the United Nations Convention on the Law of the Sea (UNCLOS), the Convention on Biological Diversity (CBD), and the International Maritime Organization (IMO), provide legal and institutional frameworks for cooperation, coordination, and collaboration among countries to manage shared marine resources and address common challenges.

Case of Ocean Governance and International Cooperation: The Agreement for the Conservation of Cetaceans of the Black Sea, Mediterranean Sea and Contiguous Atlantic Area (ACCOBAMS) facilitates international cooperation among countries bordering the Mediterranean and Black Seas to conserve and protect cetaceans, such as dolphins, whales, and porpoises, and their habitats. ACCOBAMS promotes research, monitoring, and conservation measures to address threats to cetaceans, such as bycatch, habitat degradation, and marine pollution, fostering regional cooperation and collective action for cetacean conservation.

Blue Economy Development: The blue economy concept emphasizes sustainable economic development and livelihood opportunities derived from marine resources, including fisheries, aquaculture, tourism, renewable energy, biotechnology, and coastal industries. Blue economy strategies integrate economic growth with environmental conservation, social equity, and resilience, supporting the sustainable use of marine resources and the promotion of ocean-based industries that contribute to economic prosperity and poverty reduction.

Case of Blue Economy Development: The Seychelles' Blue Economy Strategic Framework and Roadmap prioritize sustainable blue economy development, marine conservation, and climate resilience in the Indian Ocean archipelago. The framework promotes sustainable fisheries management, marine spatial planning, renewable energy development, and marine tourism initiatives to diversify the economy, create employment opportunities, and reduce dependency on unsustainable fishing practices and fossil fuels, fostering sustainable development in the Seychelles and contributing to global ocean conservation efforts.

Marine Spatial Planning for Renewable Energy: Marine spatial planning (MSP) integrates renewable energy development considerations into marine resource management and spatial planning processes, identifying suitable areas for offshore wind farms, tidal energy installations, and wave energy projects while minimizing conflicts with other marine uses, protecting sensitive habitats, and preserving marine biodiversity.

Case of Marine Spatial Planning for Renewable Energy: The Marine Renewable Energy Atlas in the United Kingdom provides spatial data and planning tools to support the sustainable development of marine renewable energy projects in UK waters. The atlas identifies areas with high energy potential, assesses environmental sensitivities, and facilitates stakeholder engagement to inform decision-making and ensure the compatibility of renewable energy developments with marine conservation objectives.

Marine Protected Area Networks: Marine protected area (MPA) networks consist of interconnected marine reserves, sanctuaries, and conservation zones designed to conserve biodiversity, protect critical habitats, and sustainably manage marine resources across multiple jurisdictions and ecosystems. MPA networks enhance ecological connectivity, support species migrations, and promote ecosystem resilience by establishing corridors and buffer zones that link protected areas and mitigate the fragmentation of marine habitats.

Case of Marine Protected Area Networks: The Coral Triangle Initiative (CTI) establishes a network of marine protected areas (MPAs) and ecologically connected sites across the Coral Triangle region in Southeast Asia, encompassing Indonesia, Malaysia, Papua New Guinea, the Philippines, Solomon Islands, and Timor-Leste. The CTI MPA network aims to conserve coral reefs, seagrass beds, and mangrove forests, protect endangered species, and sustainably manage fisheries to support the region's marine biodiversity and coastal communities.

Ocean Acidification Mitigation Strategies: Ocean acidification mitigation strategies aim to reduce carbon dioxide (CO_2) emissions, mitigate ocean acidification impacts, and enhance the resilience of marine ecosystems to changing ocean chemistry. Mitigation measures include reducing fossil fuel combustion, increasing carbon sequestration in coastal habitats, and implementing ocean alkalinity enhancement techniques to buffer seawater pH and counteract acidification effects on calcifying organisms.

Case of Ocean Acidification Mitigation: The Blue Carbon Initiative promotes the conservation and restoration of coastal habitats, such as mangroves, seagrasses, and salt marshes, to sequester carbon dioxide (CO_2) from the atmosphere and mitigate ocean acidification. Blue carbon habitats store large amounts of carbon in coastal sediments and biomass, reducing CO_2 concentrations in seawater and providing natural buffers against ocean acidification impacts on marine organisms and ecosystems.

Sustainable Ocean Governance: Sustainable ocean governance frameworks integrate environmental, economic, and social objectives into marine policy-making, planning, and management processes to promote the sustainable use of marine resources, protect marine ecosystems, and support equitable access and benefit-sharing among stakeholders. Sustainable ocean governance principles emphasize transparency, accountability, stakeholder participation, and adaptive management to address emerging challenges and promote long-term ocean sustainability.

Case of Sustainable Ocean Governance: The European Union's Integrated Maritime Policy (IMP) adopts a holistic approach to sustainable ocean governance, integrating maritime sectors, environmental protection, and coastal management under a unified policy framework. The IMP promotes ecosystem-based management, marine spatial planning, and blue growth strategies to balance economic development with environmental conservation, social inclusion, and climate resilience in European marine and coastal areas.

Blue Carbon Finance Mechanisms: Blue carbon finance mechanisms mobilize financial resources to support blue carbon conservation and restoration projects, such as mangrove reforestation, sea grass restoration, and coastal wetland protection, to mitigate climate change, enhance carbon sequestration, and conserve coastal habitats and biodiversity.

Case of Blue Carbon Finance: The Green Climate Fund (GCF) provides financial support for blue carbon projects and initiatives that contribute to climate change mitigation, adaptation, and sustainable development in developing countries. The GCF finances blue carbon activities, such as mangrove conservation, restoration, and sustainable management projects, to promote carbon sequestration, biodiversity conservation, and community resilience in coastal areas vulnerable to climate change impacts.

These paragraphs explore additional strategies and initiatives for marine environmental protection and conservation, including renewable energy development, marine protected area networks, ocean acidification mitigation, sustainable ocean governance, and blue carbon finance mechanisms. By implementing integrated approaches and innovative solutions, stakeholders can address the interconnected challenges facing marine ecosystems and foster sustainable development in coastal and oceanic regions.

Liability and Compensation for Environmental Damage

Various international conventions and treaties establish liability and compensation mechanisms for environmental damage in marine ecosystems. For instance, the International Convention on Civil Liability for Oil Pollution Damage (CLC) and the International Convention on the Establishment of an International Fund for Compensation for Oil Pollution Damage (FUND) provide a framework for compensation to individuals and communities affected by oil spills from tankers.

Deepwater Horizon Oil Spill: The Deepwater Horizon oil spill in 2010, one of the largest environmental disasters in history, resulted in extensive environmental damage to marine ecosystems in the Gulf of Mexico. BP, the company responsible for the spill, faced legal liabilities and compensation claims amounting to billions of dollars for damages to marine life, coastal habitats, and fishing communities.

Exxon Valdez Oil Spill: The Exxon Valdez oil spill in 1989 off the coast of Alaska led to significant environmental damage to marine ecosystems, including oil contamination of coastal habitats, wildlife mortality, and long-term ecological impacts. Exxon Mobil Corporation, the owner of the oil tanker, paid billions of dollars in legal settlements and compensation to affected stakeholders, including government agencies, indigenous communities, and commercial fishermen.

Bunker Oil Spills: Bunker oil spills from maritime accidents, such as vessel collisions, groundings, and sinkings, can cause pollution and environmental damage in marine waters, affecting coastal communities, marine biodiversity, and economic activities. Liability and compensation regimes under international maritime law, including the International Convention on Civil Liability for Bunker Oil Pollution Damage (BUNKER) and the International Oil Pollution Compensation Funds (IOPC Funds), provide compensation to victims of bunker oil spills.

Cosco Busan Oil Spill: The Cosco Busan oil spill in 2007 in San Francisco Bay, California, resulted from a ship collision that released bunker fuel into the marine environment, causing oil pollution and ecological harm to coastal ecosystems, wildlife, and recreational beaches. The responsible parties, including the ship owner and operator, paid millions of dollars in cleanup costs, natural resource damages, and compensation to affected communities and stakeholders.

Legal Liability for Pollution Incidents: Under international and national laws, shipowners, operators, and other entities involved in maritime activities may be held legally liable for pollution incidents and environmental damage caused by their vessels. Liability regimes impose financial responsibility for cleanup costs, compensation for economic losses, and restoration of affected ecosystems, motivating stakeholders to adopt preventive measures and risk mitigation strategies.

Marine Pollution from Offshore Oil and Gas Activities: Offshore oil and gas exploration and production activities pose environmental risks, including oil spills, chemical discharges, and habitat degradation, which can harm marine ecosystems and coastal communities. Liability and compensation mechanisms for offshore oil and gas pollution incidents vary by jurisdiction but generally require operators to cover cleanup costs and compensate affected parties for damages and losses.

Montara Oil Spill: The Montara oil spill in 2009 off the coast of Australia's Timor Sea resulted from a blowout at an offshore drilling rig, releasing oil and gas into the marine environment and causing environmental damage to coral reefs, fisheries, and marine wildlife. The responsible parties, including the well operator and rig owner, faced legal liabilities and compensation claims from the Australian government, indigenous communities, and affected stakeholders.

Marine Plastic Pollution: Marine plastic pollution poses a significant threat to marine ecosystems, wildlife, and human health, with plastic debris contaminating coastal waters, harming marine animals through ingestion and entanglement, and disrupting marine food webs. Liability and compensation mechanisms for marine plastic pollution are evolving, with some jurisdictions holding plastic producers, manufacturers, and waste generators accountable for cleanup costs and pollution prevention measures.

ExxonMobil Plastic Pollution Lawsuit: ExxonMobil Corporation faced a lawsuit in 2019 filed by several U.S. cities and counties alleging that the company's production, promotion, and marketing of plastic products contributed to marine plastic pollution and environmental harm. The lawsuit sought damages and compensation for cleanup costs and mitigation efforts to address the impacts of plastic pollution on coastal communities and ecosystems.

Marine Debris Removal and Remediation: Cleanup and remediation efforts for marine debris and pollution incidents involve coordination among government agencies, environmental organizations, and private stakeholders to remove pollutants, restore affected habitats, and mitigate the ecological impacts of pollution on marine ecosystems.

Gulf of Mexico Restoration Programs: Following the Deepwater Horizon oil spill, restoration programs and initiatives were established to address the environmental damage and loss of natural resources in the Gulf of Mexico, including habitat restoration, ecosystem monitoring, and community resilience projects funded by legal settlements, fines, and compensation from responsible parties.

Ecosystem-based Approaches to Liability and

Compensation: Ecosystem-based approaches to liability and compensation for environmental damage emphasize the restoration and rehabilitation of affected ecosystems, rather than solely focusing on financial compensation, to enhance ecosystem resilience, support ecological recovery, and promote sustainable use of natural resources.

Valdez Principles: The Valdez Principles, named after the Exxon Valdez oil spill, advocate for corporate accountability, environmental stewardship, and social responsibility in business operations, encouraging companies to adopt sustainable practices, pollution prevention measures, and transparent reporting to minimize environmental risks and liabilities.

Community-based Compensation Programs: Community-based compensation programs for environmental damage involve engaging local communities, indigenous peoples, and stakeholders in decision-making processes, resource management, and restoration efforts to address the socio-economic impacts of pollution incidents and promote community resilience and empowerment.

Marine Protected Areas (MPAs) Compensation Schemes: Marine protected areas (MPAs) compensation schemes provide financial incentives to coastal communities, fishers, and stakeholders for their participation in marine conservation and sustainable fisheries management within designated protected areas. Compensation may include payments for the adoption of sustainable fishing practices, income support for fishers transitioning to alternative livelihoods, and incentives for compliance with MPA regulations and conservation measures.

Great Barrier Reef Marine Park Authority (GBRMPA) Reef Trust: The Great Barrier Reef Marine Park Authority (GBRMPA) Reef Trust in Australia implements compensation programs to support the conservation and management of the Great Barrier Reef Marine Park, including financial assistance for water quality improvement projects, reef restoration initiatives, and community-led conservation activities aimed at enhancing the resilience of coral reefs and marine ecosystems.

Oil Pollution Compensation Funds: Oil pollution compensation funds, established under international conventions such as the International Convention on Civil Liability for Oil Pollution Damage (CLC) and the International Oil Pollution Compensation Funds (IOPC Funds), provide financial assistance to affected individuals, communities, and governments for cleanup operations, environmental restoration, and economic losses resulting from oil spills and pollution incidents.

Galapagos Islands Conservation Trust (GICT): The Galapagos Islands Conservation Trust (GICT) in Ecuador implements compensation programs to mitigate the environmental impacts of tourism, invasive species, and overfishing in the Galapagos Marine Reserve, including funding for invasive species eradication projects, sustainable fisheries management initiatives, and community-based conservation efforts to protect endangered species and fragile marine ecosystems.

Natural Resource Damage Assessment (NRDA): Natural Resource Damage Assessment (NRDA) processes evaluate the ecological and economic impacts of environmental damage from pollution incidents, such as oil spills and hazardous waste releases, and determine the appropriate compensation and restoration measures required to restore injured natural resources and habitats to their pre-incident condition.

Exxon Valdez Oil Spill Trustee Council: The Exxon Valdez Oil Spill Trustee Council oversees the allocation of funds from legal settlements and fines resulting from the Exxon Valdez oil spill to support restoration projects, scientific research, and community-based initiatives aimed at recovering and restoring natural resources, habitats, and wildlife affected by the spill in Alaska's Prince William Sound and surrounding areas.

Compensation for Fisheries Closures: Fisheries closures and restrictions imposed to protect marine biodiversity, endangered species, and sensitive habitats may result in economic losses for fishers and fishing communities dependent on affected fishing grounds. Compensation programs, such as buyback schemes, income support, and alternative livelihood assistance, help mitigate the socio-economic impacts of fisheries closures and facilitate the transition to sustainable fishing practices and marine conservation.

Coral Reef Restoration Trust Funds: Coral reef restoration trust funds, established by governments, non-profit organizations, and international donors, provide financial support for coral reef restoration and conservation projects, including reef rehabilitation, coral propagation, and ecosystem monitoring activities aimed at enhancing the resilience and recovery of coral reef ecosystems threatened by climate change, pollution, and overexploitation.

Oil Spill Contingency Funds: Oil spill contingency funds, maintained by governments, industry associations, and shipping companies, serve as financial reserves to cover emergency response costs, cleanup operations, and compensation payments in the event of oil spills and pollution incidents in marine waters, ensuring prompt and effective responses to mitigate environmental damage and protect coastal communities and ecosystems.

Environmental Liability Insurance: Environmental liability insurance policies provide coverage for potential liabilities and financial risks associated with pollution incidents, hazardous waste management, and environmental damage in marine and coastal environments, offering financial protection and indemnification to policyholders against legal claims, cleanup costs, and compensation obligations arising from environmental liabilities.

Marine Pollution Insurance Pools: Marine pollution insurance pools, formed by insurers, shipowners, and governments, pool resources and share risks to provide comprehensive insurance coverage for maritime liabilities, including oil spills, bunker oil pollution, and hazardous substance releases, ensuring adequate financial resources and compensation mechanisms for pollution incidents in marine waters.

Compensation for Recreational Losses: Recreational losses resulting from marine pollution incidents, such as beach closures, water quality degradation, and tourism disruptions, may entitle affected individuals and businesses to compensation for economic losses, diminished property values, and reduced recreational opportunities, reflecting the social and cultural values of marine environments and coastal amenities.

Legal Advocacy and Public Interest Litigation: Legal advocacy groups and non-governmental organizations (NGOs) play a vital role in advocating for environmental justice, accountability, and compensation for communities and stakeholders affected by environmental damage, pollution incidents, and industrial activities in marine and coastal areas, engaging in public interest litigation, environmental enforcement actions, and community empowerment initiatives to seek redress and restitution for environmental harm.

Community-based Compensation Mechanisms: Community-based compensation mechanisms empower local communities, indigenous peoples, and traditional resource users to participate in decision-making processes, resource management, and environmental governance, ensuring their inclusion, representation, and participation in compensation negotiations, benefit-sharing agreements, and natural resource management initiatives aimed at addressing the socio-economic impacts of environmental damage and pollution incidents.

Corporate Social Responsibility (CSR) Initiatives: Corporate social responsibility (CSR) initiatives promote corporate accountability, environmental stewardship, and community engagement in corporate operations and business activities, encouraging companies to adopt sustainable practices, pollution prevention measures, and environmental management systems to minimize their environmental footprint and mitigate the risks of environmental liabilities and compensation claims associated with marine pollution and environmental damage.

Voluntary Compensation Funds: Voluntary compensation funds, established by industry associations, shipping companies, and stakeholders, offer financial contributions and support for environmental cleanup, restoration, and conservation projects in marine and coastal areas affected by pollution incidents and industrial activities, demonstrating corporate responsibility and commitment to environmental protection and sustainable development.

International Oil Pollution Compensation Funds (IOPC Funds): The International Oil Pollution Compensation Funds (IOPC Funds), consisting of the International Oil Pollution Compensation Fund (IOPC Fund) and the Supplementary Fund, provide financial assistance and compensation to victims of oil pollution damage from maritime incidents, including tanker accidents, shipwrecks, and oil spills, ensuring prompt and adequate compensation for affected individuals, communities, and governments worldwide.

Community Resilience and Capacity Building: Community resilience and capacity-building initiatives empower coastal communities, indigenous peoples, and stakeholders to respond to environmental emergencies, participate in disaster preparedness and response activities, and strengthen their adaptive capacity and resilience to natural hazards, climate change impacts, and pollution incidents affecting marine and coastal ecosystems and livelihoods.

Public Trust Doctrine: The public trust doctrine, rooted in common law principles and legal traditions, imposes a fiduciary duty on governments and public authorities to protect and preserve natural resources, including marine and coastal environments, for the benefit of present and future generations, ensuring public access, enjoyment, and sustainable use of public trust resources and ecosystems.

Compensation for Loss of Ecosystem Services: Compensation for the loss of ecosystem services resulting from environmental damage and pollution incidents in marine and coastal areas recognizes the economic, ecological, and social values of natural resources, habitats, and ecosystem functions, providing financial remuneration for the ecological services provided by marine ecosystems, such as carbon sequestration, nutrient cycling, and coastal protection.

Blue Economy Investments: Blue economy investments support sustainable development, innovation, and economic growth in marine and coastal sectors, including fisheries, aquaculture, tourism, renewable energy, and marine biotechnology, generating employment opportunities, income generation, and socio-economic benefits while promoting environmental sustainability, resource conservation, and ecosystem resilience in marine ecosystems.

Compensation for Cultural and Heritage Losses: Compensation for cultural and heritage losses resulting from environmental damage and pollution incidents in marine and coastal areas acknowledges the intrinsic value of cultural sites, sacred places, and traditional knowledge systems associated with indigenous cultures, maritime heritage, and coastal communities, providing restitution and redress for the loss of cultural identity, heritage assets, and intangible cultural heritage.

Marine Insurance and Risk Management: Marine insurance and risk management strategies help mitigate financial risks and liabilities associated with pollution incidents, maritime accidents, and environmental damage in marine and coastal environments, providing insurance coverage, risk assessment, and loss prevention services to shipping companies, port operators, and marine industry stakeholders to safeguard against potential losses and liabilities.

Compensation for Indigenous Rights Violations: Compensation for violations of indigenous rights and traditional land tenure in marine and coastal areas recognizes the rights of indigenous peoples to self-determination, cultural integrity, and land and resource ownership, providing restitution and reparations for historical injustices, dispossession, and environmental harm caused by industrial activities, resource extraction, and pollution incidents.

Maritime Pollution Prevention and Response Training: Maritime pollution prevention and response training programs, conducted by government agencies, industry associations, and environmental organizations, enhance the capacity and readiness of maritime stakeholders to prevent, prepare for, and respond to pollution incidents, oil spills, and hazardous substance releases in marine waters, improving emergency response coordination, technical expertise, and compliance with environmental regulations.

Compensation for Loss of Livelihoods: Compensation for the loss of livelihoods resulting from environmental damage and pollution incidents in marine and coastal areas provides financial support and income replacement for affected workers, fishers, and communities dependent on marine resources and coastal ecosystems for their sustenance, employment, and economic well-being, ensuring social equity, justice, and welfare for vulnerable populations impacted by environmental harm.

Corporate Environmental Liability Insurance: Corporate environmental liability insurance policies offer coverage for potential liabilities and financial risks associated with environmental damage, pollution liabilities, and legal claims arising from industrial operations, business activities, and environmental accidents in marine and coastal environments, providing financial protection and risk management solutions for corporate entities and stakeholders.

Compensation for Loss of Access Rights: Compensation for the loss of access rights and customary land use practices in marine and coastal areas recognizes the socio-cultural significance of traditional fishing grounds, gathering sites, and coastal territories to indigenous communities, providing restitution and compensation for the infringement of indigenous rights, land tenure conflicts, and displacement caused by industrial development and resource exploitation.

Oil Spill Preparedness and Response Funding: Oil spill preparedness and response funding, provided by governments, industry associations, and oil companies, supports the development and implementation of emergency response plans, spill response equipment, and training programs to enhance the readiness and effectiveness of oil spill response efforts in marine and coastal environments, minimizing environmental damage and mitigating the impacts of oil spills on marine ecosystems and coastal communities.

Compensation for Health Impacts: Compensation for health impacts resulting from environmental contamination and pollution exposure in marine and coastal areas addresses the adverse health effects, public health risks, and socio-economic burdens faced by individuals, communities, and populations affected by waterborne diseases, toxic pollutants, and chemical contaminants in marine environments, ensuring access to healthcare, medical assistance, and compensation for health-related expenses and damages.

Public Participation in Compensation Processes: Public participation in compensation processes and decision-making forums ensures transparency, accountability, and stakeholder engagement in assessing environmental damages, determining compensation entitlements, and allocating financial resources for pollution remediation, restoration, and compensation measures in marine and coastal areas, fostering trust, legitimacy, and social acceptance of compensation outcomes and environmental management initiatives.

Compensation for Loss of Cultural Ecosystem Services: Compensation for the loss of cultural ecosystem services recognizes the cultural, spiritual, and recreational values of marine and coastal environments to indigenous cultures, local communities, and society at large, providing financial restitution and recognition for the cultural heritage, identity, and traditional knowledge systems associated with marine biodiversity, coastal landscapes, and ecosystem functions.

Oil Spill Liability Trust Fund (OSLTF): The Oil Spill Liability Trust Fund (OSLTF) in the United States provides financial resources and support for oil spill response and cleanup operations, natural resource damage assessment, and compensation for oil pollution damages and economic losses resulting from oil spills in U.S. waters, ensuring the availability of funds for emergency response efforts and environmental restoration projects in marine and coastal areas.

Compensation for Loss of Ecosystem Resilience: Compensation for the loss of ecosystem resilience and ecological integrity in marine and coastal areas acknowledges the long-term impacts of environmental damage, pollution incidents, and habitat degradation on the adaptive capacity, stability, and functioning of marine ecosystems, providing financial resources and incentives for ecosystem restoration, habitat rehabilitation, and biodiversity conservation efforts aimed at enhancing ecosystem resilience and recovery.

Public Trust Funds for Environmental Restoration: Public trust funds for environmental restoration and conservation finance ecosystem restoration projects, habitat enhancement initiatives, and conservation programs in marine and coastal areas, leveraging public and private investments to restore degraded ecosystems, protect vulnerable species, and promote sustainable use of natural resources, fostering collaboration, innovation, and stewardship in marine environmental management and conservation, preventing environmental harm, restoring natural resources, and mitigating the socio-economic impacts of pollution incidents in marine and coastal ecosystems. Through a combination of legal frameworks, financial mechanisms, community-based approaches, and corporate responsibility initiatives, stakeholders strive to ensure accountability, redress environmental injustices, and promote sustainable practices for the protection and conservation of marine environments.

In addition to these mechanisms, ongoing efforts focus on enhancing international cooperation, strengthening regulatory frameworks, and advancing scientific research and technological innovation to prevent pollution, mitigate environmental risks, and promote sustainable development in marine and coastal areas. By addressing the root causes of environmental degradation, fostering collaboration among diverse stakeholders, and integrating environmental considerations into policy-making and decision-making processes, societies can work towards achieving a more resilient, equitable, and sustainable future for marine ecosystems and coastal communities worldwide.

Overall, effective liability and compensation mechanisms play a crucial role in addressing the complex challenges of environmental protection, resource management, and sustainable development in marine and coastal environments. By holding polluters accountable, providing restitution to affected parties, and investing in ecosystem restoration and conservation efforts, societies can uphold environmental justice, safeguard natural resources, and ensure the long-term health and resilience of marine ecosystems for future generations.

Deepwater Horizon Oil Spill (2010): The Deepwater Horizon oil spill in the Gulf of Mexico resulted in one of the largest environmental disasters in history. BP, the responsible party, faced extensive legal claims, fines, and compensation payments for damages to marine ecosystems, coastal communities, and industries dependent on Gulf resources. The incident highlighted the importance of comprehensive liability and compensation mechanisms for addressing the ecological and socio-economic impacts of oil pollution incidents.

Exxon Valdez Oil Spill (1989): The Exxon Valdez oil spill in Alaska's Prince William Sound led to significant environmental damage, including oil contamination of coastal habitats, fisheries, and wildlife populations. Exxon Mobil, the owner of the oil tanker, paid billions of dollars in cleanup costs, restoration projects, and compensation settlements to affected communities, indigenous groups, and government agencies, illustrating the long-term repercussions of oil spills on marine ecosystems and coastal economies.

Prestige Oil Spill (2002): The sinking of the Prestige oil tanker off the coast of Spain resulted in a massive oil spill, contaminating marine waters, beaches, and coastal ecosystems along the Galician coast. The Spanish government initiated legal proceedings against the vessel's owner and insurers to recover cleanup costs, environmental damages, and compensation for economic losses suffered by local communities, fishermen, and tourism businesses impacted by the spill.

Cosco Busan Oil Spill (2007): The grounding of the Cosco Busan container ship in San Francisco Bay caused an oil spill, polluting marine waters, shorelines, and wildlife habitats in the vicinity. The responsible parties, including the ship's operator and pilot, faced legal actions, fines, and compensation claims from federal and state authorities, environmental organizations, and affected stakeholders for damages to natural resources, recreational areas, and commercial fisheries.

Marine Plastic Pollution: The accumulation of marine plastic debris in oceans and coastal areas poses a significant threat to marine life, ecosystems, and human health. Governments, non-profit organizations, and international agencies are exploring innovative solutions, such as extended producer responsibility schemes, pollution taxes, and cleanup initiatives, to address the environmental impacts of plastic pollution and mitigate the costs of cleanup efforts and ecosystem restoration.

Vessel Groundings and Coral Reef Damage: Incidents of vessel groundings and ship strikes on coral reefs can cause extensive damage to fragile marine ecosystems, including coral bleaching, habitat destruction, and loss of biodiversity. Ship-owners and operators may be held liable for damages under maritime law, environmental regulations, and international conventions, with compensation payments allocated for coral reef restoration, marine conservation, and ecosystem monitoring programs.

Marine Debris Cleanup Operations: Coastal cleanup programs and marine debris removal efforts, organized by government agencies, NGOs, and volunteer groups, aim to reduce the impacts of marine litter on marine wildlife, habitats, and coastal communities. Funding for cleanup operations may be sourced from public grants, corporate sponsorships, and philanthropic donations, with compensation mechanisms established to reimburse cleanup costs and support ongoing monitoring and prevention initiatives.

Fisheries Closures and Compensation Schemes: Temporary fisheries closures, implemented to protect overexploited stocks, endangered species, and sensitive habitats, may result in economic hardships for fishing communities and seafood industry stakeholders. Compensation schemes, funded by governments, fisheries management agencies, and industry associations, provide financial assistance to affected fishers, processors, and businesses during closure periods, ensuring socio-economic support and compliance with fisheries management measures.

Marine Protected Area (MPA) Compensation Funds: Compensation funds for marine protected areas (MPAs) support the conservation and management of designated marine reserves, marine parks, and protected areas, including financial incentives for sustainable fishing practices, compliance with MPA regulations, and stakeholder engagement in conservation activities. Contributions to MPA compensation funds may come from user fees, tourism revenues, and government subsidies, with funds allocated for conservation projects, research initiatives, and community development programs within MPAs.

Coastal Erosion and Shoreline Protection: Coastal erosion, exacerbated by sea level rise, storm surges, and human activities, threatens coastal infrastructure, habitats, and communities worldwide. Compensation mechanisms for shoreline protection and erosion control may involve government grants, insurance programs, and public-private partnerships to fund coastal engineering projects, beach nourishment efforts, and habitat restoration initiatives aimed at mitigating the impacts of coastal erosion and preserving coastal resilience

Chapter 8.
Dispute Settlement Mechanisms

Diplomatic Negotiation and Mediation

Diplomatic negotiation and mediation serve as primary mechanisms for resolving disputes between states and international actors in accordance with diplomatic protocols, treaties, and customary international law. One notable example is the Camp David Accords of 1978, where the United States mediated negotiations between Israel and Egypt, resulting in a peace agreement that ended decades of conflict and established diplomatic relations between the two nations.

Treaty of *Versailles* signed in 1919 at the end of World War I, included provisions for diplomatic negotiation and mediation to address territorial disputes, reparations, and disarmament measures among the Allied and Central Powers, aiming to restore peace and stability in Europe following the war.

Vienna Convention on Diplomatic Relations (1961) and the Vienna Convention on Consular Relations (1963) provide legal frameworks for diplomatic negotiation and mediation, outlining rights and obligations of states, diplomatic missions, and consular posts in conducting international relations and resolving disputes through diplomatic channels.

The United Nations Security Council, under Chapter VI of the UN Charter, has authority to recommend diplomatic negotiation and mediation as means of peaceful settlement of disputes among member states, as demonstrated in numerous resolutions addressing conflicts in regions such as the Middle East, Africa, and Asia.

Oslo Accords (1993) between Israel and the Palestine Liberation Organization (PLO) facilitated diplomatic negotiations and mediation efforts to establish interim agreements, confidence-building measures, and a framework for future peace negotiations in the Israeli-Palestinian conflict.

Dayton Agreement (1995), negotiated under the auspices of the United States, European Union, and Russia, ended the Bosnian War and established a framework for peace and reconciliation in Bosnia and Herzegovina through diplomatic negotiation and mediation among warring factions.

Good Friday Agreement (1998) in Northern Ireland, facilitated by the governments of the United Kingdom and Ireland, involved diplomatic negotiation and mediation to address political, social, and sectarian divisions and establish a power-sharing government and institutions for peace and reconciliation.

Iran Nuclear Deal, formally known as the Joint Comprehensive Plan of Action (JCPOA) (2015), involved diplomatic negotiation and mediation among the P5+1 countries (United States, United Kingdom, France, Russia, China, plus Germany) and Iran to address concerns about Iran's nuclear program and reach a mutually-agreed framework for nuclear non-proliferation.

Dayton Accords, negotiated in Dayton, Ohio, brought an end to the conflict in Bosnia and Herzegovina, which had erupted following the breakup of Yugoslavia. The agreement established a framework for peace and territorial integrity, dividing the country into two entities, the Federation of Bosnia and Herzegovina and *Republika Srpska*, and delineating power-sharing arrangements between ethnic groups.

Paris Peace Accords (1973) ended the Vietnam War and paved the way for the withdrawal of American troops from Vietnam. Negotiated in Paris, France, the accords aimed to achieve a ceasefire, the release of prisoners of war, and a political settlement between North Vietnam and South Vietnam.

Treaty of Trianon (1920) concluded World War I between Hungary and the Allied Powers, including France, the United Kingdom, and Italy. Negotiated in the Palace of Trianon at Versailles, France, the treaty established new borders and territorial arrangements in Central Europe, resulting in significant territorial losses for Hungary.

Dayton Agreement, negotiated at Wright-Patterson Air Force Base near Dayton, Ohio, involved intensive diplomatic negotiations and mediation sessions facilitated by international mediators and negotiators, including Richard Holbrooke, Christopher Hill, and Carl Bildt, leading to the successful conclusion of the peace agreement.

The United Nations has a long history of diplomatic negotiation and mediation efforts to resolve conflicts and disputes around the world, including the Korean War armistice negotiations (1951), the Cuban Missile Crisis negotiations (1962), and the Iran-Iraq ceasefire negotiations (1988), among others.

Treaty of Portsmouth (1905), negotiated in Portsmouth, New Hampshire, ended the Russo-Japanese War and established diplomatic relations between Russia and Japan, with President Theodore Roosevelt of the United States serving as a mediator and facilitating the peace negotiations.

Helsinki Accords (1975), signed by 35 countries participating in the Conference on Security and Cooperation in Europe (CSCE), included provisions for diplomatic negotiation and mediation to address human rights, security, and cooperation issues during the Cold War era, promoting dialogue and confidence-building measures among East and West European states.

Treaty of Guadalupe Hidalgo (1848), negotiated in Guadalupe Hidalgo, Mexico, ended the Mexican-American War and established diplomatic relations between the United States and Mexico, with provisions for border demarcation, territorial cessions, and compensation for Mexico's loss of territory.

Treaty of Paris (1898), negotiated in Paris, France, ended the Spanish-American War and resulted in Spain's cession of territories, including Puerto Rico, Guam, and the Philippines, to the United States, marking the beginning of American imperialism in the Asia-Pacific region.

Treaty of Ghent (1814), negotiated in Ghent, Belgium, ended the War of 1812 between the United States and Great Britain, restoring peace and diplomatic relations between the two nations and addressing issues related to territorial boundaries, maritime rights, and the impressment of American sailors.

Treaty of Wanghia (1844), negotiated in Wanghia, China, established diplomatic relations between the United States and the Qing Dynasty of China, addressing issues of trade, extraterritoriality, and consular rights, and laying the foundation for future Sino-American relations.

Treaty of Brest-Litovsk (1918), negotiated in Brest-Litovsk, Belarus, ended hostilities between Russia and the Central Powers during World War I, resulting in Russia's withdrawal from the war and territorial concessions to Germany and Austria-Hungary in Eastern Europe.

Treaty of Ghent (1814), signed in Ghent, Belgium, ended the War of 1812 between the United States and Great Britain, restoring territorial boundaries and diplomatic relations between the two nations and addressing issues related to maritime rights, imprisonment of sailors, and trade disputes.

Treaty of Paris (1783), negotiated in Paris, France, ended the American Revolutionary War and recognized the independence of the United States from Great Britain, establishing diplomatic relations and defining territorial boundaries between the newly-formed nation and the British Empire.

Treaty of Guadalupe Hidalgo (1848), negotiated in Guadalupe Hidalgo, Mexico, ended the Mexican-American War and resulted in Mexico's cession of territories, including present-day California, Arizona, New Mexico, and Texas, to the United States, expanding American territory to the Pacific Ocean.

Treaty of Portsmouth (1905), mediated by President Theodore Roosevelt, facilitated diplomatic negotiations between Russia and Japan to end the Russo-Japanese War, resulting in Japan's territorial gains in Manchuria and Korea and recognition of its dominance in East Asia by the international community.

Treaty of Paris (1815), negotiated in Paris, France, following the defeat of Napoleon Bonaparte, established a new balance of power in Europe and provided for the restoration of monarchies, territorial adjustments, and diplomatic alliances among European states to maintain peace and stability on the continent.

Treaty of Versailles (1919), negotiated in *Versailles*, France, at the end of World War I, imposed harsh terms on Germany, including territorial losses, disarmament, reparations payments, and the creation of the League of Nations, setting the stage for future diplomatic tensions and conflicts.

Treaty of Westphalia (1648), negotiated in Westphalia, Germany, ended the Thirty Years' War and the Eighty Years' War, establishing principles of state sovereignty, religious tolerance, and diplomatic immunity that shaped modern international relations and diplomacy in Europe.

Treaty of Lisbon (2007), negotiated in Lisbon, Portugal, amended the founding treaties of the European Union to streamline decision-making processes, enhance institutional cooperation, and expands the EU's role in areas such as foreign policy, security, and justice.

Treaty of Washington (1871), negotiated in Washington, D.C., resolved outstanding disputes between the United States and Great Britain, including the Alabama Claims arbitration, fisheries rights in North America, and the boundary between British Columbia and Alaska.

Treaty of Nanking (1842), negotiated in Nanking, China, following the First Opium War, ceded Hong Kong to Great Britain, opened five Chinese ports to foreign trade, and established extraterritorial rights for British subjects in China, marking the beginning of unequal treaties between China and Western powers.

Treaty of Saint-Germain-en-Laye (1919), negotiated in Saint-Germain-en-Laye, France, dissolved the Austro-Hungarian Empire and established new national boundaries and sovereign states in Central and Eastern Europe, addressing ethnic and national aspirations after World War I.

Treaty of Lausanne (1923), negotiated in Lausanne, Switzerland, replaced the Treaty of Sèvres and established peace between the Allies and the new Republic of Turkey, recognizing its sovereignty, territorial integrity, and the status of the Turkish Straits under international law.

Treaty of Riga (1921), negotiated in Riga, Latvia, between Poland and Soviet Russia, ended the Polish-Soviet War and established a ceasefire line, recognizing Poland's independence and territorial gains in Eastern Europe, while addressing minority rights and border disputes.

Treaty of Paris (1856), negotiated in Paris, France, ended the Crimean War and established principles of neutrality, territorial integrity, and free navigation in the Black Sea region, while recognizing the independence of Romania, Serbia, and Montenegro.

Treaty of Utrecht (1713), negotiated in Utrecht, Netherlands, ended the War of the Spanish Succession and reshaped the balance of power in Europe, with provisions for territorial exchanges, colonial concessions, and diplomatic alliances among European states.

Treaty of Berlin (1878), negotiated in Berlin, Germany, addressed the aftermath of the Russo-Turkish War and the Congress of Berlin, resulting in territorial adjustments, autonomy for Bulgaria, and diplomatic recognition of Serbia, Montenegro, and Romania as independent states.

Treaty of Guadeloupe Hidalgo (1848), negotiated in Guadeloupe Hidalgo, Mexico, following the Mexican-American

War, established the Rio Grande as the border between Texas and Mexico, ceded California, New Mexico, and other territories to the United States, and required the U.S. to pay Mexico $15 million in compensation.

Treaty of Sevres (1920), negotiated in Sevres, France, after World War I, imposed punitive terms on the Ottoman Empire, including territorial losses, demilitarization, and provisions for minority rights, but was never ratified and was superseded by the Treaty of Lausanne in 1923.

Treaty of Lausanne (1923), negotiated in Lausanne, Switzerland, replaced the Treaty of Sevres and established peace between the Allies and the new Republic of Turkey, recognizing its sovereignty, territorial integrity, and the status of the Turkish Straits under international law.

Treaty of Paris (1951), negotiated in Paris, France, established the European Coal and Steel Community (ECSC) among six founding member states, laying the foundation for European integration and cooperation in key economic sectors, including coal and steel production.

Treaty of Rome (1957), negotiated in Rome, Italy, created the European Economic Community (EEC) and the European Atomic Energy Community (EURATOM), advancing economic integration, free trade, and cooperation among member states in Europe.

Treaty of Maastricht (1992), negotiated in Maastricht, Netherlands, established the European Union (EU) and laid the groundwork for economic and monetary union, political integration, and the adoption of a common currency, the Euro, among participating member states.

Treaty of Nice (2001), negotiated in Nice, France, amended the founding treaties of the European Union to streamline decision-making processes, strengthen institutional capacities, and prepares the EU for enlargement by admitting new member states from Central and Eastern Europe.

Treaty of Lisbon (2007), negotiated in Lisbon, Portugal, amended the founding treaties of the European Union to streamline decision-making processes, enhance institutional cooperation, and expands the EU's role in areas such as foreign policy, security, and justice.

Treaty of Washington (1871), negotiated in Washington, D.C., resolved outstanding disputes between the United States and Great Britain, including the Alabama Claims arbitration, fisheries rights in North America, and the boundary between British Columbia and Alaska.

Treaty of Nanking (1842), negotiated in Nanking, China, following the First Opium War, ceded Hong Kong to Great Britain, opened five Chinese ports to foreign trade, and established extraterritorial rights for British subjects in China, marking the beginning of unequal treaties between China and Western powers.

Treaty of Saint-Germain-en-Laye (1919), negotiated in Saint-Germain-en-Laye, France, dissolved the Austro-Hungarian Empire and established new national boundaries and sovereign states in Central and Eastern Europe, addressing ethnic and national aspirations after World War I.

Treaty of Riga (1921), negotiated in Riga, Latvia, between Poland and Soviet Russia, ended the Polish-Soviet War and established a ceasefire line, recognizing Poland's independence and territorial gains in Eastern Europe, while addressing minority rights and border disputes.

Treaty of Paris (1856) concluded the Crimean War and introduced important principles that would influence subsequent international agreements, including the recognition of the neutrality of the Black Sea and the Danube River, as well as the establishment of new international commissions to oversee navigation and trade in these waterways.

Treaty of Tordesillas (1494) between Spain and Portugal, mediated by Pope Alexander VI, divided the newly discovered lands outside Europe between the two nations along a meridian 370 leagues west of the Cape Verde Islands, demonstrating early attempts at international cooperation and resolution of territorial disputes through diplomacy and negotiation.

Treaty of Utrecht (1713) concluded the War of Spanish Succession and had implications for maritime law by granting Britain exclusive rights to the lucrative slave trade with Spanish America, further solidifying Britain's dominance in transatlantic commerce and shaping the legal framework for colonial trade.

Treaty of Paris (1783), which ended the American Revolutionary War, recognized the independence of the United States and established its territorial boundaries, including access to the Atlantic Ocean through the Gulf of Mexico, affirming the fledgling nation's sovereignty and maritime rights.

Treaty of Trianon (1920), one of the treaties concluding World War I, addressed the disintegration of the Austro-Hungarian Empire and established new maritime boundaries in the Adriatic Sea, redistributing territory among successor states such as Yugoslavia, Italy, and Romania.

Treaty of Guadalupe Hidalgo (1848), ending the Mexican-American War, not only ceded vast territories to the United States but also addressed maritime boundaries, notably establishing the Rio Grande as the border between Texas and Mexico, affecting navigation rights and access to ports.

Treaty of Portsmouth (1905), mediated by President Theodore Roosevelt, ended the Russo-Japanese War and affirmed Japan's dominance in East Asia, granting it control over Korea, parts of Manchuria, and maritime territories, thus reshaping the balance of power in the region.

Convention for the Protection of Submarine Telegraph Cables (1884), also known as the Paris Convention, established rules for the laying and protection of undersea telegraph cables, safeguarding vital communication networks and promoting cooperation among maritime nations.

International Convention for the Safety of Life at Sea (SOLAS), first adopted in 1914 after the sinking of the Titanic, and subsequently revised and updated, sets safety standards for ships, including navigation, construction, and equipment requirements, to prevent accidents and protect lives at sea.

Convention on the International Regulations for

Preventing Collisions at Sea (COLREGs), adopted in 1972 and updated periodically, establishes rules to prevent collisions between vessels, including right-of-way, lighting, and signaling requirements, enhancing safety and reducing the risk of accidents in maritime navigation.

The Convention on the Territorial Sea and the Contiguous Zone (1958), part of the United Nations Convention on the Law of the Sea (UNCLOS), defines the breadth of a state's territorial sea and contiguous zone, establishing legal frameworks for jurisdiction and sovereignty over maritime territories.

The Convention on the High Seas (1958), another component of UNCLOS, governs the use of the high seas beyond national jurisdiction, establishing principles of freedom of navigation, overflight, fishing, and scientific research, while also outlining duties to protect the marine environment and prevent piracy.

The United Nations Convention on the Law of the Sea (UNCLOS), adopted in 1982 and considered the "constitution for the oceans," codifies principles of maritime law, including territorial sovereignty, navigation rights, marine resource management, environmental protection, and dispute resolution, providing a comprehensive framework for regulating ocean affairs.

The Antarctic Treaty System (ATS), established in 1959, designates Antarctica as a scientific preserve and prohibits military activities, territorial claims, and nuclear testing on the continent, fostering international cooperation and environmental

The Protocol on Environmental Protection to the Antarctic Treaty (1991) further strengthens environmental safeguards in Antarctica by establishing rules for waste disposal, pollution prevention, and conservation measures, reflecting global efforts to preserve fragile ecosystems and biodiversity in the Antarctic marine environment.

The Convention on Biological Diversity (CBD), adopted in 1992, promotes the conservation and sustainable use of marine biodiversity, including genetic resources and ecosystems, through measures such as protected areas, ecosystem-based management, and sustainable fisheries practices, aiming to address threats such as habitat destruction, overfishing, and climate change impacts.

The Ramsar Convention on Wetlands (1971), an international treaty for the conservation and sustainable use of wetlands, recognizes the ecological importance of coastal and marine wetlands, including estuaries, mangroves, and salt marshes, and encourages their protection, restoration, and wise use to maintain biodiversity and ecosystem services.

The Convention on International Trade in Endangered Species of Wild Fauna and Flora (CITES), established in 1973, regulates the international trade in endangered species, including marine species such as sea turtles, sharks, and corals, to prevent overexploitation and illegal trafficking, ensuring their conservation and sustainable management.

The International Maritime Organization (IMO), a specialized agency of the United Nations, sets global standards for shipping safety, security, and environmental protection through conventions such as MARPOL (preventing marine pollution), SOLAS (ensuring safety at sea), and STCW (training and certification of seafarers), promoting a safer and more sustainable maritime industry.

The International Whaling Commission (IWC), established in 1946, regulates whale hunting and conservation through agreements such as the International Convention for the Regulation of Whaling (1946) and the moratorium on commercial whaling (1986), aiming to protect whale populations and preserve marine ecosystems.

The Convention on the Conservation of Antarctic Marine Living Resources (CCAMLR), adopted in 1980, manages fisheries in the Southern Ocean surrounding Antarctica, establishing catch limits, monitoring systems, and conservation measures to sustainably manage fish stocks and protect marine ecosystems from overexploitation.

Convention on the Prevention of Marine Pollution by

Dumping of Wastes and Other Matter (London Convention), adopted in 1972 and revised in 1996, regulates the dumping of waste materials at sea, including chemicals, sewage sludge, and dredged spoils, to prevent marine pollution and protect ocean health.

The International Convention for the Control and Management of Ships' Ballast Water and Sediments (BWM Convention), adopted in 2004 and implemented in 2017, addresses the transfer of invasive species through ballast water discharge, requiring ships to adopt measures to minimize the spread of harmful organisms and pathogens in marine ecosystems.

The Convention on the Conservation of Migratory Species of Wild Animals (CMS), also known as the Bonn Convention, aims to protect migratory species and their habitats, including marine mammals, seabirds, and sea turtles, through cooperative conservation measures among range states and regional agreements.

The Agreement on the Conservation of Albatrosses and Petrels (ACAP), established in 2001, addresses the conservation of albatrosses and petrels, seabird species threatened by factors such as bycatch in fisheries, habitat loss, and climate change, promoting international cooperation and conservation action to reduce mortality and protect breeding colonies.

The Convention on the Protection of the Marine Environment of the Baltic Sea Area (Helsinki Convention), adopted in 1974 and revised in 1992, addresses pollution and environmental degradation in the Baltic Sea region, setting standards for wastewater treatment, shipping practices

The Convention for the Protection of the Marine Environment and Coastal Area of the South-East Pacific (Lima Convention), established in 1981, aims to protect and preserve the marine environment and coastal areas of the South-East Pacific region, addressing issues such as pollution, habitat destruction, and unsustainable resource exploitation.

The Convention for the Protection of the Mediterranean

Sea Against Pollution (Barcelona Convention), adopted in 1976 and amended in 1995, seeks to prevent and reduce pollution in the Mediterranean Sea through measures such as pollution control, marine spatial planning, and biodiversity conservation.

The Convention for the Protection of the Marine Environment of the North-East Atlantic (OSPAR Convention), signed in 1992, addresses marine pollution, biodiversity conservation, and ecosystem management in the North-East Atlantic region, establishing cooperative measures among coastal states to protect marine resources and habitats.

The Convention for the Protection of the Marine Environment and the Coastal Region of the Mediterranean (Barcelona Convention), adopted in 1976 and amended in 1995, aims to prevent, reduce, and control pollution in the Mediterranean Sea and its coastal areas through coordinated efforts among Mediterranean states.

The Agreement on the Conservation of Small Cetaceans of the Baltic, North East Atlantic, Irish and North Seas (ASCOBANS), established in 1992, aims to protect small cetaceans such as dolphins and porpoises in the seas around Europe, addressing threats such as bycatch, habitat degradation, and pollution.

The Convention on the Protection of the Black Sea Against Pollution (Bucharest Convention), adopted in 1992, seeks to prevent and reduce pollution in the Black Sea region through measures such as pollution monitoring, waste management, and environmental impact assessments.

The Protocol Concerning Specially Protected Areas and Biological Diversity in the Mediterranean (SPA/BD Protocol), adopted as part of the Barcelona Convention in 1995, aims to protect and conserve biodiversity in the Mediterranean Sea through the designation of specially protected areas and the implementation of conservation measures.

The Convention on the Conservation of Antarctic Marine Living Resources (CCAMLR), established in 1980, aims to conserve Antarctic marine ecosystems and regulate fishing activities in the Southern Ocean, setting catch limits, establishing protected areas, and promoting sustainable fisheries management.

The Agreement on Port State Measures to Prevent, Deter and Eliminate Illegal, Unreported and Unregulated Fishing (Port State Measures Agreement), adopted in 2009 and entered into force in 2016, aims to combat illegal fishing by preventing vessels engaged in illegal, unreported, and unregulated fishing from using ports for landing, transshipment, or processing of fish.

The Agreement for the Implementation of the Provisions of the United Nations Convention on the Law of the Sea of 10 December 1982 relating to the Conservation and Management of Straddling Fish Stocks and Highly Migratory Fish Stocks (UN Fish Stocks Agreement), adopted in 1995, seeks to ensure the long-term conservation and sustainable management of straddling and highly migratory fish stocks through cooperation among coastal states and flag states.

The International Convention for the Regulation of Whaling (ICRW), established in 1946, regulates commercial whaling to ensure the conservation of whale stocks and the orderly development of the whaling industry, setting catch limits, establishing protected areas, and promoting scientific research.

The Convention on Wetlands of International Importance especially as Waterfowl Habitat (Ramsar Convention), established in 1971, aims to conserve wetlands and their biodiversity through the designation of Ramsar Sites, promoting their wise use and sustainable management.

The Convention on the Protection of the Rhine (Rhine Convention), signed in 1999, aims to protect the Rhine River from pollution and promote sustainable development in its basin through cooperation among riparian states, implementing measures to reduce pollution, restore habitats, and improve water quality.

The Convention on the Protection and Use of Transboundary Watercourses and International Lakes (Water Convention), adopted in 1992 and revised in 2003, seeks to protect and manage transboundary water resources through cooperation among riparian states, addressing issues such as water pollution, drought, and ecosystem degradation.

The International Convention for the Control and Management of Ships' Ballast Water and Sediments (BWM Convention), adopted in 2004 and entered into force in 2017, aims to prevent the spread of invasive aquatic species through ships' ballast water by establishing standards for ballast water management and treatment.

The International Convention for the Control and Management of Ship's Ballast Water and Sediments (BWM Convention), adopted in 2004 and entered into force in 2017, aims to prevent the spread of invasive aquatic species through ships' ballast water by establishing standards for ballast water management and treatment.

The Protocol on Environmental Protection to the Antarctic Treaty (1991), also known as the Madrid Protocol, designates Antarctica as a natural reserve, devoted to peace and science, and prohibits all activities relating to mineral resources, except for scientific research.

The Convention on the Protection of the Marine Environment of the Baltic Sea Area (Helsinki Convention), adopted in 1974, aims to prevent and reduce pollution in the Baltic Sea region through cooperative measures among Baltic Sea states, addressing issues such as eutrophication, oil spills, and hazardous substances.

The OSPAR Convention (Convention for the Protection of the Marine Environment of the North-East Atlantic), signed in 1992, aims to protect and conserve the marine environment of the North-East Atlantic Ocean through cooperation among OSPAR member countries, addressing issues such as pollution, biodiversity loss, and habitat destruction.

The Protocol on Environmental Protection to the Antarctic Treaty (1991), also known as the Madrid Protocol, designates Antarctica as a natural reserve, devoted to peace and science, and prohibits all activities relating to mineral resources, except for scientific research.

The Agreement on Port State Measures to Prevent, Deter

and Eliminate Illegal, Unreported and Unregulated Fishing (Port State Measures Agreement), adopted in 2009 and entered into force in 2016, aims to combat illegal fishing by preventing vessels engaged in illegal, unreported, and unregulated fishing from using ports for landing, transshipment, or processing of fish.

The Agreement for the Implementation of the Provisions of the United Nations Convention on the Law of the Sea of 10 December 1982 relating to the Conservation and Management of Straddling Fish Stocks and Highly Migratory Fish Stocks (UN Fish Stocks Agreement), adopted in 1995, seeks to ensure the long-term conservation and sustainable management of straddling and highly migratory fish stocks through cooperation among coastal states and flag states.

The International Convention for the Regulation of Whaling (ICRW), established in 1946, regulates commercial whaling to ensure the conservation of whale stocks and the orderly development of the whaling industry, setting catch limits, establishing protected areas, and promoting scientific research.

The Ramsar Convention, established in 1971, promotes the conservation and sustainable use of wetlands worldwide, recognizing their ecological importance for biodiversity, water purification, flood control, and carbon sequestration, and encouraging international cooperation to protect and manage wetland ecosystems.

The Convention on the Protection of the Rhine, signed in 1999, aims to prevent pollution and promote sustainable development in the Rhine River basin through cooperative measures among riparian states, addressing issues such as industrial pollution, agricultural runoff, and habitat degradation.

The Convention on the Protection and Use of Transboundary Watercourses and International Lakes, adopted in 1992 and revised in 2003, seeks to promote equitable and sustainable management of transboundary water resources, fostering cooperation among riparian states to address water-related challenges such as pollution, water scarcity, and ecosystem degradation.

The International Convention for the Control and Management of Ships' Ballast Water and Sediments, adopted in 2004 and entered into force in 2017, aims to prevent the spread of invasive aquatic species through ships' ballast water by establishing standards for ballast water management and treatment.

The Protocol on Environmental Protection to the Antarctic Treaty, adopted in 1991, designates Antarctica as a natural reserve, devoted to peace and science, and prohibits all activities relating to mineral resources, except for scientific research.

The Helsinki Convention, signed in 1974, aims to prevent and reduce pollution in the Baltic Sea region through cooperative measures among Baltic Sea states, addressing issues such as eutrophication, oil spills, and hazardous substances.

The OSPAR Convention, signed in 1992, aims to protect and conserve the marine environment of the North-East Atlantic Ocean through cooperation among OSPAR member countries, addressing issues such as pollution, biodiversity loss, and habitat destruction.

The Madrid Protocol, adopted in 1991, designates Antarctica as a natural reserve, devoted to peace and science, and prohibits all activities relating to mineral resources, except for scientific research.

The Port State Measures Agreement, adopted in 2009 and entered into force in 2016, aims to combat illegal, unreported, and unregulated (IUU) fishing by preventing vessels engaged in such activities from using ports for landing, transshipment, or processing of fish. By denying port access to IUU fishing vessels, the agreement helps disrupt illegal fishing operations and strengthen fisheries management and conservation efforts.

The UN Fish Stocks Agreement, adopted in 1995, aims to ensure the long-term conservation and sustainable management of straddling and highly migratory fish stocks through cooperation among coastal states and flag states. By promoting responsible fishing practices and equitable sharing of fishery resources, the agreement seeks to prevent overfishing and depletion of fish stocks in the high seas and exclusive economic zones.

The International Convention for the Regulation of Whaling (ICRW), established in 1946, regulates commercial whaling to ensure the conservation of whale stocks and the orderly development of the whaling industry. By setting catch limits, establishing protected areas, and promoting scientific research, the convention aims to prevent the overexploitation of whale populations and protect marine ecosystems.

The Convention on the Protection and Use of Transboundary Watercourses and International Lakes, adopted in 1992 and revised in 2003, seeks to promote equitable and sustainable management of transboundary water resources. By fostering cooperation among riparian states and establishing mechanisms for joint management and dispute resolution, the convention aims to address water-related challenges and promote peace and stability in shared river basins.

The International Convention for the Control and Management of Ships' Ballast Water and Sediments, adopted in 2004 and entered into force in 2017, aims to prevent the spread of invasive aquatic species through ships' ballast water. By requiring ships to manage and treat ballast water before discharge, the convention helps protect marine biodiversity and ecosystem health from the impacts of invasive species.

The Protocol on Environmental Protection to the Antarctic Treaty, adopted in 1991, designates Antarctica as a natural reserve, devoted to peace and science. By prohibiting all activities related to mineral resources, except for scientific research, the protocol helps preserve the unique environment and ecosystems of Antarctica for scientific study and future generations.

The Helsinki Convention, signed in 1974, aims to prevent and reduce pollution in the Baltic Sea region through cooperative measures among Baltic Sea states.

Arbitration

Arbitration is a dispute resolution mechanism utilized in international law to settle disputes between states or other entities through the intervention of a neutral third party, known as an arbitrator or arbitral tribunal. One prominent example of arbitration in maritime disputes is the Permanent Court of Arbitration (PCA), established in 1899 in The Hague, Netherlands. The PCA has handled numerous maritime disputes, including those related to territorial boundaries, fishing rights, and environmental issues.

The Southern Bluefin Tuna Cases (New Zealand v. Japan; Australia v. Japan), arbitrated by the International Tribunal for the Law of the Sea (ITLOS) in 1999, involved disputes between New Zealand, Australia, and Japan over the management and conservation of Southern Bluefin Tuna stocks. The tribunal's decisions established principles for the sustainable management of shared fishery resources in the Southern Ocean, highlighting the role of arbitration in resolving complex maritime disputes.

The Arctic Sunrise Arbitration (Netherlands v. Russia), conducted under Annex VII of the United Nations Convention on the Law of the Sea (UNCLOS) in 2015, concerned the detention of the Greenpeace vessel Arctic Sunrise and its crew by Russian authorities following a protest against oil drilling in the Arctic. The arbitral tribunal ruled in favor of the Netherlands, ordering Russia to release the vessel and compensate the Netherlands for damages, demonstrating the effectiveness of arbitration in safeguarding maritime rights and freedoms.

The MOX Plant Case (Ireland v. United Kingdom), arbitrated by the International Court of Justice (ICJ) in 2001, involved a dispute between Ireland and the United Kingdom over the operation of a plutonium reprocessing plant at Sellafield, England, and its potential environmental impact on the Irish Sea. The ICJ's judgment addressed issues of environmental protection, nuclear safety, and transboundary harm, underscoring the role of arbitration in resolving disputes with significant maritime implications.

The Land Reclamation Case (Malaysia v. Singapore), arbitrated by an arbitral tribunal constituted under UNCLOS in 2003, concerned disputes between Malaysia and Singapore over land reclamation activities in the Strait of Johor, affecting maritime navigation and environmental conservation. The tribunal's decision provided clarity on the legal obligations of states regarding land reclamation projects in international waters, demonstrating the value of arbitration in resolving disputes over maritime boundaries and activities.

The Enrica Lexie Incident Arbitration (Italy v. India), conducted under Annex VII of UNCLOS in 2015, concerned the killing of two Indian fishermen by Italian marines aboard the oil tanker Enrica Lexie off the coast of Kerala, India, in 2012. The arbitral tribunal's decision addressed issues of jurisdiction, immunity, and the law of the sea, providing clarity on the legal framework governing incidents involving foreign vessels in national waters.

The ARA Libertad Case (Argentina v. Ghana), arbitrated by the ITLOS in 2012, involved a dispute between Argentina and Ghana over the detention of the Argentine naval training ship ARA Libertad in Ghanaian waters due to a commercial debt dispute. The tribunal's decision upheld Argentina's immunity as a sovereign state and ordered the release of the vessel, emphasizing the importance of respect for sovereign rights and state immunity in maritime disputes.

The Bay of Bengal Maritime Boundary Arbitration (Bangladesh v. India), conducted under UNCLOS in 2014, resolved disputes between Bangladesh and India over the delimitation of their maritime boundaries in the Bay of Bengal, including issues related to territorial waters, exclusive economic zones, and continental shelves. The arbitral tribunal's decision provided a legal framework for the equitable distribution of maritime resources and rights, contributing to regional stability and cooperation.

The Chagos Marine Protected Area Arbitration (Mauritius

v. United Kingdom), conducted under UNCLOS in 2015, concerned disputes between Mauritius and the United Kingdom over the establishment of a marine protected area around the Chagos Archipelago, including the disputed territory of Diego Garcia. The arbitral tribunal's decision invalidated the marine protected area and affirmed Mauritius' sovereignty over the Chagos Archipelago, highlighting the significance of arbitration in resolving sovereignty and territorial disputes in maritime zones.

The Annex VII Arbitration between the Republic of the Philippines and the People's Republic of China, initiated by the Philippines in 2013, concerned disputes over maritime entitlements in the South China Sea, including the legality of China's nine-dash line claim and its impact on the rights of other coastal states. The arbitral tribunal's award, issued in 2016, rejected China's historical claims and affirmed the Philippines' rights under UNCLOS, setting a precedent for the resolution of complex maritime disputes through arbitration.

The Bay of Bengal Maritime Boundary Arbitration (Bangladesh v. India), conducted under UNCLOS in 2014, resolved disputes between Bangladesh and India over the delimitation of their maritime boundaries in the Bay of Bengal. The arbitral tribunal's decision established a single maritime boundary line between the two countries, providing clarity on their respective rights and obligations in the disputed area and promoting peace between the two countries.

The Dispute Concerning Delimitation of the Maritime Boundary between Ghana and Côte d'Ivoire in the Atlantic Ocean (Ghana/Côte d'Ivoire), arbitrated by ITLOS in 2017, resolved disputes between Ghana and Côte d'Ivoire over the delimitation of their maritime boundary in the Atlantic Ocean. The arbitral tribunal's decision established a new maritime boundary line, based on equitable principles, and provided a framework for the peaceful coexistence and cooperation between the two neighboring countries.

The Enrica Lexie Incident Arbitration (Italy v. India), conducted under Annex VII of UNCLOS in 2015, addressed the killing of two Indian fishermen by Italian marines aboard the oil tanker Enrica Lexie off the coast of Kerala, India. The arbitral tribunal's decision clarified the legal obligations of the parties under UNCLOS, including the jurisdictional immunity of state vessels and the rights of coastal states to enforce their laws within their territorial waters.

The Arctic Sunrise Arbitration (Netherlands v. Russia), conducted under Annex VII of UNCLOS in 2015, involved disputes between the Netherlands and Russia over the detention of the Greenpeace vessel Arctic Sunrise and its crew following a protest against oil drilling in the Arctic. The arbitral tribunal's decision upheld the rights of states to peaceful protest and freedom of navigation in international waters, reinforcing the principles of international law governing maritime activities.

Land Reclamation Case (Malaysia v. Singapore), arbitrated by an arbitral tribunal constituted under UNCLOS in 2003, concerned disputes between Malaysia and Singapore over land reclamation activities in the Strait of Johor, affecting maritime navigation and environmental conservation. The tribunal's decision provided clarity on the legal obligations of states regarding land reclamation projects in international waters, demonstrating the value of arbitration in resolving disputes over maritime boundaries and activities.

The Annex VII Arbitration between the Republic of the Philippines and the People's Republic of China, initiated by the Philippines in 2013, concerned disputes over maritime entitlements in the South China Sea, including the legality of China's nine-dash line claim and its impact on the rights of other coastal states. The arbitral tribunal's award, issued in 2016, rejected China's historical claims and affirmed the Philippines' rights under UNCLOS, setting a precedent for the resolution of complex maritime disputes through arbitration.

The Chagos Marine Protected Area Arbitration (Mauritius v. United Kingdom), conducted under UNCLOS in 2015, concerned disputes between Mauritius and the United Kingdom over the establishment of a marine protected area around the Chagos

Archipelago, including the disputed territory of Diego Garcia. The arbitral tribunal's decision invalidated the marine protected area and affirmed Mauritius' sovereignty over the Chagos Archipelago, highlighting the significance of arbitration in resolving sovereignty and territorial disputes in maritime zones.

The Southern Bluefin Tuna Cases (New Zealand v. Japan; Australia v. Japan), arbitrated by the ITLOS in 1999, involved disputes between New Zealand, Australia, and Japan over the management and conservation of Southern Bluefin Tuna stocks. The tribunal's decisions established principles for the sustainable management of shared fishery resources in the Southern Ocean, highlighting the role of arbitration in resolving complex maritime disputes.

The ARA Libertad Case (Argentina v. Ghana), arbitrated by the ITLOS in 2012, involved a dispute between Argentina and Ghana over the detention of the Argentine naval training ship ARA Libertad in Ghanaian waters due to a commercial debt dispute. The tribunal's decision upheld Argentina's immunity as a sovereign state and ordered the release of the vessel, emphasizing the importance of respect for sovereign rights and state immunity in maritime disputes.

The Bay of Bengal Maritime Boundary Arbitration (Bangladesh v. India), conducted under UNCLOS in 2014, resolved disputes between Bangladesh and India over the delimitation of their maritime boundaries in the Bay of Bengal. The arbitral tribunal's decision established a single maritime boundary line between the two countries, providing clarity on their respective rights and obligations in the disputed area and promoting maritime stability and cooperation in the region.

The Dispute Concerning Delimitation of the Maritime Boundary between Ghana and Côte d'Ivoire in the Atlantic Ocean (Ghana/Côte d'Ivoire), arbitrated by ITLOS in 2017, resolved disputes between Ghana and Côte d'Ivoire over the delimitation of their maritime boundary in the Atlantic Ocean. The arbitral tribunal's decision established a new maritime boundary line, based on equitable principles, and provided a framework for the peaceful coexistence and cooperation between the two neighboring countries.

The Chagos Marine Protected Area Arbitration (Mauritius v. United Kingdom), conducted under UNCLOS in 2015, concerned disputes between Mauritius and the United Kingdom over the establishment of a marine protected area around the Chagos Archipelago, including the disputed territory of Diego Garcia. The arbitral tribunal's decision invalidated the marine protected area and affirmed Mauritius' sovereignty over the Chagos Archipelago, highlighting the significance of arbitration in resolving sovereignty and territorial disputes in maritime zones.

The Enrica Lexie Incident Arbitration (Italy v. India), conducted under Annex VII of UNCLOS in 2015, addressed the killing of two Indian fishermen by Italian marines aboard the oil tanker Enrica Lexie off the coast of Kerala, India. The arbitral tribunal's decision clarified the legal obligations of the parties under UNCLOS, including the jurisdictional immunity of state vessels and the rights of coastal states to enforce their laws within their territorial waters.

The MOX Plant Case (Ireland v. United Kingdom), arbitrated by the ICJ in 2001, addressed disputes between Ireland and the United Kingdom over the operation of a plutonium reprocessing plant at Sellafield, England, and its potential environmental impact on the Irish Sea. The ICJ's judgment emphasized the importance of environmental protection and the duty of states to prevent transboundary harm, setting a precedent for the resolution of disputes with significant maritime implications.

The Arctic Sunrise Arbitration (Netherlands v. Russia), conducted under Annex VII of UNCLOS in 2015, involved disputes between the Netherlands and Russia over the detention of the Greenpeace vessel Arctic Sunrise and its crew following a protest against oil drilling in the Arctic. The arbitral tribunal's decision upheld the rights of states to peaceful protest and freedom of navigation in international waters, reinforcing the principles of international law governing maritime activities.

The Southern Bluefin Tuna Cases (New Zealand v. Japan; Australia v. Japan), arbitrated by the ITLOS in 1999, involved disputes between New Zealand, Australia, and Japan over the management and conservation of Southern Bluefin Tuna stocks. The tribunal's decisions established principles for the sustainable management of shared fishery resources in the Southern Ocean, highlighting the role of arbitration in resolving complex maritime disputes.

These cases demonstrate the effectiveness of arbitration as a mechanism for resolving maritime disputes and promoting peaceful relations among states. Arbitration provides a forum for parties to present their arguments, receive impartial judgments, and reach mutually acceptable solutions, contributing to the maintenance of maritime order and the rule of law in the international community.

The ARA Libertad Case (Argentina v. Ghana), arbitrated by the ITLOS in 2012, involved a dispute between Argentina and Ghana over the detention of the Argentine naval training ship ARA Libertad in Ghanaian waters due to a commercial debt dispute. The tribunal's decision upheld Argentina's immunity as a sovereign state and ordered the release of the vessel, emphasizing the importance of respect for sovereign rights and state immunity in maritime disputes.

The Bay of Bengal Maritime Boundary Arbitration (Bangladesh v. India), conducted under UNCLOS in 2014, resolved disputes between Bangladesh and India over the delimitation of their maritime boundaries in the Bay of Bengal. The arbitral tribunal's decision established a single maritime boundary line between the two countries, providing clarity on their respective rights and obligations in the disputed area and promoting maritime stability and cooperation in the region.

The Dispute Concerning Delimitation of the Maritime Boundary between Ghana and Côte d'Ivoire in the Atlantic Ocean (Ghana/Côte d'Ivoire), arbitrated by ITLOS in 2017, resolved disputes between Ghana and Côte d'Ivoire over the delimitation of their maritime boundary in the Atlantic Ocean. The arbitral tribunal's decision established a new maritime boundary line, based on equitable principles, and provided a framework for the peaceful coexistence and cooperation between the two neighboring countries.

The Annex VII Arbitration between the Republic of the Philippines and the People's Republic of China, initiated by the Philippines in 2013, concerned disputes over maritime entitlements in the South China Sea, including the legality of China's nine-dash line claim and its impact on the rights of other coastal states. The arbitral tribunal's award, issued in 2016, rejected China's historical claims and affirmed the Philippines' rights under UNCLOS, setting a precedent for the resolution of complex maritime disputes through arbitration.

The Chagos Marine Protected Area Arbitration (Mauritius v. United Kingdom), conducted under UNCLOS in 2015, concerned disputes between Mauritius and the United Kingdom over the establishment of a marine protected area around the Chagos Archipelago, including the disputed territory of Diego Garcia. The arbitral tribunal's decision invalidated the marine protected area and affirmed Mauritius' sovereignty over the Chagos Archipelago, highlighting the significance of arbitration in resolving sovereignty and territorial disputes in maritime zones.

The Southern Bluefin Tuna Cases (New Zealand v. Japan; Australia v. Japan), arbitrated by the ITLOS in 1999, involved disputes between New Zealand, Australia, and Japan over the management and conservation of Southern Bluefin Tuna stocks. The tribunal's decisions established principles for the sustainable management of shared fishery resources in the Southern Ocean, highlighting the role of arbitration in resolving complex maritime disputes.

These cases demonstrate the effectiveness of arbitration as a mechanism for resolving maritime disputes and promoting peaceful relations among states. Arbitration provides a forum for parties to present their arguments, receive impartial judgments, and reach mutually acceptable solutions, contributing to the maintenance of maritime order and the rule of law in the international community.

The Bay of Bengal Maritime Boundary Arbitration (Bangladesh v. India), conducted under UNCLOS in 2014, resolved disputes between Bangladesh and India over the delimitation of their maritime boundaries in the Bay of Bengal. The arbitral tribunal's decision established a single maritime boundary line between the two countries, providing clarity on their respective rights and obligations in the disputed area and promoting maritime stability and cooperation in the region.

The Dispute Concerning Delimitation of the Maritime Boundary between Ghana and Côte d'Ivoire in the Atlantic Ocean (Ghana/Côte d'Ivoire), arbitrated by ITLOS in 2017, resolved disputes between Ghana and Côte d'Ivoire over the delimitation of their maritime boundary in the Atlantic Ocean. The arbitral tribunal's decision established a new maritime boundary line, based on equitable principles, and provided a framework for the peaceful coexistence and cooperation between the two neighboring countries.

The Annex VII Arbitration between the Republic of the Philippines and the People's Republic of China, initiated by the Philippines in 2013, concerned disputes over maritime entitlements in the South China Sea, including the legality of China's nine-dash line claim and its impact on the rights of other coastal states. The arbitral tribunal's award, issued in 2016, rejected China's historical claims and affirmed the Philippines' rights under UNCLOS, setting a precedent for the resolution of complex maritime disputes through arbitration.

The Chagos Marine Protected Area Arbitration (Mauritius v. United Kingdom), conducted under UNCLOS in 2015, concerned disputes between Mauritius and the United Kingdom over the establishment of a marine protected area around the Chagos Archipelago, including the disputed territory of Diego Garcia. The arbitral tribunal's decision invalidated the marine protected area and affirmed Mauritius' sovereignty over the Chagos Archipelago, highlighting the significance of arbitration in resolving sovereignty and territorial disputes in maritime zones.

These cases demonstrate the effectiveness of arbitration as a mechanism for resolving maritime disputes and promoting peaceful relations among states. Arbitration provides a forum for parties to present their arguments, receive impartial judgments, and reach mutually acceptable solutions, contributing to the maintenance of maritime order and the rule of law in the international community.

International Court of Justice (ICJ)

The International Court of Justice (ICJ), established in 1945 as the principal judicial organ of the United Nations, plays a crucial role in the settlement of disputes between states, including those related to maritime issues. The ICJ operates under the Statute of the International Court of Justice and has jurisdiction to hear cases concerning the interpretation and application of international law, including matters of maritime law.

The Corfu Channel Case (United Kingdom v. Albania), decided by the ICJ in 1949, involved disputes between the United Kingdom and Albania over incidents in the Corfu Channel, including the mining of British warships by Albanian forces. The ICJ's judgment established principles regarding the obligation of states to ensure the safety of navigation in international waters and the consequences of breaches of such obligations, contributing to the development of international maritime law.

The North Sea Continental Shelf Cases (Federal Republic of Germany v. Denmark; Federal Republic of Germany v. Netherlands), decided by the ICJ in 1969, addressed disputes between Germany, Denmark, and the Netherlands over the delimitation of their continental shelves in the North Sea. The ICJ's judgment established principles for the equitable delimitation of maritime boundaries based on geographical, geological, and geomorphological factors, shaping the practice of maritime boundary delimitation.

The Fisheries Jurisdiction Case (United Kingdom v. Iceland), decided by the ICJ in 1974, involved disputes between the United Kingdom and Iceland over the extension of Icelandic fisheries jurisdiction beyond 12 nautical miles from the baseline. The ICJ's judgment clarified the legal framework for the extension of coastal state jurisdiction over fisheries resources and the rights of other states to access those resources, influencing the development of fisheries law and practice.

The Territorial Dispute (Libyan Arab Jamahiriya v. Malta), decided by the ICJ in 1985, concerned disputes between Libya and Malta over the delimitation of their territorial waters in the Gulf of Sidra. The ICJ's judgment delineated the maritime boundary between the two states based on principles of international law, contributing to the peaceful resolution of territorial disputes in the Mediterranean region.

The Maritime Delimitation and Territorial Questions between Qatar and Bahrain (Qatar v. Bahrain), decided by the ICJ in 2001, resolved disputes between Qatar and Bahrain over the delimitation of their maritime boundaries and sovereignty over the Hawar Islands and Zubarah. The ICJ's judgment established a maritime boundary line between the two states and clarified their respective territorial claims, promoting stability and cooperation in the Persian Gulf.

The Land Reclamation Case (Qatar v. Bahrain), decided by the ICJ in 2001, addressed disputes between Qatar and Bahrain over land reclamation activities in the vicinity of the Hawar Islands. The ICJ's judgment upheld Qatar's sovereignty over the disputed territories and called for the cessation of activities that could prejudice the final delimitation of maritime boundaries, emphasizing the importance of respecting the rights of coastal states in maritime zones.

The Case Concerning Pulp Mills on the River Uruguay (Argentina v. Uruguay), decided by the ICJ in 2010, involved disputes between Argentina and Uruguay over the construction and operation of pulp mills on the River Uruguay, which forms part of the boundary between the two countries. The ICJ's judgment addressed environmental concerns raised by Argentina and Uruguay's compliance with international environmental obligations, highlighting the ICJ's role in adjudicating disputes with environmental implications in maritime areas.

The Whaling in the Antarctic Case (Australia v. Japan), which was decided by the ICJ in 2014, involved disputes between Australia and Japan regarding Japan's whaling activities in the Southern Ocean. The ICJ's judgment found that Japan's whaling program did not meet the criteria for scientific research under international law and ordered Japan to cease its whaling activities in the Antarctic region, underscoring the ICJ's role in addressing conservation and management issues in maritime zones.

The Case Concerning Certain Activities Carried Out by Nicaragua in the Border Area (Costa Rica v. Nicaragua), decided by the ICJ in 2015, involved disputes between Costa Rica and Nicaragua over Nicaragua's construction of a canal along the San Juan River, which forms part of the boundary between the two countries. The ICJ's judgment addressed issues related to environmental impact assessment, sovereignty, and navigation rights, highlighting the ICJ's jurisdiction over disputes with transboundary implications in maritime areas.

The Territorial and Maritime Dispute (Nicaragua v. Colombia), decided by the ICJ in 2012, addressed disputes between Nicaragua and Colombia over the delimitation of their maritime boundaries in the Caribbean Sea and Pacific Ocean. The ICJ's judgment established a single maritime boundary line between the two states, providing clarity on their respective rights and obligations in the disputed area and promoting maritime stability and cooperation in the region.

The South China Sea Arbitration (Philippines v. China), while not adjudicated by the ICJ, involved disputes between the Philippines and China over maritime entitlements and territorial claims in the South China Sea. The arbitral tribunal's award, issued under UNCLOS in 2016, addressed various legal issues related to maritime rights, including China's nine-dash line claim, and provided clarity on the legal status of features in the South China Sea, influencing the interpretation and application of international law in maritime disputes.

The Nuclear Tests Cases (Australia v. France; New Zealand v. France), brought before the ICJ in 1973, concerned disputes between Australia, New Zealand, and France over France's atmospheric nuclear tests in the Pacific Ocean. The ICJ's advisory opinions affirmed the obligation of states to refrain from actions that could cause environmental harm to other states and emphasized the importance of international cooperation in nuclear disarmament and environmental protection.

The Legality of the Use of Force Cases (Nicaragua v. United States), adjudicated by the ICJ in 1986, involved disputes between Nicaragua and the United States over U.S. support for armed activities in Nicaragua and the use of force in violation of international law. The ICJ's judgment condemned the United States' actions and affirmed the principle of non-intervention in the internal affairs of states, contributing to the development of international law on the use of force and state sovereignty.

The Case Concerning Certain Property (Liechtenstein v. Germany), decided by the ICJ in 2005, addressed disputes between Liechtenstein and Germany over property confiscated by East Germany after World War II, including properties located along the Danube River. The ICJ's judgment reaffirmed the principles of state responsibility and the protection of property rights under international law, highlighting the ICJ's role in resolving disputes with historical implications in maritime

The Dispute Regarding Navigational and Related Rights (Costa Rica v. Nicaragua), brought before the ICJ in 2005, involved disputes between Costa Rica and Nicaragua over navigational rights and environmental protection in the San Juan River, which forms part of the boundary between the two countries. The ICJ's judgment addressed issues related to the sovereignty of the San Juan River and the obligations of both parties under international law, contributing to the resolution of disputes affecting maritime navigation and environmental conservation.

The Case Concerning the Aerial Incident of 10 August 1999 (Pakistan v. India), adjudicated by the ICJ in 2000, addressed disputes between Pakistan and India over the downing of a

Pakistani naval aircraft by Indian fighter jets near the Sir Creek area in the Arabian Sea. The ICJ's judgment emphasized the principles of respect for sovereignty and the prohibition of the use of force in international relations, highlighting the ICJ's role in resolving disputes with security implications in maritime areas.

The Legal Consequences of the Construction of a Wall in the Occupied Palestinian Territory (Advisory Opinion), issued by the ICJ in 2004, addressed disputes between Israel and Palestine over the construction of a wall in the West Bank, including its impact on Palestinian access to maritime resources in the Mediterranean Sea. The ICJ's advisory opinion affirmed the illegality of the wall and called for its dismantlement, emphasizing the rights of Palestinians to access maritime resources and the protection of their livelihoods.

The Case Concerning Oil Platforms (Islamic Republic of Iran v. United States), decided by the ICJ in 2003, involved disputes between Iran and the United States over the destruction of Iranian oil platforms in the Persian Gulf during the Iran-Iraq War. The ICJ's judgment condemned the United States' actions as a violation of Iran's sovereignty and called for reparations for the damages caused, highlighting the ICJ's role in adjudicating disputes involving state responsibility in maritime zones.

The Case Concerning Maritime Delimitation in the Black Sea (Romania v. Ukraine), brought before the ICJ in 2004, involved disputes between Romania and Ukraine over the delimitation of their maritime boundaries in the Black Sea. The ICJ's judgment established a single maritime boundary line between the two states, based on principles of international law, and provided clarity on their respective rights and obligations in the disputed area, promoting maritime stability and cooperation in the region.

The Case Concerning Certain Activities Carried Out by Nicaragua in the Border Area (Costa Rica v. Nicaragua), decided by the ICJ in 2015, involved disputes between Costa Rica and Nicaragua over Nicaragua's construction of a canal along the San Juan River, which forms part of the boundary between the two countries. The ICJ's judgment addressed issues related to environmental impact assessment, sovereignty, and navigation rights, highlighting the ICJ's jurisdiction over disputes with transboundary implications in maritime areas.

The Case Concerning Territorial and Maritime Dispute (Nicaragua v. Colombia), decided by the ICJ in 2012, addressed disputes between Nicaragua and Colombia over the delimitation of their maritime boundaries in the Caribbean Sea and Pacific Ocean. The ICJ's judgment established a single maritime boundary line between the two states, providing clarity on their respective rights and obligations in the disputed area and promoting maritime stability and cooperation in the region.

The Case Concerning the Arctic Sunrise Incident (Netherlands v. Russia), brought before the ICJ in 2013, involved disputes between the Netherlands and Russia over the detention of the Greenpeace vessel Arctic Sunrise and its crew following a protest against oil drilling in the Arctic. The ICJ's judgment affirmed the rights of states to peaceful protest and freedom of navigation in international waters, reinforcing the principles of international law governing maritime activities.

The Case Concerning Territorial and Maritime Dispute (Nicaragua v. Honduras), decided by the ICJ in 2007, addressed disputes between Nicaragua and Honduras over the delimitation of their maritime boundaries in the Caribbean Sea. The ICJ's judgment established a single maritime boundary line between the two states, based on equitable principles, and provided a framework for the peaceful coexistence and cooperation between the two neighboring countries.

The Case Concerning Aerial Herbicide Spraying (Ecuador v. Colombia), brought before the ICJ in 2008, involved disputes between Ecuador and Colombia over Colombia's aerial spraying of herbicides in border areas, including along the Putumayo River. The ICJ's judgment addressed environmental concerns raised by Ecuador and called for the cessation of aerial spraying in border areas, highlighting the importance of environmental protection in transboundary disputes.

The Case Concerning the Arrest Warrant of 11 April 2000

(Democratic Republic of the Congo v. Belgium), decided by the ICJ in 2002, addressed disputes between the Democratic Republic of the Congo and Belgium over Belgium's issuance of an arrest warrant against the Congolese Minister of Foreign Affairs. The ICJ's judgment emphasized the principles of sovereign immunity and the need to respect the legal rights of states and their officials, contributing to the clarification of international law on immunity from legal process for state officials in the context of diplomatic relations.

The Case Concerning the Application of the Convention on the Prevention and Punishment of the Crime of Genocide (Bosnia and Herzegovina v. Serbia and Montenegro), decided by the ICJ in 2007, addressed disputes between Bosnia and Herzegovina and Serbia and Montenegro over allegations of genocide committed during the conflict in Bosnia and Herzegovina in the 1990s. The ICJ's judgment ruled that Serbia was not directly responsible for genocide but failed to prevent genocide from occurring, highlighting the obligations of states to prevent and punish acts of genocide under international law.

The Case Concerning the Legal Status of Eastern Greenland (Denmark v. Norway), decided by the ICJ in 1933, involved disputes between Denmark and Norway over the legal status of Eastern Greenland, including issues related to sovereignty and maritime rights in the Arctic region. The ICJ's judgment affirmed Denmark's sovereignty over Eastern Greenland and clarified the legal status of the territory, contributing to the settlement of disputes in the Arctic area.

The Case Concerning Armed Activities on the Territory of the Congo (Democratic Republic of the Congo v. Uganda), decided by the ICJ in 2005, addressed disputes between the Democratic Republic of the Congo and Uganda over Uganda's military intervention in the Congo during the Second Congo War. The ICJ's judgment condemned Uganda's actions as violations of the Congo's sovereignty and territorial integrity and underscored the principles of non-intervention and peaceful settlement of disputes under international law.

The Case Concerning the Gabcikovo-Nagymaros Project (Hungary v. Slovakia), decided by the ICJ in 1997, involved disputes between Hungary and Slovakia over the construction and operation of a dam system on the Danube River, known as the Gabcikovo-Nagymaros Project. The ICJ's judgment addressed environmental concerns raised by Hungary and Slovakia's compliance with international environmental obligations, highlighting the importance of sustainable development and cooperation in transboundary water management.

The Case Concerning the Frontier Dispute (Burkina Faso v. Mali), brought before the ICJ in 1986, involved disputes between Burkina Faso and Mali over the delimitation of their land and maritime boundaries. The ICJ's judgment established a single boundary line between the two states, based on historical, geographical, and equitable considerations, and provided a framework for the peaceful resolution of disputes between neighboring countries in West Africa.

The Case Concerning the Legal Consequences for States of the Continued Presence of South Africa in Namibia (South West Africa) notwithstanding Security Council Resolution 276 (1970), decided by the ICJ in 1971, addressed disputes between Namibia (then South West Africa) and South Africa over South Africa's continued administration of Namibia in defiance of UN Security Council resolutions. The ICJ's advisory opinion affirmed the illegality of South Africa's presence in Namibia and called for the decolonization and independence of Namibia, highlighting the role of the ICJ in addressing colonial and apartheid-era disputes.

The Case Concerning the Temple of Preah Vihear (Cambodia v. Thailand), decided by the ICJ in 1962, involved disputes between Cambodia and Thailand over the sovereignty of the Temple of Preah Vihear and its surrounding area. The ICJ's judgment awarded sovereignty over the temple to Cambodia and delineated the boundary between the two countries, based on historical and geographical considerations, contributing to the resolution of territorial disputes between Cambodia and Thailand.

The Case Concerning the Kasikili/Sedudu Island (Botswana

v. Namibia), decided by the ICJ in 1999, addressed disputes between Botswana and Namibia over the sovereignty of Kasikili/Sedudu Island in the Chobe River. The ICJ's judgment ruled in favor of Botswana's sovereignty over the island, based on historical and geographical factors, and provided a framework for the peaceful resolution of territorial disputes between neighboring countries in Southern Africa.

The Case Concerning the Frontier Dispute (Benin v. Niger), decided by the ICJ in 2005, involved disputes between Benin and Niger over the delimitation of their land and maritime boundaries. The ICJ's judgment established a single boundary line between the two states, based on historical, geographical, and equitable considerations, and provided a framework for the peaceful resolution of disputes between neighboring countries in West Africa.

The Case Concerning Maritime Delimitation and Territorial Questions between Qatar and Bahrain (Qatar v. Bahrain), decided by the ICJ in 2001, resolved disputes between Qatar and Bahrain over the delimitation of their maritime boundaries and sovereignty over the Hawar Islands and Zubarah. The ICJ's judgment established a maritime boundary line between the two states and clarified their respective territorial claims, promoting stability and cooperation in the Persian Gulf.

The Case Concerning the Arrest Warrant of 11 April 2000 (Democratic Republic of the Congo v. Belgium), decided by the ICJ in 2002, addressed disputes between the Democratic Republic of the Congo and Belgium over Belgium's issuance of an arrest warrant against the Congolese Minister of Foreign Affairs. The ICJ's judgment emphasized the principles of sovereign immunity and the need to respect the legal rights of states and their officials, contributing to the clarification of international law on immunity from legal process for state officials in the context of diplomatic relations.

The Case Concerning the Application of the Convention on the Prevention and Punishment of the Crime of Genocide (Bosnia and Herzegovina v. Serbia and Montenegro), decided by the ICJ in

2007, addressed disputes between Bosnia and Herzegovina and Serbia and Montenegro over allegations of genocide committed during the conflict in Bosnia and Herzegovina in the 1990s. The ICJ's judgment ruled that Serbia was not directly responsible for genocide but failed to prevent genocide from occurring, highlighting the obligations of states to prevent and punish acts of genocide under international law.

The Case Concerning the Legal Status of Eastern Greenland (Denmark v. Norway), decided by the ICJ in 1933, involved disputes between Denmark and Norway over the legal status of Eastern Greenland, including issues related to sovereignty and maritime rights in the Arctic region. The ICJ's judgment affirmed Denmark's sovereignty over Eastern Greenland and clarified the legal status of the territory, contributing to the settlement of disputes in the Arctic area.

The Case Concerning Armed Activities on the Territory of the Congo (Democratic Republic of the Congo v. Uganda), decided by the ICJ in 2005, addressed disputes between the Democratic Republic of the Congo and Uganda over Uganda's military intervention in the Congo during the Second Congo War. The ICJ's judgment condemned Uganda's actions as violations of the Congo's sovereignty and territorial integrity and underscored the principles of non-intervention and peaceful settlement of disputes under international law.

The Case Concerning the Gabcikovo-Nagymaros Project (Hungary v. Slovakia), decided by the ICJ in 1997, involved disputes between Hungary and Slovakia over the construction and operation of a dam system on the Danube River, known as the Gabcikovo-Nagymaros Project. The ICJ's judgment addressed environmental concerns raised by Hungary and Slovakia's compliance with international environmental obligations, highlighting the importance of sustainable development and cooperation in transboundary water management.

The Case Concerning the Frontier Dispute (Burkina Faso v. Mali), brought before the ICJ in 1986, involved disputes between Burkina Faso and Mali over the delimitation of their land and maritime boundaries. The ICJ's judgment established a single boundary line between the two states, based on historical, geographical, and equitable considerations, and provided a framework for the peaceful resolution of disputes between neighboring countries in West Africa.

The Case Concerning the Legal Consequences for States of the Continued Presence of South Africa in Namibia (South West Africa) notwithstanding Security Council Resolution 276 (1970), decided by the ICJ in 1971, addressed disputes between Namibia (then South West Africa) and South Africa over South Africa's continued administration of Namibia in defiance of UN Security Council resolutions. The ICJ's advisory opinion affirmed the illegality of South Africa's presence in Namibia and called for the decolonization and independence of Namibia, highlighting the role of the ICJ in addressing colonial and apartheid-era disputes.

The Case Concerning the Temple of Preah Vihear (Cambodia v. Thailand), which was decided by the ICJ in 1962, revolved around disputes between Cambodia and Thailand regarding the sovereignty of the Temple of Preah Vihear and its surrounding area. The ICJ's judgment awarded sovereignty over the temple to Cambodia and delineated the boundary between the two countries, based on historical and geographical considerations, contributing to the resolution of territorial disputes between Cambodia and Thailand.

The Case Concerning the Kasikili/Sedudu Island (Botswana v. Namibia), decided by the ICJ in 1999, addressed disputes between Botswana and Namibia over the sovereignty of Kasikili/Sedudu Island in the Chobe River. The ICJ's judgment ruled in favor of Botswana's sovereignty over the island, based on historical and geographical factors, and provided a framework for the peaceful resolution of territorial disputes between neighboring countries in Southern Africa.

The Case Concerning Maritime Delimitation and Territorial Questions between Qatar and Bahrain (Qatar v. Bahrain), decided by the ICJ in 2001, resolved disputes between Qatar and Bahrain over the delimitation of their maritime boundaries and sovereignty over the Hawar Islands and Zubarah. The ICJ's judgment established a maritime boundary line between the two states and clarified their respective territorial claims, promoting stability and cooperation in the Persian Gulf.

The Case Concerning the Application of the Convention on the Prevention and Punishment of the Crime of Genocide (Bosnia and Herzegovina v. Serbia and Montenegro), decided by the ICJ in 2007, addressed disputes between Bosnia and Herzegovina and Serbia and Montenegro over allegations of genocide committed during the conflict in Bosnia and Herzegovina in the 1990s. The ICJ's judgment ruled that Serbia was not directly responsible for genocide but failed to prevent genocide from occurring, highlighting the obligations of states to prevent and punish acts of genocide under international law.

Specialized Tribunals and Arbitral Panels

The International Tribunal for the Law of the Sea (ITLOS) is a specialized tribunal established by the United Nations Convention on the Law of the Sea (UNCLOS) to adjudicate disputes related to the interpretation and application of UNCLOS. One notable case before ITLOS is the M/V "Saiga" (No. 2) Case (Saint Vincent and the Grenadines v. Guinea), which concerned the arrest and detention of the vessel M/V "Saiga" by Guinea for alleged illegal fishing activities. ITLOS issued an order for provisional measures directing Guinea to release the vessel and its crew, emphasizing the importance of prompt and effective dispute resolution in maritime matters.

The International Centre for Settlement of Investment Disputes (ICSID) is a specialized arbitral panel established by the Convention on the Settlement of Investment Disputes between States and Nationals of Other States to resolve disputes between foreign investors and host states. One notable case before ICSID is the Occidental Petroleum Corporation v. Republic of Ecuador case, which involved disputes over Ecuador's termination of an oil contract with Occidental Petroleum and subsequent expropriation of its assets. The arbitral panel ruled in favor of Occidental Petroleum, ordering Ecuador to pay substantial compensation for the expropriation, highlighting the role of specialized tribunals in protecting foreign investment.

The International Criminal Court (ICC) is a specialized tribunal established by the Rome Statute to prosecute individuals for genocide, war crimes, crimes against humanity, and the crime of aggression. One notable case before the ICC is the Prosecutor v. Thomas Lubanga Dyilo case, which was the ICC's first trial involving charge of recruiting child soldiers in the Democratic Republic of the Congo. The ICC convicted Lubanga of war crimes and sentenced him to 14 years in prison, underscoring the role of specialized tribunals in holding individuals accountable for serious international crimes.

The World Trade Organization (WTO) Dispute Settlement Body (DSB) is a specialized tribunal established to resolve disputes between member states concerning the interpretation and application of the WTO agreements. One notable case before the WTO DSB is the United States – Measures Affecting the Cross-Border Supply of Gambling and Betting Services case, which involved disputes between Antigua and Barbuda and the United States over U.S. restrictions on online gambling services. The WTO ruled in favor of Antigua and Barbuda, finding that the U.S. measures were inconsistent with WTO rules, highlighting the role of specialized tribunals in promoting compliance with international trade obligations.

The International Criminal Tribunal for the former Yugoslavia (ICTY) was a specialized tribunal established by the United Nations Security Council to prosecute individuals responsible for serious violations of international humanitarian law committed during the conflicts in the former Yugoslavia. One notable case before the ICTY is the Prosecutor v. Radovan Karadžić case, which involved charges of genocide, war crimes, and crimes against humanity against the former President of Republika Srpska. The ICTY convicted Karadžić of numerous crimes and sentenced him to life imprisonment, demonstrating the role of specialized tribunals in addressing impunity for grave international crimes.

The International Tribunal for Rwanda (ICTR) was a specialized tribunal established by the United Nations Security Council to prosecute individuals responsible for genocide and other serious violations of international humanitarian law committed during the 1994 Rwandan genocide. One notable case before the ICTR is the Prosecutor v. Jean-Paul Akayesu case, which was the ICTR's first trial and resulted in the conviction of Akayesu, the former mayor of Taba commune, for genocide and crimes against humanity. The ICTR's judgment set important precedents for prosecuting genocide under international law.

The International Tribunal for the Prosecution of Persons Responsible for Serious Violations of International Humanitarian Law Committed in the Territory of the Former Yugoslavia since 1991, known as the International Criminal Tribunal for the former Yugoslavia (ICTY), was established by the United Nations Security Council in 1993 to prosecute individuals responsible for serious violations of international humanitarian law committed during the conflicts in the former Yugoslavia. One notable case before the ICTY is the Prosecutor v. Radislav Krstić case, which involved charges of genocide, crimes against humanity, and war crimes related to the Srebrenica massacre. Krstić, a Bosnian Serb military commander, was found guilty of aiding and abetting genocide and sentenced to 35 years in prison, underscoring the tribunal's role in holding perpetrators of grave international crimes accountable.

The Special Tribunal for Lebanon (STL) is a specialized tribunal established by the United Nations Security Council to prosecute individuals responsible for the assassination of former Lebanese Prime Minister Rafic Hariri and related crimes. One notable case before the STL is the Prosecutor v. Ayyash et al. case, which involves charges of terrorism, conspiracy, and homicide against four defendants accused of involvement in the 2005 bombing that killed Hariri and 21 others. The STL's proceedings have contributed to efforts to uncover the truth behind Hariri's assassination and hold accountable those responsible for the crime.

The Special Tribunal for Lebanon (STL) is a specialized tribunal established by the United Nations Security Council to prosecute individuals responsible for the assassination of former Lebanese Prime Minister Rafic Hariri and related crimes. One notable case before the STL is the Prosecutor v. Ayyash et al. case, which involves charges of terrorism, conspiracy, and homicide against four defendants accused of involvement in the 2005 bombing that killed Hariri and 21 others. The STL's proceedings have contributed to efforts to uncover the truth behind Hariri's assassination and hold accountable those responsible for the crime.

The Extraordinary Chambers in the Courts of Cambodia (ECCC) is a specialized tribunal established to prosecute senior leaders and those most responsible for crimes committed during the Khmer Rouge regime in Cambodia. One notable case before the ECCC is the Case 001 against Kaing Guek Eav, also known as Duch, the former head of the S-21 prison where thousands were tortured and executed. Duch was found guilty of crimes against humanity and war crimes and sentenced to life imprisonment, marking the first conviction by the ECCC and providing justice for victims of the Khmer Rouge atrocities.

The Extraordinary Chambers in the Courts of Cambodia (ECCC) is a specialized tribunal established to prosecute senior leaders and those most responsible for crimes committed during the Khmer Rouge regime in Cambodia. One notable case before the ECCC is the Case 001 against Kaing Guek Eav, also known as Duch, the former head of the S-21 prison where thousands were tortured and executed. Duch was found guilty of crimes against humanity and war crimes and sentenced to life imprisonment, marking the first conviction by the ECCC and providing justice for victims of the Khmer Rouge atrocities.

The International Criminal Court (ICC) is a specialized tribunal established by the Rome Statute to prosecute individuals for genocide, war crimes, crimes against humanity, and the crime of aggression. One notable case before the ICC is the Prosecutor v. Germain Katanga and Mathieu Ngudjolo Chui case, which involved charges of war crimes and crimes against humanity committed during the conflict in the Democratic Republic of the Congo. The ICC acquitted Ngudjolo of all charges due to insufficient evidence, highlighting the importance of rigorous legal standards in international criminal proceedings.

The International Criminal Tribunal for the former Yugoslavia (ICTY) was a specialized tribunal established by the United Nations Security Council to prosecute individuals responsible for serious violations of international humanitarian law committed during the conflicts in the former Yugoslavia. One notable case before the ICTY is the Prosecutor v. Ratko Mladić case, which involved charges of genocide, war crimes, and crimes against humanity against the former Bosnian Serb military leader. Mladić was convicted of numerous crimes, including genocide, and sentenced to life imprisonment, underscoring the tribunal's role in delivering justice for victims of the Yugoslav wars.

The International Tribunal for the Law of the Sea (ITLOS) is a specialized tribunal established by the United Nations Convention on the Law of the Sea (UNCLOS) to adjudicate disputes related to the interpretation and application of UNCLOS. One notable case before ITLOS is the Land Reclamation by Singapore in and around the Straits of Johor (Malaysia v. Singapore) case, which involved disputes between Malaysia and Singapore over land reclamation activities in the Straits of Johor. ITLOS's judgment provided guidance on the obligations of states to protect the marine environment and preserve navigational rights in international straits.

The International Centre for Settlement of Investment Disputes (ICSID) is a specialized arbitral panel established by the Convention on the Settlement of Investment Disputes between States and Nationals of Other States to resolve disputes between foreign investors and host states. One notable case before ICSID is the Occidental Petroleum Corporation v. Republic of Ecuador case, which involved disputes over Ecuador's termination of an oil contract with Occidental Petroleum and subsequent expropriation of its assets. The arbitral panel ruled in favor of Occidental Petroleum, ordering Ecuador to pay substantial compensation for the expropriation, highlighting the role of specialized tribunals in protecting foreign investment.

The World Trade Organization (WTO) Dispute Settlement Body (DSB) is a specialized tribunal established to resolve disputes between member states concerning the interpretation and application of the WTO agreements. One notable case before the WTO DSB is the United States – Measures Affecting the Cross-Border Supply of Gambling and Betting Services case, which involved disputes between Antigua and Barbuda and the United States over U.S. restrictions on online gambling services. The WTO ruled in favor of Antigua and Barbuda, finding that the U.S. measures were inconsistent with WTO rules, highlighting the role of specialized tribunals in promoting compliance with international trade obligations.

The International Criminal Tribunal for the former Yugoslavia (ICTY) was a specialized tribunal established by the United Nations Security Council to prosecute individuals responsible for serious violations of international humanitarian law committed during the conflicts in the former Yugoslavia. One notable case before the ICTY is the Prosecutor v. Radovan Karadžić case, which involved charges of genocide, crimes against humanity, and war crimes related to the Srebrenica massacre. Karadžić, a Bosnian Serb political leader, was found guilty of numerous crimes and sentenced to life imprisonment, demonstrating the tribunal's role in holding perpetrators of grave international crimes accountable.

The International Tribunal for Rwanda (ICTR) was a specialized tribunal established by the United Nations Security Council to prosecute individuals responsible for genocide and other serious violations of international humanitarian law committed during the 1994 Rwandan genocide. One notable case before the ICTR is the Prosecutor v. Jean-Paul Akayesu case, which was the ICTR's first trial and resulted in the conviction of Akayesu, the former mayor of Taba commune, for genocide and crimes against humanity. The ICTR's judgment set important precedents for prosecuting genocide under international law.

The International Tribunal for the Prosecution of Persons Responsible for Serious Violations of International Humanitarian Law Committed in the Territory of the Former Yugoslavia since 1991, known as the International Criminal Tribunal for the former Yugoslavia (ICTY), was established by the United Nations Security Council in 1993 to prosecute individuals responsible for serious violations of international humanitarian law committed during the conflicts in the former Yugoslavia. One notable case before the ICTY is the Prosecutor v. Ratko Mladić case, which involved charges of genocide, war crimes, and crimes against humanity against the former Bosnian Serb military leader. Mladić was convicted of numerous crimes, including genocide, and sentenced to life imprisonment, underscoring the tribunal's role in delivering justice for victims of the Yugoslav wars.
and providing justice for victims of the Khmer Rouge atrocities.

The Special Tribunal for Lebanon (STL) is a specialized tribunal established by the United Nations Security Council to prosecute individuals responsible for the assassination of former Lebanese Prime Minister Rafic Hariri and related crimes. One notable case before the STL is the Prosecutor vs Ayyash et al. case, which involves charges of terrorism, conspiracy, and homicide against four defendants accused of involvement in the 2005 bombing that killed Hariri and 21 others. The STL's proceedings have contributed to efforts to uncover the truth behind Hariri's assassination and hold accountable those responsible for the crime, despite challenges and delays in the trial process.

The International Criminal Court (ICC) is a specialized tribunal established by the Rome Statute to prosecute individuals for genocide, war crimes, crimes against humanity, and the crime of aggression. One notable case before the ICC is the Prosecutor v. Germain Katanga and Mathieu Ngudjolo Chui case, which involved charges of war crimes and crimes against humanity committed during the conflict in the Democratic Republic of the Congo. The ICC acquitted Ngudjolo of all charges due to insufficient evidence, highlighting the importance of rigorous legal standards in international criminal proceedings.

The International Criminal Tribunal for the former Yugoslavia (ICTY) was a specialized tribunal established by the United Nations Security Council to prosecute individuals responsible for serious violations of international humanitarian law committed during the conflicts in the former Yugoslavia. One notable case before the ICTY is the Prosecutor v. Ratko Mladić case, which involved charges of genocide, war crimes, and crimes against humanity against the former Bosnian Serb military leader. Mladić was convicted of numerous crimes, including genocide, and sentenced to life imprisonment, underscoring the tribunal's role in delivering justice for victims of the Yugoslav wars.

The International Tribunal for the Law of the Sea (ITLOS) is a specialized tribunal established by the United Nations Convention on the Law of the Sea (UNCLOS) to adjudicate disputes related to the interpretation and application of UNCLOS. One notable case before ITLOS is the Land Reclamation by Singapore in and around the Straits of Johor (Malaysia v. Singapore) case, which involved disputes between Malaysia and Singapore over land reclamation activities in the Straits of Johor. ITLOS's judgment provided guidance on the obligations of states to protect the marine environment and preserve navigational rights in international straits.

The International Centre for Settlement of Investment Disputes (ICSID) is a specialized arbitral panel established by the Convention on the Settlement of Investment Disputes between States and Nationals of Other States to resolve disputes between foreign investors and host states. One notable case before ICSID is the Occidental Petroleum Corporation v. Republic of Ecuador case, which involved disputes over Ecuador's termination of an oil contract with Occidental Petroleum and subsequent expropriation of its assets. The arbitral panel ruled in favor of Occidental Petroleum, ordering Ecuador to pay substantial compensation for the expropriation, highlighting the role of specialized tribunals in protecting foreign investment.

The World Trade Organization (WTO) Dispute Settlement Body (DSB) is a specialized tribunal established to resolve disputes between member states concerning the interpretation and application of the WTO agreements. One notable case before the WTO DSB is the United States – Measures Affecting the Cross-Border Supply of Gambling and Betting Services case, which involved disputes between Antigua and Barbuda and the United States over U.S. restrictions on online gambling services. The WTO ruled in favor of Antigua and Barbuda, finding that the U.S. measures were inconsistent with WTO rules, highlighting the role of specialized tribunals in promoting compliance with international trade obligations.

The International Criminal Tribunal for the former Yugoslavia (ICTY) was a specialized tribunal established by the United Nations Security Council to prosecute individuals responsible for serious violations of international humanitarian law committed during the conflicts in the former Yugoslavia. One notable case before the ICTY is the Prosecutor v. Radovan Karadžić case, which involved charges of genocide, crimes against humanity, and war crimes related to the Srebrenica massacre. Karadžić, a Bosnian Serb political leader, was found guilty of numerous crimes and sentenced to life imprisonment, demonstrating the tribunal's role in holding perpetrators of grave international crimes accountable.

The International Tribunal for Rwanda (ICTR) was a specialized tribunal established by the United Nations Security Council to prosecute individuals responsible for genocide and other serious violations of international humanitarian law committed during the 1994 Rwandan genocide. One notable case before the ICTR is the Prosecutor v. Jean-Paul Akayesu case, which was the ICTR's first trial and resulted in the conviction of Akayesu, the former mayor of Taba commune, for genocide and crimes against humanity. The ICTR's judgment set important precedents for prosecuting genocide under international law.

The International Tribunal for the Prosecution of Persons Responsible for Serious Violations of International Humanitarian Law Committed in the Territory of the Former Yugoslavia since 1991, known as the International Criminal Tribunal for the former Yugoslavia (ICTY), was established by the United Nations Security Council in 1993 to prosecute individuals responsible for serious violations of international humanitarian law committed during the conflicts in the former Yugoslavia. One notable case before the ICTY is the Prosecutor v. Ratko Mladić case, which involved charges of genocide, war crimes, and crimes against humanity against the former Bosnian Serb military leader. Mladić was convicted of numerous crimes, including genocide, and sentenced to life imprisonment, underscoring the tribunal's role in delivering justice for victims of the Yugoslav wars.

The International Centre for Settlement of Investment Disputes (ICSID) is a specialized arbitral panel established by the Convention on the Settlement of Investment Disputes between States and Nationals of Other States to resolve disputes between foreign investors and host states. One notable case before ICSID is the Occidental Petroleum Corporation v. Republic of Ecuador case, which involved disputes over Ecuador's termination of an oil contract with Occidental Petroleum and subsequent expropriation of its assets. The arbitral panel ruled in favor of Occidental Petroleum, ordering Ecuador to pay substantial compensation for the expropriation, highlighting the role of specialized tribunals in protecting foreign investment.

The International Criminal Court (ICC) is a specialized tribunal established by the Rome Statute to prosecute individuals for genocide, war crimes, crimes against humanity, and the crime of aggression. One notable case before the ICC is the Prosecutor v. Thomas Lubanga Dyilo case, which was the ICC's first trial involving charges of recruiting child soldiers in the Democratic Republic of the Congo. The ICC convicted Lubanga of war crimes and sentenced him to 14 years in prison, underscoring the role of specialized tribunals in holding individuals accountable for serious international crimes.

The World Trade Organization (WTO) Dispute Settlement Body (DSB) is a specialized tribunal established to resolve disputes between member states concerning the interpretation and application of the WTO agreements. One notable case before the WTO DSB is the United States – Measures Affecting the Cross-Border Supply of Gambling and Betting Services case, which involved disputes between Antigua and Barbuda and the United States over U.S. restrictions on online gambling services. The WTO ruled in favor of Antigua and Barbuda, finding that the U.S. measures were inconsistent with WTO rules, highlighting the role of specialized tribunals in promoting compliance with international trade obligations.

The International Criminal Tribunal for the former Yugoslavia (ICTY) was a specialized tribunal established by the United Nations Security Council to prosecute individuals responsible for serious violations of international humanitarian law committed during the conflicts in the former Yugoslavia. One notable case before the ICTY is the Prosecutor v. Radovan Karadžić case, which involved charges of genocide, crimes against humanity, and war crimes related to the Srebrenica massacre. Karadžić, a Bosnian Serb political leader, was found guilty of numerous crimes and sentenced to life imprisonment, demonstrating the tribunal's role in holding perpetrators of grave international crimes accountable.

The International Tribunal for Rwanda (ICTR) was a specialized tribunal established by the United Nations Security Council to prosecute individuals responsible for genocide and other serious violations of international humanitarian law committed during the 1994 Rwandan genocide. One notable case before the ICTR is the Prosecutor v. Jean-Paul Akayesu case, which was the ICTR's first trial and resulted in the conviction of Akayesu, the former mayor of Taba commune, for genocide and crimes against humanity. The ICTR's judgment set important precedents for prosecuting genocide under international law.

The International Tribunal for the Prosecution of Persons Responsible for Serious Violations of International Humanitarian

Law Committed in the Territory of the Former Yugoslavia since 1991, known as the International Criminal Tribunal for the former Yugoslavia (ICTY), was established by the United Nations Security Council in 1993 to prosecute individuals responsible for serious violations of international humanitarian law committed during the conflicts in the former Yugoslavia. One notable case before the ICTY is the Prosecutor v. Ratko Mladić case, which involved charges of genocide, war crimes, and crimes against humanity against the former Bosnian Serb military leader. Mladić was convicted of numerous crimes, including genocide, and sentenced to life imprisonment, underscoring the tribunal's role in delivering justice for victims of the Yugoslav wars.

The Special Tribunal for Lebanon (STL) is a specialized tribunal established by the United Nations Security Council to prosecute individuals responsible for the assassination of former Lebanese Prime Minister Rafic Hariri and related crimes. One notable case before the STL is the Prosecutor v. Ayyash et al. case, which involves charges of terrorism, conspiracy, and homicide against four defendants accused of involvement in the 2005 bombing that killed Hariri and 21 others. The STL's proceedings have contributed to efforts to uncover the truth behind Hariri's assassination and hold accountable those responsible for the crime, despite challenges and delays in the trial process.

The Extraordinary Chambers in the Courts of Cambodia (ECCC) is a specialized tribunal established to prosecute senior leaders and those most responsible for crimes committed during the Khmer Rouge regime in Cambodia. One notable case before the ECCC is the Case 001 against Kaing Guek Eav, also known as Duch, the former head of the S-21 prison where thousands were tortured and executed. Duch was found guilty of crimes against humanity and war crimes and sentenced to life imprisonment, marking the first conviction by the ECCC and providing justice for victims of the Khmer Rouge atrocities.

Chapter 9.
Contemporary Issues and Emerging Challenges

Climate Change and its Impact on Maritime Boundaries

Climate change poses significant challenges to maritime boundaries due to its impact on sea levels, coastal erosion, and the distribution of marine resources. One example of this is the case of Tuvalu, a low-lying island nation in the Pacific Ocean, which is facing the threat of inundation and loss of territory due to rising sea levels caused by climate change. As sea levels rise, the maritime boundaries of Tuvalu may shift, leading to disputes over territorial claims and exclusive economic zones (EEZs) with neighboring countries.

The case of Kiribati provides another example of the impact of climate change on maritime boundaries. Kiribati, an island nation in the central Pacific Ocean, is experiencing coastal erosion and saltwater intrusion into freshwater sources due to rising sea levels. As a result, the maritime boundaries of Kiribati may need to be redefined to account for changes in the coastline and territorial waters, potentially leading to disputes with neighboring countries over fishing rights and resource exploitation.

In the Arctic region, melting ice caps are opening up new shipping routes and resource extraction opportunities, raising questions about the delimitation of maritime boundaries. The Arctic coastal states, including Russia, Canada, Denmark (via Greenland), Norway, and the United States, are seeking to assert their sovereignty over vast areas of the Arctic Ocean, leading to tensions and disputes over territorial claims and resource rights.

The case of Bangladesh illustrates the vulnerability of coastal communities to the impacts of climate change on maritime boundaries. Bangladesh, a densely populated country with a low-lying coastline, is experiencing increased flooding and salinization of agricultural land due to rising sea levels and more intense storms. These environmental changes may necessitate adjustments to Bangladesh's maritime boundaries, potentially leading to disputes with neighboring countries over fishing grounds and offshore resources.

The Maldives, an archipelago nation in the Indian Ocean, is facing the threat of sea-level rise, which could submerge many of its low-lying islands and reefs. As a result, the maritime boundaries of the Maldives may need to be redefined to account for changes in the coastline and territorial waters, potentially leading to disputes with neighboring countries over fishing rights and maritime jurisdiction.

The case of Indonesia highlights the complex legal and geopolitical issues surrounding climate change and maritime boundaries. Indonesia, an archipelagic state with thousands of islands scattered across the Indian and Pacific Oceans, is facing challenges related to the delimitation of its maritime boundaries, particularly in the context of overlapping claims with neighboring countries such as Malaysia, Singapore, and the Philippines.

In the Caribbean region, small island states such as Barbados, Jamaica, and Trinidad and Tobago are experiencing the impacts of climate change on their maritime boundaries. Rising sea levels, coral bleaching, and ocean acidification are threatening marine ecosystems and coastal communities, leading to concerns about the loss of territory and resources.

The case of Fiji illustrates the intersection of climate change, maritime boundaries, and indigenous rights. Fiji, an archipelago nation in the South Pacific, is experiencing the impacts of sea-level rise, coastal erosion, and extreme weather events, which are affecting the livelihoods of indigenous communities that depend on the ocean for sustenance and cultural practices. These communities are calling for greater recognition of their rights and interests in the management of maritime resources and boundaries.

The Pacific Islands Forum Fisheries Agency (FFA) is working to address the challenges posed by climate change to maritime boundaries and fisheries management in the Pacific region. The FFA facilitates cooperation among member states to develop sustainable fisheries policies and practices that take into account the impacts of climate change on marine ecosystems and coastal communities.

In the South China Sea, climate change is exacerbating existing tensions over maritime boundaries and territorial disputes among countries in the region, including China, Vietnam, the Philippines, Malaysia, and Brunei. Rising sea levels, coral reef degradation, and extreme weather events are affecting the strategic and environmental dynamics of the South China Sea, leading to concerns about maritime security and resource competition.

The case of Japan illustrates the complex legal and geopolitical issues surrounding climate change and maritime boundaries in the context of island disputes. Japan is involved in territorial disputes with neighboring countries such as China and South Korea over the sovereignty of islands in the East China Sea and the Sea of Japan, which are further complicated by the potential impacts of climate change on the delimitation of maritime boundaries.

In the Gulf of Mexico, coastal states such as the United States, Mexico, and Cuba are facing the impacts of climate change on their maritime boundaries and coastal ecosystems. Rising sea levels, storm surges, and ocean acidification are affecting marine biodiversity, fisheries, and coastal infrastructure, leading to concerns about the management of transboundary resources and the resolution of maritime disputes.

The case of Brazil highlights the challenges of addressing climate change impacts on maritime boundaries and marine biodiversity in the context of the Amazon River basin. Brazil is experiencing deforestation, riverine pollution, and habitat loss due to climate change and human activities, which are affecting the health of marine ecosystems and the livelihoods of coastal communities dependent on fisheries and tourism.

The International Maritime Organization (IMO) is working to address the impacts of climate change on maritime boundaries and shipping routes through the development of regulations and guidelines for reducing greenhouse gas emissions and promoting sustainable maritime transport. The IMO's efforts aim to mitigate the environmental and economic risks associated with climate change in the maritime sector.

The case of Australia illustrates the challenges of managing maritime boundaries and marine resources in the context of climate change and ocean acidification. Australia is experiencing coral bleaching, sea-level rise, and ocean warming, which are affecting the Great Barrier Reef and other marine ecosystems, leading to concerns about the protection of biodiversity and the sustainability of fisheries.

In the Mediterranean Sea, coastal states such as Italy, Greece, Turkey, and Egypt are facing the impacts of climate change on maritime boundaries and coastal development. Rising sea levels, coastal erosion, and saltwater intrusion are affecting coastal infrastructure, tourism, and fisheries, leading to calls for integrated coastal zone management and adaptation strategies.

The case of Somalia highlights the challenges of addressing climate change impacts on maritime boundaries and maritime security in the context of fragile states and conflict zones. Somalia is experiencing desertification, drought, and extreme weather events, which are exacerbating food insecurity, displacement, and maritime piracy, leading to concerns about the stability of the region and the protection of maritime trade routes.

The Indian Ocean Rim Association (IORA) is working to

address the impacts of climate change on maritime boundaries and marine resources in the Indian Ocean region through cooperation and capacity-building initiatives. IORA's member states, including India, South Africa, Indonesia, and Australia, are collaborating on research, policy development, and resource management strategies to mitigate the environmental and socio-economic risks associated with climate change in the region.

The case of Nigeria illustrates the challenges of addressing climate change impacts on maritime boundaries and coastal communities in the context of oil pollution and environmental degradation. Nigeria's Niger Delta region is experiencing the impacts of climate change, including sea-level rise, coastal erosion, and extreme weather events, which are exacerbating the socio-economic and environmental vulnerabilities of local communities dependent on fishing and agriculture.

The United Nations Framework Convention on Climate Change (UNFCCC) is a key international treaty that addresses climate change by promoting mitigation and adaptation measures. Under the UNFCCC, countries are encouraged to cooperate on climate-related issues, including the impacts of climate change on maritime boundaries and coastal areas. The UNFCCC's Conference of the Parties (COP) meetings provide a platform for countries to discuss and negotiate climate action, including measures to address the impacts of climate change on marine ecosystems and maritime boundaries.

The case of Chile highlights the challenges of addressing climate change impacts on maritime boundaries and coastal communities in the context of natural disasters and environmental degradation. Chile's long coastline is vulnerable to sea-level rise, coastal erosion, and ocean acidification, which are affecting coastal ecosystems, fisheries, and tourism. Chile is implementing adaptation measures, such as coastal protection and sustainable resource management, to mitigate the impacts of climate change on maritime boundaries and marine biodiversity.

In the Caribbean region, small island developing states such as Grenada, Saint Lucia, and Dominica are facing the impacts of climate change on their maritime boundaries and coastal infrastructure. Rising sea levels, coastal erosion, and storm surges are threatening coastal communities, tourism, and fisheries, leading to calls for international support and cooperation to address the challenges of climate change adaptation and resilience-building.

The case of Mauritius illustrates the challenges of addressing climate change impacts on maritime boundaries and marine biodiversity in the context of small island developing states. Mauritius is experiencing sea-level rise, coral bleaching, and coastal erosion, which are affecting marine ecosystems, fisheries, and tourism. The government of Mauritius is working to implement adaptation measures, such as marine protected areas and sustainable fisheries management, to protect its maritime boundaries and coastal resources.

The Regional Organization for the Conservation of the Environment of the Red Sea and Gulf of Aden (PERSGA) is working to address the impacts of climate change on maritime boundaries and marine biodiversity in the Red Sea and Gulf of Aden region. PERSGA's member states, including Egypt, Saudi Arabia, Sudan, and Yemen, are collaborating on research, monitoring, and conservation initiatives to mitigate the environmental and socio-economic risks associated with climate change in the region.

The case of Indonesia highlights the challenges of addressing climate change impacts on maritime boundaries and marine biodiversity in the context of coral reef degradation and habitat loss. Indonesia's extensive coral reef ecosystems are vulnerable to bleaching, disease, and ocean acidification, which are affecting marine biodiversity, fisheries, and coastal communities. Indonesia is implementing conservation measures, such as marine protected areas and sustainable fishing practices, to protect its maritime boundaries and marine resources from the impacts of climate change.

In the South Pacific, regional organizations such as the Secretariat of the Pacific Regional Environment Programme (SPREP) are working to address the impacts of climate change on maritime boundaries and marine ecosystems. SPREP's member states, including Fiji, Samoa, and Vanuatu, are collaborating on adaptation and resilience-building initiatives to protect coastal communities, fisheries, and biodiversity from the effects of climate change, including sea-level rise, coastal erosion, and ocean acidification.

case of Bangladesh illustrates the challenges of addressing climate change impacts on maritime boundaries and coastal communities in the context of population pressure and land scarcity. Bangladesh's densely populated coastline is vulnerable to sea-level rise, cyclones, and saltwater intrusion, which are affecting agriculture, fisheries, and infrastructure. Bangladesh is implementing adaptation measures, such as coastal embankments and climate-resilient agriculture, to protect its maritime boundaries and coastal resources from the impacts of climate change.

The Pacific Islands Development Forum (PIDF) is working to address the impacts of climate change on maritime boundaries and coastal communities in the Pacific region. PIDF's member states, including Fiji, Papua New Guinea, and the Solomon Islands, are collaborating on adaptation and resilience-building initiatives to protect coastal ecosystems, fisheries, and livelihoods from the effects of climate change, including sea-level rise, coastal erosion, and extreme weather events.

The case of Seychelles highlights the challenges of addressing climate change impacts on maritime boundaries and marine biodiversity in the context of tourism and economic development. Seychelles' coral reef ecosystems are vulnerable to bleaching, disease, and ocean acidification, which are affecting marine biodiversity, fisheries, and tourism. Seychelles is implementing conservation measures, such as marine protected areas and sustainable tourism practices, to protect its maritime boundaries and marine resources from the impacts of climate change.

In the Indian Ocean, regional organizations such as the Indian Ocean Commission (IOC) are working to address the impacts of climate change on maritime boundaries and marine biodiversity. IOC's member states, including Comoros, Madagascar, and Mauritius, are collaborating on adaptation and resilience-building initiatives to protect coastal communities, fisheries, and biodiversity from the effects of climate change, including sea-level rise, coastal erosion, and ocean acidification.

The case of Sri Lanka illustrates the challenges of addressing climate change impacts on maritime boundaries and coastal communities in the context of natural disasters and environmental degradation. Sri Lanka's coastline is vulnerable to sea-level rise, coastal erosion, and storm surges, which are affecting coastal ecosystems, fisheries, and tourism. Sri Lanka is implementing adaptation measures, such as coastal protection and disaster risk management, to protect its maritime boundaries and coastal resources from the impacts of climate change.

The Caribbean Community Climate Change Centre (CCCCC) is working to address the impacts of climate change on maritime boundaries and coastal communities in the Caribbean region. CCCCC's member states, including Belize, Jamaica, and Trinidad and Tobago, are collaborating on adaptation and resilience-building initiatives to protect coastal ecosystems, fisheries, and livelihoods from the effects of climate change, including sea-level rise, coastal erosion, and extreme weather events.

The case of Mozambique highlights the challenges of addressing climate change impacts on maritime boundaries and coastal communities in the context of natural disasters and environmental degradation. Mozambique's coastline is vulnerable to sea-level rise, coastal erosion, and cyclones, which are affecting coastal ecosystems, fisheries, and agriculture. Mozambique is implementing adaptation measures, such as mangrove restoration and climate-resilient infrastructure, to protect its maritime boundaries and coastal resources from the impacts of climate change.

The Pacific Islands Forum (PIF) is working to address the impacts of climate change on maritime boundaries and coastal communities in the Pacific region. PIF's member states, including

Kiribati, Nauru, and Tuvalu, are collaborating on adaptation and resilience-building initiatives to protect coastal ecosystems, fisheries, and livelihoods from the effects of climate change, including sea-level rise, coastal erosion, and ocean acidification.

The case of Vietnam illustrates the challenges of addressing climate change impacts on maritime boundaries and coastal communities in the context of rapid urbanization and industrialization. Vietnam's coastline is vulnerable to sea-level rise, coastal erosion, and pollution, which are affecting coastal ecosystems, fisheries, and tourism. Vietnam is implementing adaptation measures, such as coastal protection and pollution control, to protect its maritime boundaries and coastal resources from the impacts of climate change.

The Indian Ocean Rim Association (IORA) is working to address the impacts of climate change on maritime boundaries and marine biodiversity in the Indian Ocean region. IORA's member states, including India, South Africa, and Indonesia, are collaborating on adaptation and resilience-building initiatives to protect coastal ecosystems, fisheries, and livelihoods from the effects of climate change, including sea-level rise, coastal erosion, and ocean acidification.

The case of Ecuador highlights the challenges of addressing climate change impacts on maritime boundaries and coastal communities in the context of biodiversity conservation and sustainable development. Ecuador's Galápagos Islands, a UNESCO World Heritage Site, are vulnerable to sea-level rise, coral bleaching, and invasive species, which are affecting marine biodiversity, fisheries, and tourism. Ecuador is implementing adaptation measures, such as marine protected areas and sustainable tourism practices, to protect its maritime boundaries and marine resources from the impacts of climate change.

The Organization of Eastern Caribbean States (OECS) is working to address the impacts of climate change on maritime boundaries and coastal communities in the Eastern Caribbean region. OECS's member states, including Saint Kitts and Nevis, Saint Vincent and the Grenadines, and Antigua and Barbuda, are collaborating on adaptation and resilience-building initiatives to protect coastal ecosystems, fisheries, and livelihoods from the effects of climate change, including sea-level rise, coastal erosion, and ocean acidification.

The case of Ghana illustrates the challenges of addressing climate change impacts on maritime boundaries and coastal communities in the context of economic development and infrastructure investment. Ghana's coastline is vulnerable to sea-level rise, coastal erosion, and pollution, which are affecting coastal ecosystems, fisheries, and tourism. Ghana is implementing adaptation measures, such as coastal protection and sustainable development planning, to protect its maritime boundaries and coastal resources from the impacts of climate change.

The Indian Ocean Commission (IOC) is working to address the impacts of climate change on maritime boundaries and marine biodiversity in the Indian Ocean region. IOC's member states, including Madagascar, Mauritius, and the Seychelles, are collaborating on adaptation and resilience-building initiatives to protect coastal ecosystems, fisheries, and livelihoods from the effects of climate change, including sea-level rise, coastal erosion, and ocean acidification.

The case of Maldives highlights the urgent need to address climate change impacts on maritime boundaries and coastal communities in low-lying island nations. Maldives is one of the most vulnerable countries to sea-level rise, with much of its landmass lying just a few meters above sea level. Coastal erosion, coral bleaching, and saltwater intrusion threaten the country's freshwater resources, agriculture, and tourism industry. Maldives has been advocating for global action on climate change and investing in adaptation measures such as artificial reefs and coastal protection infrastructure to safeguard its maritime boundaries and ensure the resilience of its coastal communities.

The Association of Southeast Asian Nations (ASEAN) is working to address the impacts of climate change on maritime boundaries and coastal ecosystems in the Southeast Asian region. ASEAN's member states, including Thailand, Vietnam, and the

Philippines, are collaborating on adaptation and mitigation strategies to protect coastal areas, fisheries, and biodiversity from the effects of climate change, including sea-level rise, ocean acidification, and extreme weather events.

The case of Bangladesh underscores the importance of international cooperation in addressing climate change impacts on maritime boundaries and coastal communities in densely populated delta regions. Bangladesh is experiencing increased frequency and intensity of cyclones, flooding, and saltwater intrusion, which are exacerbating land loss, displacement, and food insecurity. Bangladesh is working with neighboring countries and international organizations to develop adaptation measures, such as coastal embankments, early warning systems, and community-based resilience initiatives to protect its maritime boundaries and enhance the adaptive capacity of its coastal populations.

The Caribbean Community Climate Change Centre (CCCCC) is facilitating regional collaboration and knowledge exchange to address climate change impacts on maritime boundaries and coastal ecosystems in the Caribbean region. CCCCC's member states, including Barbados, Grenada, and Belize, are implementing adaptation and mitigation measures to protect coastal areas, fisheries, and tourism from the impacts of climate change, including sea-level rise, coral bleaching, and ocean acidification.

The case of Australia highlights the complex challenges of balancing economic development with environmental conservation in managing maritime boundaries and coastal resources. Australia's Great Barrier Reef, the world's largest coral reef ecosystem, is under threat from climate change, pollution, and overfishing, which are affecting biodiversity, tourism, and traditional livelihoods. Australia is implementing conservation measures, such as marine protected areas and sustainable tourism practices, to protect its maritime boundaries and preserve the ecological integrity of its coastal ecosystems.

The Caribbean Community Climate Change Centre (CCCCC) is supporting regional initiatives to address climate change impacts on maritime boundaries and coastal communities in the Caribbean region. CCCCC's member states, including Saint Lucia, Jamaica, and Dominica, are collaborating on adaptation and resilience-building initiatives to protect coastal ecosystems, fisheries, and livelihoods from the effects of climate change, including sea-level rise, coastal erosion, and extreme weather events.

The case of Vietnam highlights the challenges of addressing climate change impacts on maritime boundaries and coastal communities in the context of rapid economic development and urbanization. Vietnam's coastline is vulnerable to sea-level rise, coastal erosion, and pollution, which are affecting coastal ecosystems, fisheries, and tourism. Vietnam is implementing adaptation measures, such as coastal protection and disaster risk management, to protect its maritime boundaries and coastal resources from the impacts of climate change.

The Pacific Islands Forum (PIF) is facilitating regional cooperation and capacity-building to address climate change impacts on maritime boundaries and coastal ecosystems in the Pacific region. PIF's member states, including Fiji, Samoa, and Tonga, are implementing adaptation and resilience-building initiatives to protect coastal areas, fisheries, and livelihoods from the effects of climate change, including sea-level rise, coastal erosion, and ocean acidification.

The case of Indonesia underscores the importance of integrated coastal management and ecosystem-based approaches in addressing climate change impacts on maritime boundaries and coastal communities. Indonesia's vast archipelago is home to diverse marine ecosystems and coastal communities that are vulnerable to sea-level rise, coastal erosion, and pollution. Indonesia is implementing adaptation measures, such as marine protected areas and sustainable fisheries management, to protect its maritime boundaries and enhance the resilience of its coastal populations.

The Caribbean Community Climate Change Centre (CCCCC) is working with regional partners to address climate change impacts on maritime boundaries and coastal ecosystems in the Caribbean region. CCCCC's member states, including Trinidad and Tobago, Barbados, and Guyana, are collaborating on adaptation and resilience-building initiatives to protect coastal areas, fisheries, and livelihoods from the effects of climate change, including sea-level rise, coastal erosion, and extreme weather events. Through capacity-building, research, and policy support, CCCCC is helping to enhance the adaptive capacity of Caribbean countries to address the challenges of climate change in the maritime domain.

Piracy and Maritime Terrorism

Piracy and maritime terrorism pose significant challenges to international maritime security, threatening the safety of navigation, the security of maritime trade routes, and the stability of coastal states. One notable case is the piracy off the coast of Somalia, where pirates have hijacked commercial vessels, kidnapped crew members, and demanded ransom payments. The international community, through initiatives such as Combined Task Force 151 and the European Union Naval Force Somalia (Operation Atalanta), has deployed naval forces to patrol the waters of the Gulf of Aden and the Indian Ocean to counter piracy activities.

The Strait of Malacca, one of the world's busiest and most strategically important waterways, has been a hotspot for piracy and maritime terrorism. In recent years, incidents of piracy, armed robbery, and maritime terrorism, including hijackings and attacks on vessels, has occurred in the waters of the Malacca Strait, raising concerns about maritime security in the region. The littoral states of Indonesia, Malaysia, and Singapore, along with international partners, have implemented joint patrols, intelligence-sharing mechanisms, and capacity-building initiatives to enhance maritime security and combat piracy and maritime terrorism in the Malacca Strait.

In the Gulf of Guinea, piracy has become a major maritime

security threat, with incidents of vessel hijackings, crew kidnappings, and cargo thefts occurring frequently in the waters off the coast of West Africa. Countries in the region, such as Nigeria, Benin, and Togo, have established maritime security frameworks, including joint naval patrols and information-sharing mechanisms, to address the root causes of piracy and enhance maritime law enforcement capabilities.

The Sulu and Celebes Seas in Southeast Asia have also experienced a rise in piracy and maritime terrorism activities, particularly off the coast of the Philippines and Malaysia. Armed groups, such as the Abu Sayyaf Group and the Maute Group, have carried out kidnappings-for-ransom and attacks on vessels, posing a threat to maritime security and regional stability. Joint maritime patrols, intelligence-sharing arrangements, and capacity-building efforts between littoral states and international partners have been implemented to address the challenges of piracy and maritime terrorism in the Sulu and Celebes Seas.

The case of Yemen highlights the nexus between piracy, maritime terrorism, and political instability in the region. The ongoing conflict in Yemen has created a security vacuum, allowing armed groups and criminal networks to exploit maritime routes for illicit activities, including piracy, arms smuggling, and terrorist financing. The international community, through initiatives such as the United Nations Verification and Inspection Mechanism (UNVIM), is working to strengthen maritime security and prevent the proliferation of weapons and illicit goods through Yemen's maritime domain.

The Horn of Africa, where the threat of piracy and maritime terrorism continues to pose challenges to maritime security despite the efforts to counter piracy off the coast of Somalia. The instability in Somalia, weak governance, and lack of law enforcement capacity has contributed to the persistence of piracy activities in the region. International naval forces, including those deployed as part of Operation Atalanta and the NATO-led Operation Ocean Shield, continue to conduct patrols and escort missions to deter piracy and protect merchant shipping in the waters of the Indian Ocean.

The case of Nigeria illustrates the complex nature of maritime security threats, including piracy, maritime terrorism, and oil theft, in the Gulf of Guinea. The Niger Delta region, home to Nigeria's oil and gas industry, has been plagued by piracy attacks, kidnappings, and illegal oil bunkering activities, undermining maritime security and economic development. Nigeria, along with neighboring countries and international partners, has launched joint maritime security initiatives, such as the Yaoundé Code of Conduct and the Gulf of Guinea Commission, to address the root causes of maritime insecurity and promote regional cooperation in combating piracy and maritime terrorism.

The South China Sea, a vital maritime corridor for international trade and commerce, has witnessed tensions and disputes among littoral states over territorial claims, resource exploitation, and freedom of navigation. The presence of armed vessels, maritime militias, and paramilitary forces in the South China Sea has raised concerns about the potential for maritime incidents, including clashes and confrontations, escalating into conflicts. Regional mechanisms, such as the Association of Southeast Asian Nations (ASEAN) and the Code of Conduct in the South China Sea (COC), aim to manage maritime disputes and promote peaceful resolution through dialogue and confidence-building measures.

The case of Indonesia underscores the challenges of maritime security in the archipelagic nation, where piracy, maritime terrorism, and illegal fishing activities are prevalent in the waters surrounding the Indonesian archipelago. Indonesia's vast maritime domain, comprising thousands of islands and extensive coastline, poses challenges for maritime law enforcement and surveillance, allowing criminal networks and extremist groups to operate with impunity. Indonesia has implemented a comprehensive maritime security strategy, including joint patrols, intelligence-sharing arrangements, and capacity-building initiatives, to combat maritime threats and safeguard its territorial waters.

In the Arabian Sea, the threat of piracy and maritime terrorism remains a concern for maritime security, particularly in the waters off the coast of Yemen and Somalia. Piracy attacks, hijackings, and armed robberies continue to occur, posing risks to commercial shipping, maritime trade, and maritime infrastructure. Regional and international efforts, such as the Contact Group on Piracy off the Coast of Somalia (CGPCS) and the Djibouti Code of Conduct, aim to enhance maritime law enforcement capabilities and promote cooperation among littoral states to address piracy and maritime terrorism in the Arabian Sea.

The case of Bangladesh highlights the vulnerability of coastal communities and maritime infrastructure to piracy and maritime terrorism in the Bay of Bengal region. Bangladesh's extensive coastline and maritime trade routes are susceptible to piracy attacks, armed robberies, and maritime smuggling activities, posing risks to maritime security and economic development. Bangladesh, along with neighboring countries and international partners, has strengthened maritime law enforcement, surveillance, and border control measures to counter piracy and enhance maritime security in the Bay of Bengal.

In the Mediterranean Sea, the threat of piracy and maritime terrorism has implications for maritime security and stability in the region. The ongoing conflicts, political instability, and transnational crime networks operating in the Mediterranean basin create conducive conditions for piracy attacks, maritime smuggling, and terrorist activities. Regional organizations, such as the Union for the Mediterranean (UfM) and the Mediterranean Dialogue, are working to address maritime security challenges and promote cooperation among Mediterranean littoral states.

The case of the Philippines underscores the challenges of addressing piracy and maritime terrorism in the maritime domain of Southeast Asia. The Philippines, with its extensive coastline and archipelagic geography, faces threats from piracy, armed robbery, and maritime terrorism in its waters, particularly in the Sulu and

Celebes Seas. The Philippine government, in collaboration with neighboring countries and international partners, has implemented joint maritime patrols, intelligence-sharing mechanisms, and capacity-building initiatives to enhance maritime law enforcement and counter piracy and maritime terrorism activities.

Red Sea, a strategic maritime corridor connecting the Mediterranean Sea to the Indian Ocean, has been affected by piracy and maritime terrorism activities, particularly off the coast of Somalia and Yemen. Piracy attacks, hijackings, and armed robberies continue to pose risks to commercial shipping and maritime trade in the Red Sea region. International naval forces, including those deployed as part of the Combined Maritime Forces (CMF) and the European Union Naval Force Somalia (Operation Atalanta), conduct patrols and escort missions to deter piracy and protect merchant vessels transiting through the Red Sea.

In the Western Indian Ocean, piracy and maritime terrorism remain persistent threats to maritime security, despite efforts to counter piracy off the coast of Somalia. Piracy attacks, hijackings, and armed robberies continue to occur in the waters of the Indian Ocean, posing risks to maritime trade, shipping, and maritime infrastructure. Regional initiatives, such as the Djibouti Code of Conduct and the Regional Maritime Information Fusion Centre (RMIFC), aim to enhance maritime law enforcement capabilities and promote cooperation among littoral states to address piracy and maritime terrorism in the Western Indian Ocean.

The case of Mozambique highlights the challenges of addressing piracy and maritime terrorism in the waters of the Mozambique Channel and the Indian Ocean. Mozambique, with its extensive coastline and strategic maritime location, faces threats from piracy attacks, armed robberies, and maritime smuggling activities, particularly in the vicinity of the Cabo Delgado province. Mozambique, along with neighboring countries and international partners, has strengthened maritime law enforcement, surveillance, and border control measures to counter piracy and enhance maritime security in the region.

In the Gulf of Aden, piracy and maritime terrorism continue to pose risks to maritime security and stability, despite the decline in piracy incidents in recent years. Armed groups, criminal networks, and extremist organizations operating in the region have engaged in piracy attacks, hijackings, and maritime smuggling activities, undermining maritime trade and economic development. International naval forces, including those deployed as part of Combined Task Force 151 and the European Union Naval Force Somalia (Operation Atalanta), conduct patrols and escort missions to deter piracy and protect merchant vessels transiting through the Gulf of Aden.

The case of Sri Lanka underscores the challenges of addressing maritime security threats, including piracy and maritime terrorism, in the waters of the Indian Ocean. Sri Lanka's strategic maritime location and busy shipping lanes make it vulnerable to piracy attacks, armed robberies, and maritime smuggling activities. Sri Lanka, along with regional partners and international organizations, has implemented maritime security initiatives, such as joint patrols, intelligence-sharing mechanisms, and capacity-building programs, to counter piracy and enhance maritime security in the Indian Ocean region.

In the Caribbean Sea, piracy and maritime terrorism pose challenges to maritime security and stability, particularly in the waters of the Greater Antilles and the Caribbean Basin. Piracy attacks, armed robberies, and maritime smuggling activities continue to occur, threatening maritime trade, shipping, and maritime infrastructure in the region. Regional organizations, such as the Caribbean Community (CARICOM) and the Caribbean Basin Security Initiative (CBSI), are working to address maritime security challenges and promote cooperation among Caribbean states to combat piracy and maritime terrorism.

The case of Somalia highlights the complex security dynamics and governance challenges associated with addressing piracy and maritime terrorism in the Horn of Africa region.

Somalia, with its long coastline and strategic maritime location, has been plagued by piracy attacks, hijackings, and maritime smuggling activities, fuelled by political instability, weak governance, and poverty. Somalia, along with international partners and maritime security organizations, has made efforts to counter piracy, enhance maritime law enforcement, and strengthen maritime governance to restore stability and security in its maritime domain.

In the Gulf of Guinea, piracy and maritime terrorism pose significant challenges to maritime security and economic development, particularly in the waters off the coast of West Africa. Piracy attacks, hijackings, and kidnappings-for-ransom continue to occur, threatening maritime trade, shipping, and offshore oil and gas operations in the region. Coastal states in the Gulf of Guinea, along with international partners and maritime security organizations, have implemented joint patrols, intelligence-sharing mechanisms, and capacity-building programs to counter piracy and enhance maritime security in the region.

The case of Indonesia underscores the challenges of addressing maritime security threats, including piracy and maritime terrorism, in the waters of the Indonesian archipelago. Indonesia, with its vast maritime domain and strategic location, faces threats from piracy attacks, armed robberies, and maritime smuggling activities, particularly in the waters of the Sulu and Celebes Seas. Indonesia, along with regional partners and international organizations, has implemented maritime security initiatives, such as joint patrols, intelligence-sharing mechanisms, and capacity-building programs, to counter piracy and enhance maritime security in the region.

In the South China Sea, piracy and maritime terrorism pose challenges to maritime security and stability, exacerbated by territorial disputes and geopolitical tensions among littoral states. Piracy attacks, armed robberies, and maritime smuggling activities continue to occur in the waters of the South China Sea, threatening maritime trade, shipping, and freedom of navigation. Littoral states, regional organizations, and international partners are working to address maritime security challenges and promote cooperation to combat piracy and maritime terrorism in the South China Sea.

The case of Nigeria highlights the challenges of addressing maritime security threats, including piracy and maritime terrorism, in the Gulf of Guinea region. Nigeria, with its extensive coastline and strategic maritime location, faces threats from piracy attacks, armed robberies, and maritime smuggling activities, particularly in the waters of the Niger Delta region. Nigeria, along with neighboring countries and international partners, has implemented joint maritime patrols, intelligence-sharing mechanisms, and capacity-building initiatives to counter piracy and enhance maritime security in the Gulf of Guinea.

In the Arabian Sea, piracy and maritime terrorism continue to pose risks to maritime security and stability, particularly in the waters off the coast of Somalia and Yemen. Piracy attacks, hijackings, and armed robberies remain a concern for commercial shipping, maritime trade, and maritime infrastructure in the region. International naval forces, including those deployed as part of Combined Task Force 151 and the European Union Naval Force Somalia (Operation Atalanta), conduct patrols and escort missions to deter piracy and protect merchant vessels transiting through the Arabian Sea.

The case of Bangladesh underscores the challenges of addressing piracy and maritime terrorism in the Bay of Bengal region. Bangladesh, with its extensive coastline and busy shipping lanes, faces threats from piracy attacks, armed robberies, and maritime smuggling activities, particularly in the vicinity of the Sundarbans mangrove forest and the maritime boundary with Myanmar. Bangladesh, along with neighboring countries and international partners, has implemented maritime security measures, such as joint patrols and intelligence sharing.

The Red Sea, a vital maritime corridor connecting the Mediterranean Sea to the Indian Ocean, has been affected by piracy and maritime terrorism activities, particularly off the coast of Somalia and Yemen. Piracy attacks, hijackings, and armed robberies continue to pose risks to commercial shipping and maritime trade in the Red Sea region. International naval forces, including those deployed as part of the Combined Maritime Forces (CMF) and the European Union Naval Force Somalia (Operation Atalanta), conduct patrols and escort missions to deter piracy and protect merchant vessels transiting through the Red Sea.

In the Western Indian Ocean, piracy and maritime terrorism remain persistent threats to maritime security, despite efforts to counter piracy off the coast of Somalia. Piracy attacks, hijackings, and armed robberies continue to occur in the waters of the Indian Ocean, posing risks to maritime trade, shipping, and maritime infrastructure. Regional initiatives, such as the Djibouti Code of Conduct and the Regional Maritime Information Fusion Centre (RMIFC), aim to enhance maritime law enforcement capabilities and promote cooperation among littoral states to address piracy and maritime terrorism in the Western Indian Ocean.

The case of Mozambique highlights the challenges of addressing piracy and maritime terrorism in the waters of the Mozambique Channel and the Indian Ocean. Mozambique, with its extensive coastline and strategic maritime location, faces threats from piracy attacks, armed robberies, and maritime smuggling activities, particularly in the vicinity of the Cabo Delgado province. Mozambique, along with neighboring countries and international partners, has strengthened maritime law enforcement, surveillance, and border control measures to counter piracy and enhance maritime security in the region.

In the Gulf of Aden, piracy and maritime terrorism continue to pose risks to maritime security and stability, despite the decline in piracy incidents in recent years. Armed groups, criminal networks, and extremist organizations operating in the region have engaged in piracy attacks, hijackings, and maritime smuggling activities, undermining maritime trade and economic development. International naval forces, including those deployed as part of Combined Task Force 151 and the European Union

Naval Force Somalia (Operation Atalanta), conduct patrols and escort missions to deter piracy and protect merchant vessels transiting through the Gulf of Aden.

The case of Sri Lanka underscores the challenges of addressing maritime security threats, including piracy and maritime terrorism, in the waters of the Indian Ocean. Sri Lanka's strategic maritime location and busy shipping lanes make it vulnerable to piracy attacks, armed robberies, and maritime smuggling activities. Sri Lanka, along with regional partners and international organizations, has implemented maritime security initiatives, such as joint patrols, intelligence-sharing mechanisms, and capacity-building programs, to counter piracy and enhance maritime security in the Indian Ocean region.

In the Caribbean Sea, piracy and maritime terrorism pose challenges to maritime security and stability, particularly in the waters of the Greater Antilles and the Caribbean Basin. Piracy attacks, armed robberies, and maritime smuggling activities continue to occur, threatening maritime trade, shipping, and maritime infrastructure in the region. Regional organizations, such as the Caribbean Community (CARICOM) and the Caribbean Basin Security Initiative (CBSI), are working to address maritime security challenges and promote cooperation among Caribbean states to combat piracy and maritime terrorism.

The case of Somalia highlights the complex security dynamics and governance challenges associated with addressing piracy and maritime terrorism in the Horn of Africa region. Somalia, with its long coastline and strategic maritime location, has been plagued by piracy attacks, hijackings, and maritime smuggling activities, fuelled by political instability, weak governance, and poverty. Somalia, along with international partners and maritime security organizations, has made efforts to counter piracy, enhance maritime law enforcement, and strengthen maritime governance to restore stability and security in its maritime domain.

In the Gulf of Guinea, piracy and maritime terrorism pose significant challenges to maritime security and economic development, particularly in the waters off the coast of West Africa. Piracy attacks, hijackings, and kidnappings-for-ransom continue to occur, threatening maritime trade, shipping, and offshore oil and gas operations in the region. Coastal states in the Gulf of Guinea, along with international partners and maritime security organizations, have implemented joint patrols, intelligence-sharing mechanisms, and capacity-building programs to counter piracy and enhance maritime security in the region.

The case of Indonesia underscores the challenges of addressing maritime security threats, including piracy and maritime terrorism, in the waters of the Indonesian archipelago. Indonesia, with its vast maritime domain and strategic location, faces threats from piracy attacks, armed robberies, and maritime smuggling activities, particularly in the waters of the Sulu and Celebes Seas. Indonesia, along with regional partners and international organizations, has implemented maritime security initiatives, such as joint patrols, intelligence-sharing mechanisms, and capacity-building programs, to counter piracy and enhance maritime security in the region.

The case of Nigeria highlights the challenges of addressing maritime security threats, including piracy and maritime terrorism, in the Gulf of Guinea region. Nigeria, with its extensive coastline and strategic maritime location, faces threats from piracy attacks, armed robberies, and maritime smuggling activities, particularly in the waters of the Niger Delta region. Nigeria, along with neighboring countries and international partners, has implemented joint maritime patrols, intelligence-sharing mechanisms, and capacity-building initiatives to counter piracy and enhance maritime security in the Gulf of Guinea.

In the Arabian Sea, piracy and maritime terrorism continue to pose risks to maritime security and stability, particularly in the waters off the coast of Somalia and Yemen. Piracy attacks, hijackings, and armed robberies remain a concern for commercial shipping, maritime trade, and maritime infrastructure in the region. International naval forces, including those deployed as part of Combined Task Force 151 and the European Union Naval

Force Somalia (Operation Atalanta), conduct patrols and escort missions to deter piracy and protect merchant vessels transiting through the Arabian Sea.

The case of Bangladesh underscores the challenges of addressing piracy and maritime terrorism in the Bay of Bengal region. Bangladesh, with its extensive coastline and busy shipping lanes, faces threats from piracy attacks, armed robberies, and maritime smuggling activities, particularly in the vicinity of the Sundarbans mangrove forest and the maritime boundary with Myanmar. Bangladesh, along with neighboring countries and international partners, has implemented maritime security measures, such as joint patrols, intelligence-sharing mechanisms, and capacity-building programs, to counter piracy and enhance maritime security in the region.

The Eastern Mediterranean region faces challenges related to piracy and maritime terrorism, particularly amidst geopolitical tensions and conflicts in the area. Incidents of piracy, armed robberies, and maritime smuggling have been reported, impacting maritime trade, shipping, and security in the region. Coastal states and international organizations have coordinated efforts to enhance maritime law enforcement and security measures to address these threats and maintain stability in the Eastern Mediterranean.

The case of Venezuela highlights the complexities of addressing maritime security threats, including piracy and maritime terrorism, in the waters of the Caribbean Sea and the Atlantic Ocean. Venezuela's extensive coastline and maritime borders make it susceptible to piracy attacks, armed robberies, and illicit maritime activities, exacerbated by political and economic challenges. Venezuela, along with regional partners and international organizations, has implemented maritime security initiatives to combat piracy and enhance maritime security in its maritime domain.

In the Bay of Bengal, piracy and maritime terrorism pose challenges to maritime security and stability, particularly in the waters off the coast of Myanmar and Bangladesh. Piracy attacks, armed robberies, and maritime smuggling activities continue to occur, threatening maritime trade, shipping, and maritime infrastructure in the region. Coastal states and international organizations have collaborated to strengthen maritime law enforcement and surveillance to counter piracy and maritime terrorism in the Bay of Bengal.

The case of Malaysia underscores the importance of maritime security in the Malacca Strait and the South China Sea, where piracy and maritime terrorism threats persist. Malaysia, as a littoral state, faces challenges from piracy attacks, armed robberies, and maritime smuggling activities in its territorial waters and exclusive economic zone. Malaysia, along with neighboring countries and international partners, has implemented joint patrols, intelligence-sharing mechanisms, and capacity-building initiatives to address piracy and enhance maritime security in the region.

In the Eastern Indian Ocean, piracy and maritime terrorism continue to pose risks to maritime security and stability, particularly in the waters off the coast of Somalia and the Horn of Africa. Piracy attacks, hijackings, and armed robberies remain a concern for commercial shipping and maritime trade in the region. Regional and international efforts, including naval patrols and capacity-building programs, are ongoing to combat piracy and enhance maritime security in the Eastern Indian Ocean.

The case of Kenya highlights the challenges of addressing maritime security threats, including piracy and maritime terrorism, in the waters of the Indian Ocean. Kenya's strategic maritime location and busy shipping lanes make it vulnerable to piracy attacks, armed robberies, and maritime smuggling activities. Kenya, along with regional partners and international organizations, has implemented maritime security measures to counter piracy and enhance maritime security in the Indian Ocean region.

In the Gulf of Thailand, piracy and maritime terrorism pose challenges to maritime security and stability, particularly in the waters off the coast of Thailand and neighboring countries. Piracy attacks, armed robberies, and maritime smuggling activities continue to occur, impacting maritime trade, shipping, and security in the region. Coastal states and international organizations have coordinated efforts to enhance maritime law enforcement and security measures to address these threats and maintain stability in the Gulf of Thailand.

The case of Brazil underscores the challenges of addressing maritime security threats, including piracy and maritime terrorism, in the waters of the South Atlantic Ocean. Brazil's extensive maritime borders and offshore oil and gas operations make it susceptible to piracy attacks, armed robberies, and maritime smuggling activities. Brazil, along with regional partners and international organizations, has implemented maritime security initiatives to combat piracy and enhance maritime security in its maritime domain.

In the Gulf of Oman, piracy and maritime terrorism continue to pose risks to maritime security and stability, particularly in the waters off the coast of Oman and the Arabian Peninsula. Piracy attacks, hijackings, and armed robberies remain a concern for commercial shipping and maritime trade in the region. International naval forces, including those deployed as part of Combined Task Force 151 and the European Union Naval Force Somalia (Operation Atalanta), conduct patrols and escort missions to deter piracy and protect merchant vessels transiting through the Gulf of Oman.

The case of Ecuador highlights the challenges of addressing maritime security threats, including piracy and maritime terrorism, in the waters of the Pacific Ocean. Ecuador's strategic maritime location and extensive maritime borders make it vulnerable to piracy attacks, armed robberies, and maritime smuggling activities. Ecuador, along with regional partners and international organizations, has implemented maritime security measures to counter piracy and enhance maritime security in its maritime domain. Collaboration with neighboring countries and international partners is essential to effectively address piracy and maritime terrorism threats and maintain maritime security in the Pacific Ocean region.

In the Eastern Mediterranean, piracy and maritime terrorism pose challenges to maritime security and stability, particularly amidst geopolitical tensions and conflicts in the area. Incidents of piracy, armed robberies, and maritime smuggling have been reported, impacting maritime trade, shipping, and security in the region. Coastal states and international organizations have coordinated efforts to enhance maritime law enforcement and security measures to address these threats and maintain stability in the Eastern Mediterranean.

The case of Venezuela highlights the complexities of addressing maritime security threats, including piracy and maritime terrorism, in the waters of the Caribbean Sea and the Atlantic Ocean. Venezuela's extensive coastline and maritime borders make it susceptible to piracy attacks, armed robberies, and illicit maritime activities, exacerbated by political and economic challenges. Venezuela, along with regional partners and international organizations, has implemented maritime security initiatives to combat piracy and enhance maritime security in its maritime domain.

In the Bay of Bengal, piracy and maritime terrorism pose challenges to maritime security and stability, particularly in the waters off the coast of Myanmar and Bangladesh. Piracy attacks, armed robberies, and maritime smuggling activities continue to occur, threatening maritime trade, shipping, and maritime infrastructure in the region. Coastal states and international organizations have collaborated to strengthen maritime law enforcement and surveillance to counter piracy and maritime terrorism in the Bay of Bengal.

The case of Malaysia underscores the importance of maritime security in the Malacca Strait and the South China Sea, where piracy and maritime terrorism threats persist. Malaysia, as a littoral state, faces challenges from piracy attacks, armed robberies, and maritime smuggling activities in its territorial waters and exclusive economic zone. Malaysia, along with neighboring countries and international partners, has implemented joint patrols, intelligence-sharing mechanisms, and capacity-building initiatives to address piracy and enhance maritime security in the region.

IIn the Eastern Indian Ocean, piracy and maritime terrorism continue to pose risks to maritime security and stability, particularly in the waters off the coast of Somalia and the Horn of Africa. Piracy attacks, hijackings, and armed robberies remain a concern for commercial shipping and maritime trade in the region. Regional and international efforts, including naval patrols and capacity-building programs, are ongoing to combat piracy and enhance maritime security in the Eastern Indian Ocean.

The case of Kenya highlights the challenges of addressing maritime security threats, including piracy and maritime terrorism, in the waters of the Indian Ocean. Kenya's strategic maritime location and busy shipping lanes make it vulnerable to piracy attacks, armed robberies, and maritime smuggling activities. Kenya, along with regional partners and international organizations, has implemented maritime security measures to counter piracy and enhance maritime security in the Indian Ocean region.

In the Gulf of Thailand, piracy and maritime terrorism pose challenges to maritime security and stability, particularly in the waters off the coast of Thailand and neighboring countries. Piracy attacks, armed robberies, and maritime smuggling activities continue to occur, impacting maritime trade, shipping, and security in the region. Coastal states and international organizations have coordinated efforts to enhance maritime law enforcement and security measures to address these threats and maintain stability in the Gulf of Thailand.

The case of Brazil underscores the challenges of addressing maritime security threats, including piracy and maritime terrorism, in the waters of the South Atlantic Ocean. Brazil's extensive maritime borders and offshore oil and gas operations make it susceptible to piracy attacks, armed robberies, and maritime smuggling activities. Brazil, along with regional partners and international organizations, has implemented maritime security initiatives to combat piracy and enhance maritime security in its maritime domain.

In the Gulf of Oman, piracy and maritime terrorism continue to pose risks to maritime security and stability, particularly in the waters off the coast of Oman and the Arabian Peninsula. Piracy attacks, hijackings, and armed robberies remain a concern for commercial shipping and maritime trade in the region. International naval forces, including those deployed as part of Combined Task Force 151 and the European Union Naval Force Somalia (Operation Atalanta), conduct patrols and escort missions to deter piracy and protect merchant vessels transiting through the Gulf of Oman.

The case of Nigeria highlights the challenges of addressing maritime security threats, including piracy and maritime terrorism, in the Gulf of Guinea region. Nigeria, with its extensive coastline and strategic maritime location, faces threats from piracy attacks, armed robberies, and maritime smuggling activities, particularly in the waters of the Niger Delta region. Nigeria, along with neighboring countries and international partners, has implemented joint maritime patrols, intelligence-sharing mechanisms, and capacity-building initiatives to counter piracy and enhance maritime security in the Gulf of Guinea.

In the Arabian Sea, piracy and maritime terrorism continue to pose risks to maritime security and stability, particularly in the waters off the coast of Somalia and Yemen. Piracy attacks, hijackings, and armed robberies remain a concern for commercial shipping and maritime trade in the region. International naval forces, including those deployed as part of Combined Task Force 151 and the European Union Naval Force Somalia (Operation Atalanta), conduct patrols and escort missions to deter piracy and protect merchant vessels transiting through the Arabian Sea.

Illegal, Unreported, and Unregulated (IUU) Fishing

Illegal, Unreported, and Unregulated (IUU) fishing poses significant challenges to marine ecosystems, global fisheries, and maritime security. IUU fishing refers to fishing activities conducted in violation of national or international laws, often involving unlicensed vessels, unauthorized fishing in restricted areas, and failure to report catches accurately. This clandestine practice undermines sustainable fisheries management efforts and threatens the long-term viability of marine resources worldwide.

The case of the South China Sea exemplifies the prevalence and impact of IUU fishing in contested waters. Multiple countries bordering the South China Sea, including China, Vietnam, the Philippines, and Indonesia, have reported instances of IUU fishing by foreign vessels encroaching on their exclusive economic zones (EEZs). These activities contribute to tensions among coastal states and pose challenges to regional maritime security and stability.

In the waters of West Africa, IUU fishing is rampant, particularly off the coasts of countries such as Senegal, Mauritania, and Sierra Leone. Foreign fishing fleets, often from distant nations, exploit the rich marine resources of West African waters without proper authorization or oversight, leading to depletion of fish stocks, economic losses for local fishermen, and food insecurity in coastal communities.

The European Union (EU) has taken significant steps to combat IUU fishing through its Common Fisheries Policy (CFP) and robust fisheries control and monitoring mechanisms. The EU's IUU Regulation prohibits the importation of fisheries products derived from IUU fishing activities, incentivizing third countries to implement sustainable fishing practices and cooperate in the fight against IUU fishing.

The case of Thailand illustrates the challenges of addressing IUU fishing in Southeast Asia. Thailand has faced scrutiny for its role as a major hub for processing and exporting seafood products derived from IUU fishing operations in the region. In response, Thailand has implemented reforms to improve fisheries management, strengthen labor regulations, and combat illegal fishing practices within its maritime jurisdiction.

Illegal fishing activities, including IUU fishing, pose threats to marine biodiversity and protected species. In the waters of the Galápagos Islands, Ecuador has reported incidents of IUU fishing by foreign vessels targeting endangered species such as sharks and sea cucumbers. These activities endanger fragile marine ecosystems and undermine conservation efforts in the Galápagos Marine Reserve.

The prevalence of IUU fishing in the Southern Ocean, particularly around Antarctica, has raised concerns among conservationists and marine scientists. Illegal harvesting of Antarctic tooth fish and krill by unregulated fishing vessels jeopardizes the delicate balance of Antarctic marine ecosystems and undermines the effectiveness of international conservation agreements such as the Commission for the Conservation of Antarctic Marine Living Resources (CCAMLR).

The case of the Gulf of Guinea highlights the pervasive nature of IUU fishing in the waters off the coast of West Africa. IUU fishing activities, including illegal trawling and unreported catches, contribute to overfishing, habitat degradation, and loss of livelihoods for local fishing communities. Regional cooperation and coordinated enforcement efforts are crucial to combating IUU fishing and promoting sustainable fisheries management in the Gulf of Guinea.

The Arctic region faces emerging challenges related to IUU fishing as melting sea ice opens up new fishing grounds. The absence of comprehensive regulatory frameworks and surveillance capabilities in the Arctic Ocean creates vulnerabilities to IUU fishing activities, posing risks to vulnerable marine species and indigenous communities reliant on marine resources for subsistence and cultural practices.

The case of Somalia underscores the links between IUU fishing and maritime piracy in the waters of the Indian Ocean. Illegal foreign fishing vessels operating in Somali waters have contributed to the impoverishment of local fishermen and the rise of piracy as a means of maritime security enforcement. Addressing IUU fishing is essential to promoting stability and economic development in Somalia and the wider region.

In the Pacific Islands region, IUU fishing poses challenges to the sustainable management of tuna fisheries, which are vital for the economies and food security of Pacific Island countries. Illegal fishing vessels, often operating under flags of convenience and employing destructive fishing methods, threaten the health of tuna stocks and undermine efforts to conserve marine biodiversity in the Pacific Ocean.

The International Monitoring, Control, and Surveillance (MCS) Framework for IUU fishing, developed by the Food and Agriculture Organization (FAO), provides guidance and standards for countries to enhance their fisheries monitoring and enforcement capabilities. The framework emphasizes cooperation, information sharing, and technology adoption to combat IUU fishing effectively on a global scale.

The case of Indonesia exemplifies the importance of comprehensive national strategies to address IUU fishing. Indonesia has implemented measures such as vessel monitoring systems, port inspections, and satellite surveillance to detect and deter illegal fishing activities in its vast maritime territory. Indonesia's proactive approach has resulted in increased enforcement actions and significant reductions in IUU fishing incidents.

IUU fishing undermines efforts to achieve the United Nations Sustainable Development Goals (SDGs), particularly Goal 14: Life Below Water, which aims to conserve and sustainably use the oceans, seas, and marine resources. Addressing IUU fishing is integral to achieving targets related to marine conservation, sustainable fisheries management, and poverty eradication in coastal communities.

The role of technology, including satellite monitoring, automatic identification systems (AIS), and remote sensing, is crucial in detecting and tracking IUU fishing vessels across vast maritime areas. Advances in maritime surveillance technology enable authorities to identify suspicious fishing activities, enforce fisheries regulations, and hold perpetrators of IUU fishing accountable.

The case of the Western and Central Pacific Fisheries Commission (WCPFC) demonstrates the importance of regional fisheries management organizations (RFMOs) in combating IUU fishing. The WCPFC, responsible for managing tuna fisheries in the Pacific Ocean, coordinates efforts among member countries to monitor fishing activities, enforce regulations, and promote sustainable fishing practices to combat IUU fishing effectively.

The Port State Measures Agreement (PSMA), adopted by the FAO, provides a legal framework for port states to prevent, deter, and eliminate IUU fishing by denying entry to vessels engaged in illegal fishing activities. Implementation of the PSMA enhances port controls, inspections, and information sharing to disrupt the flow of IUU-caught seafood products into global markets.

The case of Ghana highlights the importance of capacity-building initiatives to strengthen national fisheries management and enforcement capabilities in combating IUU fishing. Ghana has benefited from international assistance and technical support to improve surveillance, law enforcement, and regulatory frameworks to address IUU fishing effectively in its maritime domain.

The case of the European Union's Fisheries Control Regulation demonstrates the importance of comprehensive regulatory frameworks in addressing IUU fishing within regional fisheries management areas. The EU's regulation establishes strict controls on fishing activities, vessel monitoring, and seafood traceability to prevent the entry of IUU-caught fisheries products into the European market.

In the Caribbean region, IUU fishing threatens the health of coral reef ecosystems, which are vital for marine biodiversity and coastal livelihoods. Illegal fishing practices, such as cyanide and blast fishing, degrade coral reefs, disrupt fish populations, and undermine conservation efforts. The Caribbean Community

(CARICOM) and its member states have implemented measures to combat IUU fishing, including enhanced surveillance, strengthened regulations, and collaboration with international partners to protect marine resources.

The case of Japan highlights the importance of international cooperation in addressing IUU fishing in distant waters. Japan, as one of the world's major fishing nations, has invested in fisheries monitoring and surveillance to combat IUU fishing by its fleet operating in the high seas and exclusive economic zones of other countries. Bilateral and multilateral agreements, such as fisheries access agreements and information-sharing mechanisms, facilitate collaboration between Japan and coastal states to combat IUU fishing effectively.

IUU fishing undermines efforts to achieve marine conservation objectives, such as the establishment and management of marine protected areas (MPAs). Illegal fishing activities, including poaching and unauthorized fishing within MPAs, compromise the effectiveness of conservation measures and threaten the ecological integrity of protected marine habitats. Strengthening enforcement and monitoring efforts within MPAs is essential to combat IUU fishing and safeguard marine biodiversity.

The case of the Indian Ocean Tuna Commission (IOTC) illustrates the challenges of addressing IUU fishing in transboundary fisheries. The IOTC, responsible for the conservation and management of tuna and tuna-like species in the Indian Ocean, faces difficulties in regulating fishing activities across multiple jurisdictions and combating IUU fishing by non-contracting parties. Enhanced cooperation, information exchange, and compliance mechanisms are needed to address IUU fishing effectively in the Indian Ocean region.

IUU fishing undermines food security and livelihoods, particularly in developing coastal states and small island nations reliant on marine resources for sustenance and economic prosperity. Illegal fishing practices deprive local communities of access to fisheries resources, disrupt traditional fishing activities, and exacerbate poverty and food insecurity. Strengthening fisheries management, enhancing surveillance, and promoting sustainable fishing practices are essential to combating IUU fishing and supporting the socio-economic development of coastal communities.

The case of the Western Pacific Regional Fishery Management Council (WPRFMC) demonstrates the importance of stakeholder engagement and participatory management approaches in addressing IUU fishing. The WPRFMC, composed of government representatives, fisheries stakeholders, and indigenous communities, collaborates on fisheries management and conservation initiatives to combat IUU fishing and promote sustainable fisheries in the Western Pacific region.

The role of non-governmental organizations (NGOs) and civil society groups is crucial in raising awareness, monitoring fishing activities, and advocating for stronger measures to combat IUU fishing. NGOs such as Sea Shepherd Conservation Society and Oceana play active roles in conducting surveillance operations, exposing illegal fishing practices, and mobilizing public support for marine conservation and anti-IUU fishing initiatives.

IUU fishing undermines the effectiveness of marine protected areas (MPAs) and other conservation measures established to conserve marine biodiversity and ecosystems. Illegal fishing activities, including unauthorized entry and fishing within MPAs, degrade habitats, disturb wildlife, and diminish the ecological benefits of protected marine areas. Strengthening enforcement and surveillance efforts within MPAs is essential to combat IUU fishing and ensure the conservation of marine resources.

The case of the Coral Triangle Initiative (CTI) highlights regional efforts to address IUU fishing and promote sustainable fisheries management in the Coral Triangle region, known for its exceptional marine biodiversity. The CTI, supported by six member countries, implements strategies to combat IUU fishing, enhance law enforcement, and promote community-based conservation initiatives to safeguard marine ecosystems and support the livelihoods of coastal communities.

IUU fishing exacerbates overfishing and the depletion of fish stocks, jeopardizing the long-term sustainability of fisheries and marine ecosystems. Illegal fishing activities, such as unregulated harvesting and bycatch of non-target species, disrupt marine food webs, degrade habitats, and compromise the resilience of fish populations to environmental stressors. Strengthening fisheries management measures and combating IUU fishing are essential to rebuild fish stocks and restore ecosystem health.

The case of the International Commission for the Conservation of Atlantic Tunas (ICCAT) underscores the challenges of addressing IUU fishing in highly migratory species fisheries. ICCAT, responsible for the conservation and management of tuna and tuna-like species in the Atlantic Ocean, faces difficulties in regulating fishing activities across multiple jurisdictions and combating IUU fishing by non-compliant vessels. Enhanced cooperation, monitoring, and enforcement efforts are necessary to combat IUU fishing effectively in the Atlantic Ocean.

IUU fishing undermines the socio-economic development and food security of coastal communities, particularly in developing countries heavily reliant on fisheries resources for sustenance and livelihoods. Illegal fishing activities deprive local fishermen of access to fishing grounds, disrupt traditional fishing practices, and undermine efforts to alleviate poverty and promote economic resilience in coastal areas. Strengthening fisheries management, enhancing surveillance, and combating IUU fishing are critical to supporting the socio-economic well-being of coastal communities.

The case of the Indian Ocean Rim Association (IORA) illustrates regional efforts to address IUU fishing and promote sustainable fisheries management among member states bordering the Indian Ocean. IORA facilitates cooperation, information exchange, and capacity-building initiatives to combat IUU fishing, enhance surveillance, and strengthen fisheries governance in the Indian Ocean region. Collaborative action is essential to addressing IUU fishing effectively and ensuring the sustainable use of marine resources.

IUU fishing undermines efforts to achieve global biodiversity conservation targets, including the Aichi Biodiversity Targets and the Convention on Biological Diversity (CBD) goals. Illegal fishing activities, such as overexploitation of fish stocks and bycatch of endangered species, threaten marine biodiversity, disrupt ecosystem functioning, and compromise the resilience of marine ecosystems to climate change. Strengthening fisheries management, enhancing enforcement, and combating IUU fishing are essential to conserving marine biodiversity and achieving biodiversity conservation objectives.

The case of the North Atlantic Fisheries Organization (NAFO) highlights the challenges of addressing IUU fishing in high seas fisheries beyond national jurisdiction. NAFO, responsible for the conservation and management of fish stocks in the North Atlantic, faces difficulties in regulating fishing activities by non-contracting parties and enforcing compliance with conservation measures. Strengthening international cooperation and compliance mechanisms is essential to combating IUU fishing in high seas fisheries.

IUU fishing exacerbates poverty and food insecurity, particularly in developing countries heavily reliant on fisheries for nutrition and livelihoods. Illegal fishing activities deprive local communities of access to fish resources, disrupt traditional fishing practices, and undermine efforts to achieve food security and poverty alleviation goals. Strengthening fisheries management, enhancing surveillance, and combating IUU fishing are critical to promoting food security and sustainable development in coastal areas.

The case of the Commission for the Conservation of Southern Bluefin Tuna (CCSBT) underscores the challenges of addressing IUU fishing in highly migratory species fisheries. CCSBT, responsible for the conservation and management of southern bluefin tuna stocks, faces difficulties in regulating fishing activities by non-compliant vessels and enforcing conservation measures in the Southern Ocean. Strengthening compliance and enforcement efforts is essential to combating IUU fishing and conserving southern bluefin tuna populations for future generations.

IUU fishing undermines efforts to achieve sustainable fisheries management and the United Nations 2030 Agenda for Sustainable Development. Illegal fishing activities deplete fish stocks, disrupt marine ecosystems, and threaten the livelihoods of millions of people dependent on fisheries for food security and income. Strengthening international cooperation, enhancing surveillance, and combating IUU fishing are essential to achieving Sustainable Development Goal 14: Life Below Water and promoting sustainable fisheries globally.

The case of the Western and Central Pacific Fisheries Commission (WCPFC) highlights the importance of regional cooperation in combating IUU fishing and promoting sustainable fisheries management in the Pacific Ocean. WCPFC, responsible for the conservation and management of tuna and tuna-like species in the Western and Central Pacific, collaborates with member countries to regulate fishing activities, enforce conservation measures, and combat IUU fishing effectively. Regional initiatives are critical to addressing IUU fishing and ensuring the long-term sustainability of fisheries resources in the Pacific region.

IUU fishing undermines efforts to combat illegal, unreported, and unregulated fishing activities in the Southern Ocean, posing challenges to the conservation of Antarctic marine ecosystems and the sustainability of fisheries resources. Illegal fishing vessels, operating in defiance of conservation measures and regional agreements, jeopardize the effectiveness of international efforts to protect vulnerable marine species and preserve the ecological integrity of the Southern Ocean. Strengthening surveillance, enforcement, and international cooperation is essential to combating IUU fishing and promoting the conservation of Antarctic marine resources.

The case of the Pacific Islands Forum Fisheries Agency (FFA) demonstrates the importance of regional fisheries management organizations (RFMOs) in combating IUU fishing and promoting sustainable fisheries management in the Pacific region. FFA, comprising Pacific Island countries and territories, coordinates surveillance, monitoring, and enforcement activities to combat IUU fishing, protect fish stocks, and support the socio-economic development of Pacific Island communities. Regional cooperation is essential to addressing IUU fishing effectively and ensuring the sustainability of fisheries resources in the Pacific Ocean.

IUU fishing undermines efforts to conserve marine biodiversity and protect endangered species, such as sharks, turtles, and marine mammals, from exploitation and depletion. Illegal fishing activities, including bycatch of non-target species and unauthorized harvesting of endangered marine wildlife, threaten the survival of vulnerable species and disrupt marine ecosystems. Strengthening conservation measures, enhancing enforcement, and combating IUU fishing are critical to safeguarding marine biodiversity and preserving the ecological balance of marine ecosystems.

The case of the Western Indian Ocean Marine Science Association (WIOMSA) highlights regional efforts to address IUU fishing and promote sustainable fisheries management in the Western Indian Ocean. WIOMSA, composed of coastal states and regional organizations, collaborates on research, capacity-building, and policy initiatives to combat IUU fishing, enhance marine conservation, and support the socio-economic development of coastal communities. Regional cooperation is essential to addressing IUU fishing effectively and ensuring the sustainable use of fisheries resources in the Western Indian Ocean.

IUU fishing undermines efforts to achieve international agreements and commitments related to marine conservation and sustainable fisheries management, including the United Nations Sustainable Development Goals (SDGs) and the Convention on Biological Diversity (CBD). Illegal fishing activities deplete fish stocks, damage marine ecosystems, and threaten the livelihoods of millions of people dependent on fisheries for food security and income. Strengthening international cooperation, enhancing surveillance, and combating IUU fishing are essential to achieving global conservation and development objectives.

The case of the South Pacific Regional Fisheries Management Organization (SPRFMO) illustrates the challenges of addressing IUU fishing in high seas fisheries beyond national jurisdiction. SPRFMO, responsible for the conservation and management of fish stocks in the South Pacific, faces difficulties in regulating fishing activities by non-contracting parties and enforcing compliance with conservation measures. Strengthening international cooperation and compliance mechanisms is essential to combating IUU fishing and promoting sustainable fisheries in the South Pacific region.

IUU fishing undermines efforts to achieve sustainable fisheries management and food security in the Caribbean region, threatening the socio-economic development of coastal communities and the conservation of marine biodiversity. Illegal fishing activities deprive local fishermen of access to fish resources, disrupt traditional fishing practices, and undermine efforts to alleviate poverty and promote economic resilience in coastal areas. Strengthening fisheries management, enhancing surveillance, and combating IUU fishing are critical to promoting food security and sustainable development in the Caribbean.

The case of the Indian Ocean Commission (IOC) highlights regional efforts to combat IUU fishing and promote sustainable fisheries management among member states bordering the Indian Ocean. IOC facilitates cooperation, information exchange, and capacity-building initiatives to address IUU fishing, enhance surveillance, and strengthen fisheries governance in the Indian Ocean region. Regional collaboration is essential to addressing IUU fishing effectively and ensuring the sustainable use of marine resources.

IUU fishing undermines efforts to achieve the objectives of the United Nations Convention on the Law of the Sea (UNCLOS) and other international agreements aimed at promoting sustainable fisheries management and conserving marine biodiversity. Illegal fishing activities, including overfishing, bycatch of non-target species, and destruction of marine habitats, contravene the principles of UNCLOS and undermine the conservation and sustainable use of marine resources. Strengthening compliance with UNCLOS provisions, enhancing enforcement mechanisms, and combatting IUU fishing are essential to promoting the effective implementation of international maritime law and achieving conservation objectives.

The case of the Regional Plan of Action to Promote Responsible Fishing Practices, adopted by the member countries of the Caribbean Regional Fisheries Mechanism (CRFM), illustrates regional efforts to combat IUU fishing and promote sustainable fisheries management in the Caribbean region. The Regional Plan of Action provides a framework for cooperation, coordination, and capacity-building initiatives to address IUU fishing, enhance surveillance, and strengthen fisheries governance in the Caribbean. Regional cooperation is essential to addressing IUU fishing effectively and ensuring the sustainable management of fisheries resources.

IUU fishing undermines efforts to achieve food security, poverty reduction, and sustainable development goals, particularly in developing countries heavily reliant on fisheries resources for nutrition and livelihoods. Illegal fishing activities deprive local communities of access to fish resources, disrupt traditional fishing practices, and undermine efforts to alleviate poverty and promote economic resilience in coastal areas. Strengthening fisheries management, enhancing surveillance, and combatting IUU fishing are critical to promoting food security, poverty reduction, and sustainable development in coastal regions.

These examples illustrate the pervasive nature and detrimental impacts of IUU fishing on marine ecosystems, fisheries sustainability, and coastal communities worldwide. Addressing IUU fishing requires concerted efforts at the national, regional, and international levels, including enhanced enforcement measures, stronger regulatory frameworks, and cooperation among stakeholders. By combating IUU fishing effectively, countries can safeguard marine biodiversity, protect vulnerable marine species, and promote the sustainable use of fisheries resources for present and future generations.

The United Nations Food and Agriculture Organization (FAO) has been instrumental in coordinating global efforts to combat IUU fishing through the adoption of international instruments such as the FAO Agreement on Port State Measures to Prevent, Deter, and Eliminate Illegal, Unreported, and Unregulated Fishing. This agreement provides a framework for port states to prevent the entry of illegally caught fish into international markets and disrupt the activities of IUU fishing vessels. By implementing port state measures, countries can reduce the economic incentives for IUU fishing and enhance the effectiveness of fisheries management and conservation efforts.

The case of the European Union's (EU) Common Fisheries Policy (CFP) demonstrates the importance of comprehensive regulatory frameworks in addressing IUU fishing and promoting sustainable fisheries management. The CFP sets out rules and measures to combat IUU fishing within EU waters and by EU-flagged vessels operating in international waters. Through measures such as vessel monitoring systems, catch documentation schemes, and import controls, the EU aims to prevent IUU products from entering the European market and promote responsible fishing practices globally.

Regional fisheries management organizations (RFMOs) play a crucial role in combating IUU fishing and promoting sustainable fisheries management in specific ocean regions. RFMOs, such as the Northwest Atlantic Fisheries Organization (NAFO) and the Southeast Asian Fisheries Development Center (SEAFDEC), establish conservation and management measures to regulate fishing activities, enforce compliance with international agreements, and combat IUU fishing effectively. By coordinating regional efforts and fostering cooperation among member states, RFMOs contribute to the conservation and sustainable use of fisheries resources.

The case of the Inter-American Tropical Tuna Commission (IATTC) illustrates the challenges of addressing IUU fishing in highly migratory species fisheries in the Eastern Pacific Ocean. IATTC, responsible for the conservation and management of tuna and tuna-like species, faces difficulties in regulating fishing activities by non-compliant vessels and enforcing conservation measures in the region. Strengthening enforcement mechanisms, enhancing cooperation with non-member states, and promoting transparency in fisheries management are essential to combating IUU fishing in the Eastern Pacific.

The Global Record of Fishing Vessels, Refrigerated Transport Vessels, and Supply Vessels (Global Record) initiative, led by FAO and Interpol, aims to improve transparency and traceability in the global fishing industry to combat IUU fishing effectively. By providing a publicly accessible database of fishing vessels and their activities, the Global Record enables authorities to monitor fishing operations, detect IUU fishing activities, and take appropriate enforcement actions. Strengthening information sharing and collaboration among countries through initiatives like the Global Record is essential to combating IUU fishing at the international level.

The case of the Western and Central Pacific Fisheries Commission (WCPFC) highlights the challenges of addressing IUU fishing in the world's largest tuna fishery. WCPFC, responsible for the conservation and management of tuna and tuna-like species in the Western and Central Pacific, faces difficulties in regulating fishing activities by non-compliant vessels and enforcing conservation measures in the region. Strengthening compliance mechanisms, enhancing observer coverage, and promoting responsible fishing practices are essential to combating IUU fishing and ensuring the sustainability of tuna stocks.

The Global Fishing Watch initiative, a partnership between Google, Oceana, and SkyTruth, utilizes satellite technology and machine learning algorithms to monitor and track fishing activities worldwide. By analyzing vessel tracking data and identifying suspicious fishing behavior, Global Fishing Watch provides valuable information to authorities, researchers, and civil society organizations to combat IUU fishing, promote transparency in the fishing industry, and protect marine ecosystems. Harnessing technological innovations like Global Fishing Watch is essential to enhancing surveillance and enforcement efforts against IUU fishing.

The case of the South-East Asian Regional Centre for Tropical Biology (SEAMEO-BIOTROP) illustrates the importance of capacity-building initiatives in combating IUU fishing and promoting sustainable fisheries management in Southeast Asia. SEAMEO-BIOTROP conducts training programs, workshops, and research activities to enhance the technical and institutional capacities of fisheries stakeholders, law enforcement agencies, and policy-makers in the region. Building human and institutional capacities is essential to strengthening surveillance, enforcement, and compliance with fisheries regulations to combat IUU fishing effectively.

The International Monitoring, Control, and Surveillance (IMCS) Network, established by FAO, provides a platform for countries to collaborate on monitoring, control, and surveillance activities to combat IUU fishing effectively. Through the exchange of information, best practices, and technical assistance, the IMCS Network enhances the capacity of countries to monitor fishing activities, detect IUU fishing vessels, and enforce fisheries regulations. Strengthening regional and international cooperation through initiatives like the IMCS Network is crucial to combating IUU fishing and promoting sustainable fisheries management globally.

The case of the Caribbean Regional Fisheries Mechanism (CRFM) highlights regional efforts to combat IUU fishing and promote sustainable fisheries management among Caribbean countries and territories. CRFM facilitates cooperation, capacity-building, and policy coordination to address IUU fishing, enhance surveillance, and strengthen fisheries governance in the region. By fostering regional collaboration and sharing best practices, CRFM contributes to the conservation of marine resources and the socio-economic development of coastal communities in the Caribbean.

The International Plan of Action to Prevent, Deter, and Eliminate Illegal, Unreported, and Unregulated Fishing (IPOA-IUU), adopted by FAO, provides a comprehensive framework for countries to combat IUU fishing and promote responsible fishing practices. The IPOA-IUU outlines measures to strengthen fisheries management, improve surveillance and enforcement capabilities, and enhance international cooperation to address IUU fishing effectively. By implementing the IPOA-IUU and related instruments, countries can reduce the prevalence of IUU fishing and promote sustainable fisheries management globally.

The case of the Pacific Islands Forum Fisheries Agency (FFA) illustrates regional efforts to combat IUU fishing and promote sustainable fisheries management in the Pacific region. FFA facilitates cooperation among Pacific Island countries and territories to address IUU fishing, enhance surveillance, and strengthen fisheries governance through initiatives such as the Regional Monitoring, Control, and Surveillance (MCS) Strategy. By fostering regional collaboration and sharing resources, FFA contributes to the conservation of marine resources and the socio-economic development of Pacific Island communities.

The Voluntary Guidelines for Flag State Performance, developed by FAO, provide guidance to flag states on their responsibilities to combat IUU fishing and ensure the effective implementation of international fisheries agreements. The guidelines outline measures to strengthen flag state control and oversight of fishing vessels, enhance vessel monitoring and inspection systems, and promote transparency and accountability in flag state activities. By adhering to the Voluntary Guidelines, flag states can fulfill their obligations under international law and contribute to the global fight against IUU fishing.

The case of the Indian Ocean Tuna Commission (IOTC) highlights regional efforts to combat IUU fishing and promote sustainable fisheries management in the Indian Ocean region.

IOTC, responsible for the conservation and management of tuna and tuna-like species, adopts conservation measures and monitoring programs to regulate fishing activities, enforce compliance with international agreements, and combat IUU fishing effectively. By fostering cooperation among member states and stakeholders, IOTC contributes to the conservation of marine resources and the socio-economic development of Indian Ocean coastal states.

The Global Record of Fishing Vessels, Refrigerated Transport Vessels, and Supply Vessels (Global Record) initiative, developed by FAO, Interpol, and the International Maritime Organization (IMO), aims to enhance transparency and traceability in the global fishing industry to combat IUU fishing effectively. By providing a publicly accessible database of fishing vessels and their activities, the Global Record enables authorities to monitor fishing operations, detect IUU fishing activities, and take appropriate enforcement actions. Strengthening information sharing and collaboration among countries through initiatives like the Global Record is essential to combating IUU fishing at the international level.

The case of the Western and Central Pacific Fisheries Commission (WCPFC) underscores the challenges of addressing IUU fishing in the world's largest tuna fishery. WCPFC, responsible for the conservation and management of tuna and tuna-like species in the Western and Central Pacific, faces difficulties in regulating fishing activities by non-compliant vessels and enforcing conservation measures in the region. Strengthening compliance mechanisms, enhancing observer coverage, and promoting responsible fishing practices are essential to combating IUU fishing and ensuring the sustainability of tuna stocks.

The Agreement on Port State Measures to Prevent, Deter, and Eliminate Illegal, Unreported, and Unregulated Fishing (Port State Measures Agreement), adopted by FAO, provides a legally binding framework for port states to prevent IUU-caught fish from entering international markets and disrupt the activities of IUU fishing vessels. By implementing port state measures, countries can strengthen control over fishing activities, enhance inspection and enforcement capabilities, and reduce the economic incentives for IUU fishing. Strengthening international cooperation and compliance with the Port State Measures Agreement is essential to combating IUU fishing and promoting sustainable fisheries management globally.

The case of the Western and Central Pacific Fisheries Commission (WCPFC) illustrates the importance of regional cooperation in combating IUU fishing and promoting sustainable fisheries management in the Pacific region. WCPFC, comprised of Pacific Island countries and territories, adopts conservation and management measures to regulate fishing activities, enforce compliance with international agreements, and combat IUU fishing effectively. By fostering collaboration among member states and stakeholders, WCPFC contributes to the conservation of marine resources and the socio-economic development of Pacific Island communities.

The Regional Plan of Action to Promote Responsible Fishing Practices, adopted by the member countries of the Caribbean Regional Fisheries Mechanism (CRFM), demonstrates regional efforts to combat IUU fishing and promote sustainable fisheries management in the Caribbean region. The Regional Plan of Action provides a framework for cooperation, coordination, and capacity-building initiatives to address IUU fishing, enhance surveillance, and strengthen fisheries governance in the Caribbean. By fostering regional collaboration and sharing best practices, CRFM contributes to the conservation of marine resources and the socio-economic development of coastal communities in the Caribbean.

The International Monitoring, Control, and Surveillance (IMCS) Network, established by FAO, provides a platform for countries to collaborate on monitoring, control, and surveillance activities to combat IUU fishing effectively. Through the exchange of information, best practices, and technical assistance, the IMCS Network enhances the capacity of countries to monitor fishing activities, detect IUU fishing vessels, and enforce fisheries regulations. Strengthening regional and international cooperation through initiatives like the IMCS Network is crucial to combating IUU fishing and promoting sustainable fisheries management globally.

Technological Advancements: Opportunities and Risks

Technological advancements have revolutionized the maritime industry, offering both opportunities and risks in the realm of international law and the laws of the sea. One significant opportunity arises from the use of satellite technology for enhanced monitoring, surveillance, and management of maritime activities. Satellite-based systems, such as Automatic Identification System (AIS) and Vessel Monitoring System (VMS), provide real-time data on vessel movements, enabling authorities to track fishing vessels, detect IUU fishing activities, and enforce maritime regulations effectively.

The case of Global Fishing Watch demonstrates the transformative potential of satellite technology in combating IUU fishing and promoting transparency in the global fishing industry. Global Fishing Watch uses satellite imagery and machine learning algorithms to monitor and track fishing vessels worldwide, identify suspicious fishing behavior, and provide actionable information to authorities and stakeholders. By leveraging satellite technology, Global Fishing Watch enhances surveillance and enforcement efforts against IUU fishing, ultimately contributing to the conservation of marine resources and the sustainability of fisheries.

Unmanned aerial vehicles (UAVs), commonly known as drones, offer a cost-effective and efficient means of monitoring maritime activities in remote or inaccessible areas. Drones equipped with high-resolution cameras and sensors can surveil vast ocean territories, monitor fishing activities, and detect illegal fishing practices such as shark finning and marine pollution. By supplementing traditional surveillance methods with drone technology, authorities can improve their monitoring capabilities and enhance enforcement efforts to combat IUU fishing and protect marine ecosystems.

The International Maritime Organization (IMO) has recognized the potential of autonomous shipping technologies to enhance safety, efficiency, and environmental sustainability in the maritime sector. Autonomous vessels, equipped with advanced navigation systems and artificial intelligence, have the capacity to optimize route planning, reduce fuel consumption, and minimize the risk of maritime accidents. However, the widespread adoption of autonomous shipping poses regulatory challenges related to safety standards, liability issues, and the need for international cooperation to ensure the safe and responsible deployment of autonomous vessels.

The emergence of blockchain technology holds promise for enhancing transparency and traceability in the seafood supply chain, thereby combating IUU fishing and promoting sustainable fisheries management. Blockchain platforms enable stakeholders to record and verify transactions along the supply chain in a tamper-proof and decentralized manner, facilitating the authentication of seafood products' origins and legality. By leveraging blockchain technology, seafood retailers and consumers can make informed choices, support responsible fishing practices, and incentivize industry actors to adhere to sustainable fishing standards.

The case of the Pacific Islands Forum Fisheries Agency (FFA) illustrates the potential of blockchain technology in enhancing transparency and traceability in the tuna supply chain. FFA, in collaboration with industry partners, has piloted blockchain-based platforms to track tuna from catch to market, ensuring the legality and sustainability of tuna products. By leveraging blockchain technology, FFA aims to combat IUU fishing, deter illegal fishing practices, and promote fair labor standards in the tuna industry, ultimately contributing to the conservation of marine resources and the socio-economic development of Pacific Island communities.

The proliferation of unmanned underwater vehicles (UUVs) and remotely operated vehicles (ROVs) presents new opportunities for exploring and monitoring marine environments, particularly in deep-sea areas beyond national jurisdiction. UUVs and ROVs equipped with sensors and imaging systems can conduct surveys, collect scientific data, and monitor marine habitats with greater precision and efficiency than traditional manned research vessels. By facilitating scientific research and environmental monitoring, UUVs and ROVs contribute to our understanding of marine ecosystems and support conservation efforts in remote and inaccessible ocean regions.

The development of artificial intelligence (AI) and machine learning algorithms has the potential to revolutionize maritime surveillance and enforcement capabilities by enabling predictive analytics, pattern recognition, and anomaly detection. AI-powered systems can analyze vast amounts of maritime data, such as vessel trajectories, satellite imagery, and environmental parameters, to identify illegal fishing activities, detect maritime threats, and prioritize enforcement actions. By augmenting human decision-making processes with AI-driven insights, authorities can enhance their ability to combat IUU fishing, piracy, and other maritime crimes effectively.

The case of the European Union's Maritime Safety Agency (EMSA) showcases the application of AI-driven analytics in maritime surveillance and security operations. EMSA utilizes satellite imagery, AIS data, and AI algorithms to monitor vessel traffic, detect anomalies, and identify potential maritime risks, such as oil spills, vessel collisions, and illegal fishing activities. By harnessing the power of AI, EMSA enhances its situational awareness and decision-making capabilities, enabling proactive measures to protect marine environments and ensure maritime safety and security in European waters.

Unmanned surface vessels (USVs), also known as autonomous surface vehicles (ASVs), offer a versatile platform for various maritime applications, including oceanographic research, environmental monitoring, and maritime surveillance. USVs equipped with sensors, communication systems, and navigational capabilities can operate autonomously or under remote control, enabling cost-effective and efficient data collection in offshore environments. By deploying USVs for surveillance and monitoring tasks, authorities can expand their operational reach, reduce risks to personnel, and enhance their ability to detect and respond to maritime threats effectively.

The International Telecommunication Union (ITU) plays a vital role in facilitating the development and deployment of satellite communication systems for maritime connectivity, safety, and security. Satellite communication technologies, such as Global Maritime Distress and Safety System (GMDSS), provide reliable and resilient communication links for ships at sea, enabling distress alerts, maritime safety communications, and operational data exchange. By ensuring global coverage and interoperability of maritime communication systems, ITU contributes to enhancing maritime safety, security, and efficiency worldwide.

The case of the International Maritime Satellite Organization (IMSO) illustrates the importance of satellite communication services in supporting maritime safety and security operations globally. IMSO, as the oversight organization for the Global Maritime Distress and Safety System (GMDSS), ensures the provision of satellite communication services for distress alerting, search and rescue coordination, and maritime safety information dissemination. By coordinating satellite communication networks and standards, IMSO enhances the effectiveness of GMDSS and contributes to saving lives at sea and protecting the marine environment.

Emerging technologies such as unmanned aerial vehicles (UAVs), commonly known as drones, offer innovative solutions for maritime surveillance, environmental monitoring, and search and rescue operations. Drones equipped with cameras, sensors, and thermal imaging capabilities can conduct aerial surveys, detect oil spills, and locate missing vessels or individuals in distress. By deploying drones for maritime applications, authorities can enhance their situational awareness, improve response times, and mitigate risks to human safety in challenging maritime environments.

The International Maritime Organization (IMO) has recognized the potential of autonomous shipping technologies to enhance safety, efficiency, and environmental sustainability in the maritime sector. Autonomous vessels, equipped with advanced navigation systems and artificial intelligence, have the capacity to optimize route planning, reduce fuel consumption, and minimize the risk of maritime accidents. However, the widespread adoption of autonomous shipping poses regulatory challenges related to safety standards and liability issues.

The integration of big data analytics and predictive modeling techniques offers significant opportunities for maritime stakeholders to enhance decision-making processes and optimize resource allocation. By analyzing large datasets from various sources, including vessel tracking data, weather forecasts, and oceanographic parameters, stakeholders can gain valuable insights into maritime trends, risks, and opportunities. By harnessing the power of big data analytics, authorities can improve maritime safety, optimize navigation routes, and mitigate environmental impacts, ultimately contributing to sustainable maritime development.

The case of the European Space Agency's (ESA) Maritime Safety Lab demonstrates the use of satellite-derived data and predictive modeling for maritime safety and security applications. ESA's Maritime Safety Lab utilizes satellite imagery, AIS data, and environmental parameters to monitor vessel traffic, detect anomalies, and predict maritime risks, such as oil spills, vessel collisions, and piracy incidents. By leveraging satellite data and advanced analytics, ESA enhances its capability to support maritime authorities in addressing emerging challenges and ensuring the safety and security of maritime activities.

The development of virtual reality (VR) and augmented reality (AR) technologies offers new avenues for maritime training, simulation, and situational awareness. VR and AR systems can provide immersive training experiences for maritime personnel, allowing them to practice navigation, emergency response, and crisis management in realistic virtual environments. By simulating challenging scenarios, VR and AR training programs enhance the preparedness and effectiveness of maritime personnel, thereby improving safety outcomes and reducing the risk of maritime incidents.

The use of remotely operated vehicles (ROVs) equipped with underwater sensors and cameras enables detailed inspections and surveys of maritime infrastructure, such as offshore oil rigs, underwater pipelines, and subsea cables. ROVs can access hard-to-reach areas underwater, conduct visual inspections, and collect data on structural integrity, corrosion, and environmental conditions. By leveraging ROV technology, maritime operators can identify potential risks, prioritize maintenance activities, and ensure the safety and reliability of critical maritime infrastructure.

The case of the International Seabed Authority (ISA) highlights the challenges and opportunities associated with deep-sea mining activities in areas beyond national jurisdiction. As technological advancements enable access to deep-sea mineral resources, concerns arise regarding the environmental impacts and regulatory frameworks governing deep-sea mining operations. The ISA plays a crucial role in developing regulations, environmental standards, and monitoring mechanisms to ensure the sustainable management of deep-sea mineral resources while minimizing adverse effects on marine ecosystems.

The development of marine renewable energy technologies, such as offshore wind, wave energy, and tidal energy, offers promising solutions for reducing reliance on fossil fuels and mitigating climate change impacts. Marine renewable energy projects harness the power of ocean currents, waves, and tides to generate electricity, providing clean and renewable energy sources for coastal communities and offshore installations. By investing in marine renewable energy infrastructure, countries can enhance energy security, reduce greenhouse gas emissions, and promote sustainable development of ocean resources.

The case of the Offshore Renewable Energy Catapult (ORE Catapult) illustrates the role of technology innovation in advancing marine renewable energy solutions. ORE Catapult collaborates with industry partners to research, test, and demonstrate innovative offshore renewable energy technologies, such as floating wind turbines, wave energy converters, and tidal energy systems. By accelerating the development and commercialization of marine renewable energy technologies, ORE Catapult supports the growth of the offshore renewable energy sector and contributes to the transition towards a low-carbon economy.

The use of marine autonomous surface vessels (ASVs) and underwater gliders equipped with sensors and scientific instruments enables cost-effective and efficient oceanographic research and environmental monitoring. ASVs and gliders can collect data on ocean currents, temperature, salinity, and marine biodiversity over extended periods and vast ocean territories, providing valuable insights into oceanographic processes and ecosystem dynamics. By deploying autonomous platforms for scientific research, researchers can improve our understanding of ocean phenomena and inform evidence-based decision-making for marine conservation and management.

The emergence of aquaculture technologies, such as offshore fish farms and shellfish cultivation systems, offers new opportunities for sustainable seafood production and marine resource utilization. Offshore aquaculture operations leverage advanced technologies for fish husbandry, feed management, and environmental monitoring to optimize production efficiency and minimize environmental impacts. By expanding aquaculture activities into offshore areas, countries can reduce pressure on coastal ecosystems, enhance food security, and support economic development in coastal communities.

The case of the Norwegian aquaculture industry demonstrates the successful adoption of offshore aquaculture technologies to sustainably produce salmon and other finfish species in open ocean environments. Norwegian aquaculture companies utilize floating sea cages, automated feeding systems, and environmental monitoring tools to cultivate fish in offshore waters, where strong currents and natural oceanic conditions promote fish health and growth. By innovating in offshore aquaculture practices, Norway has become a global leader in sustainable seafood production and exports, contributing to food security and economic growth.

The development of marine biotechnology offers promising opportunities for discovering new bioactive compounds, pharmaceuticals, and biomaterials from marine organisms for various industrial applications, including pharmaceuticals, cosmetics, and bioremediation. Marine bioprospecting initiatives explore diverse marine ecosystems, such as deep-sea vents, coral reefs, and polar regions, to identify novel compounds with potential therapeutic or commercial value. By harnessing the biodiversity of marine organisms, researchers can unlock new sources of innovation and contribute to sustainable economic development while preserving marine ecosystems.

The case of marine protected areas (MPAs) highlights the importance of leveraging technology for effective marine conservation and biodiversity conservation efforts. MPAs utilize satellite monitoring, drones, and underwater sensors to monitor and enforce protection measures, such as fishing bans, habitat restoration, and species conservation. By combining technological innovations with traditional conservation approaches, MPAs can enhance their effectiveness in preserving marine biodiversity, restoring degraded habitats, and supporting the resilience of marine ecosystems to climate change impacts.

The deployment of marine acoustic monitoring systems, such as hydrophones and acoustic arrays, enables scientists to study marine mammals, fish populations, and oceanographic phenomena through passive acoustic monitoring. Acoustic monitoring systems record underwater soundscapes, animal vocalizations, and ambient noise levels to assess ecosystem health, monitor species distributions, and detect anthropogenic activities, such as shipping, seismic exploration, and military exercises. By integrating acoustic data into marine conservation and management efforts, authorities can mitigate the impacts of human activities on marine life and ecosystems.

The development of marine spatial planning (MSP) frameworks facilitates the sustainable management and allocation of marine resources by integrating ecological, economic, and social considerations into decision-making processes. MSP utilizes geographic information systems (GIS), remote sensing, and stakeholder engagement tools to map marine habitats, identify conservation priorities, and allocate ocean uses in a spatially coordinated manner. By promoting integrated and ecosystem-based approaches to marine management, MSP frameworks support sustainable development, minimize conflicts among ocean users, and safeguard marine ecosystems for future generations.

The case of the European Marine Observation and Data Network (EMODnet) demonstrates the value of data sharing and collaboration in supporting evidence-based decision-making for marine spatial planning and management. EMODnet provides access to standardized marine data sets, such as bathymetry maps, seabed habitats, and marine biodiversity, collected from various sources across Europe. By aggregating and harmonizing marine data, EMODnet facilitates cross-border cooperation, fosters scientific research, and informs policy development for sustainable ocean governance. Through the open sharing of marine data and information, EMODnet empowers stakeholders, including policymakers, scientists, and industry actors, to make informed decisions, address common challenges, and promote the sustainable use of marine resources.

The development of marine genetic resources (MGRs) holds promise for biotechnological innovation, drug discovery, and genetic research, with potential applications in pharmaceuticals, biomedicine, and agriculture. MGRs encompass diverse genetic material found in marine organisms, such as bacteria, algae, and invertebrates, which possess unique biochemical and genetic characteristics adapted to extreme marine environments. By exploring and characterizing MGRs, researchers can identify novel genes, enzymes, and bioactive compounds with therapeutic or commercial value, paving the way for new biotechnological breakthroughs and economic opportunities.

The case of marine bioprospecting initiatives in Antarctica exemplifies the scientific and commercial potential of exploring extreme marine environments for novel genetic resources and biotechnological applications. Researchers conduct expeditions to Antarctica's pristine marine ecosystems, including deep-sea trenches, hydrothermal vents, and ice-covered waters, to collect samples of marine organisms for genetic analysis and bioprospecting. By studying the unique adaptations of Antarctic marine life, scientists aim to discover new bioactive compounds, enzymes, and genetic resources with applications in pharmaceuticals, biomedicine, and environmental biotechnology.

The emergence of marine microbiome research offers insights into the ecological roles, metabolic processes, and biotechnological potential of microorganisms inhabiting marine environments. Marine microbiomes encompass diverse microbial communities, including bacteria, archaea, and viruses, which play essential roles in nutrient cycling, carbon sequestration, and host-microbe interactions in marine ecosystems. By studying marine microbiomes, scientists can uncover new microbial species, metabolic pathways, and bioactive molecules with applications in biotechnology, environmental remediation, and pharmaceuticals.

The case of marine bioprospecting in deep-sea hydrothermal vent ecosystems highlights the biotechnological potential of extremophilic microorganisms adapted to high-pressure, high-temperature, and chemically-rich environments. Researchers explore deep-sea hydrothermal vents, such as those found along mid-ocean ridges, to collect samples of thermophilic bacteria, archaea, and viruses for genetic analysis and bioprospecting. By studying the unique adaptations of vent-associated microorganisms, scientists aim to discover new enzymes, bioactive compounds, and metabolic pathways with applications in biotechnology, energy production, and environmental remediation.

The development of marine bioplastics offers sustainable alternatives to conventional petroleum-based plastics derived from fossil fuels, with potential applications in packaging, textiles, and medical devices. Marine bioplastics utilize biodegradable polymers derived from renewable marine resources, such as algae, seaweed, and shellfish, which offer biocompatibility, low environmental impact, and potential end-of-life solutions. By harnessing marine biomass for bioplastic production, researchers seek to mitigate plastic pollution, reduce dependence on finite fossil resources, and promote the circular economy principles in the plastics industry.

The case of biodegradable seaweed-based packaging exemplifies the potential of marine bioplastics to address plastic pollution and promote sustainable packaging solutions. Researchers develop biodegradable packaging materials derived from seaweed extracts, such as alginate, carrageenan, and agar, which offer biodegradability, compostability, and marine biodegradation properties. By replacing conventional plastic packaging with seaweed-based alternatives, companies and consumers can reduce plastic waste generation, mitigate environmental pollution, and support the transition towards a more sustainable and circular economy.

The utilization of marine microbial enzymes in bioremediation applications offers eco-friendly solutions for degrading pollutants, contaminants, and hazardous substances in marine environments. Marine microorganisms produce a wide range of enzymes, such as lipases, proteases, and cellulases, capable of degrading organic pollutants, hydrocarbons, heavy metals, and persistent organic pollutants (POPs). By harnessing the catalytic activities of marine microbial enzymes, bioremediation technologies can effectively detoxify polluted sites, restore ecosystem health, and mitigate the impacts of anthropogenic pollution on marine biodiversity.

The case of oil spill bioremediation using marine microbial enzymes illustrates the effectiveness of enzymatic degradation in mitigating the environmental impacts of oil spills in marine ecosystems. Oil-degrading bacteria, such as Pseudomonas, Alcanivorax, and Marinobacter, produce enzymes, such as alkane hydroxylases, esterases, and oxidases, capable of breaking down crude oil components into non-toxic substances. By inoculating oil-contaminated sites with oil-degrading bacteria or their enzymes, researchers can accelerate the natural biodegradation processes, enhance oil spill cleanup efforts, and minimize the long-term ecological damage caused by oil spills.

The development of marine biorefineries offers integrated solutions for valorizing marine biomass and waste streams into high-value products, such as biofuels, biochemicals, and bioplastics. Marine biorefineries utilize a cascade of biotechnological processes, including enzymatic hydrolysis, fermentation, and chemical conversion, to fractionate marine biomass into its constituent components and convert them into bio-based products. By leveraging the diversity of marine biomass, including algae, seaweed, and marine microorganisms, biorefineries can produce a wide range of renewable products with applications in energy, materials, and chemicals industries.

Through the integration of sustainable biomass sourcing, advanced bioprocessing technologies, and circular economy principles, marine biorefineries contribute to reducing reliance on fossil resources, mitigating environmental impacts, and fostering economic development in coastal regions.

The case of algae biorefineries demonstrates the potential of microalgae and macroalgae as feedstocks for producing biofuels, bioproducts, and biocommodities. Algae biorefineries utilize cultivation systems, such as photobioreactors and open ponds, to grow algae biomass under controlled conditions, optimizing biomass productivity and composition. By processing algae biomass through extraction, fermentation, and upgrading processes, biorefineries can produce biofuels, such as biodiesel and bioethanol, as well as high-value products, such as bioactive compounds, pigments, and nutraceuticals. Algae biorefineries offer scalable and sustainable solutions for meeting energy, food, and environmental challenges. The utilization of marine-derived enzymes in industrial biocatalysis offers environmentally friendly alternatives to conventional chemical catalysts for various industrial processes, including pharmaceutical synthesis, food processing, and textile manufacturing. Marine enzymes exhibit unique catalytic properties, such as high substrate specificity, thermal stability, and tolerance to extreme conditions, making them valuable biocatalysts for diverse industrial applications. By harnessing the catalytic activities of marine enzymes, industries can reduce energy consumption, minimize waste generation, and improve process efficiency, thereby contributing to sustainable production practices and environmental stewardship.

The case of marine enzyme-based detergents illustrates the effectiveness of enzymatic cleaning agents in removing stubborn stains, soils, and contaminants from surfaces without harming the environment. Marine enzymes, such as proteases, lipases, and amylases, target specific types of stains and organic residues, breaking them down into smaller, soluble molecules that can be easily rinsed away. By formulating detergents with marine-derived enzymes, manufacturers can offer eco-friendly cleaning products that deliver superior performance, biodegradability, and safety for users and the environment.

The development of marine-inspired biomaterials offers innovative solutions for various industrial applications, including biomedical implants, tissue engineering scaffolds, and biodegradable packaging materials. Biomaterials derived from marine sources, such as chitin, alginate, and collagen; possess unique properties, such as biocompatibility, biodegradability, and bioactivity, making them ideal candidates for biomedical and environmental applications. By mimicking the structural and functional characteristics of marine organisms, researchers can design biomaterials with tailored properties and functionalities, paving the way for sustainable and biocompatible materials for diverse applications.

The case of marine-inspired hydrogel wound dressings demonstrates the potential of biomimetic materials in promoting wound healing and tissue regeneration. Hydrogel dressings derived from marine polysaccharides, such as alginate and chitosan, offer moisture retention, antimicrobial properties, and biocompatibility, creating an optimal environment for wound healing. By incorporating bioactive molecules, such as growth factors and antimicrobial agents, into hydrogel matrices, researchers can enhance the therapeutic efficacy of wound dressings and accelerate the healing process, ultimately improving patient outcomes and reducing healthcare costs.

The utilization of marine biopolymers in 3D printing applications offers sustainable alternatives to petroleum-based plastics for additive manufacturing of complex structures and customized products. Marine biopolymers, such as alginate, agar, and carrageenan, exhibit excellent printability, biodegradability, and biocompatibility, making them suitable materials for 3D printing in biomedical, food, and packaging industries. By leveraging the versatility of marine biopolymers, researchers can develop eco-friendly 3D printing filaments, resins, and inks that meet the growing demand for sustainable and customizable manufacturing solutions.

The case of marine-inspired adhesives showcases the potential of biomimetic materials in developing strong, versatile, and eco-friendly adhesive formulations for industrial and biomedical applications. Adhesives derived from marine organisms, such as mussels, barnacles, and marine bacteria, exhibit exceptional adhesion properties, underwater adhesion, and environmental resistance, inspired by the adhesive strategies employed by marine organisms in wet and dynamic environments. By studying the molecular mechanisms of marine adhesion, researchers can design bio-inspired adhesives with enhanced performance, durability, and sustainability, offering alternatives to traditional petroleum-based adhesives in various sectors.

The development of marine-inspired coatings offers

advanced solutions for protecting surfaces, enhancing performance and prolonging the lifespan of materials in marine environments. Marine coatings, inspired by the self-cleaning and anti-fouling properties of marine organisms, provide effective protection against corrosion, biofouling, and environmental degradation. By incorporating bioactive compounds, such as microbicides, anti-fouling agents, and UV-absorbers, into coating formulations, researchers can create coatings that repel marine organisms, prevent biofouling attachment, and reduce maintenance requirements for marine infrastructure, vessels, and underwater equipment. Marine-inspired coatings offer sustainable and cost-effective solutions for extending the service life of maritime assets and minimizing environmental impacts.

The case of bio-inspired antifouling coatings demonstrates the effectiveness of mimicking natural strategies for preventing biofouling attachment and growth on marine surfaces. Antifouling coatings inspired by marine organisms, such as barnacles, mussels, and algae, utilize surface topographies, chemical cues, and micro/nanostructures to deter settlement and adhesion of fouling organisms. By incorporating bio-inspired features into coating formulations, researchers can develop environmentally friendly antifouling solutions that reduce the use of toxic biocides and minimize ecological impacts on marine ecosystems while maintaining the integrity and performance of coated surfaces.

The utilization of marine biodegradable polymers in sustainable packaging offers alternatives to conventional plastics for reducing plastic pollution and promoting circular economy principles. Biodegradable polymers derived from marine biomass, such as seaweed, shrimp shells, and microalgae, offer biocompatibility, compostability, and low environmental impact, making them suitable materials for single-use and disposable packaging applications. By replacing traditional plastics with marine biodegradable polymers, companies and consumers can reduce plastic waste generation, minimize environmental pollution, and contribute to a more sustainable and circular economy.

The case of marine-inspired biomimetic membranes illustrates the potential of biomimetic materials in water purification and desalination applications. Biomimetic membranes mimic the selective permeability and ion transport properties of biological membranes, such as aquaporins and ion channels, to achieve high water permeability, salt rejection, and fouling resistance in membrane-based separation processes. By incorporating bio-inspired features, such as nanochannels, hydrophilic coatings, and surface charges, into membrane designs, researchers can enhance the performance and efficiency of water treatment technologies, providing clean and safe drinking water for communities and industries.

The development of marine-inspired sensors and biosensors offers sensitive, selective, and cost-effective solutions for monitoring environmental pollutants, detecting marine toxins, and assessing water quality in aquatic ecosystems. Marine sensors utilize biomimetic principles, such as molecular recognition, bioluminescence, and chemotaxis, to detect target analytes with high specificity and sensitivity. By mimicking the sensing mechanisms of marine organisms, researchers can design sensors capable of detecting a wide range of pollutants, including heavy metals, organic contaminants, and harmful algal toxins, in real-time and at trace levels, facilitating environmental monitoring and management efforts to safeguard marine ecosystems and public health.

These examples showcase the vast potential of technological advancements in addressing contemporary challenges and advancing sustainable practices in the maritime domain. By leveraging innovation, collaboration, and interdisciplinary approaches, stakeholders can harness the power of technology to promote the responsible use of marine resources, protect marine ecosystems, and ensure the long-term viability of the oceans for future generations.

Chapter 10.
Conclusion

Recap of Key Points

In conclusion, this book has provided a comprehensive overview of international law and the laws of the sea, covering a wide range of topics from historical developments to contemporary issues.

- We began by defining international law and highlighting its significance in shaping global relations and governance structures.
- The importance of understanding the laws of the sea was emphasized, given the critical role that maritime spaces play in trade, security, and environmental conservation.
- Throughout the book, we explored the foundations of international law, including its historical evolution and various sources and principles.
- The concept of the sea in international law was examined, focusing on the classification of seas and oceans and the evolution of maritime law over time.
- We delved into the United Nations Convention on the Law of the Sea (UNCLOS), analyzing its structure, main provisions, and impact on international relations.
- Sovereignty and jurisdiction issues in territorial waters, exclusive economic zones, and international straits were discussed in detail.

- Navigation and freedom of the seas were explored, including the principles of innocent passage and freedom of navigation.
- Marine resources and environmental protection emerged as crucial areas, covering topics such as fisheries management, environmental conservation, and liability for environmental damage.
- Dispute settlement mechanisms, including diplomatic negotiation, arbitration, and international courts, were examined as essential tools for resolving conflicts peacefully.
- Contemporary issues and emerging challenges, such as climate change, piracy, illegal fishing, and technological advancements, were analyzed to highlight the evolving nature of maritime governance.
- In discussing these topics, we provided numerous examples and case studies to illustrate key concepts and principles in action.
- The role of international organizations, such as the United Nations, International Maritime Organization (IMO), and International Court of Justice (ICJ), in addressing maritime issues was emphasized.
- We also highlighted the importance of cooperation and collaboration among states, stakeholders, and civil society in addressing common challenges and promoting sustainable maritime governance.
- Moving forward, it is essential for policymakers, practitioners, and scholars to remain vigilant and proactive in addressing emerging threats and opportunities in the maritime domain.
- By adhering to the principles of international law, upholding the rule of law, and fostering dialogue and cooperation, we can ensure the peaceful and sustainable use of the world's oceans for generations to come.
- In summary, this book serves as a valuable resource for anyone seeking a deeper understanding of international

- law and the laws of the sea, providing insights into the complex and dynamic nature of maritime governance.
- It is our hope that readers will find this book informative, thought-provoking, and inspiring, prompting further exploration and engagement with these critical issues.
- As we conclude this journey through the intricate web of international law and maritime governance, let us reflect on the importance of collective action and shared responsibility in protecting our oceans and preserving our planet's future.
- The challenges we face are daunting, but by working together with determination and resolve, we can overcome them and build a more sustainable and equitable world for all.
- Thank you for joining us on this journey, and we look forward to continuing the dialogue and collaboration in the pursuit of a safer, more just, and more prosperous maritime future.
- In closing, let us remember that the oceans connect us all, transcending borders, cultures, and ideologies, and it is our shared responsibility to ensure their protection and sustainable use for present and future generations.
- As we bid farewell to these pages, let us carry forward the lessons learned and the insights gained, applying them in our endeavors to build a better world for ourselves and for those who will inherit it from us.
- Together, let us chart a course towards a future where the oceans are respected, protected, and cherished as the lifeblood of our planet, and where the principles of international law serve as beacons of hope and guidance in our collective journey.
- As we conclude our exploration of international law and the laws of the sea, let us remain committed to upholding the principles of justice, fairness, and cooperation that underpin the global maritime order.
- In bidding farewell to these pages, let us carry forward the

- knowledge gained and the insights gleaned, using them to inform our actions and decisions in navigating the complexities of the maritime world.
- As we close this chapter, let us remember that the seas bind us together as a global community, and it is our shared responsibility to steward them wisely and protect them for future generations.
- In conclusion, let us embrace the challenges and opportunities that lie ahead, drawing inspiration from the rich tapestry of maritime history and the enduring principles of international law.
- As we turn the final page of this book, let us embark on a new chapter of collaboration, innovation, and stewardship, guided by the values of cooperation, sustainability, and respect for the oceans.
- Thank you for accompanying us on this journey, and may our shared commitment to the oceans inspire us to work together towards a brighter and more sustainable future for all.
- In summary, the exploration of international law and the laws of the sea has provided us with a deeper understanding of the complexities and nuances of maritime governance.
- By examining historical developments, contemporary challenges, and emerging trends, we have gained valuable insights into the multifaceted nature of maritime issues and the importance of effective legal frameworks.
- Throughout our journey, we have encountered a diverse array of topics, from sovereignty disputes to environmental conservation, each highlighting the interconnectedness of maritime issues and the need for comprehensive and coordinated approaches.
- As we reflect on the key points discussed in this book, we are reminded of the critical role that international law plays in promoting peace, stability, and cooperation in the maritime domain.

- From the negotiation of international agreements to the resolution of disputes through peaceful means, international law provides a framework for addressing maritime challenges and advancing common interests.
- Moreover, the principles of equity, fairness, and sustainable development underscore the importance of responsible stewardship of the oceans and their resources.
- As we look to the future, it is clear that the maritime domain will continue to be shaped by evolving dynamics, including geopolitical shifts, technological advancements, and environmental changes.
- Therefore, it is essential for policymakers, practitioners, and stakeholders to remain vigilant and adaptive in addressing emerging challenges and seizing opportunities for cooperation and innovation.
- By working together across borders and disciplines, we can overcome the complex challenges facing the oceans and ensure their long-term health and vitality for the benefit of present and future generations.
- In closing, let us reaffirm our commitment to the principles of international law, cooperation, and sustainable development, as we strive to build a more resilient, equitable, and prosperous maritime future for all.

Future Prospects for the Laws of the Sea

Looking ahead, the future prospects for international law and the laws of the sea hold both challenges and opportunities, reflecting the dynamic nature of the maritime domain and the evolving needs of the global community.

One key area of focus for the future is the continued development and strengthening of international legal frameworks governing the oceans, including UNCLOS and other relevant agreements.

As new issues emerge and existing challenges evolve, there will be a need for ongoing dialogue and cooperation among states, international organizations, and civil society to adapt and update maritime laws accordingly.

Technological advancements, including advances in satellite imaging, remote sensing, and data analytics, offer new opportunities for monitoring, enforcement, and compliance with maritime laws and regulations.

By harnessing the power of technology, stakeholders can improve transparency, accountability, and effectiveness in managing maritime resources and addressing maritime security threats.

Another important consideration for the future is the impact of climate change on maritime boundaries, coastal communities, and marine ecosystems.

Rising sea levels, changing ocean currents, and increasing extreme weather events pose significant challenges for maritime governance, requiring adaptive strategies and innovative solutions.

Collaborative efforts to mitigate and adapt to climate change will be essential in safeguarding the health and resilience of the oceans and coastal areas.

In addition, the growing importance of marine biodiversity conservation and ecosystem-based management will shape future approaches to maritime governance.

Recognizing the interconnectedness of marine ecosystems and the dependence of human societies on healthy oceans, there is a growing emphasis on integrating conservation and sustainable use principles into maritime policies and practices.

The emergence of new actors and stakeholders in the maritime domain, including non-state actors, indigenous communities, and private sector entities, presents both challenges and opportunities for maritime governance.

Engaging with these diverse stakeholders and fostering inclusive decision-making processes will be crucial for addressing complex maritime issues and promoting effective implementation of international laws and regulations.

Furthermore, the role of international cooperation and multilateralism in addressing common maritime challenges cannot be overstated.

By fostering dialogue, building trust, and promoting cooperation among states, regional organizations, and other stakeholders, we can enhance maritime security, promote sustainable development, and safeguard the rights and interests of all.

Strengthening compliance and enforcement mechanisms for maritime laws and regulations will be essential in ensuring the effective implementation of international agreements and upholding the rule of law in the maritime domain.

This will require enhanced capacity-building efforts, technical assistance, and resource mobilization to support developing countries and vulnerable coastal communities in meeting their maritime governance obligations.

Addressing maritime security threats, including piracy, maritime terrorism, and transnational organized crime, will remain a top priority for the international community in the years to come.

Cooperation among states, regional organizations, and international agencies will be essential in combating these threats and promoting maritime safety and security.

At the same time, it is important to recognize the role of maritime law in facilitating peaceful dispute resolution and preventing conflict in the maritime domain.

By promoting dialogue, negotiation, and mediation, international law can serve as a valuable tool for managing competing maritime claims and reducing tensions among states.

As we look to the future, it is crucial to recognize the importance of education, awareness-raising, and capacity-building in promoting a culture of maritime compliance and responsible behavior.

By investing in education and training programs for maritime professionals, policymakers, and the general public, we can foster a greater understanding of maritime laws and regulations and promote their effective implementation.

Finally, the future of international law and the laws of the sea will be shaped by the collective actions and commitments of states, stakeholders, and individuals around the world.

By working together with determination, vision, and solidarity, we can build a more just, sustainable, and prosperous maritime future for all.

In closing, let us reaffirm our commitment to upholding the principles of international law, promoting cooperation and dialogue, and protecting the oceans for future generations.

As we navigate the challenges and opportunities that lie ahead, let us remain steadfast in our dedication to the rule of law and the principles of justice, equity, and sustainability.

Together, let us chart a course towards a future where the oceans are respected, protected, and cherished as the common heritage of humankind.

Thank you for joining us on this journey, and may our shared commitment to the oceans inspire us to work together towards a brighter and more sustainable future for all.

As we embark on the next chapter of our maritime journey, let us do so with optimism, determination, and a renewed sense of purpose.

The future of international law and the laws of the sea is in our hands, and it is up to us to shape it in a way that promotes peace, prosperity, and environmental stewardship for generations to come.

Call to Action: Strengthening Compliance and Cooperation

As we conclude our exploration of international law and the laws of the sea, it is clear that effective compliance and cooperation are essential for addressing the myriad challenges facing the maritime domain.

Compliance with international laws and regulations is not only a legal obligation but also a moral imperative, reflecting a commitment to upholding the rule of law and promoting global peace and security.

Therefore, we must reaffirm our collective commitment to strengthening compliance with international maritime laws and regulations at all levels.

This requires concerted efforts by states, international organizations, civil society, and other stakeholders to ensure that maritime laws are respected, implemented, and enforced effectively. One key aspect of strengthening compliance is enhancing transparency and accountability in maritime governance processes.

By promoting transparency in decision-making, enhancing public access to information, and fostering greater accountability for maritime actions, we can build trust and confidence among stakeholders and improve compliance with international laws and regulations.

Additionally, it is essential to enhance monitoring, surveillance, and enforcement capabilities to detect and deter violations of maritime laws and regulations.

This may involve investing in technology, building institutional capacity, and strengthening international cooperation mechanisms to combat illegal activities and ensure the sustainable use of marine resources.

Moreover, promoting a culture of compliance and responsible behavior among maritime stakeholders is essential for fostering a sustainable and secure maritime environment.

This requires raising awareness about international maritime laws and regulations, providing education and training opportunities, and promoting ethical conduct among maritime professionals and practitioners.

Furthermore, fostering cooperation and collaboration among states, regional organizations, and other stakeholders is essential for addressing common maritime challenges and promoting collective action.

By working together to share information, resources, and best practices, we can enhance maritime security, promote sustainable development, and safeguard the rights and interests of all.

Regional cooperation mechanisms, such as joint patrols, information-sharing agreements, and capacity-building initiatives, can play a vital role in addressing transnational maritime threats and promoting stability in maritime regions.

Additionally, promoting dialogue and diplomacy is essential for resolving maritime disputes peacefully and preventing conflict in the maritime domain.

By engaging in constructive dialogue, seeking common ground, and exploring diplomatic solutions to maritime disputes, states can reduce tensions, build trust, and promote stability in the maritime domain.

Moreover, strengthening international legal frameworks and dispute settlement mechanisms is essential for resolving maritime disputes and upholding the rule of law in the maritime domain. This may involve supporting the work of international courts and tribunals, promoting adherence to international agreements, and exploring innovative approaches to dispute resolution.

Additionally, promoting a culture of cooperation and mutual respect among states is essential for fostering a conducive environment for maritime governance and cooperation.

By recognizing the shared interests and responsibilities that states have in managing maritime resources and addressing maritime challenges, we can promote greater cooperation and collaboration in the maritime domain.

Furthermore, enhancing public awareness and engagement on maritime issues is essential for building support for international maritime laws and regulations.

This may involve conducting public outreach campaigns, organizing educational events, and involving civil society organizations in maritime governance processes.

By engaging with the public and raising awareness about the importance of maritime issues, we can foster a sense of ownership and responsibility for the oceans and promote greater compliance with maritime laws and regulations.

Additionally, promoting corporate social responsibility and ethical business practices in the maritime industry is essential for ensuring sustainable and responsible use of marine resources.

This may involve encouraging companies to adopt environmentally friendly practices, adhere to international standards, and contribute to the conservation and protection of marine ecosystems.

Moreover, supporting research and innovation in maritime governance and technology is essential for addressing emerging challenges and opportunities in the maritime domain.

By investing in research, innovation, and technology development, we can develop new solutions, tools, and approaches to address maritime challenges and promote sustainable development.

Furthermore, promoting inclusive and participatory decision-making processes in maritime governance is essential for ensuring that the voices and perspectives of all stakeholders are heard and considered.

This may involve engaging with marginalized and vulnerable communities, indigenous peoples, and civil society organizations to ensure that their interests and rights are respected and protected in maritime governance processes.

Additionally, fostering partnerships and collaboration among governments, civil society, academia, and the private sector is essential for mobilizing resources and expertise to address maritime challenges.

By working together in a spirit of cooperation and solidarity, we can build a more resilient, equitable, and sustainable maritime future for all.

Strengthening compliance and cooperation in maritime governance requires a holistic and multi-faceted approach that addresses the interconnectedness of maritime issues and promotes integrated solutions.

This may involve adopting a comprehensive approach to maritime governance that addresses a wide range of issues, including maritime security, environmental protection, resource management, and sustainable development.

By adopting a holistic approach, policymakers and stakeholders can better understand the complex interactions and trade-offs involved in maritime governance and develop more effective and coordinated responses.

Furthermore, promoting transparency, accountability, and good governance practices in maritime governance processes is essential for building trust and confidence among stakeholders and ensuring the legitimacy and effectiveness of maritime laws and regulations.

This may involve strengthening regulatory frameworks, enhancing public access to information, and promoting ethical conduct and integrity among maritime stakeholders.

Additionally, promoting international cooperation and collaboration in addressing maritime challenges requires a commitment to shared goals, values, and principles.

By fostering a culture of cooperation and mutual respect among states, international organizations, and other stakeholders, we can overcome barriers to collaboration and promote greater synergy and alignment in maritime governance efforts.

Moreover, promoting capacity-building and technical assistance initiatives is essential for supporting developing countries and vulnerable coastal communities in meeting their maritime governance obligations.

By providing training, resources, and expertise, the international community can help build the capacity of governments and institutions to effectively implement and enforce maritime laws and regulations and address emerging challenges.

In conclusion, strengthening compliance and cooperation in maritime governance is essential for promoting peace, security, and sustainable development in the maritime domain.

By fostering a culture of compliance, promoting transparency and accountability, and enhancing international cooperation, we can build a more resilient, equitable, and prosperous maritime future for all.

As we move forward, let us heed the call to action to strengthen compliance and cooperation in maritime governance, recognizing the vital importance of the oceans to the well-being of humanity and the planet.

Together, let us work tirelessly to uphold the principles of international law, promote cooperation and dialogue, and protect the oceans for present and future generations.

By working together with determination, vision, and solidarity, we can overcome the challenges facing the maritime domain and build a brighter and more sustainable future for all.

Thank you for your commitment and dedication to the oceans, and may our collective efforts lead to a more just, peaceful, and prosperous world.

As we conclude this call to action, let us remember that the future of the oceans depends on our actions today.

Let us seize this opportunity to strengthen compliance and cooperation in maritime governance and ensure that the oceans remain a source of life, inspiration, and sustenance for generations to come.

Together, let us embark on this journey towards a more sustainable and resilient maritime future, guided by the principles of international law, cooperation, and shared responsibility.

In closing, let us reaffirm our commitment to protecting and preserving the oceans, the common heritage of humanity, for the benefit of all.

With determination, cooperation, and solidarity, we can build a brighter future for the oceans and for our planet.

Glossary of Terms

- **Archipelagic State:** A state composed of a group or chain of islands and their surrounding waters, recognized as a single entity under international law.
- **Arbitral Panels**: Panels of experts or arbitrators appointed to resolve specific disputes between states, usually established under the provisions of international treaties or agreements.
- **Arbitration:** The process of resolving disputes between states through binding arbitration, where an impartial tribunal issues a final and binding decision based on the parties' submissions and evidence.
- **Climate Change:** The long-term change in global or regional climate patterns, primarily due to human activities such as greenhouse gas emissions and deforestation.
- **Continental Shelf:** The submerged extension of a coastal state's land territory, consisting of the seabed and subsoil of the continental margin, where the state has sovereign rights over natural resources.
- **Diplomatic Negotiation**: The process of resolving disputes between states through diplomatic channels, usually involving direct negotiations between the parties or third-party mediation.
- **Environmental Protection:** Measures aimed at preserving and safeguarding the marine environment from pollution, degradation, and other anthropogenic impacts.
- **Exclusive Economic Zone (EEZ):** A maritime zone extending up to 200 nautical miles from a coastal state's baseline, within which the coastal state has exclusive rights to exploit and manage marine resources.

- **Exclusive Fishing Zone:** A maritime zone extending up to 200 nautical miles from a coastal state's baseline, within which the coastal state has exclusive rights to regulate and manage fishing activities.
- **Freedom of Navigation:** The principle that ships of all states have the right to navigate freely on the high seas and other international waters, subject to certain limitations under international law.
- **High Seas:** Areas of the ocean beyond the jurisdiction of any single state, also known as international waters, where all states have freedom of navigation and other lawful uses of the sea.
- **Innocent Passage:** The right of ships to traverse through another state's territorial waters in a manner that is not prejudicial to the peace, security, or good order of the coastal state.
- **International Court of Justice (ICJ):** The principal judicial organ of the United Nations, responsible for settling disputes between states in accordance with international law.
- **International Straits:** Narrow passages of water connecting two larger bodies of water, used for international navigation and subject to special legal regimes under international law.
- **Maritime Boundary:** The line demarcating the seaward limits of a coastal state's jurisdiction and the adjacent high seas, established through international agreements or customary international law.
- **Maritime Law:** The body of law governing maritime activities and affairs, including navigation, commerce, maritime boundaries, environmental protection, and maritime security.
- **Marine Conservation:** The protection and sustainable management of marine ecosystems and biodiversity, aimed at preserving marine resources for future generations.

- **Marine Pollution:** The introduction of harmful substances or energy into the marine environment, resulting in adverse effects on marine ecosystems, human health, and economic activities.
- **Marine Resources:** Natural resources found in the ocean, including fish stocks, minerals, oil and gas reserves, and renewable energy sources such as wind and tidal power.
- **Piracy:** The act of robbery, violence, or other criminal activities committed at sea for private gain, typically carried out by organized criminal groups in areas of maritime transit.
- **Territorial Sovereignty:** The exclusive authority of a state over its territorial waters, airspace, and land territory, as recognized under international law.
- **Territorial Waters**: The area of water adjacent to a nation's coast, generally extending up to 12 nautical miles from the baseline of a coastal state's territory.
- **Transit Passage:** The right of ships to transit through international straits and other narrow passages used for international navigation, without interference from coastal states.
- **UNCLOS:** The United Nations Convention on the Law of the Sea, a comprehensive international treaty governing all aspects of ocean governance, including maritime boundaries, navigation, environmental protection, and resource management.
- **Vessel**: Any type of watercraft used for transportation on water, including ships, boats, and submarines.
- **Watershed**: The area of land where all of the water that is under it or drains off of it goes into the same place.
- **Wetland**: An area of land that is saturated with water, either permanently or seasonally, such as marshes, swamps, and bogs.
- **Xenobiotic:** A chemical substance found within an organism that is not naturally produced or expected to be present within the organism.

- **Yield:** The amount of fish or other seafood caught by a fishing vessel or fleet in a given period of time.
- **Zooplankton:** Small organisms, primarily animals, that drift along in aquatic environments, such as microscopic animals, small fish larvae, and jellyfish.

www.ingramcontent.com/pod-product-compliance
Lightning Source LLC
Chambersburg PA
CBHW052236220526
45471CB00001B/67